THE CIVIL WAR
MILITARY MACHINE

WEAPONS AND TACTICS OF THE UNION AND CONFEDERATE ARMED FORCES

THE CIVIL WAR
MILITARY MACHINE

WEAPONS AND TACTICS OF THE UNION AND CONFEDERATE ARMED FORCES

Ian Drury & Tony Gibbons

SMITHMARK

This edition published in 1993 by SMITHMARK Publishers Inc.,
16 East 32nd Street, New York, NY 10016.

SMITHMARK Books are available for bulk purchase for sales promotion
and premium use. For details write or call the manager of special
sales, SMITHMARK Publishers Inc., 16 East 32nd Street, New York,
NY 10016; (212) 532-6600.

Produced by	Dragon's World Ltd.
Address:	26 Warwick Way
	London SW1V 1RX
	England
Editor:	Patricia Burgess
Designer:	Tony Gibbons
Editorial Director:	Pippa Rubinstein
Art Director:	Dave Allen
ISBN	0-8317-1325-9
Printed in:	Portugal

10 9 8 7 6 5 4 3 2 1

DEDICATION
To Dee and especially to our friend Ollie.
The light that burns twice as bright
burns but half as long.

Library of Congress Cataloging-in-Publication Data

Gibbons, Tony.
    The Civil War military machine : weapons and tactics of the Union
and Confederate armed forces / by Tony Gibbons & Ian Drury.
      p.   cm.
    Includes index.
    ISBN 0-8317-1325-9 : $24.98
    1. United States. Army—History—Civil War, 1861-1865. 2. United
States.   Army—Drill and tactics—History—19th century. 3. United
States.   Army—Weapons systems—History—19th century.
4. Confederate States of America.   Army—Weapons systems.
5. Confederate States of America.   Army—Drill and tactics.
6. United States—History—Civil War, 1861-1865—Campaigns.
I. Drury, Ian. II. Title.
E491.G53   1992
973.7—dc20   92-37948
                                                        CIP

CONTENTS

Introduction

Walking along the sunken lane at Antietam or over the jumbled rocks of Devil's Den, visitors to the Civil War battlefields pause to imagine the scene at the height of the fighting. We draw our images from movies, photographs, paintings, and books, all with different perspectives. *Civil War Military Machine* explains how battles were fought – how the armies and navies harnessed new technology and new weapons in a conflict of unprecedented innovation.

The horrific casualties of the Civil War battles dwarfed those of all previous warfare in the western hemisphere. Were they the result of amateur generals leading untrained volunteers into battle? Or were they the inevitable product of more accurate weapons, one step further on the road to the holocaust of World War I?

The Civil War has frequently been described as the first modern war. Strategic movements were controlled and carried out by the new combination of telegraph and railroad. Rifle- and carbine-armed cavalry operated in a manner unknown in Europe, where horsemen still expected to charge, sword in hand. The terrible power of Civil War rifles and artillery drove both armies to make extensive use of fieldworks, cumulating in the infamous trench lines around Petersburg.

This book examines the full range of military equipment used by the Union and Confederate forces. From pistols to siege cannon and ironclad warships, these are the weapons that helped shape American history. Lack of space prevents the inclusion of every single weapon – after all, the Federal government bought at least 54 different types of pistol during the war and no one ever knew how many different weapons were acquired by the Confederate States. Nevertheless, all significant weapons are here in one volume.

While we study the technology that created a generation of revolutionary weapons, it is important not to lose sight of the men. Superior equipment does not guarantee victory (as the Army of the Potomac demonstrated for several years). The precise effectiveness of Civil War weapons continues to be debated, with historic weapons being fired under test conditions and casualty figures studied exhaustively. Since the records of both armies were inevitably imprecise, exact computation of weapons' lethality is impossible. There is a well-known story of a guest at West Point who asked a Southern cadet about a monument to the Union graduates who were killed during the Civil War: "A monument to the accurate shooting of the Confederate soldier, sir!" While we can arrive at only a rough estimate of exactly *how* accurate, more American soldiers died in one day at Antietam than in the first month of fighting following the Normandy landings in 1944. Civil War weapons were undoubtedly more effective than those of earlier conflicts. It is no wonder that their deadly effects came as a surprise to the soldiers who marched to war in 1861.

The Shenandoah Valley was the scene of some of the Civil War's most dramatic moments. The 165-mile corridor between the Blue Ridge Mountains and the Alleghenies ran from the heart of the Confederacy all the way to Harper's Ferry; it was the back door to the North or a gateway to the South, and an obvious pathway for invasion. An army posted in the valley could pass through one of the Blue Ridge gaps to strike the flank of an enemy operating in Virginia, just 60 miles away. The very soil of the Shenandoah was a key strategic asset, for the valley was the breadbasket of the Army of Northern Virginia. It was here that Thomas J. Jackson conducted one of the most outstanding campaigns in military history in 1862.

Stonewall's valley campaign linked his name with that of the Shenandoah forever, and after his tragic death in May 1863, his body was returned to Lexington. Within a few weeks long columns in gray headed down the valley for to meet their destiny at Gettysburg. In 1864 John C. Breckinridge saved the valley again with his sparkling victory at New Market; but it was only a matter of time. In 1865 the valley was systematically devastated by a new generation of Union officers that had replaced gallant bumblers like Franz Sigel. Today there is no trace of Phil Shenandoah is at peace. Several of the key battlefields are well preserved, especially New Market, which is graced with an excellent museum commemorating the gallant charge of the VMI cadets.

The South in the Civil War

Panoramic view of the Confederacy from Galveston to Mobile. Clearly shown is the twisting coastline with numerous inlets favoured by blockade runners. It was at New Orleans near the mouth of the Mississippi that the Union made one of its earliest moves to split the Confederacy in two; this was designed to keep the supplies produced in the western states from reaching the Southern armies fighting in the east.

Levenworth

Fort Worth   Dallas

Kansas City

Clarksville

Montgomery

Bentonville   Little Rock

Trinity

Huntsville   Shrevenport

Boonville

Hempstead

Bellville

Liberty

Houston   Crowley's

Wallisville   Beaumont
Orange

Wharton   *Sabine River*

Galveston Bay

Brazos River   Galveston

The South in the Civil War

The Mississippi valley at the heart of the Confederacy, showing Vicksburg and the surrounding country. The long Union campaign against Vicksburg was mainly an army operation. The navy supported Grant's force, and Union warships tried to get behind the strong Vicksburg defenses through the twisting bayous, but without success. As Union naval forces controlled much of the Mississippi, their presence enabled Grant to move a large force across the river at Hard Times Landing, capturing Jackson before finally taking Vicksburg on July 4, 1863.

Bartholomew

Pine Bluff

Washington Landing

Steele's Bay

Floyd

Monticello

Millikens Bend

Yazoo River

Richmond

Vicksburg

Mississippi River

New Carthage

Warrenton

Hankinson's Ferry

Rocky Spring

Hard Times Landing

Grand Gulf

Willow Spring

Port Gibson

Memphis

Little Rock

Arkansas Post

Oxford

Coffeeville

Fort Pemberton

Grenada

Yazoo Pass

Columbia

Greenville

Tallahatchie River

Yazoo River

Little River

Yazoo City

Haynes Bluff

Cardiff

Chickasaw Bluffs

Benton

Big Black River

Livingston

Brownsville

Battle Springs

New Auburn

Clinton

Jackson

Crystal Springs

The South in the Civil War

Charleston, reckoned by the North as the seat of the rebellion in the South, was able to withstand all the naval attacks made upon it. It was only toward the end of the war that it fell to an army approaching from the rear.

Atlanta

Madison

Milledgeville

Macon

Davidsborough

Marion

Dublin

Warrenton

Hawkinsville

Mount Vernon

Louisville

Augusta

Armenia

Blacksville

Reidsville

Millen

Eden

Branchville

Hinesville

Morton Hall

Marlow

Blufton

Medway River

Savannah

Brunswick

Savannah River

St Catherine's Strait

Warsaw Sound

Ossabaw Island

Wilmington Island

Hilton Head

12

Pickens

Greenville

Chester

Lancaster

Newberry

Abbeyville

Columbia

Hamburg

Edgefield

Barnwell

Aiken

Blacksville

Orangeville

Pineville

Branchville

Laurence

Waltonborough

Summerville

Combahee

Jacksonboro

Glovers Mill

Charleston

Logansville

Sumter

Fort Moultrie

Port Royal

Edisto Island

Light House Inlet

St Helena Sound

Stono Inlet

The South in the Civil War

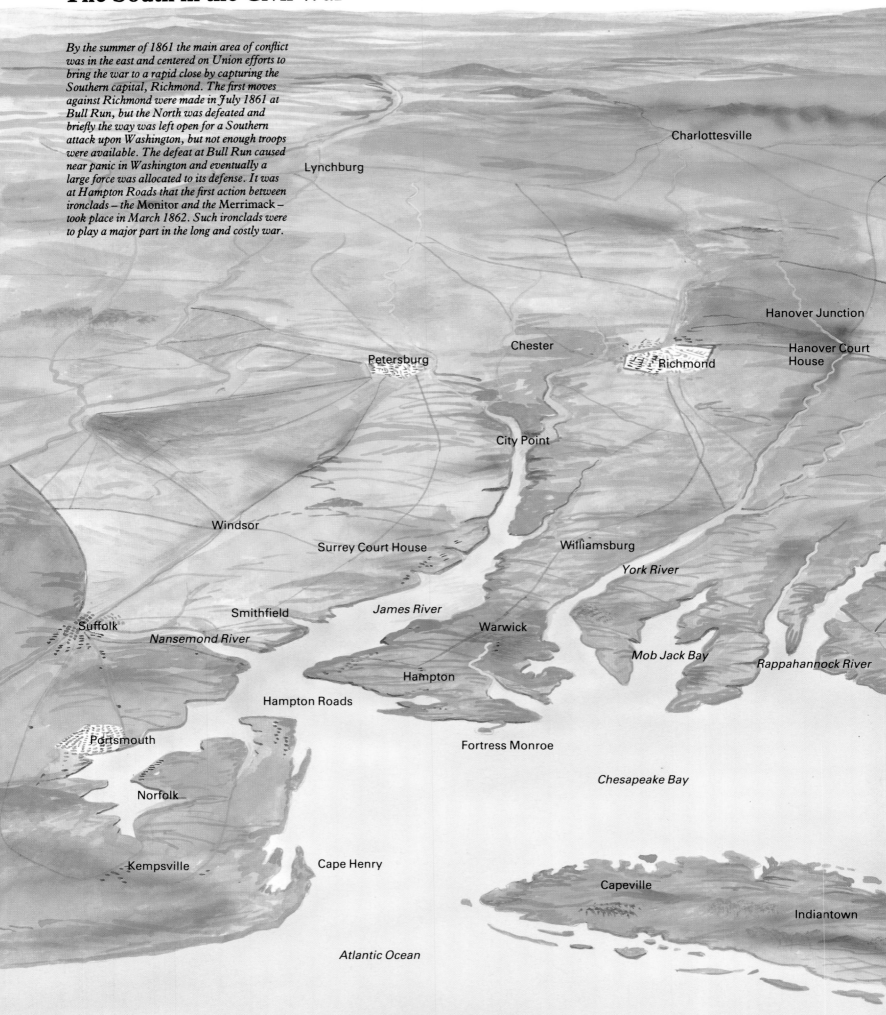

By the summer of 1861 the main area of conflict was in the east and centered on Union efforts to bring the war to a rapid close by capturing the Southern capital, Richmond. The first moves against Richmond were made in July 1861 at Bull Run, but the North was defeated and briefly the way was left open for a Southern attack upon Washington, but not enough troops were available. The defeat at Bull Run caused near panic in Washington and eventually a large force was allocated to its defense. It was at Hampton Roads that the first action between ironclads – the Monitor and the Merrimack – took place in March 1862. Such ironclads were to play a major part in the long and costly war.

Charlottesville

Lynchburg

Hanover Junction

Chester

Hanover Court House

Petersburg

Richmond

City Point

Windsor

Williamsburg

Surrey Court House

York River

James River

Warwick

Smithfield

Mob Jack Bay

Rappahannock River

Suffolk

Nansemond River

Hampton

Hampton Roads

Fortress Monroe

Portsmouth

Chesapeake Bay

Norfolk

Kempsville

Cape Henry

Capeville

Indiantown

Atlantic Ocean

Culpepper

Pittsburg

Wheeling

Bull Run

Bedford

Falmouth

Fairfax

Harper's
Ferry

Fredericksburg

Warrenton

Winchester

Cumberland

Dumfries

Brentsville

Potomac River

Fairfax

Washington

Frederick

Alexandria

Port Tobacco

Upper Marlborough

Newport

Leonardstown

Frederickstown

Baltimore

Patuxent River

Annapolis

Eastern Bay

Choptank River

Cambridge

Easton

Dover

New Town

Drummondtown

Camden

Delaware Bay

Salem

15

The Savage Wars of Peace

The US Army and the western frontier, 1848–60

President Lincoln's initial call for 75,000 volunteers has always looked naively optimistic with the advantage of hindsight. The Union would have a million men under arms by the end of the war. Yet this first call to arms represented a seven-fold expansion of the US Army. The rapidity with which the Regular Army was swamped by the mass of volunteers was a key feature of the first six months of the war. The Regular regiments were not broken up to provide cadres of trained men to stiffen the green units appearing in 1861 – they soldiered on throughout the war. But their officers, serving and retired, found themselves catapulted to ranks they could never have dreamed of achieving in the army of the 1850s. Their combat experience – or lack of it – was to have profound consequences during the first campaigns of the Civil War.

Rudyard Kipling coined the expression, "the savage wars of peace" in his poem "The White Man's Burden," written in reference to the US campaigns in the Philippines in 1899. His description of the army's potential enemies then – "new-caught, sullen peoples, half devil and half child" – applies equally to the Indian peoples, who suddenly found themselves under nominal US jurisdiction from 1845. Indian resistance east of the Mississippi had all but ceased during the 1840s, apart from the Seminole wars in Florida. The US Army's eight infantry, four artillery, and three cavalry regiments represented the minimum military force necessary for national security. Manning coastal forts, the Canadian frontier, and the Permanent Indian Frontier, the troops were scattered along the periphery of the United States.

The US Army's role was vastly complicated in the three years up to 1848. The annexation of Texas in 1845, resolution of the Oregon border dispute the following year, and Mexico's ceding of California, the Great Basin, and the Rio Grande southwest added a million square miles to the United States. The California Gold Rush drove white settlement deep into unfamiliar territory and vastly over-extended the army's responsibilities. The army established regional defense systems to protect the emigrants from increasingly unimpressed tribes. An uneasy relationship was established between the army and the indigenous population. Sometimes friendly, sometimes hostile, and always unpredictable, the Indian tribes were locked in a fatal embrace with white civilization.

The Regular infantry regiments consisted of 10 companies lettered A through K with the letter J omitted. They were armed with the M1842 musket, although some individual companies received the M1841 Mississippi Rifle. In 1855 the capable secretary of war, Jefferson Davis, succeeded in expanding the army by two infantry and two cavalry regiments. Weapons were also modernized: regiments one through eight were armed with the Springfield M1855 .58-caliber rifled musket. The new 9th and 10th Regiments, modelled on the French chasseurs (light infantry) received the M1855 rifle.

The artillery regiments had 12 companies lettered A through M, omitting J. Ten companies in each regiment were classed as "heavy artillery" and were employed on the coastal forts and permanent defenses. Equipped and trained like the infantry, they fought as such in Mexico and Florida. The remaining two companies in each regiment were organized as light artillery batteries. Each had six guns, usually four six-pounder M1841 smoothbore cannon and two 12-pounder M1841 howitzers. Sporting fancier uniforms and inheriting a light artillery tradition (no sidearms other than swords), they regarded themselves as the elite of the artillery.

The 1st and 2nd Dragoons were raised in 1833 and 1836 respectively. Known as "light dragoons" until 1850, they were organized into 10 companies, A-K, yet usually scattered in troop-sized detachments all over the frontier.

Congress restricted the number of horsemen in the army because cavalry was at least twice as expensive to maintain and because "the man on horseback" remained a bugbear of the democratic conscience. European-style hussars and the like were viewed with suspicion as the potential strong-arm of an autocrat. Nevertheless, the men aped European light cavalry fashion – mustaches were almost compulsory and gold earrings were sported by those who could afford them.

Raised in 1846 to guard the Oregon Trail, the third cavalry formation fielded by the US Army was the Mounted Rifles. It was organized like the dragoons, only its companies were theoretically 64-strong as opposed to 50-strong. Armed with Mississippi rifles and Colt revolvers, it quickly established a strong sense of unit pride.

Jefferson Davis's greatest achievement as secretary of war was to cajole Congress into authorizing the 1st and 2nd Cavalry Regiments. Modelled on the dragoons, they carried a wide mixture of carbines, as the Ordnance Department spent the five years before the Civil War testing different weapons. Equipped with the Springfield M1854 rifled carbine and pistol carbine, companies of these regiments also carried Burnside, Perry, and Merill carbines, as well as Colt Navy pistols.

Between the Mexican War and the Civil War, the US Army deployed its major formations together on only one occasion. This was the 1857 expedition against the Mormon settlements in Utah. Commanded by Colonel Albert S. Johnston, concentration included the 5th and 10th Infantry supported by the 2nd Dragoons and elements of two other infantry regiments and two light batteries. Eventually comprising 20 percent of the US Army's strength, the expedition survived the "war" without casualties. For the rest of the time, the army was deployed in small units, tied to a dull routine of frontier garrison duty.

Touring the west in 1866, Major-General William T. Sherman expressed his astonishment at the living conditions of America's frontier soldiers: ". . . had the Southern planters put their negroes in such hovels, a sample would, ere then, have been carried to Boston and exhibited as illustration of the cruelty and inhumanity of the man-masters." The reality of frontier soldiering was not the smart wooden fort beloved of Hollywood, but a sod or adobe shack, baking hot in summer, freezing cold in winter, and crawling with vermin all year round.

The vast enlargement of the United States placed a heavy burden on the US Army but Congress steadfastly refused to accept this. Military spending rose, but by nowhere near enough to satisfy the incessant demands of the frontier. Policing such vast lands on a shoestring budget proved a disheartening experience for officers and men alike. Enthusiastic officers, fresh from the glories of the Mexican War, were frustrated by the dismal reality of the frontier. Their career commitment was gradually whittled away by humdrum duties in isolated forts, low pay, poor housing, and little prospect of advancement.

Lieutenant David D. Porter of USS Spitfire *in action during the Mexican War of 1847. General Winfield Scott landed his army at Vera Cruz and marched to Mexico City, winning a series of victories against the Mexican forces along the way. Many senior commanders of the Civil War fought in Mexico as junior officers; this understanding of each other, their strengths and weaknesses, was a unique feature of the War Between the States. Scott's army was small by Civil War standards, never exceeding 14,000 men, but it was the largest concentration of US troops before 1861.*

The Savage Wars of Peace

Future Confederate general Ambrose P. Hill was not the husband Captain Randolph Marcy wanted for his daughter. He warned her not to marry a soldier since "his pay could hardly give you a miserable living, with a house that a man in civilized society would actually be ashamed to keep a horse in." Pay scales had hardly altered in 50 years. Colonels could earn $75 a month, second lieutenants like Hill made $25 per month, while infantry and cavalry/artillery earned $7 and $8 respectively. Pay was usually in arrears and generally in paper currency, which tended to be discounted by 10–20 percent on the frontier. Sutlers, settlers, Indians, and whores preferred gold or silver coin.

By the mid-1850s 73 percent of the officer corps had been educated at West Point. Yet the college concentrated on engineering and on full-scale military operations against a European-style opponent. It developed a spirit of professionalism and military thought, but on the subject of Indian-fighting West Point maintained a deafening silence. Its graduates had to learn the hard way. Unfortunately, since officers advanced strictly by seniority and there was no retired list, the West Point graduate's career was blocked by a body of aging officers. The glacial slowness of promotion is nowhere better illustrated than by the 19 regimental colonels in office at the beginning of the Civil War. Eleven of them were veterans of the war of 1812 and only four had served for less than 40 years!

Commanding tiny detachments with long spells of inactivity drove many officers to resign their commissions. Future generals McClellan, Bragg, Halleck, Buckner, Sherman, Burnside, and Jackson all left the service. So too did Grant. He left as captain of Company E, 4th Infantry – in theory a force of three officers, eight NCOs, and 74 enlisted men. In fact, there were only 34 men all told, including just 26 private soldiers. Their number was further reduced by sickness and daily routine duties. Although the three lieutenants present included George Crook and, fresh from West Point, John B. Hood, they had a force of three NCOs and 11 privates able to take the field. It was an underwhelming deterrent to Indian – or white settler – misbehavior.

The Duke of Wellington once described the men who won him the battle of Waterloo as "the scum of the earth." Congressmen, Secretary of War Floyd, and even enlisted soldiers shared similar sentiments about the US Army's rank and file. Alcoholism was endemic among officers and men alike. Many soldiers had certainly enlisted because they were unable to find any other work. Little over 30 percent of the soldiers were born in the USA. Of the rest, at least half hailed from Ireland and the rest from western Europe, with Germans predomi-

nating. They were a wild mixture: young, restless spirits, drunken toughs, and aging deadbeats held together by a leavening of older soldiers with re-enlistment stripes on their faded sleeves. The latter provided the NCOs, who are the backbone of any army.

Most recruits were signed up in eastern cities and were supposed to be trained before they were posted to their units. But the frontier demanded a constant flow of new blood to maintain formations weakened by disease and desertion. Recruits were often hurried to their units with the minimum of training in the optimistic belief that they would have plenty of time to learn their drill and weapons handling once they arrived. By Murphy's Law, semi-trained recruits often found themselves in some desperate skirmish with hostile forces before this was possible.

If a recruit was really unlucky he could find himself at the mercy of an aging officer who maintained discipline with the full spectrum of savage field punishments allowed by the Articles of War. Whipping, suspension on ropes, endless marching with a pack full of bricks – all manner of tortures could be ordered by company officers who usually skipped the tedious formality of a court martial.

Condemned to a dreary diet in dismal surroundings, where boredom and disease were bigger threats than hostile Indians, many soldiers voted with their feet. Every year between

10 and 20 percent of the US Army's enlisted men deserted. Although the reliability of immigrant soldiers with comical German accents was widely questioned, native-born Americans were actually more prone to desertion. Local factors determined the exact rate – bad officers or proximity to mining centers with their lure of easy money could dramatically weaken a fort's garrison.

Despite all the tribulations of an enlisted man's career, hardly a man of the Regular Army elected to join the Confederacy. Just 26 out of 15,000 enlisted men are known to have turned in their blue coats for gray. The officers were far more evenly divided, which led to accusations that West Point was a secessionist institution, despite the fact that the majority of its graduates sided with the Union. Relations on many army posts were very strained in the late 1850s, as tension developed between North and South. In April 1861 some 313 officers

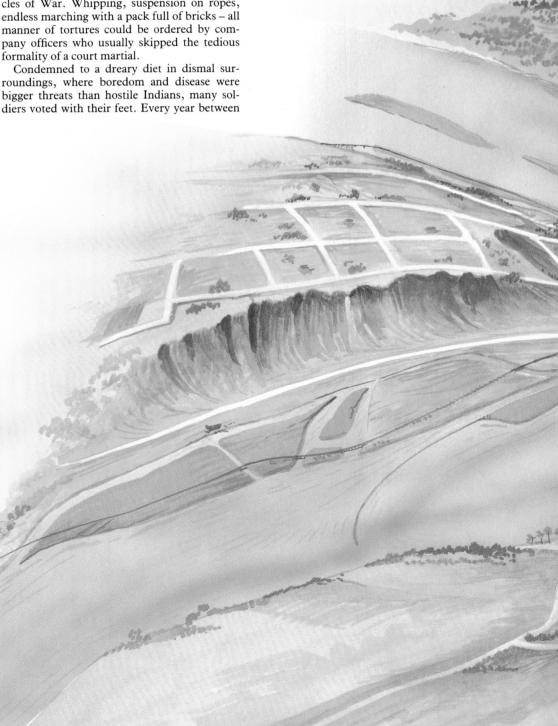

resigned as their home states seceded – thus, at a stroke, the US Army lost a third of its officer corps.

The Regular Army was rapidly dwarfed by the volunteer formations raised in 1861. Although it retained its separate identity throughout the war, it could not compete with the wages and enlistment bounties offered by state volunteer regiments. Despite this obstacle to recruitment, the regulars fought with high distinction. However, many regular officers moved into volunteer service, where their prospects of high rank were infinitely superior. The Regular Army was expanded by nine infantry regiments, one artillery regiment, and one cavalry regiment. In addition, the cavalry

was reorganized and re-numbered as cavalry regiments one through six. All the old titles were abolished.

Combat experience of the Indian wars was poor preparation for high command in the Civil War. Yet many future leaders saw some tough action before facing each other across a battlefield. Characteristically, J.E.B. Stuart took part in one of the few classic saber charges ever made against an Indian foe. The battle took place in Colorado in 1856 and Stuart was wounded by a pistol ball. He was serving with a small column commanded by Edwin V. Sumner, cooperating with a similar force under John Sedgwick. Both men were future Union corps commanders.

Harper's Ferry was of enormous strategic importance during the war and also the scene of John Brown's famous raid during 1859. The fanatical abolitionist attempted to seize the Federal armory there, but was overwhelmed by US Marines directed by the then Lieutenant Colonel Robert E. Lee, 2nd US Cavalry, and his aide, Lieutenant J.E.B. Stuart. Brown was hanged for his crimes, but his last note, written only an hour or so before his death, was strangely prophetic: "I, John Brown, am quite certain that the crimes of this guilty land will never be purged away; but with blood, I had as I now think, vainly flattered myself that without very much bloodshed, it might be done."

Land Battle in the Civil War

Over 623,000 Americans died in the Civil War, which remains America's bloodiest conflict. Only the death toll from World War II approaches this figure: between 1941 and 1945 the US forces sustained 407,000 fatal casualties. The Civil War casualty list dwarfs those incurred in World War I (106,000); Vietnam (57,000), and Korea (55,000). For Americans of the 1860s the casualties were simply unprecedented. Total casualties in the Mexican War had been just over 13,000, and fewer than 2000 of these were battle deaths. The US armed forces had lost fewer than 5000 men during the entire history of the American Revolution.

While between 65 and 70 percent of the Civil War deaths were caused by disease, the carnage inflicted by mid-nineteenth century weapons was an icy shock. Both sides began the conflict with volunteer armies that anticipated a decisive result during the summer of 1861. Casualties would be inevitable, but few men were bold enough to predict the true length of the struggle. Battle succeeded battle, but few engagements seemed to produce a significant result. The succession of clashes in the eastern theater left the Union forces with a healthy respect for the Army of Northern Virginia, but they always returned to fight another day. Lee's victories won the South time, but they could

not inflict a fatal blow on the Army of the Potomac. For both sides decisive victories proved illusive. Was this the fault of the generals? Or the volunteer soldiers? Or had the weapons of the 1860s so increased the power of the defense that an overwhelming victory like Jena or Waterloo was no longer possible?

Since the tiny US Regular Army was swamped immediately by the vast volunteer armies, many descriptions of the Civil War battles were penned by civilians in uniform. Since not even the regular soldiers had ever seen more than a few thousand troops assembled together, no one was prepared for the sheer scale of Civil War battles. While armies of more than 100,000 men had been seen in Europe since the seventeenth century, such concentration of military force was unheard of in America. Not surprisingly, this led to understandable exaggeration from time to time. This caused some European military commentators to disregard the evidence of the Civil War, but the more perceptive, like the British officer G.R.F. Henderson, were impressed with American honesty. Many American soldiers were brutally frank in their memoirs – if their regiment ran away during an action, they openly said so. This contrasted sharply with German accounts of their war with France in

1870. Here, most writers glossed over any failures in order to present a smug story of unbroken military success. American descriptions of the chaos of battle were mocked as proof of US amateurishness. In fact, they were far more accurate, but it is essential to remember this difference in approach when comparing the battles of the Civil War to combat in nineteenth-century Europe.

Infantry

With few exceptions, Civil War battles were dominated by infantry armed with rifled muskets. The Springfield .58-caliber and similar weapons inflicted the majority of battlefield casualties and largely determined the tactics adopted. Although the rifled musket was longer ranged and more accurate than the smoothbores it replaced, it still had to be concentrated for its fire to be effective. The French-inspired manuals used by both sides still relied on a two-deep line of troops, more or less shoulder to shoulder, as the final arbiter of land battle. The battle line was to be preceded by skirmishers who took every advantage of the ground, but only a relatively dense line of troops could develop the firepower necessary in defense and the momentum to break through in an attack.

ABOVE: *Infantry regiments fought in a two-deep line to maximize their firepower. Each man in the formation took up about 2 feet when fighting in close order. The 10 companies of a regiment would maneuver independently if in broken ground, but only a shoulder-to-shoulder line could develop the weight of fire to drive back the enemy.*

BELOW: *A regiment deploys for battle with two companies skirmishing ahead of the main line and another two retained as a reserve. Major-General Lew Wallace likened a regiment's skirmishers to the antennae of an insect, probing ahead to locate the enemy and prevent a surprise attack. In early battles many regiments failed to deploy skirmishers or posted them too close to the main body. This left them vulnerable to a deadly volley at close range from an undetected enemy.*

Land Battle in the Civil War

The strength of Civil War infantry regiments varied enormously. The 1697 volunteer infantry regiments created by the Union were authorized by Congress in 1862 to have a headquarters section of 13 regimental officers and 1024 officers and men. The latter were formed into 10 companies, each 101 strong. In reality, few regiments could muster more than 450 men in action. A young man who had volunteered for the Union or Confederacy usually found himself in an infantry company of about 40 individuals. His company would probably march into action in two ranks with the other companies prolonging the regiment's line of battle to either side.

The companies were known by letter, with A company (the senior) in the place of honor, the right flank. B company took the left and so on. In the center stood the regimental color party, which played a crucial role. Raising aloft the national flag and a regimental flag, it led the soldiers forward in the attack and served as a rallying point in defense. Bearing the colors was probably the riskiest job in the regiment and soldiers of both sides would take on hopeless odds to defend their standard or to seize that of an enemy.

An infantry company was commanded by a captain with a 1st lieutenant, a 2nd lieutenant, a 1st sergeant, four sergeants, and eight corporals. But just as the companies were invariably short of half their private soldiers, officers and NCOs were in similarly short supply. Companies were also supposed to include two musicians. In the noise and smoke of a Civil

War battlefield, officers and NCOs could shout themselves hoarse and still fail to make themselves heard. The shrill notes of bugles and fifes, and the rhythmic pounding of drums were useful because they could pierce the din.

Maintaining this simple two-rank formation was not easy, even when the regiment crossed tidy Pennsylvannia farmland. Among the twisted branches of the Wilderness or the steep slopes of Lookout Mountain it was another matter altogether. Civil War soldiers spent far more time practicing their drill movements than they did firing their rifles. Unless a regiment could retain its cohesion in action, it was doomed to defeat at the hands of a better organized enemy. A disordered regiment was unlikely to be able to coordinate its fire or maneuver quickly and effectively. Unless order could be re-established, the regiment would take cover and stay there, unable to deliver an attack yet unwilling to give up its ground without a fight. The result would be a long casualty list with little to show for it.

Armies screened themselves with cavalry patrols, keeping their own movements secret and trying to discover those of the enemy. The Confederacy was fortunate in having two of the greatest cavalry generals in military history – J.E.B. Stuart and Nathan Bedford Forrest. Until 1864 the well-led Southern cavalry was able to dominate the better equipped but poorly led Union horsemen. However, the promotion of men like George A. Custer and Philip Sheridan, and an overwhelming numerical superiority, eventually gave the advantage to the North. Here a cavalry regiment is deployed on picket duty. Half the troopers remain with the "grand guard," while the rest disperse into small patrols and ultimately to a chain of individual riders. Note the detachments of infantry posted in close support: this made it impossible for a superior cavalry force to push through without a serious fight.

Land Battle in the Civil War

Although the regiment was often the limit of the ordinary soldier's horizon, it was merely one cog in a very large machine. For senior officers, the basic tactical unit was the brigade of between three and six regiments. In the Union forces this was commanded by a colonel, in the Confederacy, a brigadier-general. Several brigades combined to make a division commanded by a US brigadier-general or a Confederate major-general. Divisions were assembled into corps, which were more formally organized in the Union Army. Given numbers and allotted symbols in the Army of the Potomac, some like the I Corps were destined for fame. Others, notably the ill-fated XI Corps, were not so successful.

Confederate corps were simply known by their commanders' names and, indeed, their entire structure depended on the senior Confederate leadership. After Thomas Jackson's death, Lee reorganized the Army of Northern Virginia from two into three corps, accepting that no other officer could perform the same role as Stonewall himself.

Weaponry

Civil War rifled muskets were far more effective weapons than the smoothbores they replaced. In competent hands they were capable of deadly accuracy at surprising ranges – as the unfortunate Union general Sedgwick discovered. But although the practiced sniper could hit a man at over 600 yards, the ordinary soldier's fire was much less precise. When the skirmish line was halted and the main battle lines engaged, precision shooting was impossible. Indeed, it was considered a major achievement to impose any fire control on a regiment once it became locked in combat with the enemy. In theory, the men were supposed to fire their rifles in crisp, disciplined volleys. But while a regiment might manage to open a fight with a well-timed volley, this was usually followed by an uncontrolled fusillade. Soldiers loaded, aimed, and fired at will. Some emptied their cartridge boxes with bewildering speed; others remained in cover, only loosing off a round when the enemy's fire appeared to slacken.

Infantrymen carried between 60 and 100 rounds when they went into action. Carrying any more ammunition was physically difficult,

and pointless unless the soldiers were able to clean their rifles. The fouling from black powder accumulates rapidly in a rifle barrel, making it increasingly difficult to load. After between 20 and 30 shots, the barrel becomes so choked that the rammer needs to be hammered down to get the ball right down to the breech. Weapons fired with the ball not fully seated in the breech were liable to misfire or bulge their barrels. The recoil increases in direct proportion to the fouling. After 40 rounds it becomes a major effort to raise the brass-backed rifle stock to a bruised and battered shoulder.

In the intense stress of combat, these physical limitations of the weapon were compounded by human error. Some 37,000 muskets were salvaged from the Gettysburg battlefield. Of these, 24,000 were loaded, three-fourths of them with more than one round. The 6000 with just the one round loaded included many weapons with the whole cartridge rammed down unopened, or with the bullet behind the powder charge instead of in front. Some of the multiple-loaded muskets had over half a dozen cartridges hammered down their barrels. Their owners had presumably been going through the motions, but the deafening noise and mind-numbing pressure had dulled their senses. If it is assumed that for every incorrectly loaded rifle left on the field, there was another still slung over someone's shoulder, over a third of the infantry at Gettysburg finished the battle with a disabled weapon.

Tactics

Since a regiment's firepower was inevitably degraded as the soldiers tired and the barrels clogged, the first few shots were very important. If the regiment could deliver a very accurate opening volley, it might be able to defeat its opposite number in short order. Failure would mean a protracted shooting match, unlikely to prove decisive. This encouraged regimental commanders to reserve their fire for close range rather than fritter away the advantage. Leading several regiments forward in the Union counter-attack at Shiloh, U.S. Grant himself went in front of the troops to prevent long-range firing.

A surprise volley, delivered from cover and followed up with a charge, proved to be a better

recipe for success than a long-range firefight. At Antietam the corn was higher than men's heads and able to shelter major bodies of troops. One Confederate attack came badly unstuck when their advance ran into the 9th New York Volunteers, who gave them a volley at point-blank range. Elsewhere, A.P. Hill's Confederates used the Indian corn to mask their arrival on the battlefield. John C. Starkweather's 28th Brigade (3rd Division, US I Corps) marched his men 12 miles to reach the Perryville battlefield, where he lay in wait for the Confederate onslaught. The corps commander's report describes how the 21st Wisconsin Regiment was deployed "in a cornfield, lying down, awaiting the approach of the enemy, and when he approached with his overwhelming force, this new regiment poured into his ranks a most withering fire."

Infantry regiments endeavored to protect themselves against this sort of unpleasant surprise by detaching skirmishers ahead of the main body. Typically, two of the 10 infantry companies would be sent ahead, spread out so that they screened the whole front. The frontage of a regiment formed in line of battle was calculated at 2 feet per man. A 450-strong regiment would thus occupy 150 yards if all 10 companies were in a two-deep line. Sending two companies forward to skirmish would contract the line to 120 yards, and the 90 skirmishers would advance on a slightly wider frontage to cover the main body to the flank as well as from ahead.

Major-General Lew Wallace said that the skirmishers were to the main body what antennae are to insects. Unlike sharp-shooters who acted almost individually, skirmishers maneuvered as a body, probing ahead of the main line. In defensive actions they formed the rearguard, seeking to delay the enemy and gain time for a counter-blow to be assembled or for their comrades to make good their retreat. This could be a hazardous undertaking if the attack was pressed home. Colonel B.B. Gayle of the 12th Alabama brought forward some troops in support of his skirmishers, driven back during the battle of South Mountain. Cut off by the Federal advance, he yelled, "We're flanked boys, but let's die in our tracks!" He drew his pistol and fought on until shot dead.

RIGHT: *A gun deploys for action, with the limber bearing ammunition close behind. Artillery regulations called for guns to be posted at 14-yard intervals, so a six-gun battery occupied a frontage of about 80 yards. When the section or battery commander gave the order, "Commence firing," the gunner in charge of each individual cannon ordered, "Load." The gun was sponged while the vent was blocked by an artillerist's thumb, otherwise the rush of air could be enough to re-ignite smoldering debris inside the tube. The gunner personally aimed the gun and inspected the fuses. If a gun fired from the same position for any length of time, the repeated recoil churned up the ground. Running a gun back into position again and again was exhausting work and nearby infantrymen were often used to assist the artillerymen.*

BELOW: *Although the line of cannon with their crews clustered around them presented a relatively scattered target to enemy fire, if the limbers and caissons could not be concealed behind a hill crest, the battery was hard to miss. At regulation intervals the limber was 6 yards behind the gun. With six horses, it occupied a depth of 11 yards; another 11 yards behind was the 14-yard-long caisson. A six-gun battery thus occupied a frontage of 80 yards and a depth of 47 yards. Batteries often had more horses than men, and they frequently suffered heavy losses.*

25

Land Battle in the Civil War

In Napoleonic times attacking troops had frequently advanced in dense columns. European battalions, similar in strength to Civil War regiments, fought nine ranks deep and they were often stacked one behind the other to assault an enemy position. If the enemy was unable to concentrate its artillery on this large and splendid target, such a massed column was difficult to stop with musketry alone. Defending troops would have time for only a few volleys before they were face to face with the attackers' bayonets. Only the best disciplined infantry – like the British – proved able to volley and counter-charge to defeat a deep column.

Mass-assault columns were seldom employed during the Civil War. Whereas the effective range of a smoothbore musket was between 50 and 100 yards, rifled muskets were effective at about 250 yards. In the disastrous assault on Marye's Heights at Fredericksburg in December 1862, the Federal infantry had gotten to a ravine some 300 yards in front of the stone wall held by Cobb's Confederates. There was no cover the rest of the way. Six times a line of blue-uniformed figures rose from that ravine to hurl themselves against the Confederate defenses and six times the result was the same. A thick carpet of bodies lay sprawled in front of Cobb's brigade.

A handful of desperate individuals made it to within 30 yards. General McClaw's report recorded, "single bodies were scattered at increased distances until the main mass of the dead lay thickly strewn at something like 100 yards off and extending to the ravine." Marye's Heights proved beyond doubt that the rifled

musket had changed the rules. Wave after wave of troops had been shot down *outside* the effective range of smoothbore muskets.

Civil War attacks were usually conducted in successive waves of men. Although rifled muskets had much greater range than smoothbores, they were still relatively low-velocity weapons and their bullets traveled over a high trajectory to reach their target. A bullet aimed at an enemy formation 300 yards away by a kneeling rifleman would pass over 6½ feet above the ground at 200 yards. Dropping low enough to hit a standing man at 250 yards, it would strike the ground 100 yards further on. This relatively high trajectory meant it was vitally important to estimate the range correctly.

Marcellus Hartley, the New York gun dealer appointed as the Union's purchasing agent in Europe during 1862, was told that the weapons he had bought in Belgium could not be issued immediately. The assistant secretary of war insisted that their crude block sights be replaced by elevating rear sights so that the soldiers could aim correctly. However, this concern was not shared by everyone. An Englishman who served with a Confederate regiment observed them removing the elevating rear sights on the Enfields. All experienced rifle shots, the soldiers were accustomed to adjusting their aim by eye!

Infantry brigades and divisions usually fought in waves separated by about 200 yards in open country. Sumner's and Hancock's divisions attacked Marye's Heights with their brigades formed into single lines of battle, following each other at 200-yard intervals. The

leading brigade ground to a halt in the face of the Confederates' furious musketry and was succeeded by the second, which met a similiar fate. The process was repeated. Each brigade, in the poignant words of Major-General Couch, "would do its duty and melt like snow coming down on warm ground."

Hood's Confederate division advanced with its brigades at 200-yard intervals when they marched on the Union right flank on the second day of Gettysburg. During Pickett's immortal charge the following day, the Confederate formation disintegrated rapidly as the Union artillery opened fire with canister. His division began the assault in two waves about 100 yards apart, with a skirmish line in front. The brigades lost formation as they crossed the Emmitsburg road and they overran their skirmishers who had slowed down under fire. Union infantry opened fire at 200 yards range, although some regiments deliberately held their fire until the Confederates were within 100, or even 50, yards. As they reached the crest of the ridge, the Confederates were crowded together many ranks deep – a terribly vulnerable target.

The famous Union assault at Cold Harbor was defeated in similar circumstances. Withdrawing from a salient where his entrenchments jutted out toward the Union lines, Major-General Law deployed his Confederates across the neck of the position, wrong-footing the assault before it began. When the Union troops attacked, they swarmed over the aban-

doned entrenchments only to run into a fresh trench line spitting fire. The first wave halted in confusion, so the following wave of troops cannoned into them. Succeeding lines of Union soldiers followed them but no one could advance against the Confederate musketry. The Union soldiers found themselves in a deep mass, a splendid target which Law's men could hardly miss. Unable to advance under such heavy fire, unable to maneuver and unwilling to retreat, the Federals suffered over 3000 casualties. Law described the action as even more dreadful than Marye's Heights at Fredericksburg, or on the old railroad cut where Stonewall Jackson's men inflicted heavy execution at Second Manassas.

The attack on Law's position at Cold Harbor was not intended to be made by a deep formation of infantry; they were funnelled together as the frontline stalled and successive waves merged in front of the Confederate line. It was an accident. But on several occasions troops were deliberately concentrated in this way in an effort to punch through the enemy line. Against a thin line of troops unsupported by artillery, a massed formation could succeed. Even if the defenders' fire was accurate, they could not hit a high enough proportion of the attacking troops to halt their advance. Yet because such a massed formation was more vulnerable to fire, it was a bold gamble indeed.

The Union II Corps at Antietam advanced in columns of brigades, changing front opposite the Dunker church so that they were formed in three lines of brigades no more than 70 yards apart. Promptly caught in the flank by McLaw's and Walker's Confederates, they were driven from the field.

At the battle of Corinth in 1862 Confederate infantry attacked the Union entrenchments in relatively dense formations, which were slowed by the fallen timber in front of the enemy line. Columns of regiments about 100 yards apart were eventually repulsed, although they reached the parapet of the Union battery Robinett.

However, a well-timed advance *en masse* could be a battle-winning stroke. In the wooded battlefield of Chickamauga James Longstreet assembled his corps in columns of brigades at half distance. Hood's division was massed five brigades deep and, in compact formation, the Confederates thundered through the forest to strike the weakest point in the Union line. The Union troops were taken by surprise and Rosecrans's army was driven from the field.

Faced by infantry armed with rifles, cavalry had few opportunities for a straightforward saber charge. Unlike European cavalry, which clung to outdated notions of mounted action, American horsemen tended to dismount for combat. Under the command of a man like Bedford Forrest, cavalry could exploit its superior mobility to concentrate its strength at the vital point. One man in four remained to hold the horses, while the rest of the regiment skirmished forward. Confederate cavalry relied on a mixture of shotguns, rifles, and muzzleloading carbines. Their US opponents soon began to acquire breechloaders and, ultimately, repeaters. As Buford's men demonstrated at Gettysburg, cavalry could plug a gap and win vital time for the rest of the army.

Land Battle in the Civil War

Trench warfare

In his book *Elements of Military Art and Science* Major-General Halleck rated one infantryman well entrenched as equivalent to six men attacking. The US Army's chief of staff, Halleck's belief in the defensive value of entrenchments was to be proved correct. Their importance had been an article of faith at West Point after Mahan began teaching there, but not all commanders rated them so highly. General Lee, who attended West Point before Mahan's time, did not entrench his men at Antietam and the Army of Northern Virginia suffered more casualties than the Union attackers. The 40,000-strong Confederate Army lost nearly 14,000 men, whereas the 75,000 Union troops sustained about 12,500 casualties. Contrast this to the Wilderness, where Lee's men made extensive use of fieldworks. Grant's 100,000 Federals suffered nearly 18,000 casualties on May 5–6, 1864. Lee's 60,000 Confederates lost 7500.

Entrenched troops enjoyed a psychological as well as physical advantage over their opponents. Sheltered from the worst effects of the enemy's fire, they were able to take better aim than soldiers crouching in an open field with bullets whistling past their ears. One of Meade's staff officers recalled that the Confederates could fortify their line with rifle pits in one day. If left undisturbed in their position for a second day, the defenses would be augmented to a regular parapet with artillery batteries in line. A third day would see an abatis of chopped trees and brush placed just in front of their parapet. This obstacle would slow the attackers down at point-blank range, breaking the momentum of the assault at the last and most vital moment. The artillery batteries would be sited in strong redoubts angled to sweep the cleared ground in front of the entrenchments. "Sometimes," the officer lamented, "they put this three days' work into the first twenty-four hours."

The likely consequences of an assault on an enemy trench line became more universally accepted as the war progressed. Lee's attacks on the Federal defenses at Malvern Hill were repulsed with casualties the Confederacy could ill afford, and he never assaulted so strong a position again. After Sherman's unsuccessful attack on Kenesaw Mountain, Major-General Howard observed, "We realized now, as never before, the futility of direct assaults upon entrenched lines." Sherman's infantry had attacked the Confederate defenses after a heavy artillery bombardment, but the Union troops were halted before the felled trees in front of the Confederate line. Many officers died trying to rally their men and press the attack home, but to no avail. They were beaten back.

The formidable rate of fire achieved by the Confederate defenders in several battles was not only due to the security afforded by their entrenchments. At Marye's Heights Cobb's brigade had already occupied the whole front when Kershaw's men arrived and doubled on to them. They fought the whole battle with a four-deep firing line. Kershaw was impressed that no one was injured accidentally. In the Wilderness some Confederate regiments sent men forward of their entrenchments after the first Union attacks had been repelled. Gathering up the muskets of the dead and wounded, they distributed them among themselves and

faced the next assault with several loaded muskets each.

For all their importance, entrenchments could not win a battle unaided. Halleck's equation of one man dug in equalling six attackers only held true if both sides were equally determined and the assault did not come as a surprise. Prolonged artillery bombardments rarely damaged a trench line; instead, they telegraphed the attackers' intentions, allowing the defenders to concentrate their reserves close to the threatened point. This was one respect in which the Civil War anticipated later conflicts. The Russians would encounter the same problem fighting the Turks in 1877. Other European armies were to discover it in 1914.

Entrenched positions could be taken by surprise. Two brigades of Jubal Early's corps were overwhelmed in their fortified bridgehead over the Rappahannock on November 7, 1863. Russell's division attacked late in the afternoon under the direction of General Sedgwick. More

than 1600 Confederate soldiers were captured just half an hour after one of their commanders had personally told Lee that he could hold the position against the whole Union Army.

This attack was intended as the prelude to a full-scale attack on Lee, but the Army of the Potomac did not maneuver with the necessary vigor to catch the Confederates. Instead of turning Lee's position and possibly splitting the Army of Northern Virginia as intended, Meade found himself confronting 7 miles of entrenchments at Mine Run. He prepared to attack nevertheless, while his soldiers were to be seen writing their names and addresses on slips of paper to identify them should the worse happen. Some even added the words, "Killed in action, November 30, 1863!" His corps commanders opposed an assault and Meade had no intention of fighting a futile battle to please bellicose New York newspapermen and politicians. He called it off and retreated, just as Lee began to maneuver against his flank, possibly seeking a second Chancellorsville.

The most successful attack on an entrenched position occurred just a week earlier at Missionary Ridge above Chattanooga. Braxton Bragg's Confederate Army was strongly posted atop a rocky slope rising up to 400 feet above the Union lines. It was a disagreeable prospect, and Grant's plan called for flanking attacks around both ends while Thomas's troops pressed the

The first Union assault on Bloody Lane at Antietam, shortly after 9.00 a.m., demonstrates the deadly power of muzzleloading rifles. Some 1900 Confederates lining the sunken road were attacked by a shoulder-to-shoulder line of Union infantry. There was little artillery support and the Union brigade advanced as if on parade without a skirmish line in front. The Confederates held their fire until the Union troops were within 100 yards, then shot them down. The 1st Delaware in the center foreground lost half its 900 men in a matter of minutes. On the left of the Union line, the 4th New York lost 187 out of 450.

Land Battle in the Civil War

Confederate center. In the event, Sherman and Hooker's flanking assaults were beaten back but, in an unauthorized maneuver, Thomas's leading troops lowered their heads and charged full tilt. Scrambling up the brush-covered incline, they drove back the Confederate skirmish line toward the main position. The Confederates found some of their artillery pieces could not be depressed low enough to hit the attackers, so the whole line wavered and eventually ran. Casualties in this assault were comparatively slight – testimony to the rapid Confederate collapse.

Artillery

Although relatively ineffective against dug-in infantry, artillery could be murderous indeed if the target were unprotected. It was one of the key reasons for entrenching in the first place, and a lynchpin of the defense throughout the war. Field guns were organized into four- or six-gun batteries; the Union forces standardized on the latter, while the Confederates' strength varied. In the fall of 1862 the Army of Northern Virginia included 16 batteries with six guns, four five-gun batteries, and 34 four-gun units. An individual battery was usually divided into two-gun sections and was manned by 3–5 officers, 12–20 NCOs, and 58–122 privates. Batteries were attached to infantry brigades, divisions, and corps, so each infantry formation had its own integral artillery. In addition, several armies formed an artillery reserve, the Confederates being quicker off the mark. During the Seven Days Campaign, Lee retained six battalions of artillery as an army reserve. An Antietam he did the same, each reserve artillery battalion consisting of five or six batteries, although by Gettysburg he had reduced the reserve and allotted more guns to the three corps in which he had reorganized the army. The Army of Northern Virginia's artillery reserve was eventually abolished in 1863 and corps artillery battalions created to provide each of Lee's senior commanders with a powerful concentration of guns.

Artillery batteries in the Union forces progressively standardized their equipment until it was unusual to find two different types of gun within the same battery. All batteries engaged at Gettysburg were uniformly armed. Far less well equipped than their enemies, the Confederates invariably had several different cannon within their batteries. It was normal for a four-gun battery to consist of two sections with dissimilar guns, typically a pair of 12-pounder Napoleon smoothbores and a pair of 10-pounder Parrott rifles. Numerous combinations existed during the war, with some batteries at Antietam fielding up to four types of cannon, each with widely varying characteristics. It was a logistic nightmare.

The advent of rifled cannon had increased the effective range of artillery in the same way that rifled muskets had lengthened the reach of the infantry. At Gaines Mill the heavy guns with the Union Army engaged Confederate infantry north of the Chickahominny at 2½ miles, making them fall back and seek another route of attack. At Knoxville, Tennessee, the Union frontline trenches were under disagreeably accurate Confederate sniper fire from a brick

house about 750 yards away. The infantrymen complained to their artillery and the gunners took careful aim with a 20-pounder Parrott rifle. Fired from Fort Sanders, at a range of 2500 yards, the first shell scored a direct hit.

When the infantry advanced to attack the enemy line, their supporting artillery batteries often remained a mile from their targets. At Crampton's Gap on September 14, 1862, Slocum's division of the US VI Corps stormed the Confederate positions with artillery firing in their support from a flanking position. The Union gunners drove off their opposite numbers, preventing the Confederate artillery from firing effectively on the attacking infantry. Lee, Longstreet, and D.H. Hill came forward to observe Union movement at Antietam, Hill remaining mounted despite a warning from Longstreet. As they studied the Federal deployment through their telescopes, they saw a puff of white smoke from a Union battery about a mile away. Several seconds later Hill's horse lost its front legs and the general was left trapped in the reins although not injured

himself. General Leonidas Polk was not so lucky. Reconnoitering more closely with generals Johnston and Hardee, he was studying the Federal lines from Pine Mountain on June 14, 1864, when a battery of Parrott rifles opened fire at a range of about 500 yards. The round passed clean through his chest, killing him instantly.

These spectacular examples of accuracy illustrate the potential of Civil War artillery, but it was only fully realized during a minority of battles. The gunners labored under two difficulties: unsuitable ground and the rifled muskets of the infantry. Very few battlefields offered long, clear fields of fire like the ½-mile killing zone at Malvern Hill where D.H. Hill lost a third of his 6500 men. He described it as murder, not war, a situation destined to be replayed at Fredericksburg. Longstreet asked E.P. Alexander, his artillery commander, whether he needed more cannon on his front. Alexander refused, saying, "General, we cover that ground now so well that we will comb it as with a fine toothcomb. A chicken could not live on that field when we open on it."

The charge of the Union cavalry at the battle of New Market is repulsed by the 22nd and 23rd Virginia infantry regiments (about 1200 men in total) and 16 field guns. Stahel's cavalry division had about 2000 men, and the formation took its time preparing for the attack. The Confederates had time to bring forward their artillery and double-shot the guns with canister. When the horsemen finally emerged from the wooded hillside, they came under a hail of fire and were taken in the flank by McClanahan's battery firing across Smith Creek. Attacking in three lines, the cavalry were immediately disordered and within moments the whole formation turned and fled. The division lost 107 men in the attack – a low proportion of its total strength.

Land Battle in the Civil War

His chilling prophesy proved correct, but such killing grounds were to prove a rarity. In densely wooded battlefields like the Wilderness, Chancellorsville, Chickamauga and others, gunners were lucky to find a clearing in which to deploy. When they did, they found that the increased range of rifled muskets had reduced the effect of their primary close range weapon, canister.

Solid shot fired from cannon was very effective against deep columns of troops. But, as we have seen, Civil War commanders rarely obliged the enemy gunners by deploying their men in this manner. Instead, successive waves of two-rank lines came forward, separated by several hundred yards if fighting in the open. Such a shallow formation could easily take cover and presented a relatively poor target. Since Civil War shells included modest bursting charges, and their fuses, especially in Confederate service, were unreliable, they too were usually ineffective.

Not only were they unlikely to inflict significant damage on entrenchments, infantry could also take cover by using the lie of the land. At Antietam, Stonewall Jackson's troops defending the "east" and "west" woods took advantage of a slight ridge after the "east" wood had fallen. This almost imperceptible rise in the ground was some 70–80 yards in front of the Confederate infantry, who took cover among the boulders and trees. Incoming Federal artillery rounds struck the ridge and went hurtling above the Confederates' heads. The Union infantry awaiting Pickett's charge at Gettysburg enjoyed a similar immunity from artillery fire as they lay behind the crest.

So the artillery's most effective projectile was the shotgun blast effect produced by case-shot: tin cylinders or linen bags packed with musket balls. Its effective range was around 300 yards, slightly longer for larger caliber cannon firing heavier loads. In the Napoleonic wars artillery had been able to blast enemy infantry with canister from beyond the effective range of the hapless foot soldiers' muskets. In the 1860s this was seldom possible. With rifled muskets, infantry could shoot back with every hope of killing the gunners and the horses they needed to maneuver the cannon.

When infantry happened across enemy artillery in the close terrain of many battles, they could fire or they could charge. Charging was not necessarily suicidal. If the infantry were close enough, they could be among the gunners at bayonet point before the artillery had time to fire more than a few rounds. The fate of Union

batteries in the first phase of Shiloh and those guns deployed on Little Round Top on July 2 illustrate what could happen when determined infantry boiled out of the woods.

Other charges were less successful. Major-General Alfred Pleasanton managed to stop Jackson's exultant Confederates at Chancellorsville by forming a gun line at Hazel Grove. Consisting of 24 cannon, six 3-inch Ordnance rifles, six 10-pounder Parrotts, six light 12-pounders, and six Napoleons, it was a powerful line but perilously close to the forest edge. When the Confederates swarmed out of the woods, they were crowded five or six ranks deep, their formations disordered by hard fighting and rapid pursuit through the trees. Although they held aloft a Union flag, the deception did not work and the gun line opened fire.

The volley of shot was deliberately aimed at the ground 100 yards in front. Striking the earth, the projectiles bounced up to fly into the Confederate formation at waist height. Pleasanton's defense was considered so successful by some captured Confederates that they assumed the rout of the US XI Corps to have been a ruse. The Union gunners considered themselves lucky that the Confederates had pressed

home their charge and fired their rifles wildly. The bullets passed harmlessly above the gun crew. Had they managed a well-aimed volley, they might have broken through.

Union infantry from the II and VI Corps were driven off in much the same way on May 18, 1864, when they attacked part of Ewell's corps at Spotsylvania. Some 30 guns had been deployed to sweep all approaches to the Confederate position and the Federals never made it to musket range.

However, rifled muskets were certainly able to drive off artillery in certain circumstances, although it helped if the infantry were on the defensive. The new-found power of infantry to protect itself against close range artillery fire was demonstrated at dawn on November 21, 1862. A detachment of Morgan's cavalry attacked the 31st Ohio Infantry at Cage's Ford on the Cumberland River. They brought up two 12-pounder howitzers and fired over the water, but heavy fire from the Union infantry compelled the gunners to withdraw.

Even when protected by fieldworks, gunners could suffer badly from rifle fire if the enemy infantry was allowed to establish itself within about 300 yards. The Washington Artillery,

formed in 1840, claimed to be the oldest military organization in Louisiana and it provided four companies to the Army of Northern Virginia. At Fredericksburg it occupied redoubts built by the engineers but made improvements before the battle. Firing on the Union assaults against Marye's Heights, it began to take steady losses from riflemen posted in the ravine, from which each attacking wave rose and charged to its destruction. The Louisiana gunners lost 24 men wounded and three dead. Toward the end of the action they needed help from nearby infantry to work the guns in the mud and slush of their redoubts.

Preparing a redoubt for an artillery battery was a major work of field engineering, which took even the most mole-like gun crew a good 48 hours. Where entrenching was not feasible, the experienced gunners could still achieve some protection by exploiting the lie of the land. In the same way that Jackson's infantry sheltered from the barrage at Antietam, an artillery battery could shelter behind the crest of a hill. Brigadier-General John Imboden recalled the position of his battery at First Bull

Run, unerringly selected by Brigadier-General Bee: "We were almost under cover by reason of a slight swell in the ground immediately to our front and not 50 feet away. Our shot passed not 6 inches above the surface of the swell and the recoil ran the guns back to still lower ground where we loaded, as only the heads of my men were visible to the enemy."

Imboden's battery of four 6-pounder smoothbores then engaged a Federal battery of six Parrott rifles at 1500 yards, which was soon supported by another Parrott battery which also included two howitzers. Only the latter were effective since the rifles' shells continued to bury themselves deep in the ground before exploding. "After the action," Imboden remarked, "the ground looked as though it had been rooted up by hogs." Further combat experience convinced Imboden that this was no accident. He suggested that over open ground a battery of 6-pounder smoothbores would take about an hour to defeat twice their own number of rifled cannon at up to 1000 yards. Twelve-pounder Napoleon smoothbores could do the same at 1500–1800 yards, all because a rifled

gun was helpless if the target lay behind sloping ground. Rifled projectiles striking at an angle much over 15 or 20 degrees would plough into the earth. The shot from a smoothbore would bounce and continue towards the target with lethal energy.

Taking cover behind a slope could also be employed against enemy artillery in fortifications. McAllister's Illinois battery engaged Confederate guns in Fort Donelson by loading his guns in the lee of a ridge. They were then run up by hand and fired, the recoil hurling the cannon back into cover.

Sedgwick's division attacks the West Woods at Antietam with its three brigades one behind the other at intervals of only 75 paces. There was no skirmish line ahead or to either flank. Gorman's brigade led the attack and was the only one able to return the fire of the Confederate troops to the front. Undetected by Sedgwick, fresh Confederate troops were arriving to his front and flank. Shortly after entering the woods, the Union troops were caught in a deadly crossfire and routed, with severe casualties.

Land Battle in the Civil War

Counter-battery fire, which used artillery to silence that of the enemy, had always been fairly difficult with smoothbore guns firing solid shot. A six-gun battery occupied an 82-yard frontage if deployed according to regulations, and this presented a dispersed target. To strike another gun with a cannonball was no easy matter; howitzers were more effective. It was a first-round hit from one that drove McAllister to site his guns behind the ridge line in the first place. Spherical case, sometimes called after its English inventor Captain Shrapnel, was designed to explode in the air, showering the target with fragments. This was most effective against enemy gun crew. It was not widely used in the Civil War, although it would become the most common field artillery round by the end of the century. Spherical case required good quality fuses, which were in very short supply in the Confederacy.

The technical difficulties involved made counter-battery fire an indulgence for those gunners with ammunition to spare. Even Union artillery with their much better stocked caissons were reluctant to bother. At Perryville they terminated a gun duel with their Confederate opposite numbers and waited for Bragg's infantry to show itself. The much larger Union gun line at Gettysburg did the same, reserving its fury for Pickett's division.

The Confederate artillery at Perryville advanced, with the infantry fighting well to the fore. The Union infantry took cover behind stone walls and fences, but the Confederate batteries were maneuvered up to take them in the flank. Artillery was at its most valuable acting in this close support role, but it was only really feasible when the enemy was not properly entrenched.

In a well-known episode in US Artillery history, a two-gun section of 12-pounders belonging to the 5th Regular Artillery galloped forward to support the attack at Cold Harbor on May 10, 1864. One officer and one NCO led the 23 gunners into action and they were the only men to walk back. Sixteen of the enlisted men were wounded and the other seven killed. All the horses died. The gun carriages were so badly damaged as to be beyond repair. Sergeant Lines discovered 27 bullet holes in the lid of the limber chest, which had been raised while ammunition was brought up to the guns, and the iron sponge bucket (⅛ inch thick) had 39 holes in it. They managed to deploy with the muzzles of their cannon projecting over the first line of Confederate breastworks. One gun fired nine rounds of canister and the other 14, before they were silenced by the storm of rifle fire.

Cavalry

The Union Army enjoyed a more plentiful supply of modern rifles and its artillery batteries had an even more pronounced edge with their conspicuous superiority in rifled cannon and far more reliable ammunition. However, there was one element of the army in which the Confederacy began the war with a distinct advantage. "The young bloods of the South . . . are brave, fine riders, bold to rashness and dangerous subjects in every sense . . . as long as they have good horses, plenty of forage, and an open country, they are happy . . . they are the most dangerous set of men that this war has turned loose upon the world. They are splendid riders, first-rate shots, and utterly reckless. Stuart, John Morgan, Forrest, and Jackson are the types and leaders of this class." The writer was Sherman and he was describing the men who formed the Confederate cavalry.

The South's great strength in cavalry was an enormously valuable asset. As the Union armies penetrated the Confederacy through Mississippi and via Kentucky and Tennessee, they were forced to detach an ever-increasing proportion of their strength to protect their supply lines.

Unless close to a major river, Federal forces had a serious logistic headache. Their wagon trains were bushwhacked, small parties of troops overrun, and the railroad lifeline ripped up. Confederate horsemen seemed to strike at will and some of their commanders, Morgan and Forrest especially, demonstrated a genius for guerrilla warfare.

The North began and ended the war with a shortage of horses suitable for the cavalry. In the first two years of the war the Union also lacked suitable riders. There were horses aplenty in the North, but most of them pulled carriages. Fox-hunting was popular in parts of the South, especially Virginia, and in the eastern theater the Confederacy could call upon the fine horses bred in Virginia and Kentucky.

The men who joined the colors riding these splendid hunters were a far cry from their Northern opponents. The Union cavalry raised in 1861 exhibited all the failings of cavalry recruited from a population not at home in the saddle. They lacked the training and confidence for rapid mounted maneuvers and ignorance of

horses led to a lot of sore backs and unnecessary casualties among the horses. Before the war the US Army accepted that it took three years to train a good cavalryman. Major-General William Averell recalled with some weariness his experience in the Peninsula campaign. Most of the Union cavalry force consisted of volunteers with just six months' service behind them. None of them had previous experience of caring for a horse or riding one, let alone fighting mounted. Some authorities recognized the folly of recruiting cavalry from urban areas; the governor of Pennsylvania refused applications to form volunteer cavalry companies from major towns and cities.

The situation was more evenly balanced in the west. Here both sides relied less on European-style horses and more on the Texan type raised on the western plains. Descended from horses originally brought to America by the Spanish, they had run wild in Mexico and spread northwards. Standing a little over 14 hands, they were used on the frontier by the regular US cavalry which was deployed there during the 1850s.

The most famous assault of the war: Pickett's charge at Gettysburg. The Confederates attacked in three waves of shoulder-to-shoulder infantry with a skirmish line ahead. The skirmishers ground to a halt along the Emmitsburg road as they came under increasingly heavy fire. The successive waves of Confederates bunched up as the leading troops slowed down. The massed Union artillery tore great gaps in the formation and the infantry regiments opened fire according to their colonels' tactical ideas. Some, like the 7th Michigan, opened fire at 200 yards; others waited until the gray line was less than 100 yards away. A regiment's first volley was usually its most effective, and it was not unusual for commanders to deliberately hold their fire to maximize its effect.

Land Battle in the Civil War

Nevertheless, thanks to their superior horsemanship, Southern cavalry dominated the fighting in both theaters for the first two years of the war. Both sides used the same weapons, relying on rifles, carbines, and pistols. Sabers were issued and a handful of units carried lances in 1861 – the famous 6th Pennsylvania Cavalry (Rush's Lancers) retained theirs until May 1863. But Civil War cavalry never adopted contemporary European tactics, which had changed little since the Napoleonic wars. American horsemen never attempted the sort of gallant, but usually futile saber charges that French and German troopers made in 1870. Small parties of cavalry would certainly charge an isolated artillery battery if they could flank it, but mass assaults by whole brigades were not contemplated.

There were two main reasons for this different approach. First of all, American cavalry was not hostage to several hundred years of battlefield tradition. In 1870, and even in 1914, French cavalry rode into action wearing armor that had proved of questionable value at Waterloo in 1815. The US Army was fortunately free of the conservative cavalry lobby which closed its eyes to the improvements in infantry weapons. With their much longer effective range, rifled muskets could inflict much more damage on charging cavalry than smoothbores. The appearance of breechloaders and repeating rifles tipped the scales still further.

Infantry had customarily adopted a square formation to defeat cavalry. This worked, provided the horsemen were not supported by mobile artillery which could massacre the foot soldiers, crammed together into an unmissable target. This was still in the drill book in 1861 and it was used on a few occasions during the Civil War, but generally as a result of a mistake! At the battle of Olustee in February 1864 the inexperienced colonel of the 64th Georgia Infantry Regiment formed square, fearing a charge by Union cavalry. The Federal artillerymen were cranking their pieces around when General Colquitt countermanded the order.

Neither side bothered to mass its cavalry for use on the battlefield. Those mounted charges that were made were usually the work of quite small bodies of horsemen. At Pea Ridge as few as 22 Confederate cavalrymen dashed at an advancing Union regiment in a gallant attempt to win time for their artillery to withdraw. This tiny force included several former British cavalrymen who had charged at Balaclava, and its advance was fortunately screened by the thick smoke shrouding the battlefield. They burst upon several hundred Federal infantry who were surprised and obviously did not expect these men to be on their own. The Union troops fell back into some woods.

The 5th US Cavalry Regiment made a classic saber charge at Gaines Mill, again to save their comrades in the artillery from being overrun by enemy infantry. Some 300 horsemen counterattacked the leading elements of Longstreet's corps. Confederate rifle fire hit 50 troopers and six out of the seven officers, dispersing the attack without loss to themselves. The true value of the charge was disputed by different Union officers, largely because General Fitz John Porter claimed the cavalry's subsequent retreat caused him to lose 22 cannon as his command fell back before the Confederate onslaught.

Colonel Joseph Wheeler's Confederate cavalry was more successful at Perryville, skirmishing with Union cavalry at dawn and finally charging them after the Federals had received support from both infantry and artillery. Dispersing the Union cavalry, Wheeler's men drove them back through their own infantry and took 140 prisoners.

More typical was the experience of the Union cavalry shot down and driven off by Branch's brigade at Second Manassas, or the destruction of Farnsworth's cavalry in their charge at Gettysburg. Kilpatrick's cavalry division menaced the right flank of the Confederates attacking Little Round Top. Some troopers were dismounted to skirmish with the Confederate infantry but were driven back. Kilpatrick, not for nothing called "Kill Cavalry" by some of his men, ordered a charge by the 1st West Virginia and 1st Vermont cavalry regiments. The West Virginias were launched against the 1st Texas infantry and were driven off by the main body of the Texans. The Vermont cavalry struck and passed through the Texans' skirmish line, which extended to the left.

Those Union cavalry who made it past the Confederate front line then maneuvered frantically as infantry regiments emerged from cover and batteries were turned on them. They eventually escaped with surprisingly light casualties, considering the odds – about 65 of the 300 charging cavalry were lost, but their commander, Brigadier-General Elon Farnsworth, died from multiple gunshot wounds.

Cavalrymen of both sides preferred to maneuver mounted, but to fight on foot. One man in four held the horses, so a regiment dismounting for action lost 25 percent of its theoretical firepower. However, the Union cavalry was more than able to compensate for this as it steadily acquired Sharps or Spencer carbines. Confederate cavalry continued to rely on a wild mixture of handguns, carbines, rifles and even shotguns.

Cavalry's primary function was to provide reconnaissance information for the army. Like Lew Wallace's skirmishers, they were antennae probing ahead to detect and evaluate enemy activity. Of course, a determined enemy could repel these antennae by judicious use of his infantry. When D.H. Hill was transferred to the Army of the Tennessee he was disappointed to find that the Confederate commander, Braxton Bragg, relied solely on his cavalry for information. Since the Union forces were supporting their cavalry outposts with detachments of infantry, the Confederate cavalry was unable to get close enough to the enemy main body to provide the best intelligence. In the east Robert E. Lee supplemented his cavalrymen's reports with a well-developed intelligence network. Gregarious agents drank with Union officers in Washington bars and kept the Army of Northern Virginia reasonably well informed of future Federal activity.

Reconnaissance by cavalry and reports from agents could never provide a commander with more than a fragment of the intelligence picture. Civil War generals conducted their operations in a perpetual state of uncertainty. The "fog of war" was an inescapable part of military operations but it affected some men more than others. McClellan habitually overestimated the Confederate forces opposed to him. At Perryville Bragg believed he was facing only part of the much larger Union Army, so he stayed and offered battle. His opponent, General Rosecrans, had concentrated most of his troops but thought Bragg's army was little smaller than his own. Stonewall Jackson's celebrated campaign in the Shenandoah was a classic example of a bold and enterprising commander relying on speedy maneuver to remain one step ahead of his enemies' intelligence.

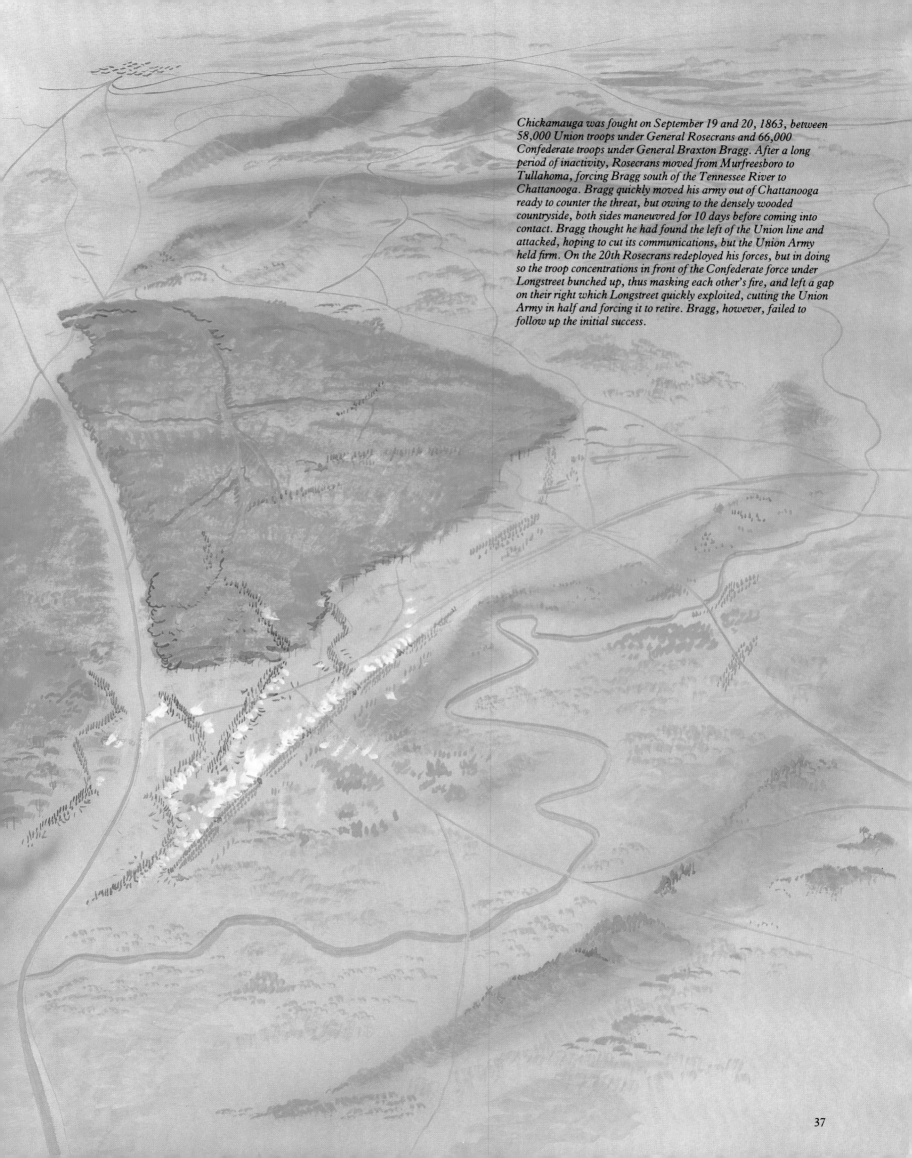

Chickamauga was fought on September 19 and 20, 1863, between 58,000 Union troops under General Rosecrans and 66,000 Confederate troops under General Braxton Bragg. After a long period of inactivity, Rosecrans moved from Murfreesboro to Tullahoma, forcing Bragg south of the Tennessee River to Chattanooga. Bragg quickly moved his army out of Chattanooga ready to counter the threat, but owing to the densely wooded countryside, both sides maneuvred for 10 days before coming into contact. Bragg thought he had found the left of the Union line and attacked, hoping to cut its communications, but the Union Army held firm. On the 20th Rosecrans redeployed his forces, but in doing so the troop concentrations in front of the Confederate force under Longstreet bunched up, thus masking each other's fire, and left a gap on their right which Longstreet quickly exploited, cutting the Union Army in half and forcing it to retire. Bragg, however, failed to follow up the initial success.

Land Battle in the Civil War

The difficulties of command

While the exact strength of the enemy was often a mystery, the weaknesses of a commander's own army were much too clear. Great strength of character was required for a general to press on, banking on the enemy being in a worse position. Lee's handling of the Chancellorsville battle – facing Hooker's full strength with fewer than 20,000 men, while Jackson maneuvered against the Union flank – shows enormous confidence and an accurate assessment of his opponent's character.

One reason for Lee's confidence was the inherent strength of the defensive and the time taken to overcome a major force. With cavalry banished to the fringes of the battlefield and artillery frustrated by bad terrain and enemy rifle fire, infantrymen usually had to settle the issue themselves. Unless there was a great disparity in troop quality, tactical leadership or armament, this took time. Infantry lines frequently shot it out for hours before either side gave way.

The battle fought in early May 1864 in the rough, tangled woodland known as the Wilderness was a direct result of Grant, who had taken overall command of the Army of the Potomac, trying to turn the right flank of the Confederate Army under Lee. After a great deal of confused fighting, both sides had exhausted themselves with no appreciable gains. On May 7 both armies improved their defensive positions, but Grant now moved his army toward New Spotsylvania Court House for what would prove to be the last action fought in the many confused battles that made up the Wilderness Campaign. Losses were heavy after several days' hard fighting, and many of the wounded were left in the tangled mass of woods which were often ablaze as a result of the fierce bombardment. In fact, many of the 17,666 Union soldiers listed as missing perished in the burning woods.

Confederate troops kept up their attacks on the Hornets' Nest at Shiloh for about five hours. The slaughter at the Burnside Bridge at Antietam went on for three hours before Union troops finally rushed it successfully. Even minor actions were seldom resolved any faster. At the battle of new Berne, North Carolina, on March 14, 1862 three Union regiments, with one in reserve behind, attacked the left flank of the Confederate position. This was held by a single infantry regiment. Across the rest of the front, a more equal firefight took place without any decisive results. After some 3½ hours of fighting, the attackers' ammunition was running low and the reserve regiment, the 51st Pennsylvania, was brought forward. Relieving the exhausted 51st New York Regiment, the Pennsylvanian troops advanced, fired a full volley, and charged. The Confederate defenders broke, which exposed the rest of their line to a flanking attack that led to the capture of the whole position.

As an illustration of the tempo of Civil War battle, the example of New Berne is interesting. Even if they had carried a heavy ammunition load of 80–100 rounds each, the Union infantry took 3½ hours to run low. If they fired 50 rounds apiece, their rate of fire averages at less

than one shot every four minutes. During the action the four regiments suffered 199 casualties – 169 wounded and 30 killed. Worn down by this protracted shooting match, the Confederates' morale failed when the 51st Pennsylvania intervened.

In a close action with the enemy, regiments lost their officers and their best men first. The majority struggled on, fatigue increasing as muskets thudded into shoulders with increasingly vicious recoil. Eyes became sore and reddened by the acrid smoke swirling around them. Nerves frayed little by little as a constant stream of enemy bullets passed by. Every few moments someone else would drop his musket to roll around in pain. The large-caliber lead bullets inflicted horrible, gaping wounds. Thus, the arrival of fresh troops was often decisive, even if they had had to march all day to reach the battle. In proper order and with clean weapons, they could still fire coordinated volleys and deliver a charge.

Although the deployment of reserves was straightforward in a small action like New Berne, it became increasingly hard with larger armies. Unless in close terrain like the Wilderness, brigade commanders could see all their regiments and maneuver them accordingly. A

competent divisional commander could sometimes switch an exhausted brigade out of line and replace it with fresh troops. But at corps or army level it proved very difficult to deploy reserves in the right place at the right time. The "fog of war" thickened during a battle. It was very difficult to see behind the enemy front line. Every tree line, every fold in the ground could conceal a powerful enemy force. The clouds of white smoke produced by black powder weapons produced a literal fog to compound the problem.

Many commanders could not tell where the front line was. At Mill Springs Confederate Brigadier-General Zollicoffer rode up to an officer to stop the infantry behind him firing on their fellow Confederates by mistake. Unfortunately, the mistake was Zollicoffer's. The officer was a Union colonel who promptly shot him. The Union lost the talented Philip Kearny at Second Manassas when he rode into some Confederates in error; General McPherson died in similar circumstances during the battle of Atlanta. General Mansfield had just stopped part of his XII Corps firing at Antietam, believing their target to be Duryea's Union brigade, when the supposed Federals opened fire and killed him.

The Confederate bishop-general Leonidas Polk was luckier at Perryville; he too rode over to stop supposed Confederates firing on his own men, only to discover the regiment he was ordering about came from Indiana. Polk bluffed it out, issuing loud orders as he trotted further down the line and into the sanctuary of a small wood. Earlier in the same action a Union officer had reported to Polk, asking for orders, only to be forced to surrender. Longstreet nearly never made it to the battle of Chickamauga. He got off the train at Catoosa with his staff, missed the Confederate Army, and rode into the Federal lines. He too adopted a bold front when he realized the error and his party slipped away without drawing attention to themselves.

If the commanders were not clear what was going on, their troops were none too sure either. Stonewall Jackson's death at the hands of Confederate infantry is perhaps the best known example, but it was not unique. Longstreet's luck ran out in the Wilderness when he was badly wounded by Confederate pickets, and General Jenkins, riding with him, was shot to death. It is easy to criticize the infantrymen from the comfort of an armchair, but keyed-up soldiers surrounded by enough underbrush to

conceal a division are prone to shoot first and shout a challenge afterwards.

Some officers were shot quite deliberately. John Reynolds was picked off by a Confederate sharpshooter at Gettysburg. Fellow corps commander John Sedgwick died the same way at Spotsylvania, seconds after he had chided his skirmishers for taking cover with the sadly mistaken remark that "they can't hit an elephant at this distance." The spectacular deaths of these two senior Union officers represent the summit of the sharpshooters' achievement. How many regimental and brigade commanders were killed or wounded by aimed fire as opposed to a random shot from a volley it is naturally difficult to discover. Wherever the terrain suited their trade, sharpshooters would issue forth from infantry regiments to pick off officers, color parties, or artillery crew. The experience of the Washington Artillery at Fredericksburg, described earlier, was shared by many a battery during the war. Confederate sharpshooters ensconced themselves in Devil's Den at Gettysburg and picked off numerous Union troops on Little Round Top.

Land Battle in the Civil War

Most generals, intent on directing their troops and usually on horseback, had little choice but to accept the risk from enemy snipers. However, some officers gave as good as they got. Brigadier-General Law was shouted at by the men of his brigade as he stood near the Richmond and Fredericksburg Railroad during the battle of the Wilderness. He ducked in time and the Minié ball passed by his head. Taking cover behind the log breastwork his troops were building, the general seized a rifle and shot it out with the Union sniper. He wounded the man with his second shot and the unfortunate sharpshooter was captured by the Confederates the following morning.

Even when the senior commanders managed to escape the lethal attentions of enemy sharpshooters, coordinating large forces proved extraordinarily difficult. The poor intelligence picture, blurred front lines, and broken ground that frustrated so many generals could have been compensated by an efficient staff system. But the tiny US Army in 1860 had no such administrative machinery and even the powerful armies fielded toward the end of the war

were prone to embarrassing breakdowns in communications.

The chaos was understandable in 1861. Confederate congressman and sometime chief of staff of the Army of the West, Colonel Thomas L. Snead, remembered the situation in Missouri. "No better proof could be given of the dearth of material for the staff than the fact that I was myself assigned to duty by General Price as chief of ordnance of the army, though I told him at the time that I did not know the difference between a howitzer and a siege gun, and had never seen a musket cartridge in all my life." Ignorance of the technicalities of military hardware was sadly matched by inadequate knowledge of the ground. The Confederates suffered heavy losses at Gaines Mill, primarily because the area occupied by the Union forces was pretty much a blank space on their maps.

Weak administration combined with green troops to waste a lot of time on Civil War battlefields. Mansfield's XII Corps got into a

horrible muddle at Antietam as undrilled infantry regiments became tangled as they hurried forward. Vital moments were lost as the formation shook itself out. Their commander was dead before the process was completed. But the problem at the top remained. Brigadier-General Jacob Cox described the "strange tardiness in sending orders" at all levels of the Army of the Potomac at Antietam.

An astonishing number of Civil War battles did not get under way until well into the afternoon, despite both sides being in contact early in the morning. No one was immune: Lee's Confederate attacks during the Peninsula Campaign are a classic example. In almost every major action large formations received their orders late or not at all. Infantry divisions frequently never moved when they were supposed to and attacks supposed to start together

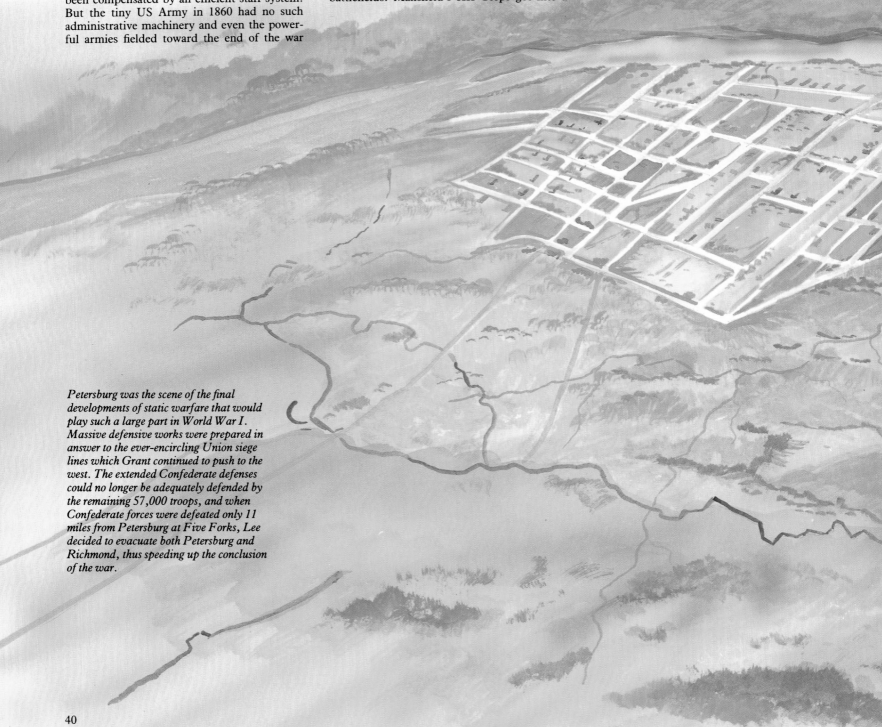

Petersburg was the scene of the final developments of static warfare that would play such a large part in World War I. Massive defensive works were prepared in answer to the ever-encircling Union siege lines which Grant continued to push to the west. The extended Confederate defenses could no longer be adequately defended by the remaining 57,000 troops, and when Confederate forces were defeated only 11 miles from Petersburg at Five Forks, Lee decided to evacuate both Petersburg and Richmond, thus speeding up the conclusion of the war.

often ended up as attacks in succession. Sometimes the individual officers were to blame; Cheatham was almost certainly drunk at Murfreesboro and Bragg never forgave him for his tardiness. Gallons of ink were expended after the war by commanders who blamed their subordinates for slowness, and by officers of all ranks explaining the reasons for apparent inactivity. President Lincoln never ceased to be amazed by the torpor which seemed to afflict successive commanders of the Army of the Potomac.

To give some idea of the size of the problem at the highest level, Halleck directed the US Army with just seven officers and 16 enlisted men. Between the end of July and September 12, 1862 his headquarters dispatched 421 telegrams but received enough signals to fill a 524-page bound volume. By comparison, von Moltke had 92 men on his staff during the invasion of France in 1870. Yet increasing the staff did not automatically increase its capacity. Although the Army of the Potomac's staff expanded steadily, it was duplicated from 1864 when Grant brought his own headquarters into the field. This seems to have added to the difficulties and the opening campaigns of that year were marked by map-reading errors and poorly disseminated orders.

In both the Union and the Confederacy the politicians and the general public expected decisive battles. Sir Edward Creasy's *Fifteen Decisive Battles* was published in London and New York in 1851. From Marathon to Saratoga and Waterloo it described a series of overwhelming victories, reflecting a popular notion that good generalship could always produce a clear-cut result. Small wonder that U.S. Grant's "no terms except unconditional and immediate surrender can be accepted" caught the public imagination after the disappointments of 1861. Yet no major army was ever destroyed in a single action throughout the Civil War. Even Hood's disastrous leadership of the Army of Tennessee, which led to the stinging defeats of Franklin and Nashville, did not remove his troops from the military balance. Hood's forces were depleted in battle, but were weakened still further by their retreat over a barren land in the dead of winter. From the shambles at Bull Run to the strategic stagnation at Petersburg, a knock-out blow in the field proved impossible.

The contemporary explanation often took the form of a diatribe against the generals. In the North, West Pointers were singled out for criticism – that they were obsessed with defensive tactics or even harbored sympathy for the South. But although both sides were saddled with some dim bulbs throughout the war, even when the light of military genius blazed brightly, truly annihilating victories still failed to materialize.

Land Battle in the Civil War

The disagreeable truth was that mid-nineteenth-century armies were harder to destroy than those of the Napoleonic era. Indeed, the ease with which earlier armies could be destroyed has been exaggerated. Large forces rarely disintegrated without a social or political dimension that multiplied the effect of a defeat. Both sides in the Civil War proved able to recruit and arm military forces on a vast scale. Unfortunately, the size of the armies and the frontages they occupied took them to the limit of what could be controlled by men on horseback. Frequently operating in terrain that frustrated reconnaissance, and armed with weapons that kept cavalry at a distance, Civil War armies could not be ruptured. Even when badly defeated, like Rosecrans's troops at Chickamauga, the retreating forces could always outpace their pursuers. Troops who had managed to break through often found themselves as disorganized as their opponents.

The power of the rifled musket made it difficult for artillery to provide the sort of intimate support occasionally achieved during the Napoleonic wars. Artillery only inflicted massive casualties when enemy infantry obligingly attacked massed batteries head-on. The heavy execution inflicted by the Union gun line

at Malvern Hill showed what happened then and it was seldom repeated. Concentrated artillery greatly aided the defense, but attacking armies found it very hard to tear a hole in an enemy position with even the heaviest bombardment. If the defenders entrenched themselves properly, field artillery was powerless to shift them.

American armies lacked the divisions of heavy cavalry trained to charge *en masse* in the European manner. But their performance in the Crimean War and subsequent European conflicts in 1859, 1866, and 1870 does not suggest that they would have made much difference.

With artillery kept at bay and cavalry banished to the wings, it fell to the infantry to win the battles of the Civil War. Since they could not overhaul a beaten enemy, decisive results would only have been possible if one side could inflict substantially more casualties than it received. The best ratios were certainly impressive – at Cold Harbor and Kennesaw Mountain Confederate forces inflicted about five times as many casualties as they suffered themselves. Yet these were unusual battles in which the attacking forces were shot to pieces without making any real impression on the

defense. Normally an attack would achieve at least partial success, compelling the defenders to counter-attack to restore the line. This often cost them dearly and evened out the losses.

Even without fighting a major battle, Civil War armies could sustain surprisingly heavy losses. The daily clashes between outposts between Sherman's and Johnston's armies in May 1864 cost both sides dearly, although neither mounted a full-scale assault. The Army of the Tennessee lost over 9000 killed and wounded, while the Union forces pressing them suffered nearly 12,000. The steady attrition from these continual exchanges of fire reduced the Confederate forces by 18 percent.

Civil War land battles were chaotic, confusing, and bloody affairs. Volunteer soldiers learned their trade the hard way – by experience. Mistakes were certainly made. But the great German military theorist Carl von Clausewitz likened warfare to movement in a resistant medium. Getting anything done in war is slower and more difficult than in peace; it is the difference between strolling along a sidewalk and wading through chest-deep water. Warfare produces friction which slows everything up. In the 1860s the timeless problems of soldiering were complicated by new developments in

weapons. The tactical certainties of the flintlock musket era were gone. By the end of the war some American units were among the most combat-experienced formations in the world. "Go to your homes," Lee said to his men at Appomattox, "and resume your occupations. Obey the laws and become as good citizens as you were soldiers." He could have been speaking to them all.

The defenses of Petersburg consisted of a series of artillery redoubts connected by trenches that gradually lengthened during the 10-month stalemate. Coehorn mortars were fired from the front line, lobbing their bombs into the enemy positions like the trench mortars of World War I. The Union artillery batteries were rotated between those redoubts in constant action and those on quieter sectors. In this way the wear on individual guns was kept about the same. The Union mine, fired under the Confederate lines, was the most serious attempt to break into Lee's defenses. The detonation of 900 lb of gunpower under a Confederate redoubt left a huge crater, but the infantry assault went badly wrong thanks to inept leadership.

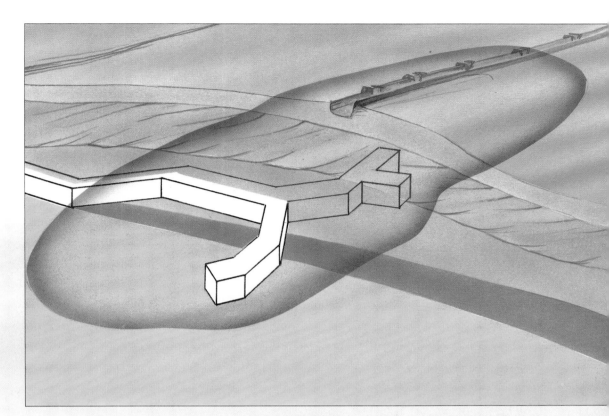

Pistols

Although revolvers had already proved themselves highly effective weapons in certain circumstances, the US Army Ordnance Department did not support their general issue. Reporting in 1850, the chief of ordnance argued that "repeating pistols cannot be advantageously used by the mass of our private soldiers for want of the necessary discretion, coolness, and skill." While accepting that pistols could be of service in the hands of certain selected men, he saw no point in the army buying Samuel Colt's patents and manufacturing its own revolvers. Instead, the army bought limited numbers of Colt's revolvers and they were still under examination at the outbreak of war.

Of all firearms used by the military, pistols require the most practice to be at all effective. Issuing them as last-ditch, personal defensive weapons is only worthwhile if the individual trains regularly. No amateur pistol shot can hope to hit a target unless in the same room. However, pistols were acquired in tens of thousands during the war. They were carried by almost all cavalrymen, officers, artillery crew, and other specialists. Their limitations have often been emphasized, but from the perspective of the 1860s they were a welcome source of handy firepower. Given the slow rate of fire of the infantry's rifled muskets, one cornered man with a revolver could even have the advantage. However, any attempt to take on rifled armed infantry *en masse* was a different matter, as the US sailors discovered when they attacked Fort Fisher in 1865.

The typical Civil War revolver took some time to load. Each chamber had to be filled with a measure of powder and the spherical lead pistol ball rammed down using the lever under or beside the barrel. When all five or six chambers were loaded, the soldier placed percussion caps over the nipples on the rear of the cylinder and he was ready to fire. The better makes of Civil War revolver could group their shots on a playing card at up to 25 yards. This assumes the shooter was not under pressure and the target remained obligingly still. However, in practice a competent pistol shot could be confident of hitting a man-sized target within that sort of range under battlefield conditions.

Civil War revolvers were prone to several problems. Percussion caps often disintegrated when they fired (not a problem on a rifle or carbine), and pieces of cap could fall between the cylinder and the frame, preventing it from rotating properly. Add to this the fouling from

Colt revolvers (and copies of them) were the most widely carried handguns of the Civil War. In 1857 Congress had refused to renew Colt's patent on revolving firearms. But although he had lost his monopoly, Samuel Colt was the only gunmaker with the production facilities to meet the demand for weapons in 1860. He had patented a revolver designed by John Pearson in 1834–5. Successive designs had become popular thanks to a shrewd advertising program; consequently, by the outbreak of war, his guns were already the most popular pistols in the USA.

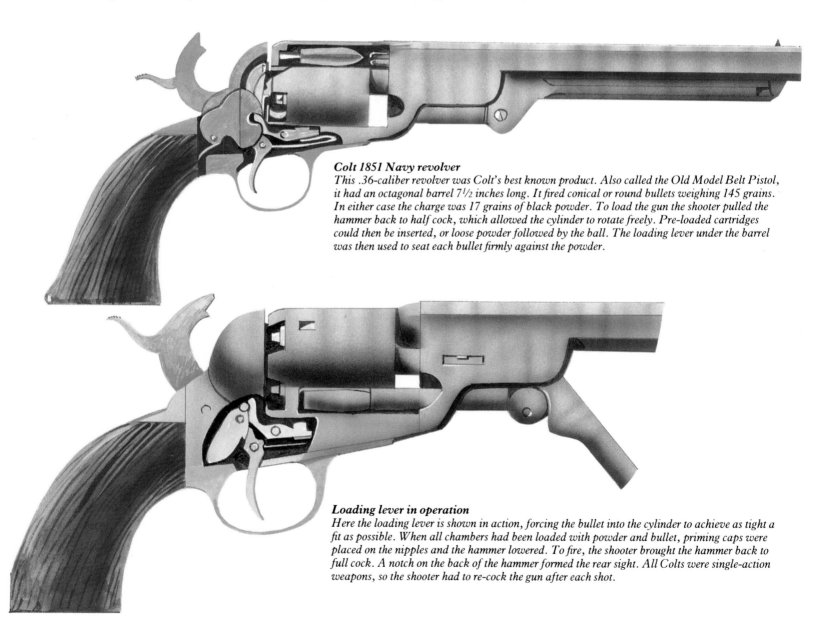

Colt 1851 Navy revolver
This .36-caliber revolver was Colt's best known product. Also called the Old Model Belt Pistol, it had an octagonal barrel 7¹/₂ inches long. It fired conical or round bullets weighing 145 grains. In either case the charge was 17 grains of black powder. To load the gun the shooter pulled the hammer back to half cock, which allowed the cylinder to rotate freely. Pre-loaded cartridges could then be inserted, or loose powder followed by the ball. The loading lever under the barrel was then used to seat each bullet firmly against the powder.

Loading lever in operation
Here the loading lever is shown in action, forcing the bullet into the cylinder to achieve as tight a fit as possible. When all chambers had been loaded with powder and bullet, priming caps were placed on the nipples and the hammer lowered. To fire, the shooter brought the hammer back to full cock. A notch on the back of the hammer formed the rear sight. All Colts were single-action weapons, so the shooter had to re-cock the gun after each shot.

the black powder and it did not take long for a cylinder to jam solid. On some pistols the shooter was lucky to get all six shots off. To overcome the resistance caused by the fouling it was sometimes necessary to use both thumbs to force the hammer back. As reloading was time-consuming and fiddly, the prudent cavalryman carried spare cylinders – or a spare revolver.

The single most widely used revolver in the Civil War was the Colt Army Model 1860. After some experiment with Colt revolvers, the Ordnance Department requested a modified weapon and Colt responded by fitting a cylinder chambered for .44-caliber balls to the frame of his popular .36-caliber revolvers. With a streamlined barrel, loading lever group, and an extended grip, it was an excellent compromise between weight and bore size. From late 1861 Lieutenant-Colonel Ripley constantly pressed Colt to increase production and the Hartford factory rose to the challenge. By the end of 1862 it was producing 1000 weapons a week and double that by early 1863.

Samuel Colt dominated the early war revolver production largely because he alone had the capacity to satisfy the US Government. Yet he may have cut his own throat by overcharging. Although Colt patriotically raised a regiment at his own expense and provided it with his revolving rifles in 1861, he was charging the government $25 for his pistols. This was approximately double what they cost him to produce, and since he sold the US Army and Navy some 145,000 revolvers in the first 30 months of the war (two-thirds of the pistols supplied to the Union forces), he was making a tidy profit. Competition from Remington forced the price down to $14.50 in June 1862, shortly after Colt's death. The company was taken over by Colt's chief assistant, E.K. Root, but it completed its final contract for the army in November 1863 and was never given another.

BELOW: ***Remington New Model Army .44 revolver***
The US Army preferred the solid frame of the Remington to the Colt design and offered no more contracts to Colt after November 1863. Remingtons were stronger and cheaper. The New Model was a development of the 1858 Old Model, also known as Beal's revolver. The majority of these – some 1000

Colt 1849 pocket revolver
Sometimes referred to as the "Wells Fargo" after the famous stagecoach company, the Model 1849 was 3-inch barrel revolver designed for concealed carry in the same way as modern "snub-nosed" pistols. It was issued to Wells Fargo employees. The most common version had five cylinders and no reloading lever, although six-shot models and ones with loading levers were manufactured. The 1849 fired a .31-caliber ball.

Remington rolling block pistol
Remington finished the Civil War as the largest producer of pistols in the world. Defeating Colt in the struggle for US government orders during 1863, Remington supplied over 250,000 handguns by 1865. Almost all were revolvers, but in 1865 Remington introduced this .50-caliber, single-shot pistol. It employed the same breechloading mechanism as the Remington rolling block rifles patented in 1863. Further models of this weapon were introduced: the 1867 Navy and 1871 Army.

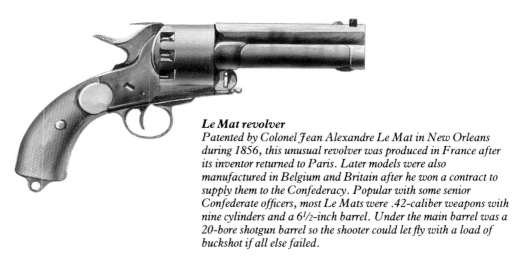

Le Mat revolver
Patented by Colonel Jean Alexandre Le Mat in New Orleans during 1856, this unusual revolver was produced in France after its inventor returned to Paris. Later models were also manufactured in Belgium and Britain after he won a contract to supply them to the Confederacy. Popular with some senior Confederate officers, most Le Mats were .42-caliber weapons with nine cylinders and a 6½-inch barrel. Under the main barrel was a 20-bore shotgun barrel so the shooter could let fly with a load of buckshot if all else failed.

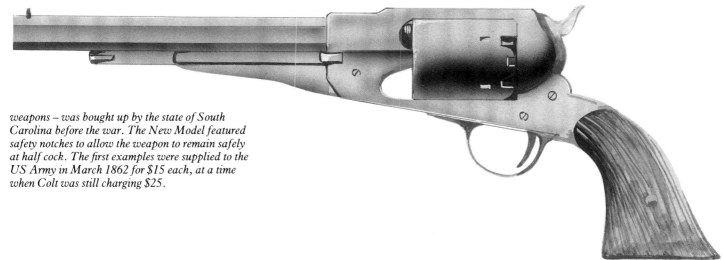

weapons – was bought up by the state of South Carolina before the war. The New Model featured safety notches to allow the weapon to remain safely at half cock. The first examples were supplied to the US Army in March 1862 for $15 each, at a time when Colt was still charging $25.

Pistols

Dissatisfaction with Colt's prices was one reason for the army's reluctance to reorder, but they had another practical reason: combat experience led many officers to prefer revolvers with a solid frame. Remington presented samples of his 1861 Army Model revolver to Lieutenant-Colonel Ripley in July 1861 and secured an order for 5000. Their solid frame with top strap followed the style of British revolvers like the Adams. Making the frame and grip from a single high-grade iron forging greatly increased the strength of the weapon. Remingtons required less machining than Colts, and the base pin which held the cylinder in line was an independent steel rod requiring no screws or wedges like the Colt design. On the enormously popular New Model Army of 1863 this pin was securely anchored by the butt end of the loading lever.

Like Colt, Remington delivered .36-caliber "Navy" revolvers, as well as .44-caliber "Army" weapons. But although Remington was supplying 250 Navy Models per week during 1861, the army had to wait until March 1862 before it received its first .44s. The good news was that Remington wanted only $15 each and Samuel Remington testified before the 1862 Ordnance commission hearings that he could produce his revolvers for as little as $12 on large contracts. He added that he could also manufacture any other design, such as a Colt, for the same price. Colt's $25-a-gun bonanza was at an end. By 1865 Remington had supplied 125,000 Army Model revolvers, mostly the 1863 version, and 133,000 others. At the time it was undoubtedly the largest producer of pistols in the world.

Colt and Remington dominated the pistol market during the Civil War but there were many other manufacturers active in both Union and Confederacy. The next most widely used weapons were produced by the Starr Arms Company of Binghamton and Yonkers, New York. Like many pistol firms, it started life in the late 1850s when Samuel Colt's patent on revolving firearms expired. By the beginning of the war Starr had manufactured some 1500 .36-caliber double-action revolvers, of which 1000 were delivered to the US Army under an 1858 contract.

The Starr Army Model was unusual in being double-action only, i.e. the hammer could not be thumbed back to cock the weapon as on

Savage .36 Navy revolver
The US Army bought 11,000 of these unusual weapons at the beginning of the war but did not persevere with them. The lower part of the "8" ring worked the cylinder and cocked the hammer. The upper ring then operated the trigger. This gun was designed by H.S. North between 1856 and 1861, and manufactured by E. Savage of Middletown, Connecticut.

Kerr's .44 revolver
In 1858 James Kerr, superintendent of the London Armoury Company, patented a six-shot percussion revolver that saw extensive service with Confederate forces in the Civil War. Similar to the Adams revolver, its main feature was an easily detachable sidelock of the sort found on shotguns or rifles. With an equally straightforward cylinder-locking mechanism, Kerr's revolver was designed for ease of repair (to suit people who might not have access to a gunsmith). This obviously suited Southern units, who found the Kerr an ideal pistol.

Adams' .32 pocket revolver
Robert Adams was a partner in the London company of Deane, Adams & Deane. His revolvers were the most serious rival faced by Colt before the war. They were double-action: pulling the trigger rotated the cylinder, cocked the hammer, and allowed it to fall. Frame and barrel were made in one piece and the cylinders were easy to detach. Produced in .50, .44 and .32 caliber, the Adams design was modified in 1857 to allow the gun to be fired single- or double-action. Combat experience in the Crimea and Indian Mutiny led British officers to prefer the Adams to the Colt. Both sides imported the Adams during the war, and some were manufactured under license in Massachusetts.

single-action revolvers. In fact, it could not be cocked in the true sense of the word; instead, squeezing the trigger caused the hammer to rise and fall while the cylinder rotated. Like the British Adams, this made it much better suited to a desperate fight at close quarters when a split second's delay in firing could be the difference between life and death. Although accuracy at longer ranges compared unfavorably with a good single-action, the triggers on most Starrs were fairly smooth and even. Although the Ordnance Department remained hostile to anything unnecessarily complicated, the shortage of weapons helped spur it to order another 12,000 Starrs in .44-caliber. This con-tract, issued in September 1861, was increased by another 8000 in January 1862.

Unfortunately for Starr, it failed to deliver on schedule and the order was subsequently reduced to 15,000 and the price cut from $25 to $20. But in December 1863 Starr introduced a conventional single-action .44, which it could supply at $12 each. By April 1865 Starr had supplied 58,000 revolvers.

Between them, Colt, Remington, and Starr supplied 90 percent of the American-made revolvers bought by the Union during the Civil War. Ordnance Department records show a total of 359,000 revolvers purchased in the USA and just 14,000 from Europe. The supply of European revolvers was largely taken up by one purchase of 10,000 weapons from France. These were 12-mm Lefaucheaux pin-fire revolvers. Using metallic cartridges, they were far ahead of the standard cap and ball percussion revolvers, although supplying ammunition for them was not easy.

The main reason for the longevity of the percussion revolvers was a patent granted in 1855 to Rolling White of Hartford, Connecticut. The patent applied to an unsuccessful invention which did not actually work but was stated to include "extending the chambers through the rear of the cylinder for the purpose of loading them at the breech from behind."

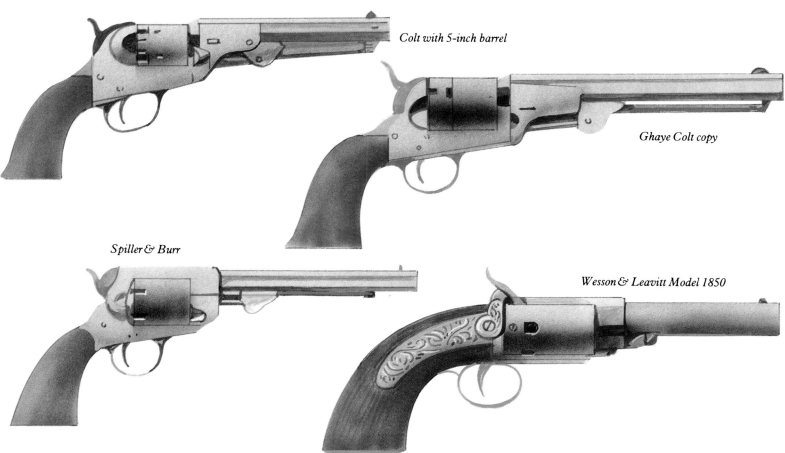

Colt with 5-inch barrel

Ghaye Colt copy

Spiller & Burr

Wesson & Leavitt Model 1850

Colt Model 1849 with 5-inch barrel
This is the most common version of the Model 1849, of which Colt manufactured over 325,000 between 1850 and 1873. Essentially a reduced-size Model 1851 Navy, more of these pistols were produced than any other Colt percussion firearm and there was a tremendous variety of minor variations – over 200 according to the best estimates.

Spiller and Burr .36 revolver
Spiller and Burr manufactured an estimated 1450 revolvers based on the Whitney Navy design after the company secured a Confederate Government contract for 15,000 pistols. Half were made in Richmond, then the firm moved to Atlanta in 1862. The pistol has a six-shot cylinder and a 6-inch octagonal barrel.

Colt copy
Colt's revolvers were widely copied before the war and Colt was continually engaged in lawsuits to prevent patent infringement. Many copiers were in the South and were well placed to manufacture their products when the war began. Colt copies included the Shawk & McLanahan, built in St Louis between 1858 and 1860; the Spiller & Burr; and the Leech & Rigdon. Metropolitan Arms built copies of the Model 1851 in New Orleans. Griswold & Grier produced several thousand well-finished copies before Union cavalry reached Griswoldville, Georgia, and burned the factory.

Wesson & Leavitt Model 1850
Daniel Leavitt designed a six-shot revolver with hand-rotated cylinder in 1837. Manufactured by Wesson, Stephens & Miller at Hartford, Connecticut, it was another local challenge to Colt. Edward Wesson affected a number of improvements after Leavitt's death and the resulting Wesson-Leavitt series of revolvers was manufactured by the newly created Massachusetts Arms Company at Chicopee Falls. However, their commercial prospects were blighted by a lawsuit mounted by Colt. Although small numbers of these weapons were used in the war, they were not ordered by the US government.

Pistols

Thus, the next logical development in the revolver – a metallic cartridge with an integral primer – was potentially frustrated. Smith and Wesson had just developed such a cartridge and were on the brink of marketing it when the patent was granted.

The patent was open to challenge since Hertog and Devos had already developed a revolver with a bored-through cylinder in Belgium by 1853. The Lefaucheaux pepper-box revolver had its barrels bored through and loaded from the rear. This had been in existence since 1845 and was shown at the London Exhibition in 1851. But Smith and Wesson adopted a cunning plan indeed. Instead of demolishing the patent in the courts, they struck a deal with Rollin White, paying him a royalty and planning to monopolize the market by championing the existing patent.

Smith and Wesson's gambit succeeded. Other manufacturers did challenge them, but in the Massachussetts Circuit Court during November 1863, the patent was upheld. In fact, the case went to appeal but did not reach the Supreme Court until 1869, two months before the patent expired. Although both Houses of Congress granted White's patent a seven-year extension, President Grant vetoed it, saying, "the government suffered inconvenience and embarrassment enough during the war in consequence of the inability of manufacturers to use this patent."

Smith and Wesson concentrated on smaller calibers and their .22- and .32-caliber pistols were not powerful enough to attract government orders. The .32-caliber No.2 revolver was a fine weapon, its rimfire copper cartridges anticipating later weapons, but although carried by some Union officers as a back-up weapon, it lacked the potency of the .44-caliber

and could never match the popularity of conventional percussion weapons.

The Confederacy had no standard pistol in reality but captured Colts and Colt copies made in the South were the most commonly used revolvers. During their ride around McClellan's army in the Peninsula Campaign, Jeb Stuart's cavalry were delighted to capture a wagonload of new Colt revolvers, "A prize indeed," observed Colonel Robins, "as in those days we were poorly armed." The Model 1851 Colt .44 was copied by several companies, including the Augusta Machine Works, the Columbus Firearms Manufacturing Company, and Griswold and Gunnison of Griswoldville, all in Georgia. Colts were also copied by Schnieder and Glassick in Memphis, Tennessee, and at least two firms in Texas.

The Confederacy acquired several types of European revolver, of which several British types were the most prized. The Adams double-action .49-caliber Dragoon was a very stoutly built weapon indeed. Since, in the last resort, a pistol is only worthwhile if it can also double as a club, the Adams' value was indisputable. James Kerr was the superintendent of the London Armoury Company, which supplied many Enfield rifles to both sides. He patented an excellent revolver in 1858–9 which became popular with the Confederates because it used a back-action lock as sometimes fitted to rifles and shotguns. This had the great advantage that it was easily detachable and if the lock

mechanism malfunctioned it could be fixed by a local blacksmith with no need for the specialized knowledge or tools demanded by the normal locks.

Pistol shots accounted for several leading figures in the Civil War. The short-sighted Brigadier-General Felix Zollicoffer rode right up to a Union officer at Fishing Creek, believing him to be a fellow Confederate. The Federal shot him dead with a revolver. General Earl Van Dorn's women-chasing days were terminated in Spring Hill, Tennessee, in 1863. Dr George B. Peters shot the Confederate commander as he sat at his desk after discovering Van Dorn had been having an affair with his wife. The Union general William Nelson was shot to death by fellow Union general Jefferson C. Davis after a bitter argument. The pistol's reputation as "the devil's right hand" was already established before those fatal shots in Ford's Theater on April 14, 1865.

Tranter .44 revolver
William Tranter, a Birmingham gunmaker who manufactured the Adams, introduced his own revolver in 1853. This had a double-action mechanism in which the weapon was cocked by pulling the lower trigger and fired by pulling the upper. This was for deliberate shooting. When fast shooting was demanded, both triggers could be pulled together. Manufactured in quantity from 1856 to 1863, Tranters were imported to the USA and used by officers on both sides.

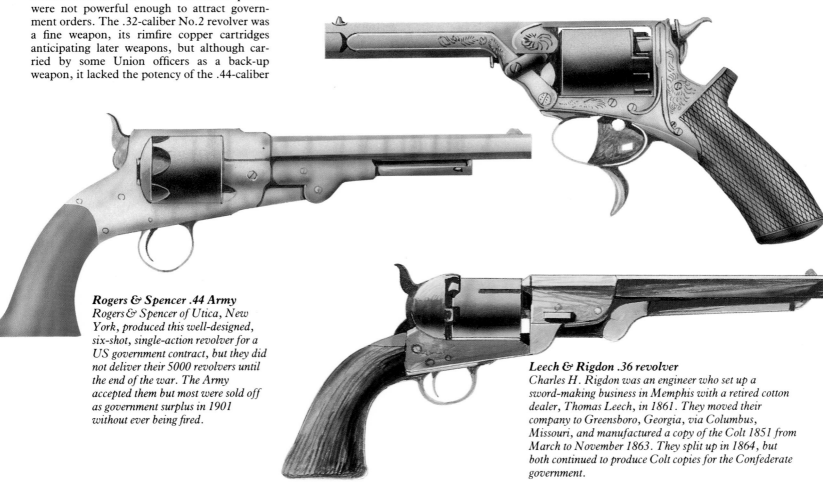

Rogers & Spencer .44 Army
Rogers & Spencer of Utica, New York, produced this well-designed, six-shot, single-action revolver for a US government contract, but they did not deliver their 5000 revolvers until the end of the war. The Army accepted them but most were sold off as government surplus in 1901 without ever being fired.

Leech & Rigdon .36 revolver
Charles H. Rigdon was an engineer who set up a sword-making business in Memphis with a retired cotton dealer, Thomas Leech, in 1861. They moved their company to Greensboro, Georgia, via Columbus, Missouri, and manufactured a copy of the Colt 1851 from March to November 1863. They split up in 1864, but both continued to produce Colt copies for the Confederate government.

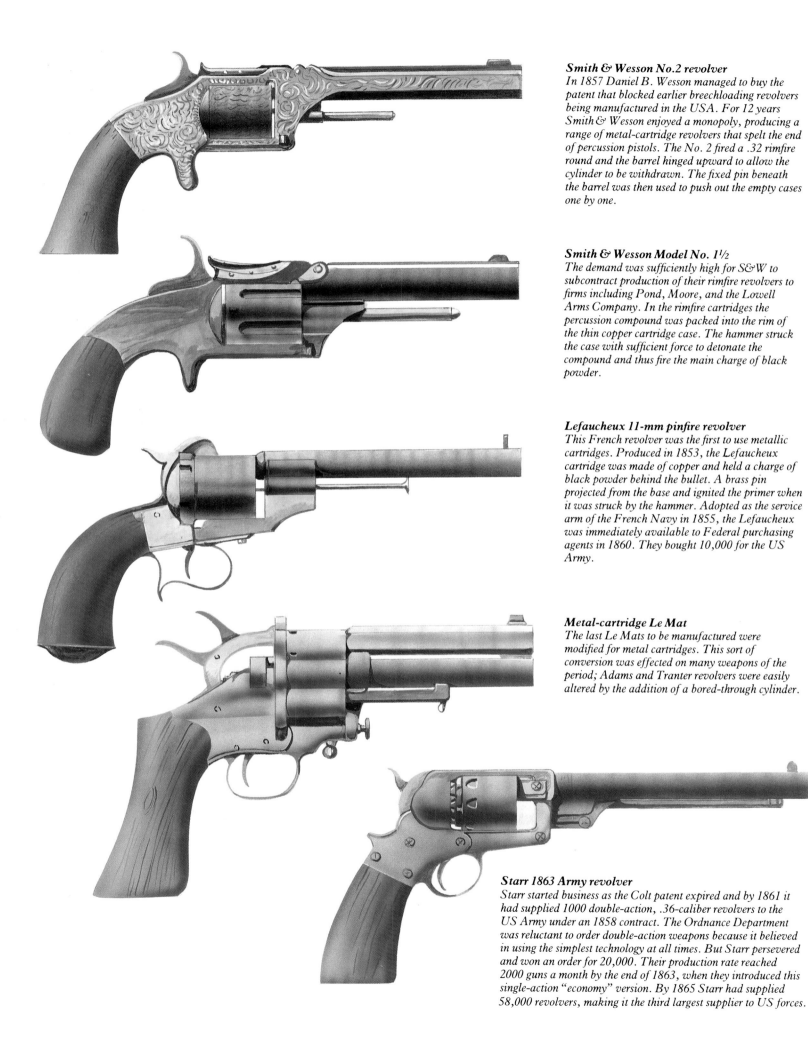

Smith & Wesson No.2 revolver
In 1857 Daniel B. Wesson managed to buy the patent that blocked earlier breechloading revolvers being manufactured in the USA. For 12 years Smith & Wesson enjoyed a monopoly, producing a range of metal-cartridge revolvers that spelt the end of percussion pistols. The No. 2 fired a .32 rimfire round and the barrel hinged upward to allow the cylinder to be withdrawn. The fixed pin beneath the barrel was then used to push out the empty cases one by one.

Smith & Wesson Model No. 1½
The demand was sufficiently high for S&W to subcontract production of their rimfire revolvers to firms including Pond, Moore, and the Lowell Arms Company. In the rimfire cartridges the percussion compound was packed into the rim of the thin copper cartridge case. The hammer struck the case with sufficient force to detonate the compound and thus fire the main charge of black powder.

Lefaucheux 11-mm pinfire revolver
This French revolver was the first to use metallic cartridges. Produced in 1853, the Lefaucheux cartridge was made of copper and held a charge of black powder behind the bullet. A brass pin projected from the base and ignited the primer when it was struck by the hammer. Adopted as the service arm of the French Navy in 1855, the Lefaucheux was immediately available to Federal purchasing agents in 1860. They bought 10,000 for the US Army.

Metal-cartridge Le Mat
The last Le Mats to be manufactured were modified for metal cartridges. This sort of conversion was effected on many weapons of the period; Adams and Tranter revolvers were easily altered by the addition of a bored-through cylinder.

Starr 1863 Army revolver
Starr started business as the Colt patent expired and by 1861 it had supplied 1000 double-action, .36-caliber revolvers to the US Army under an 1858 contract. The Ordnance Department was reluctant to order double-action weapons because it believed in using the simplest technology at all times. But Starr persevered and won an order for 20,000. Their production rate reached 2000 guns a month by the end of 1863, when they introduced this single-action "economy" version. By 1865 Starr had supplied 58,000 revolvers, making it the third largest supplier to US forces.

Muskets and Rifles

Soldiers in the mid-nineteenth century lived in a rapidly changing world. Weapons technology was evolving at a bewildering pace, upsetting the tactical assumptions of the Napoleonic wars. Different soldiers and different armies reacted in a variety of ways. The Prussian Army adopted new weapons and a fresh set of tactics which would bring it spectacular triumphs the year after Appomattox and again in 1870. The Russian Army had already paid the price for technological inferiority in its bloody defeats in the Crimea. Armed with obsolete smoothbore muskets, its courageous soldiers had suffered heavy losses at the hands of British and French regiments equipped with Minié rifles.

The eerie whistling sound of a Minié bullet in flight was to become disagreeably familiar to American soldiers. Fired by the standard rifle used by both sides during the Civil War, it was probably the single greatest cause of battlefield casualties.

The US Army had standardized its infantry shoulder arms in 1855, adopting a muzzleloading, .58-inch caliber rifle which replaced the existing .69-caliber smoothbore musket and the .54-caliber rifle. Developed at the Springfield armory in Massachusetts, it entered production in September 1855 and plans were drawn up to modify the now-obsolete weapons still in service. The changeover could not take place overnight and it was accepted that several years would pass before all infantry regiments would receive the new rifle. The state militias would have to wait even longer.

The Springfield was a finely engineered and handsomely finished weapon. Two basic versions were manufactured: the rifle and the rifled musket. The former had a 33-inch barrel, the latter a 40-inch, but they were otherwise very similar. The very first model was designed to be fired by the automatic priming device developed by Dr Edward Maynard, but all subsequent versions reverted to using copper primers individually placed for each shot.

The standard of accuracy demanded of the Springfield was a far cry from the days of the smoothbore musket in which aimed fire at much over 100 yards was a futile business. At 100 yards the Springfield had to group its shots within a 4-inch bull's eye, 9-inch at 200 yards, 11-inch at 300 yards, 18½-inch at 400 yards, and 27-inch at 500 yards. Against a mass target its range was even greater. Firing on a target the size of an infantry company (52 feet wide and 6 feet high), a Springfield rifled musket could hit with every round at a range of 1000 yards. While no weapon will ever perform anything like as well on a battlefield as opposed to a firing range, the improvement in infantry firepower represented by the muzzleloading rifle is undeniable. Close-order formations of infantry could no longer maneuver unhindered within a few hundred yards of their opponents. Mass assaults were stopped in their tracks at ranges unheard of in Napoleonic battles.

The fact that imparting a spin to the bullet vastly improved the accuracy of any firearm had been known since the seventeenth century. During the English Civil War snipers used rifled fowling pieces to pick off enemy officers, and Prince Rupert demonstrated his skill by shooting a church weathervane with his pistol. But rifles had never been able to overcome one critical problem: their rate of fire. As the bullet needed to fit tightly into the rifling, it had to be

Springfield Model 1855 percussion rifle musket
From 1857 through 1861 the Harper's Ferry and Springfield armories manufactured 59,273 M1855 rifle muskets. The first US military rifle to fire the .58-inch Minié cartridge, they used the Maynard tape primer system. The metal parts were left bright rather than blued. This is a later model which lacks the large rear sight of the early examples. The lid of the tape primer box was stamped with the US eagle and the lockplate displayed the weapon's origin and date of manufacture just behind the hammer. The Model 1855 was one of the standard infantry weapons for the early part of the war.

laboriously hammered down the barrel. After a few shots the inevitable fouling would add to the difficulty, which is why rifles tended to be used by hunters rather than soldiers.

There were two solutions: either design a bullet which could be slipped down the barrel like a musket ball and then forced into the rifling, or adopt a breechloading rifle. Breechloaders had already appeared in America. The ingenious English captain Ferguson of the 70th Foot had invented a flintlock weapon and led a company armed with his creation against American forces at Brandywine Hill in 1777. But Ferguson was killed in action in 1780 and the weapon failed to dislodge the smoothbore musket. It was complicated, less reliable, and more expensive. In 1826 the US Army became the first in the world to adopt a breechloader –

The Maynard tape primer system
Dr Edward Maynard was a New York dentist who also designed firearms and ignition systems. The tape primer worked rather like a child's roll-cap pistol: a paper tape containing fulminate patches was fed over the nipple by the action of the hammer. The system was used on sporting guns, as well as carbines and the M1855 rifle musket. Maynard claimed many advantages for his system: conventional priming caps cost $1.00 per thousand – his primers were 10–20 cents per thousand. Fitting a percussion cap was a fiddly business, especially with cold hands, or when under stress. Maynard's primers were cranked into place automatically. To fit a percussion cap, the hammer had to be at half cock and rifle muskets carried with a cap in place were often fired accidentally. Maynard's system was safer. Unfortunately, it was not wholly reliable, since if the paper tape became damp, it failed to feed properly. The system was rejected by the US Army after experience with the Model 1855 and the percussion cap was re-adopted for the Model 1861 rifle musket.

the Hall rifle. Patented in 1811, it was issued in only small numbers and staunch opposition from many quarters eventually killed it off. In fact, until an alternative to the flintlock mechanism had been developed, a breechloading rifle was not a practical proposition.

The Minié bullet was invented by a French army captain 15 years before the war. The bullet had a hollow base with an iron plug inserted. Although it did not engage the rifling on its way down the barrel, the moment the rifle was fired, the bullet expanded. The hard iron plug was driven violently into the softer lead, forcing it against the sides of the barrel as it raced toward the muzzle. Without reducing the rate of fire, this simple yet clever system substantially increased the accuracy and effective range of the infantryman.

Yet the smoothbore musket did not vanish

overnight. At the beginning of the war it was still the standard weapon of the state militias. Congress had baulked at the idea of providing the new rifles – at the unprecedented cost per weapon of $13.93 – to the militia. (Smoothbore muskets made in the early 1850s cost less than $9.00 each.) As the nation stood on the brink of civil war, the strategically vital state armories were filled with obsolete weapons. In some cases the smoothbores had not yet been converted to percussion, forcing certain units to go to war with weapons all but identical to those used in the War of Independence almost 100 years earlier.

When any military weapon is replaced, there are always those who argue against the prevailing wisdom. It is worth noting that a minority of officers criticized the new muzzleloading rifle, using arguments that have been revived in

more recent times. Arguing that the most infantry fighting would still take place within 100 yards, they pointed out that the smoothbore could be loaded and fired faster than the rifled musket. Also, at such close quarters, the smoothbore's ability to fire "buck and ball" (several .30-caliber balls added to the .69-ball) was likely to be decisive. The shotgun effect and rate of fire would triumph against the new weapon.

Major G.L. Willard accepted the longer range of the rifled musket but qualified this by doubting whether ordinary soldiers could understand how to use the sights. A smoothbore musket was merely brought to the shoulder and fired. To shoot accurately at much over 100 yards, a soldier with a rifled musket had to estimate the range and elevate his rear sight accordingly. Believing this to be beyond the American private soldier, Willard argued for a

TOP: *Model 1861 percussion rifle musket*
Over 1,000,000 rifle muskets were manufactured to this pattern during the Civil War. The Springfield Armory made 265,129 during 1861–2, and the rest were made under contract by over 20 different companies. All metal parts were left bright, although the rear sight was often blued. The front sight doubled as a lug for the 18-inch triangular bayonet. On the Springfield-made rifle muskets, the lock was marked with the eagle motif forward of the hammer, and the date of manufacture (1861 or 1862) was stamped behind.

CENTER: *Model 1840 flintlock musket*
The last standard production flintlock adopted by the US Army, this .69-inch caliber smoothbore was originally designated the Model 1835, but five years of tinkering with the design led to its acceptance as the Model 1840. Springfield Armory built 30,141, of which 26,841 were altered to percussion between 1849 and 1851. Because the vast majority of these weapons were converted, surviving flintlocks are rare. Many percussion conversions have been refitted as flintlocks over the past few years to be sold as originals to unwary collectors.

BOTTOM: *Sharps Model 1855 British carbine*
The British government ordered 6000 .577 carbines from Sharps, and some were used by British cavalry regiments during the Indian Mutiny. Half had 18-inch barrels and half had 21-inch barrels. Metal parts were blued and the carbines were fitted with the Maynard tape primer system. Units issued with the Sharps were happy with the gun, but disliked the Maynard primer, which became damp in tropical conditions and brittle when used in the heat of central India.

Muskets and Rifles

mixed brigade structure. While most regiments retained their smoothbores, each brigade would have a picked unit of light infantry, which would be trained in skirmishing tactics and armed with rifled muskets.

Colonel Craig, the chief of ordnance in the US Army on the outbreak of war, reported the numbers of government firearms in November 1859 as follows:

Rifles: 1385 .54-caliber rifles, now converted to .58-caliber; 43,375 .54-caliber rifles still awaiting conversion; 4102 .58-caliber Springfield Model 1855 rifles

Rifled muskets: 33,631 .69-caliber smoothbores, now rifled and with percussion locks added; 24,105 .58-caliber Springfield rifled muskets

Smoothbore muskets: 275,744 original flintlocks, now converted to percussion; 14,765 flint-locks fitted with the Maynard lock; 213,155 built as percussion muskets

From a total of 610,598 shoulder arms, only 28,207 were the latest .58-caliber weapons. The remainder were not especially ancient; over half had been manufactured within the previous 20 years and none pre-dated 1822, but the government was in the process of reducing this stock when the war broke out. The total reserve had actually declined to 576,800 by the end of 1860 because over 30,000 smoothbore muskets had been sold to private dealers and to individual states. This was the beginning of a program to sell up to a quarter of a million smoothbore muskets, but the plan was revoked by the secretary of war as the secession crisis loomed in January 1861.

By the time the fatal shots rang out in Charleston harbor, the US Government had no more than 40,000 .58-caliber rifles and rifled muskets out of a total stock of some 437,000 shoulder arms. Worse, nearly 15,000 of the .58-caliber rifles were at the Harper's Ferry Arsenal, burned and abandoned by Union forces on May 18, 1861. The weapons were destroyed, but the machinery was not and Confederate troops under Colonel Jackson removed it to Winchester and Strassburg shortly afterwards.

If the Federal supply of infantry weapons was an immediate source of worry to Washington, the Confederacy came into existence with an even more pitiful arms supply. Less than 25 percent of Federal weapons were stored within the Confederate States. The Confederate Ordnance Department, headed by Major Josiah Gorgas, inherited the following weapons from United States arsenals taken over in 1861:

Rifles: 8990 .54-caliber rifles

Rifled muskets: 1765 .58-caliber rifled muskets; 972 .69-caliber rifled muskets

When the various state arsenals were included, the Confederacy started the war with fewer than 20,000 modern, rifled firearms. The Union had about 100,000.

The Confederacy was fortunate that during the last year of John B. Floyd's administration of the War Department he sent 105,000 smoothbore muskets and over 10,000 .54-caliber rifles to Southern states. Small wonder Floyd had no desire to be captured in a Confederate uniform at Fort Donelson. In fact, it is very difficult to prove a Southern conspiracy here. It is unlikely that Floyd was deliberately arming the South in readiness for conflict, but he did not stand in the way of requests from Southern states' governors when they asked for weapons.

By contrast, the elderly Colonel Craig at the US Ordnance Department was certainly doing the opposite. Perhaps sensing the inevitable, he ensured that as few weapons went South as he could. While he was in no position to prevent Southern states receiving their allotted quota of weapons during 1860, he took care that the bureaucratic machine remained in low gear. He certainly assured several governors that weapons shipments were on their way when they had not even left the armories. This "the check's in the mail" approach succeeded in causing considerable delay.

Once the shooting started the Federal Government's stock of weapons was rapidly exhausted. The latest .58-caliber rifles disappeared first, followed by the .69-caliber rifled muskets. By the end of May 1861 the Ordnance Department, now headed by Lieutenant-Colonel James W. Ripley, could supply only smoothbore percussion muskets. With Harper's Ferry lost to the secessionists, the Springfield Armory hurried to rifle the existing stocks of .69-caliber smoothbores and, above all, to accelerate production of the .58-caliber rifled musket.

By midsummer 1861 the Federal Government had emptied almost every arsenal and even the smoothbore muskets were all issued. The government turned to private sources, buying everything from sporting guns and condemned weapons. It was a seller's market in which many people made a great deal of money. For example, John C. Frémont, the infamously inept "political general," bought several thousand .52-caliber Hall carbines for which he paid $22 each. These weapons had only just been sold for $3.00 apiece by the Ordnance Department as part of its drive to standardize on .58-caliber weapons.

Both sides soon looked across the Atlantic to supplement their inadequate supplies of infantry weapons. The Europeans were not slow to take advantage of this welcome demand for guns at (almost) any price, especially as several European armies were in the process of adopting new weapons and needed somewhere to unload the old. They were aided by the fact that not only were Confederate representatives bidding against those of the Union, but private arms dealers and officials from individual states were pitching in too. The Union missed one golden opportunity in August 1861 when F.H. Morse, the US consul in London, managed to secure all production of the prized Enfield rifled musket not going to the British Army. But his deal for 15,000 weapons per month collapsed after he was told to leave this sort of arrangement to the War Department.

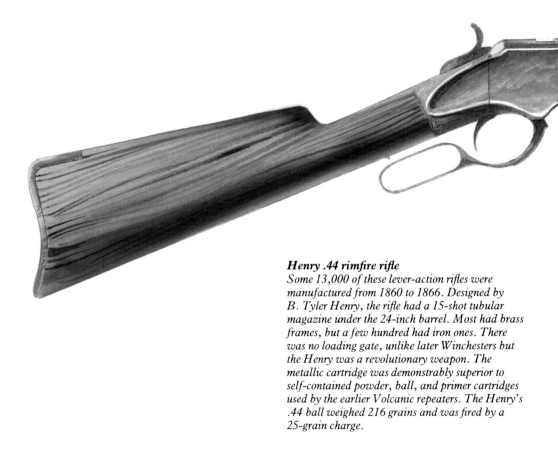

Henry .44 rimfire rifle
Some 13,000 of these lever-action rifles were manufactured from 1860 to 1866. Designed by B. Tyler Henry, the rifle had a 15-shot tubular magazine under the 24-inch barrel. Most had brass frames, but a few hundred had iron ones. There was no loading gate, unlike later Winchesters but the Henry was a revolutionary weapon. The metallic cartridge was demonstrably superior to self-contained powder, ball, and primer cartridges used by the earlier Volcanic repeaters. The Henry's .44 ball weighed 216 grains and was fired by a 25-grain charge.

Colonel George L. Schuyler was commissioned as the first agent of the War Department the previous month. He too was let down when War Department credits were delayed in arrival, ruining a contract with the Birmingham Small Arms company (BSA) for up to 7000 Enfields per month. Caleb Huse, the Confederate purchasing agent, seized his chance and offered BSA 50 cents a gun more. He clinched the deal. But Schuyler eventually managed to obtain over 120,000 rifles, rifled muskets, and carbines and did succeed in securing 15,000 Enfields.

The British .577-caliber Enfield was the single most popular foreign weapon to see service in the Civil War. The US Government bought a total of 1,165,000 rifles, muskets, and carbines from Europe, mostly during 1861–2. Enfield rifles accounted for 436,000 of the total and both sides continued to import them to the end of the war. Unlike several of the European weapons, Enfields were manufactured to as high a standard as the Springfield, so first impressions were good. Other European

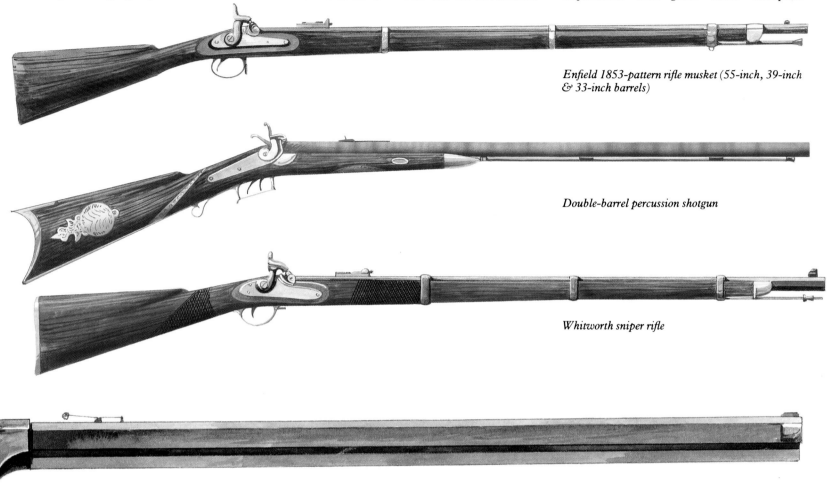

Enfield 1853-pattern rifle musket (55-inch, 39-inch & 33-inch barrels)

Double-barrel percussion shotgun

Whitworth sniper rifle

Henry .44 rimfire rifle (24-inch barrel)

Enfield 1853-Pattern rifle musket
The Federal government bought 428,292 British .577-inch rifle muskets and 8000 1858-pattern Short Sea Service rifle muskets. The dimensions of the British rifle were almost identical to the 1861 Springfield. Both were 55 inches long; at 8.6 lb, the British rifle was a few ounces lighter; the Enfield's 39-inch barrel was an inch shorter than the Springfield. Rifled with three grooves, it was sighted to 900 yards. The rear sight was raised and the slider used for ranges of 400 yards or more. The Short Sea Service version had a 33-inch barrel, but its rifling had five grooves and a faster twist: one turn in 48 inches rather than one in 78. This actually made it more accurate than the longer rifle.

Double-barrel percussion shotgun
In 1860 the overwhelming majority of American households owned at least one shotgun. Throughout rural America all manner of shotguns and fowling pieces were in use, mainly 10 or 12 gauge. Although mostly assembled in America, many parts were imported from Europe. English-made barrels were very common since their quality and price could not be matched by US gunmakers until well after the war. Shotguns were pressed into military service by ill-armed volunteer units early in the war and were retained by many Confederate cavalry outfits. But it is unlikely that shotguns were ever issued by the Confederate government: nineteenth-century shotguns bearing CSA stamps are commonly found but invariably fake.

Whitworth sniper rifle
Joseph Whitworth was a British engineer who produced rifles and cannon using a mechanically-fitted projectile. The barrel was hexagonal, with a slow twist to impart a spin to the bullet. Whitworth produced some 8000 .451-caliber rifles for the British Army, but they were rejected because they fouled badly and were difficult to load after only a dozen shots. However, they were superbly accurate – capable of a head shot at 500 yards in the right hands. They were imported in small numbers and used as sniper rifles.

Muskets and Rifles

weapons were crude by comparison, with poorly finished stocks and second-rate locks, sights, and barrels.

The Enfield Pattern 1853 rifle had a 39-inch barrel with three grooves of rifling, which made one turn in 78 inches. Weighing 8.6 pounds, it was robust yet elegant. The best rifles supplied to the Union came from the London Armoury Company. They had smart, tough, walnut stocks and machine-made parts which were interchangeable and were rated by the British Army as almost equal to these produced at the Royal Small Arms Factory at Enfield itself. The other main supplier to the US forces was the Birmingham Small Arms company. Parts for BSA weapons were not always interchangeable.

The Enfield's ladder backsight allowed the soldier to advance the slider for ranges of 100, 200, and 400 yards. For longer ranges the ladder was flipped into the vertical position.

The 530-grain bullet was designed to grip the rifling without recourse to a Minié-style plug. Instead, its base was hollow, which theoretically produced the same expansion effect, but early combat experience in the Crimea revealed several problems with the ammunition. The bullets were manufactured by compressing lead sections in a press. This eliminated the air bubbles and inconsistencies sometimes encountered with cast bullets, but the rounds were found to work better with a burnt clay or boxwood plug nevertheless.

There were several versions of the Enfield in service during the Civil War. The three bands holding the barrel to the stock were altered in 1859 and the backsight was changed in 1861 since the British had adopted a better grade of powder which produced a lower trajectory. In the same way that the US Army had adopted the Springfield .58 rifle as opposed to the rifled musket, the British introduced a short Enfield intended for light infantry.

The British Army's Rifle Brigade and the 60th Rifle Regiment's Enfields had a 33-inch barrel to make skirmishing through rough terrain rather easier. Between 1857 and 1858 the Royal Navy adopted a similar version but with significantly improved rifling. With five grooves instead of three, and turning much faster (one turn in 48 instead of 78 inches), it proved so much more accurate that the army promptly adopted it as well in 1860. However, only 8000 of all the Enfields bought by the Union were of the shorter pattern.

Prices paid for the Enfield reflect the panic demand for weapons early in the war. In July 1861 the British were taking $18 each; by August the price had risen to $25 and did not fall to $19 until February 1862.

Unfortunately for other European manufacturers, the weapons they supplied to the desperate American purchasers during 1861 included a proportion of old, rusty, and virtu-

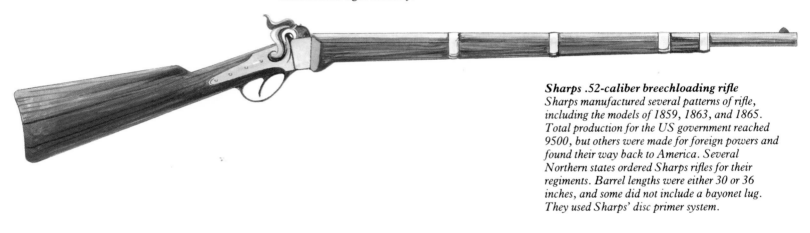

Sharps .52-caliber breechloading rifle
Sharps manufactured several patterns of rifle, including the models of 1859, 1863, and 1865. Total production for the US government reached 9500, but others were made for foreign powers and found their way back to America. Several Northern states ordered Sharps rifles for their regiments. Barrel lengths were either 30 or 36 inches, and some did not include a bayonet lug. They used Sharps' disc primer system.

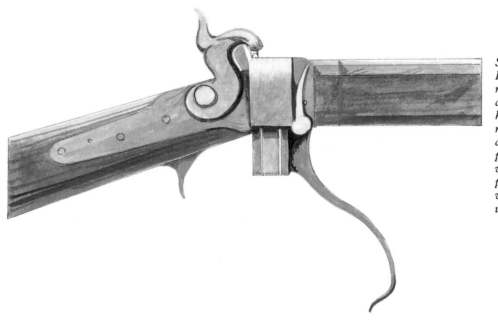

Sharps disc priming device
Fitted to Sharps sporting guns, as well as military rifles and carbines, the disc primer held a column of copper priming caps. As the hammer fell, it pushed the top cap on to the nipple and fired it. The caps were positioned above a feed spring, which pushed up the next priming cap ready for the next shot. This system was an important advance over the tape priming mechanisms like the Maynard. Not vulnerable to water, it was much more reliable under adverse conditions.

ally useless firearms. Seizing this heaven-sent opportunity to rid themselves of old stock, however, proved a shortsighted decision. Although in their haste to acquire weapons some American buyers did not inspect consignments too closely and often rushed them off to the armies without proper examination, there was uproar when they were eventually issued to the troops. Consequently, the reputation of all foreign rifles, except the British, was irretrievably tarnished.

The proportion of poor-quality weapons in the rifle and musket deliveries from Europe was exaggerated at the time. No one wanted an old smoothbore musket of unfamiliar construction when they might have a new Springfield. Some US volunteer units deliberately broke the muskets issued to them in the hope of receiving better weapons instead. It did not require many weapons to misfire consistently or fall apart in action to destroy the soldiers' confidence. Once a soldier begins to doubt the effectiveness of his

weapon he is halfway defeated before a shot has been fired.

The only other European weapon not to be thoroughly damned was the Austrian Lorenz Model 1854 muzzleloading rifle. Colonel Schuyler bought the first 70,000 in 1861 and they proved hardy and reliable in service, becoming known as "Austrian Enfields." Unfortunately, their caliber varied; they were originally .54 but the barrels had been reamed out to .58 to accept standard US Army ammunition. However, the conversion was not uniform and their true caliber varied from batch to batch.

They also had a *tige* breech. This was an alternative method of forcing a muzzleloaded bullet to engage the rifling, one which the Minié had been developed to replace. The breech had a short spike parallel to the axis of the bore, and the bullet, once rammed down the barrel, came to rest against it. The soldier then hammered the ramrod, which was special-

ly curved to fit the nose of the bullet. Thus, the bullet was impaled on the spike and, being made from relatively soft lead, it expanded at the base, fitting into the rifling.

Excellent in theory and on a target range, the *tige* was open to several objections in practice. It fouled badly and was difficult to clean. Standing up to hammer the bullet into shape was a disagreeable activity under effective enemy fire and if the soldier neglected to do so, accuracy fell off rapidly. In view of these limitations it is perhaps surprising to note that it did prove very effective in 1859, better than the French troops' Miniés. It seems, according to British tests at their School of Musketry, that the Austrian's secret lay in using a high-quality powder which did not foul the breech as badly.

Unfortunately for the Confederacy, 80 percent of the US arms industry was concentrated in the Connecticut valley in 1860. With such a weak manufacturing base, the Confederacy relied heavily on imported and captured

TOP: **Greene bolt-action rifle**
Patented in 1857 by Lieutenant-Colonel J. Durrell Greene, US Army, this .53-caliber, bolt-action, under-hammer rifle was the most peculiar infantry weapon of the war. It had an oval bore that twisted to impart spin to the bullet. While the Greene was the first bolt-action rifle used by US infantry, its operation was unique. The combustible paper cartridge had the powder charge in front of the bullet! The firer started by opening the bolt and inserting a hollow-base expanding bullet, pushing the bolt forward to seat the bullet, and opening it again to insert this odd cartridge.

The shooter was left with two bullets in the gun, sandwiching a powder charge. When fired, the rearmost bullet functioned as a gas check, while the foremost one exited the barrel. Loading another Greene cartridge continued the cycle. The Ordnance Department bought 900 Greene rifles, while orders from individual states brought total production to about 4000. It was not a success: some US troops dumped theirs in Antietam creek in 1862. Some Confederates believed this strange cartridge to carry poison!

ABOVE: **Remington "Zouave" rifle musket**
Officially known as the Remington Model 1863 Percussion Contract Rifle, this .58-caliber, muzzleloading rifle was manufactured from 1862 to 1865. Only 12,501 were made, and the majority of those in existence today are in such good condition that a high proportion of Zouave muskets were probably never issued. The quality of manufacture was excellent. Note the brass patch box on the side of the butt.

Muskets and Rifles

weapons before its own industry could develop. The Enfield was a perennial favorite, carried by many Confederate soldiers, both infantry and even cavalry. It did not take long for the Confederacy to produce copies; for example, the Asheville Armory in North Carolina built its own versions of the shorter Enfield rifle. Others were manufactured in New Orleans, Athens, and Macon in Georgia, and Tyler, Texas, which also produced Lorenz copies.

Fayetteville, North Carolina, soon became one of the most important sources of the Confederacy's infantry weapons. Starting by assembling components captured at Harper's Ferry, the Fayetteville Armory was soon manufacturing direct copies of the US M1861 rifled musket. Marked CSA Fayetteville, the locks carried the date of construction and an eagle. The biggest Confederate rifle producer was the Richmond Armory, which supplied a 40-inch barrel version of the US M1861 rifle, a 30-inch barreled "musketoon," and a cavalry carbine with a 24-inch barrel. South Carolina had the advantage of her own Palmetto Armory at Columbia, which produced weapons before the war for the state forces. Already turning out M1842 percussion muskets and M1841 rifles, they simply increased production.

For all the well-known problems the Confederates faced in arming and equipping their armies, it is to their eternal credit that they never lost a major battle through lack of guns or ammunition. Indeed, the war was an incredible stimulus to Southern industry. In its Augusta Powder Works in Georgia, the Confederate Government created the largest nationally owned factory system in the world. Richmond, Augusta, Columbus, Macon, Atlanta, and Selma rapidly turned into major industrial centers.

Union weapons production accelerated rapidly, so the unpopular European muskets were no longer being purchased by late 1862. Although the initial belief that the war would last only a matter of months delayed the Federal arms program, once the need was recognized, the factories soon made up for lost time. Production at Springfield itself was about 40 .58-caliber rifles per day in August 1861. This had doubled a year later and reached 200,000 per annum by the fall of 1862. But a 10-hour working day was not enough. By 1864 a double shift system and better tooling plant was producing over 300,000 weapons per annum. By April 1865 Springfield had manufactured a total of 820,000 rifles at an average cost of $11.97.

As so much of Federal rifle production was concentrated at Springfield, the fear of sabotage or some ghastly accident led the US Government to construct a second national arsenal at Rock City, Illinois, but it was not operational until the end of the war. Since even Springfield's colossal production figures could not satisfy the insatiable demand of the US Army, private companies were soon contracted to build them under license. Colt and the Providence Tool Company built 70,000 each; Lamson, Goodnow, and Hale manufactured 50,000, and Remington 40,000. Significantly, these privately-produced Springfields cost the government an average $19.52.

The desperate rush to arm the volunteer soldiers in both armies led to a bewildering number of weapons entering service side by side. Since very few officers, even from the pre-war regular army, had seen many of these weapons, great confusion resulted. The Ordnance Department was traditionally blamed for delays and errors such as supplying a regiment with the wrong type of ammunition. This was not uncommon since the US Army used 25 different types of rifle cartridges during the war. However, volunteer officers did not help matters by requesting "Minié musket ammunition" or bullets for "the Austrian rifle" or "Prussian musket." Inexact terminology was often the source of the problem. This was even more so with privately produced breechloaders or carbines adopted during the war. Some manufacturers did not name the individual parts, so ordering spares became a nightmare for quartermasters.

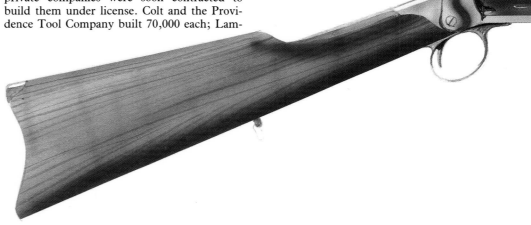

The astonishing variety of firearms used during the Civil War was matched by an equally daunting selection of ammunition. It was a nightmare for quartermasters. Although many Civil War cartridges anticipate today's self-contained cartridge, it was not until the advent of the Winchester .44/40 in 1873 that the world had a truly modern firearm. The cartridges illustrated here are all different solutions to the problem solved by the introduction of center-fired metallic cartridges.

Maynard
The Maynard cartridge is metal but has no primer. It relied on either a copper cap or Maynard's tape primer to fire the charge. The small hole in the base of the cartridge was sealed by wax paper and the cases could be re-used. Maynard's sporting rifles were popular before the war both for their accuracy and the ease with which the cartridge could be reloaded to achieve a consistent performance.

Burnside
The Burnside was loaded base-first into the lowered breech block; raising the carbine's trigger guard moved the breech block forward and seated the bullet in the chamber. This provided a very good seal, preventing the worrying discharge of gas that took place with linen or paper cartridges.

Henry
The copper rimfire Henry .44 cartridge allowed soldiers to have a magazine-loading rifle capable of rapid fire, but the copper case had to be very thin to allow the striker to indent it enough to fire the fulminate. This limited the charge that the cartridge could take and the weight of the bullet.

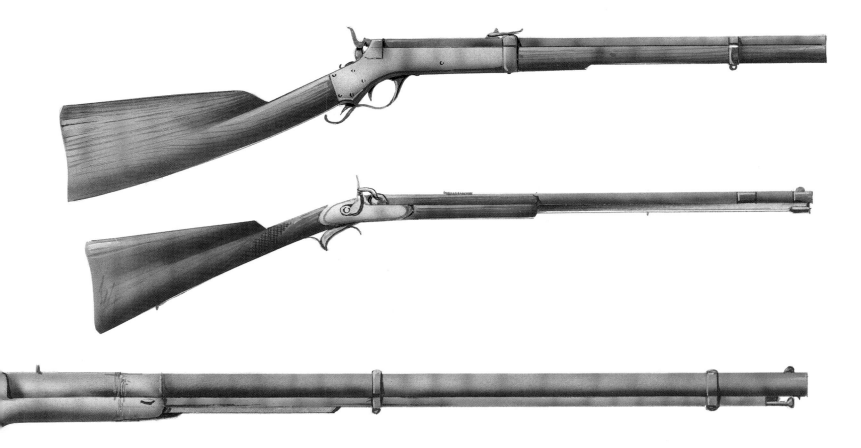

TOP: *Sharps & Hankins Model 1861 Navy rifle*
Manufactured during 1861–2, this .52-caliber, rimfire breechloader was one of Christian Sharps's designs during his brief (1862–66) partnership with William Hankins. Opening the trigger-guard lever slid the barrel forward to allow a fresh cartridge to be loaded. The Model 1861 had a brass buttplate and steel mountings. There was no ramrod provided, but a bayonet lug was fitted under the muzzle on most of them.

CENTER: *Custom-made rifle for Jefferson Davis*
This muzzleloading percussion sporting rifle was owned by the Confederate president. By his own admission more comfortable as a soldier than as a politician, Davis had won his military fame commanding a rifle regiment in the Mexican War. The 1841 Model percussion rifle became known as the "Mississippi rifle" because of its use by Davis's regiment.

ABOVE: *Colt Model 1855 revolving rifle*
Colt manufactured revolving rifles, carbines, and shotguns. The Model 1855 rifle held five rounds in the cylinder and weighed a fraction under 10 lb. It was also produced in a six-shot, .44-caliber version. Estimated production figures are just over 9000 between 1856 and 1864. The Colt had several drawbacks, including the occasional discharge of several cylinders at once, but it was used by Berdan's Sharpshooters before they obtained their Sharps rifles.

Sharps' linen cartridge
The US government bought more than 16 million of these during the war. The base of the cartridge was covered with thin paper, so the flash from the cap ignited the charge. However, the nitrated linen case was not always completely consumed and burning residue could still be in the chamber when it was opened for reloading!

Whitworth "bolt"
Test firings of 1860s' vintage Whitworth ammunition show this 530-grain, .45-caliber hexagonal bullet was the best long-range rifle of the war. It produces groups of less than 5 inches at 100 yards and, in capable hands, can hit man-sized targets at 1000 yards.

Spencer carbine
The Spencer was another copper-cased rimfire round. The .52-caliber Spencer fired a 385-grain bullet with 48 grains of powder behind it. Spare seven-round tubes allowed US cavalry regiments to deliver a tremendous volume of fire when necessary.

Carbines

The US Army had recognized the need to arm its cavalry with something other than the old muzzleloading carbines before the war. Loading such a weapon on horseback was an almost impossible act of dexterity and quite out of the question at close quarters with the enemy. What was required was a short and handy weapon that could be used by mounted troops, yet accurate enough to enable them to use it effectively while fighting on foot. Two types of carbine were being issued in 1860: the Sharps and the Burnside. So popular did these weapons prove that no less than 60 different types had been tested by 1865, and 18 had actually entered service.

To make the soldiers' and historians' task more challenging, the names of the many carbines are a source of great confusion. For instance, the "Gwyn and Campbell" carbine, the "Union" and "Ohio" carbines, and the "Cosmopolitan" carbine are four names for the same weapon. Sharps carbines were not manufactured by the same company that built Sharps and Hawkins carbines. Although both weapons were designed by Christian Sharp, they were entirely different. The Smith and Wesson carbine was not made by the famous pistol manufacturer but by another company which happened to have the same name!

In December 1861 the US Ordnance Department reported that it had 73,000 breechloading weapons on order, but only 9000 had actually been delivered. Of these, 6000 were Sharps carbines and the rest were mostly Burnsides.

The Sharps carbine was a .52-caliber single shot weapon with a 21¼-inch barrel. Flipping down the trigger guard lowered the breech block to expose the end of the chamber. After inserting the paper cartridge, the soldier raised the trigger guard, which brought the breech block back up and sheered off the end of the cartridge to expose the powder. Ignition was by the standard copper percussion cap or by the Maynard tape primer. The latter worked much like a strip of caps in a modern child's toy and was much easier to use than fiddly individual caps, especially for a mounted soldier. The inventor, Dr Edward Maynard, was a New York dentist who numbered several presidents among his clients. He made several medical discoveries and his primer system was one of several important contributions to the development of firearms.

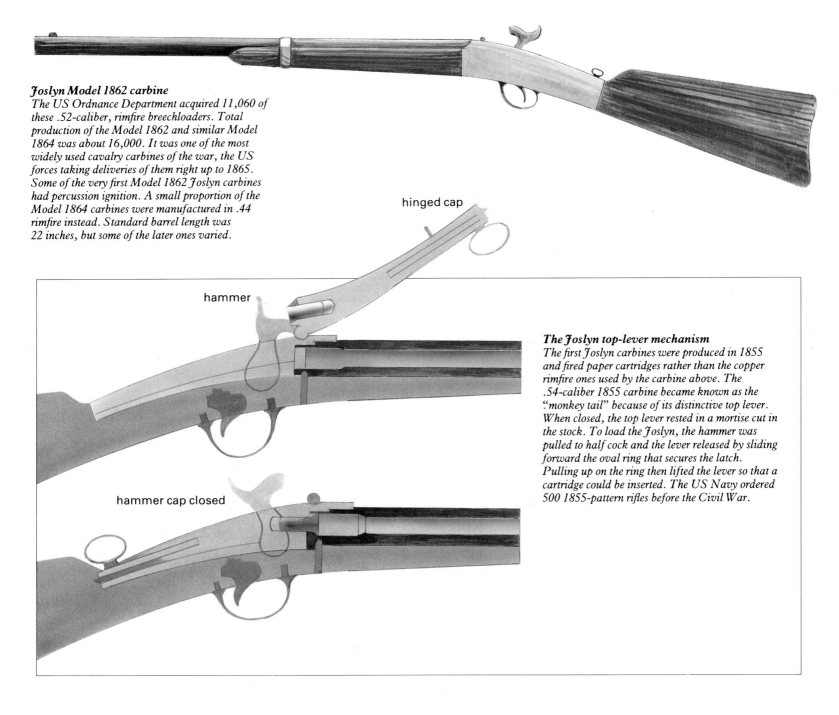

Joslyn Model 1862 carbine
The US Ordnance Department acquired 11,060 of these .52-caliber, rimfire breechloaders. Total production of the Model 1862 and similar Model 1864 was about 16,000. It was one of the most widely used cavalry carbines of the war, the US forces taking deliveries of them right up to 1865. Some of the very first Model 1862 Joslyn carbines had percussion ignition. A small proportion of the Model 1864 carbines were manufactured in .44 rimfire instead. Standard barrel length was 22 inches, but some of the later ones varied.

hinged cap

hammer

hammer cap closed

The Joslyn top-lever mechanism
The first Joslyn carbines were produced in 1855 and fired paper cartridges rather than the copper rimfire ones used by the carbine above. The .54-caliber 1855 carbine became known as the "monkey tail" because of its distinctive top lever. When closed, the top lever rested in a mortise cut in the stock. To load the Joslyn, the hammer was pulled to half cock and the lever released by sliding forward the oval ring that secures the latch. Pulling up on the ring then lifted the lever so that a cartridge could be inserted. The US Navy ordered 500 1855-pattern rifles before the Civil War.

The Sharps carbines had already seen action in the hands of British cavalry during the later stages of the Indian Mutiny. The British generally liked the weapon but complained that the tape primer became brittle in the intense heat of the Indian plains and soggy in damp conditions. But the Sharps was reliable and effective. Fouling did accumulate in the chamber, making it progressively more difficult to load, but the early models were provided with ramrods so the carbine could be muzzleloaded in an emergency. The M1859 Sharps carbines were distinguished by brass barrel bands and furniture; the M1863 substituted iron as a wartime economy. Of the 90,000 breechloaders supplied by Sharps to the US Government, 80,000 were carbines, sold for $2.2 million.

Ambrose E. Burnside was a talented young officer in the US Army who resigned his commission in 1852 to devote all his energy to the carbine he had invented. Patented four years later, his carbine won a competitive evaluation at West Point in 1857, defeating 17 other breechloading carbine designs. But Burnside obviously failed to impress the right people and his gun secured only token government orders and his firm went into bankruptcy. Fortunately for him, the outbreak of war revived his company and his career. The carbine was used by the Union cavalry with the total order reaching 55,000 weapons. Burnside rose so rapidly that he was promoted beyond his ability and led the Army of the Potomac to bloody disaster at Fredericksburg. He was later elected governor of Rhode Island.

The Burnside carbine was a .54-caliber, single-shot weapon which fired a cartridge of Burnside's own invention. This was a conical brass case containing a charge of black powder with a hole in the base exposed to the flame produced by the percussion cap. At the moment of firing the cartridge's metal case sealed the joint between the barrel and breech block, preventing the disagreeable blast of hot gas produced by carbines that relied on paper or linen cartridges.

Of the approximately one million rifles and carbines produced by private companies in the North during the war, over 400,000 were breechloaders. Given the stubborn opposition from the Ordnance Department and other quarters, it is unlikely that this transition would have occurred so rapidly but for the war. The most successful of all these weapons was the Spencer repeating carbine, a weapon which gave Union cavalry clear fire superiority over their Confederate enemies.

The Spencer carbine had a tubular magazine inserted via a trap door in the butt. This was spring-loaded and contained seven cartridges

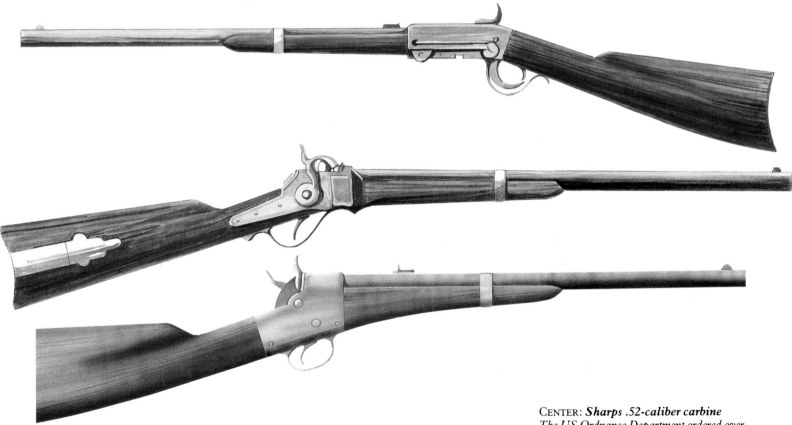

ABOVE: *Remington "split-breech" carbine*
This single-shot breechloader was the forerunner of the famous rolling block rifles. One of Remington's first metallic cartridge designs, they were the last weapon to be ordered for US troops before the end of the Civil War. About 5000 were made in .46 rimfire in 1865. This is one of the 15,000 .50-caliber rimfire carbines built between 1864 and 1865. Most were re-sold to France after the war.

TOP: *Burnside carbine*
One of the most widely used carbines of the war, the Burnside was designed by Ambrose E. Burnside, better known as a Union major-general. Pressing the two trigger guards together allowed the firer to lower them, rotating the block to allow the insertion of the special Burnside percussion cartridge. Over 55,000 Burnside carbines were bought by the US Ordnance Department. Burnside may have been a mediocre field commander, but his carbine was a great success.

CENTER: *Sharps .52-caliber carbine*
The US Ordnance Department ordered over 80,000 carbines for Federal mounted troops. A single-shot, percussion breechloader, it used the same priming system as the Sharps rifle. The carbine was 39 inches long, the rifle, 47 inches long. Lowering the trigger guard dropped the breech block, allowing the insertion of a linen cartridge. When the block rose again, a knife edge sliced off the rear of the case, exposing the powder to the flash from the percussion cap. The action tended to leak gas. Total production of the Sharps Models of 1859, 1863, and 1865 ran to 115,000.

Carbines

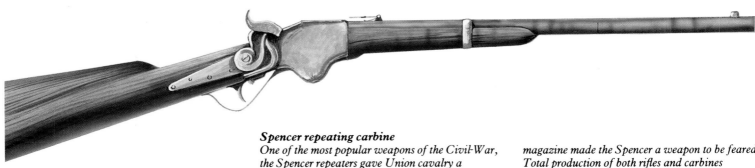

Spencer repeating carbine

One of the most popular weapons of the Civil-War, the Spencer repeaters gave Union cavalry a significant tactical advantage. While demonstrating his carbine to the Navy, Spencer fired at a rate of 21 rounds per minute. While actual rate of fire in action was obviously much lower, the rapid fire allowed by its seven-shot magazine made the Spencer a weapon to be feared. Total production of both rifles and carbines exceeded 144,000, with 107,372 going to the US Ordnance Department. Winning the personal endorsement of President Lincoln, the Spencer was widely used by US cavalry in the Indian wars.

The Spencer repeating action

The Spencer fired a .52-caliber copper rimfire case containing a 385-grain lead bullet with a 48-grain powder charge behind. The complete round weighed about an ounce and, containing its own primer, it was much more reliable than ignition systems that required primer caps or tapes. The magazine tube was loaded through the center of the buttstock. Spencer carbines and rifles always had six grooves, but those manufactured under license by Burnside had three. The lock and breechloading systems were not connected; working the lever chambered a fresh cartridge, then the hammer had to be manually cocked. The Confederacy had no facilities for manufacturing Spencer cartridges, so if Southern soldiers captured a Spencer it was very difficult for them to obtain ammunition.

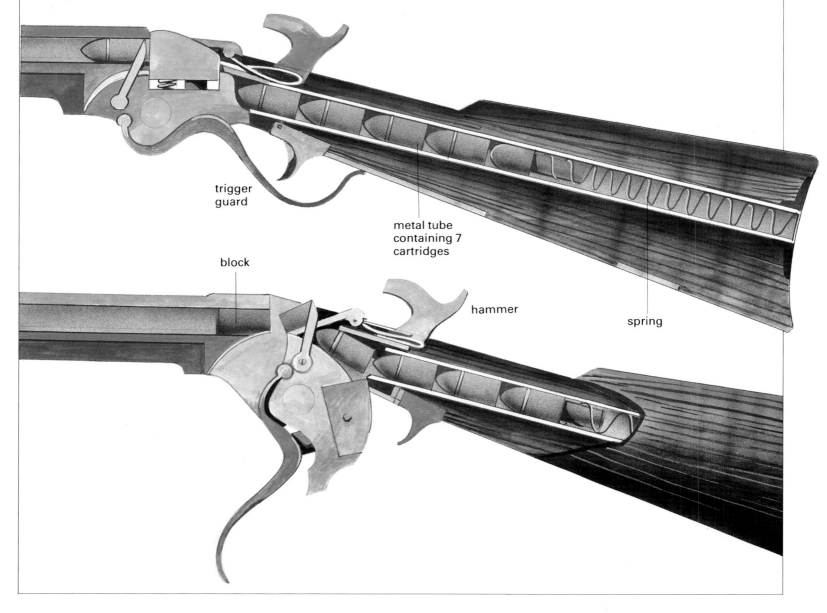

trigger guard

metal tube containing 7 cartridges

block

hammer

spring

which were rimfire, i.e. the base contained a primer which fired the black powder charge when it was struck by the firing pin. Thus, the soldier did not have to worry about priming each shot with a cap or tape primer.

Twenty-seven-year-old Christopher M. Spencer had no factory at the beginning of the war, but he had a valuable friend in Charles Cheney, a neighbor of Gideon Welles, secretary of the navy. Leasing premises from the Chickering Piano Company in Boston, Spencer secured his first order – 700 carbines for the US Navy – in July 1861. By June 1863 he had delivered 7500 weapons to the US Army and that winter he won a contract for 34,500. By the end of the war he had supplied about 85,000 of his carbines.

The first unit to use the Spencer carbine was Colonel John T. Wilder's "Hatchet" brigade of cavalry who fought with their new weapons at

Hoover's Gap in June 1863. Impatient for the best guns available, they had bought the carbines with their own money, each trooper giving up three months' pay. Renamed the "Lightning" brigade, they went on to inflict heavy losses on Longstreet's men at Chickamauga, which led the Confederates to overestimate greatly the strength of Wilder's command. Other early users of the Spencer include George A. Custer's Michigan brigade, who used them against Stuart's cavalry at Hannover Station, and Buford's cavalry at Gettysburg. In the last 18 months of the war Union cavalry became difficult for the Confederates to stop.

The Spencer had two rivals at the beginning of the war: the Henry and the Ball. The latter came into production too late to be a threat but the Henry presented a serious challenge. Chambered for the lighter .44 cartridge, it allowed the soldier to carry much more ammunition for

a given weight and the weapon itself had a 16-round magazine. This was easier to load, the soldier merely feeding the rounds in rather than having to extract the whole tube as on the Spencer. Dropping the trigger guard ejected the spent case, chambered the next one, and cocked the weapon. The Spencer had to be manually cocked.

Fortunately for Christopher Spencer, Oliver Winchester's New Haven Arms Company was simply unable to manufacture the Henry in the quantity demanded. Production never exceeded 260 guns per month, whereas Spencer was delivering 3500 weapons a month by 1865. The US Government bought 1730 Henry rifles in all, but the total order for Spencers was 105,000, of which 60,000 had been delivered. The US Ordnance Department bought 4.6 million .44 Henry cartridges, but a staggering 58 million .56-caliber Spencer cartridges.

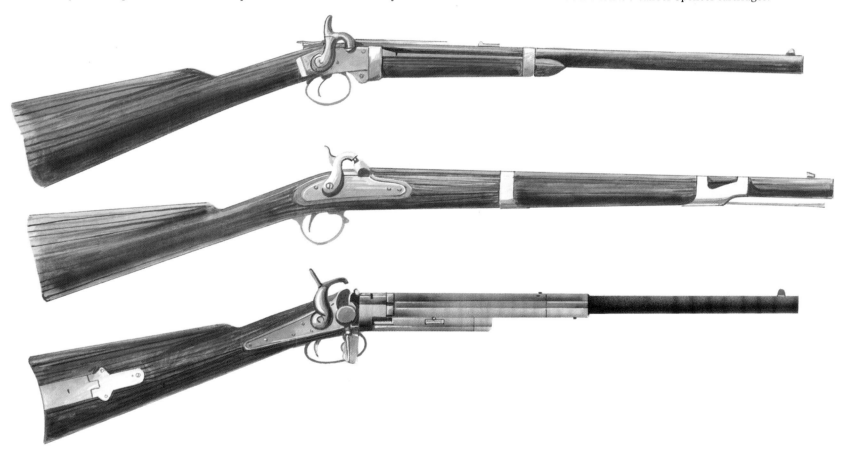

TOP: **Smith percussion breechloader**
This was a .50-caliber, single-shot breechloader loaded by depressing a latch forward of the trigger that allowed the barrel to pivot downward rather like a shotgun. It fired a variety of cartridges: brass, paper, coiled brass, and even rubber. The brass ones had flash holes in the rear for ignition from the percussion cap. Total production of the Smith is estimated at 30,000.

CENTER: **J.P. Murray percussion carbine**
Manufactured at Columbus, Georgia, Murray's carbine was one of several types produced for the Confederate government. Metal parts are believed to have had a bright finish. Three versions have been identified: this cavalry carbine with a 23-inch barrel; an artillery "musketoon" with a 23½- or 24-inch barrel; and rifle with a 33-inch barrel. A few hundred of each type were made between 1862 and 1864.

BOTTOM: **Greene carbine**
A rare Union weapon, only about 300 Greenee carbines were made between 1855 and 1857. This .54-caliber, percussion breechloader used the Maynard tape primer system. Some 170 Greene carbines were made for the 1857 Ordnance Department trials, so some examples have Army stamps on them. The British Army bought over 2000 Greene carbines and some are alleged to have returned to the USA during the Civil War, but there is no firm evidence of this. British examples, bearing the cypher of Queen Victoria and British proof marks, survive today.

Carbines

Just as some officers had opposed the replacement of smoothbore muskets by muzzle-loading rifles, the introduction of breechloaders was only achieved in the face of bitter opposition. James Ripley argued against the new weapons on several grounds, his opposition representing the last stand of a department which had steadfastly resisted breechloading weapons since the demise of the Hall rifle many years earlier. Ripley wrote Oliver Winchester in early 1861 saying that his department had not the time or the personnel to test the Henry repeating rifle. This 67-year-old officer, who had been one of the prime movers behind the adoption of the Springfield rifled musket, remained entrenched in his position. Breechloaders, he argued, were more fragile than

muzzleloaders since they have many more moving parts. Arming troops with them would tempt them to fire too quickly and not take proper aim.

Meanwhile, navy tests in 1861 showed the Spencer and Henry to be robust enough for service. Their rate of fire was certainly impressive: the Henry fired 125 rounds in five minutes and 40 seconds. But they could be accurate too, and reliable: the Spencer fired 500 rounds with only one misfire. It proved capable of shooting all its seven rounds in 10 seconds. General McClellan appointed a board of officers under future cavalry commander Captain Alfred Pleasanton to examine both weapons. The report recommended both. Ripley was removed from office in September 1863.

The Ordnance Departments of both North and South were the butt of much criticism during the war, but in fact they performed very well indeed. While the Confederacy could never match the quantity of Northern arms production, it did manage to fulfil its own needs. On occasion it even surpassed them. When Bragg invaded Kentucky in September 1862, few Kentuckians responded to his call and he ended the campaign with 15,000 more rifles than he had soldiers. The Confederacy's most serious weakness in small arms was its inability to match the Union cavalry's breechloaders. But this did not become significant until well into 1864 when the strategic situation was already bleak indeed.

Neither army seemed to rate the work of

Starr percussion carbine
This single-shot breechloader fired a .54-caliber bullet from a linen cartridge. In tests the Starr performed better than the Sharps, but it never achieved the fame or popularity of weapons like the Burnside, Sharps, or Spencer. Total production was 20,000 percussion carbines and 5000 very similar weapons that fired a .52-caliber rimfire cartridge.

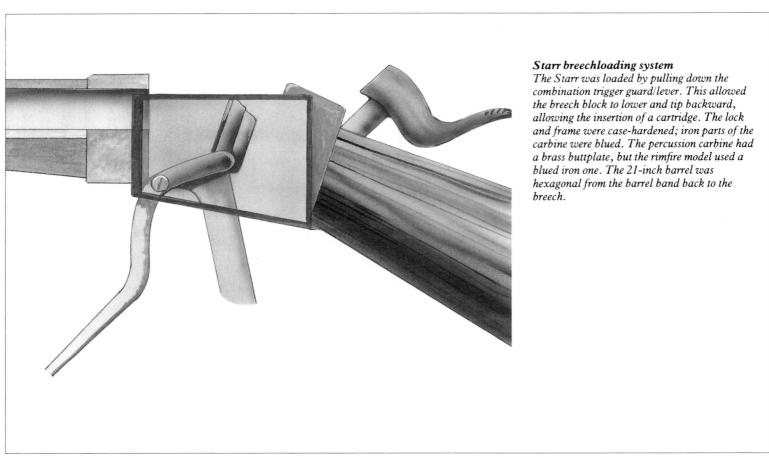

Starr breechloading system
The Starr was loaded by pulling down the combination trigger guard/lever. This allowed the breech block to lower and tip backward, allowing the insertion of a cartridge. The lock and frame were case-hardened; iron parts of the carbine were blued. The percussion carbine had a brass buttplate, but the rimfire model used a blued iron one. The 21-inch barrel was hexagonal from the barrel band back to the breech.

their ordnance experts very highly. In 1860 there were 41 officers in the US Army Ordnance Department, but this had increased to only 45 by the time of Gettysburg, with at least a dozen of these seconded to field commands. Several of the original ordnance officers hurriedly resigned in 1861, seeking more glamorous service in the field – these included Captain Oliver O. Howard and Lieutenant Jesse Reno, who both became generals! Such promotion was denied even to the head of the Ordnance Department. Alexander B. Dyer, who took over in 1864, directed the Springfield Armory, the largest arms manufacturer in the world, and commanded 3000 men, yet he held the rank of captain for most of the war and never rose higher than major. A similar-sized command in the field would have merited at least the rank of brigadier-general.

Evidently, military technology – and experts in this field – were not held in great esteem. In the Ordnance Department's Washington headquarters before the war, eight civilian clerks dealt with some 300 quarterly returns of stores and handled money disbursements amounting to $1.2 million. By January 1863 the 300 returns had grown to a total of 14,000 and $38 million passed through the department, yet just 10 temporary staff had been added. The paperwork got behind and front line troops cursed the inefficiency, assuming that a bloated bureaucracy was behind it all. In fact, the army had only itself to blame.

American soldiers ended the war with weapons the equal of anything in Europe. In 1866 the breechloader controversy was finally resolved and, like the British, the US Army adopted a breechloading conversion of its muzzleloading rifle. The "Trapdoor" Springfield served until 1894, although some volunteer units were still using them in Cuba four years later. After the war American manufacturers sold their guns all over the world. The Russian cavalry and rifle regiments adopted a rifle designed by Colonel Berdan; the Turks and Egyptians bought Remingtons and Winchesters. In the fall of 1870 American manufacturers sold their guns to the desperate French republicans, fighting the Prussians, a neat reversal of the situation 10 years earlier.

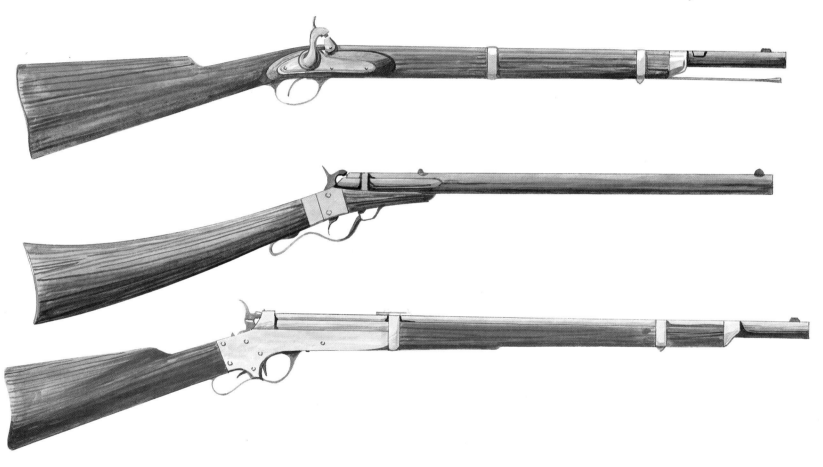

TOP: *Enfield "musketoon"*
This was a British muzzleloading carbine issued to the Royal Artillery in 1853. It had a 30-inch barrel and was issued with a sword bayonet. It was imported by the Confederacy for cavalry and artillery units. Gunners required a weapon for personal defense and it was common practice in European armies to issue a short rifle, longer than cavalry carbines but shorter than the infantry's rifles. In 1860 the British Artillery carbines were altered to the faster twist, which made them more accurate than the infantry rifle.

CENTER: *Maynard carbine*
Designed by Dr Maynard, inventor of the Maynard tape primer, this carbine was issued to Union cavalrymen, but so many were captured by the Confederacy that the Maynard was listed in Confederate ordnance manuals as an official weapon. From 1860 to 1865 just over 20,000 Maynard carbines were produced, all firing a .50-caliber cartridge. Some of the 400 first models made in 1857 were of .35 caliber. Lowering the trigger guard tipped the barrel down like a Smith carbine.

ABOVE: *Sharps & Hankins carbine*
This was manufactured from 1862 to 1867 in three types: an Army carbine with a 24-inch barrel; a Navy carbine with a 24-inch barrel and leather covering to protect it from salt spray; and a Short Cavalry-type, also known as the 11th New York Volunteer Cavalry Model since that unit was issued with it. The US Army bought 1467 Army carbines, the Navy purchased 6686 Navy carbines, and the short Cavalry model's production run was about 1000. Opening the trigger guard slid the barrel forward for loading. It had a floating firing pin mounted in the frame.

Machine Guns

The American Civil War was the first conflict to involve the use of machine guns, although they were not automatic. None of them used the force of the discharge to operate the weapon; they were cranked by hand. Machine guns of the Civil War are better described as mechanically operated repeaters. They did break new ground, but the use of a percussion-fired black powder cartridge severely restricted their performance. True automatic weapons would have to wait until the development of smokeless powder and jacketed bullets.

The most widely used Civil War machine gun was invented by Captain Williams of Covington, Kentucky. Mounted on a one-horse, double-shafted carriage like a mountain howitzer, it had a 48-inch barrel. It fired 1-pound bolts or buckshot charges and was operated by three men. Self-consuming paper cartridges were fed into the breech by hand and a percussion cap was placed on a nipple to the left of the chamber. The gun was operated by a crank and connecting rod that forced the breech block back and forth. By moving the crank the breech block was moved forward, chambering the cartridge and tripping the hammer. As the block came back, the hammer rose clear of the nipple once more and the process was repeated.

The Williams gun was first used by Pickett's brigade at Fair Oaks in 1862. The Ordnance Department ordered 42 guns to make seven six-gun batteries and they were manufactured at Lynchburg and Richmond, Virginia, and at Mobile, Alabama. Captain Williams continued to command a detachment of his guns attached to Pickett's brigade. The gun could fire 60 rounds a minute with a well-drilled crew, but this could not be sustained for long. The relatively poor quality steel used in the gun's construction meant that the breech tended to expand after repeated firing, preventing rounds from chambering properly.

The US Ordnance Department's opposition to breechloading rifles did not augur well for the exponents of even more revolutionary firearms. Although several inventors offered machine guns to the Union at the beginning of

the war, it was only after intense lobbying and presidential intervention that any such weapons were ordered. In the fall of 1861 the US Army purchased 10 Agar machine guns for $1300 and they were tested in the field without delay.

The Agar machine gun had a single barrel fed via a prominent hopper that led it to be called a "coffee grinder." It fired special cartridges: steel cases with a percussion cap at the rear that were either loaded with loose powder and ball or with a standard .58-caliber rifle cartridge. These were fed into the hopper above the breech. Each crank of the handle drew the breech block to the rear, allowing one round to drop into the feedway. As the handle turned further, the cartridge was driven into the chamber and a hammer automatically fired the percussion cap. As the handle continued to rotate, the bolt was opened and the empty tube ejected. The empty tubes needed to be collected for reloading. So, like sports shooters today, the Federal gunners spent as much time scrambling in the grass for their empty cases as they did firing them!

The Agar gun was adopted as the "Union Repeating Gun" but only 63 were officially purchased. Those tested in early 1862 received highly critical reports, complaining about their lack of reliability and questioning their safety. Several were captured by the Confederates and two were used against their former owners during the siege of Petersburg. The Agar gun's cost certainly counted against it; priced at $850, it was more expensive than a Parrott rifled field gun. It also depreciated quickly after the war. In a surplus sale at Fort Monroe in 1865 Agar guns were sold for as little as $5 each.

Richard J. Gatling of North Carolina was working on machine-gun designs before the war. He took out his first patents in 1862 when he demonstrated his first prototype at Indianapolis. The Gatling gun was a six-barrelled version of the Agar system. Each barrel had its own bolt and a gear drive arrangement cocked and fired each one in succession. The use of so many barrels was a simple solution to the problem of overheating that is still employed today. Gatling first fired his creation for the

benefit of the governor of Indiana, Oliver P. Morton, who wrote the War Department suggesting an official trial.

Twelve Gatlings were manufactured in 1862. Fed from steel chambers like the Agar, they fired .58-caliber cartridges and were bought by General Ben Butler for $1000 each after the Ordnance Department rejected them. They were used during the Petersburg siege operations and were the only Gatlings to see action during the war. In 1864 Gatling modified the design to use copper rimfire cartridges and it was tested in January 1865. It was immediately recognized as a vast improvement on the steel cylinder system and further trials were ordered. It finally went into service in August 1866.

Two other weapons should be mentioned while on the subject of machine guns, since they were used in the same role during the war. The Billinghurst-Requa "covered bridge gun" employed 25 .58-caliber barrels fixed in parallel. Cartridges were held in clips and a handle operated a sliding breech. A channel behind the cartridges was filled with loose powder and detonated by a percussion cap, which it was hoped would fire all the barrels together. Since this channel was open to the elements, it was vulnerable to wind and rain, but on a good day it could blaze off half a dozen volleys a minute – a fearsome barrage which suited it to the defense of static positions.

Similar in concept, the Vandenberg volley gun was a multi-barrelled weapon but the barrels were enclosed in a tube to give the appearance of a stubby, large-caliber howitzer. A screw breech held the cartridges in their individual chambers. Closing the breech forced copper sleeves into a counter-bored chamber, creating a gas-tight seal. Several models were produced with 85, 191, and even 451 barrels all fired together. However, the Vandenberg's recoil was ferocious, despite its weight, so it was another technological blind alley.

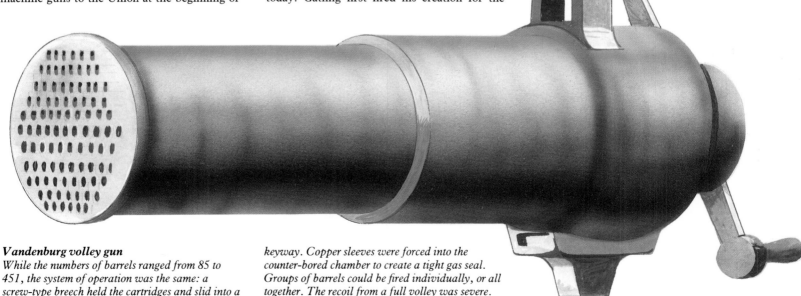

Vandenburg volley gun
While the numbers of barrels ranged from 85 to 451, the system of operation was the same: a screw-type breech held the cartridges and slid into a keyway. Copper sleeves were forced into the counter-bored chamber to create a tight gas seal. Groups of barrels could be fired individually, or all together. The recoil from a full volley was severe.

The only Gatling guns to see action during the Civil War were a handful of model 1862 weapons. These fired .58-caliber paper cartridges rather than the copper rimfire cases used in the more successful 1865 model. Twelve early-model Gatlings were bought by General Ben Butler and used during his inept operations against Richmond and Petersburg.

LEFT: *Billinghurst-Requa volley gun*
The so-called "covered bridge gun," this was a simple arrangement of 25 .58-caliber barrels. A thin metal strip holding 25 steel cartridges was used to load the gun and all barrels were discharged simultaneously. The empty cases were all pulled out together and another volley could be reloaded very quickly.

BELOW: *Agar "Coffee Mill" gun*
The Agar was tested in the field by Union troops in 1862, but proved too unreliable and was not taken into service. The tall hopper that gave rise to its nickname fed .58-caliber cartridges in steel cases down to the feedway. Cranking the handle fed rounds into the breech, fired them, and ejected the empty steel case. If it did not break down, an Agar could fire about 120 rounds per minute.

CENTER: *Williams machine gun*
Mounted on a one-horse split trail carriage like the 12-pounder mountain howitzer, the Confederate Williams gun fired either 16-ounce iron bolts or an equivalent charge of buckshot. Self-consuming paper cartridges were used, fed by hand into the breech. These were manually primed with a cap placed over the nipple on the left of the chamber. Cranking the handle closed the breech and dropped the hammer on the cap. Prolonged firing heated the breech to the point where it would not seat rounds properly. But for a short spell the Williams could fire up to 60 rounds a minute.

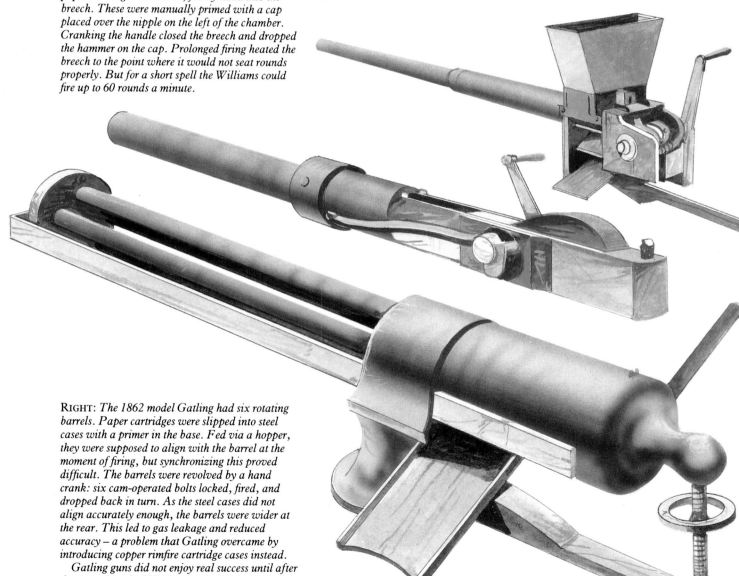

RIGHT: The 1862 model Gatling had six rotating barrels. Paper cartridges were slipped into steel cases with a primer in the base. Fed via a hopper, they were supposed to align with the barrel at the moment of firing, but synchronizing this proved difficult. The barrels were revolved by a hand crank: six cam-operated bolts locked, fired, and dropped back in turn. As the steel cases did not align accurately enough, the barrels were wider at the rear. This led to gas leakage and reduced accuracy – a problem that Gatling overcame by introducing copper rimfire cartridge cases instead.

Gatling guns did not enjoy real success until after the war when the US Navy ordered some in 1-inch caliber. Subsequently, the British and Turkish armies bought Gatlings in .45-caliber. The Russians built them under license and eventually developed a model of their own with 10 barrels.

Field Artillery

Writing at West Point in 1859, 1st Lieutenant John Gibbon of the 4th Artillery Regiment observed in his *Artillerist's Manual*: "Artillery becomes of so much more importance when placed with raw and undisciplined troops; when the batteries, well posted and served, will atone in some measure for the deficiencies of the rest of the troops." He cited Washington's, Bragg's, and Sherman's batteries at Buena Vista, little imagining that Americans would soon demonstrate the wisdom of his words while fighting against each other.

The US Artillery was in the process of upgrading its equipment in 1860. Its standard weapons were the 6- and 12-pounder guns; 12-, 24-, and 32-pounder howitzers; and a light 12-pounder mountain howitzer. In 1857 the artillery had adopted the 12-pounder "Napoleon" (named after Emperor Napoleon III of France) to replace the existing mixture of guns and howitzers. It was destined to become the single most widely used artillery piece of the

Civil War. By the time hostilities began, the US Army had abandoned the old howitzers, but the Confederates could not afford to be choosy. They retained small numbers of them throughout the war and even acquired extra ones from Europe.

The US Army possessed just 163 field guns and howitzers when the war began. The expansion of the artillery park was rapid indeed and represented a considerable bonanza for those factories able to manufacture heavy ordnance. Between New Year's Day 1861 and June 30, 1866 the Federal Ordnance Department purchased a total of 4048 field guns. Two types predominated: the 3-inch Ordnance rifle and the 12-pounder Napoleon gun/howitzer. Respectively, these cannon made up 41 and 39 percent of the Army of the Potomac's artillery at Gettysburg. The rest of Meade's guns were almost exclusively 10-pounder Parrott rifles. Predictably, the Confederate Artillery had to rely on a much wider mixture of cannon and

they seldom managed to standardize their batteries on the same gun.

Artillery pieces were described by the weight of the cannonball they fired. The only major exception was the 3-inch Ordnance Rifle, patented by John Griffen in 1855. Adopted in early 1861, this fired shells weighting 8 or 9 pounds and could, in an emergency, fire those manufactured for the 10-pounder Parrotts. With two notable exceptions, all Civil War field guns were muzzleloaders and they were made of bronze, cast iron, or wrought iron.

With its much greater manufacturing base, the North enjoyed a major advantage in artillery throughout the conflict, Union forces had more field guns available than the Confederates and could afford to abandon obsolete cannon like the 6-pounder field gun or the old howitzers. It also had a much superior supply of ammunition. Although artillery was to remain classified by the weight of its solid shot for some years to come, artillery ammunition included explosive shells. More time-consuming and complex to manufacture, they were a problem for the Confederate Ordnance Department since their effect depended on reliable fuses. Brigadier-General E.P. Alexander emphasized how disheartening it was for a gun crew to see their shells failing to go off, or tumbling through the air in an erratic trajectory because they were improperly manufactured. Once the gunners lost confidence in their ammunition, they lost interest in aiming properly and felt very handicapped in a duel with their opposite numbers. Confederate gunners serving in batteries equipped with rifled cannon were highly envious of their Union opponents who had plentiful stocks of reliable shells.

Guns and howitzers

The division into guns and howitzers dated back to the eighteenth century when explosive shells came into widespread use. Cannon which fired conventional solid cannonballs were known as guns; those designed to fire shells were called howitzers. Guns fired their solid

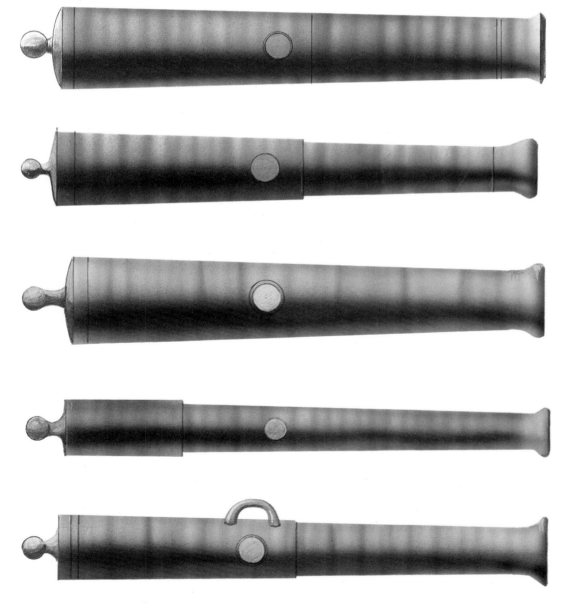

LEFT, TOP TO BOTTOM: *1841 pattern 6-pdr field gun; 1840 pattern experimental 6-pdr field gun; 1851 pattern bronze 6-pdr field gun; 1851 pattern iron 6-pdr field gun; 1836 pattern 12-pdr field gun. Six-pounders were widely used during the Napoleonic wars but were obsolete by 1861. The 1841 pattern bronze 6-pdrs were used by both sides in the first years of the war because they were the only cannon available. But as the rival armies re-equipped with 12-pdr Napoleons, even the Confederates began melting them down to provide bronze for larger guns.*

Many 6-pdrs in Federal service were rifled using the James system. Civil War bronze field guns were made from a mixture of 100 parts copper to between 8 and 13 parts tin. Bronze guns cost 45 cents per pound just before the war; iron guns could cost as little as 6 cents per pound, but iron was liable to rust, and several types of iron gun were infamous for exploding unexpectedly.

projectiles on a relatively flat trajectory and took full advantage of the spherical shape of their ammunition. On gently sloping, hard ground gunners learned to bounce their shot according to the range so that it could plough into closely packed infantry formations at chest height. The faster the shot traveled, the further it could reach. Even rolling along the ground, a cannonball could be deceptively dangerous: their momentum could smash the unwary ankle or break a carriage wheel.

The first shells were fired from smoothbore cannon, so they retained the spherical shape but contained a filling of black powder. High velocity was not required; the trick was to lob the shell into the midst of the enemy with the greatest accuracy. Howitzers were shorter barrelled than guns of equivalent shot weight and they employed much lighter charges of gun powder to fire the round. Their carriages were built to allow the tube to be elevated at higher angles. Howitzers were thus closely related to mortars – indeed, some European armies designated theirs as such. The German heavy howitzers used in both world wars were officially still classified as mortars. Lobbing their shells high in the air allowed howitzers to engage targets behind fieldworks or among buildings.

Wooden peg fuses, filled with fine-grade power, were cut to length according to the time delay required before detonation. They were ignited by the propellant flash in the gun and gave howitzer shells a peculiar fizzing sound. When they struck the ground they rolled erratically, emitting their ominous noise and spitting sparks and smoke. Shells were rated as particularly effective against cavalry since the explosion terrified horses.

If the gunners underestimated the range to the target when firing solid cannonballs, it did not necessarily matter. The shot was still likely to plough into the enemy. But a shell landing short was a shell wasted, and although the fragments from a US 24-pounder howitzer shell could be flung up to 600 yards, the effective danger area was of a much smaller radius. Single shells broke into only 19 fragments on average. Landing a shell on target required

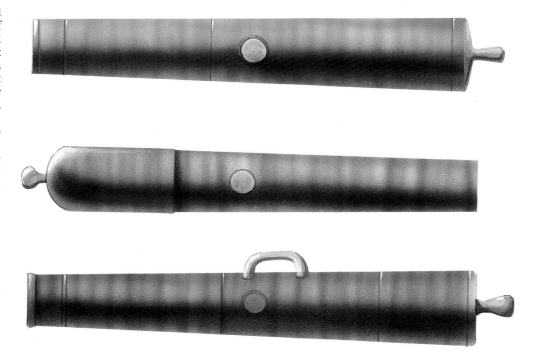

accurate range estimation, correct fuse cutting and not a little luck. As a rule of thumb, US gunners rated solid shot as one and a half times more effective than shell.

The answer adopted by the European armies during the Napoleonic wars was to form mixed batteries of guns and howitzers. The French liked to deploy their howitzers in the center of a six- or more usually eight-gun battery. Perhaps placing a higher value on their howitzers, the US Army tended to deploy them on the flanks so that if a two-gun section had to be detached, it would include a howitzer.

The 12-pounder Napoleon gun-howitzer was not a hybrid combining the essential elements of both types of weapon. It was simply a smoothbore field gun which was also able to fire shells. It lacked the high elevation characteristic of a true howitzer but it represented a

TOP: *1841 pattern 12-pdr field howitzer. This 4.62-inch caliber howitzer was supposed to be replaced by the 12-pdr Napoleon, and the Federal armies did abandon them by the middle of the war. The Confederates retained them, for want of anything better, and they were encountered in Southern batteries until the end of the war. They fired shell or spherical case to a maximum range of 1072 or 1050 yards respectively.*

CENTRE AND ABOVE: *A Confederate iron howitzer made in 1861 and a 24-pdr bronze smoothbore howitzer of the 1841 pattern. The latter fired its 5.68-inch caliber shell to 1322 yards. Its spherical case round took four seconds to reach 1050 yards. The shot fired by 24-pdr howitzers weighed 24.4 lb, the shell 17 lb, and the spherical case round 11.8 lb.*

LEFT: *Confederate bronze 6-pdr gun and an iron 12-pdr made in 1864. Although they rarely burst, bronze guns lost their accuracy as the repeated impact of the iron shot tended to wear the tube unevenly. Cannon barrels were cast in molds made from sand and clay and then bored out, rotating on a track against a fixed boring head. Pre-war experiments with forged iron guns had been conducted for many years, but failed to produce a serviceable weapon.*

Field Artillery

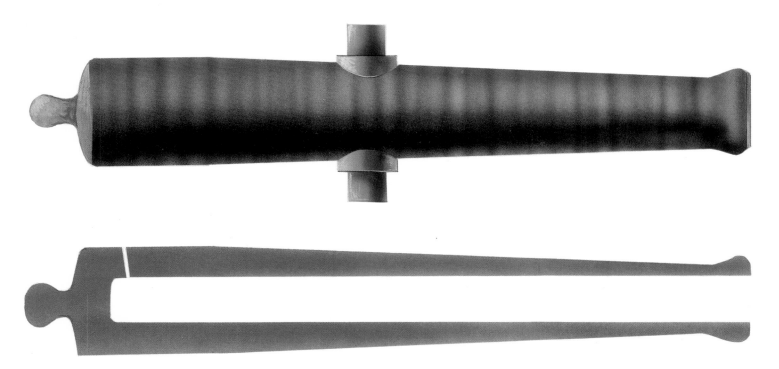

satisfactory compromise. It was demonstrably superior to the old 6-pounder and Confederate gunners found themselves outmatched when they used the older weapon against Union Napoleons. Robert E. Lee wrote the secretary for war in December 1862 explaining this inequality. The Confederacy was soon manufacturing its own Napoleons, which can be distinguished by their lack of a swell at the muzzle. By the time of Gettysburg, Lee's gunners had exactly the same proportion of Napoleons as their Union opponents.

Batteries were supposed to be commanded by a captain with a lieutenant in charge of each two-gun section. All field guns were towed into action behind a limber pulled by a horse team – generally six horses in the Union Army and four in the Confederate service. A limber had an iron pin at the rear, which fitted through the ring on the end of the gun's trail. The ammunition chests also contained friction primers and fuses.

Each gun was accompanied by a caisson, also attached to a limber towed by a four- or six-horse team. The caisson carried extra ammunition, plus a spare wheel and other

Target's view of a 12-pdr Napoleon. In 1861 the US Army ordered 179 Napoleons, 422 in 1862, and 512 in 1863. US Napoleons were produced by five privately-owned foundries, and the total production for the army was 1131 Napoleons. At least 26 more were ordered by various states: Ohio (2), Massachusetts (18), and New Jersey (6). There were probably more orders from state governors, but the exact number is uncertain. About 630 Napoleon copies were produced by the Confederacy; these are generally distinguished by the lack of flare at the muzzle. The Napoleon's higher rate of fire complemented the rifled field guns' greater accuracy at long range. Wherever possible the guns were sited so that the muzzle just cleared the ground, thus providing some cover for the crew and the horse-teams behind.

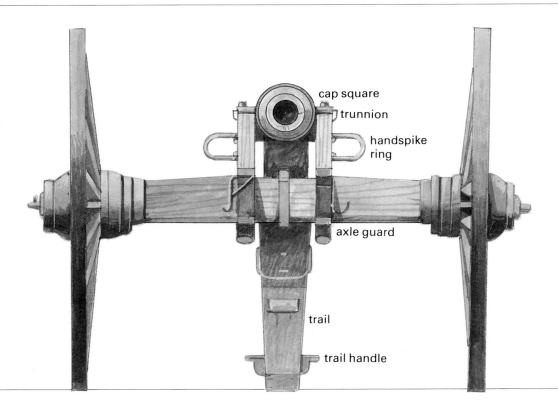

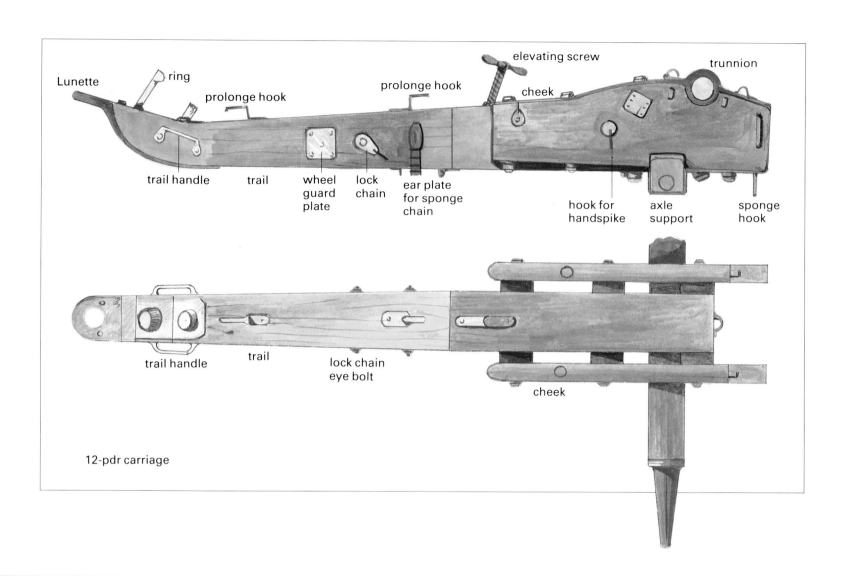

Lunette ring

prolonge hook

prolonge hook

elevating screw

trunnion

cheek

trail handle   trail   wheel
guard
plate

lock
chain

ear plate
for sponge
chain

hook for
handspike

axle
support

sponge
hook

trail handle   trail   lock chain
eye bolt

cheek

12-pdr carriage

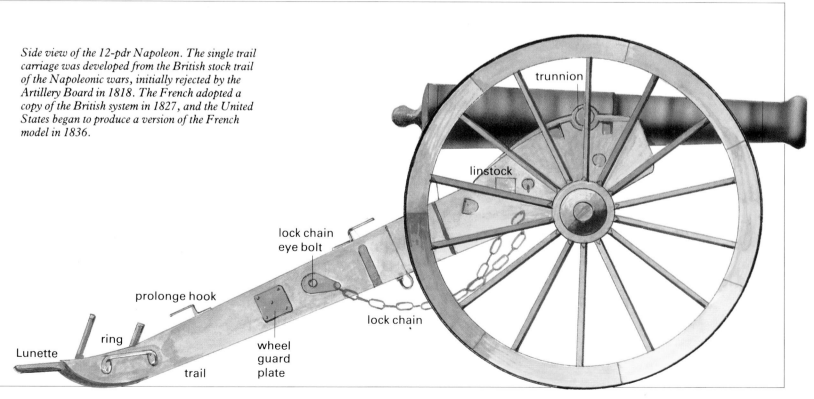

*Side view of the 12-pdr Napoleon. The single trail
carriage was developed from the British stock trail
of the Napoleonic wars, initially rejected by the
Artillery Board in 1818. The French adopted a
copy of the British system in 1827, and the United
States began to produce a version of the French
model in 1836.*

trunnion

linstock

lock chain
eye bolt

prolonge hook

lock chain

ring

Lunette

wheel
guard
plate

trail

Field Artillery

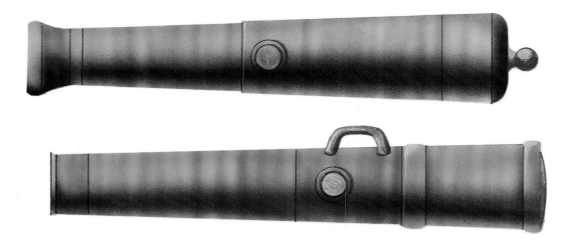

TOP: *Confederate 24-pdr field howitzer*
Although the 12-pdr howitzer was the most commonly encountered field howitzer in Confederate service, small numbers of 24-pdrs continued to serve. At least two Confederate batteries included a pair of 24-pdr howitzers at Antietam.

ABOVE: *Confederate 32-pdr howitzer*
The heaviest piece to be classified as field artillery of the 1841–44 models, the 32-pdr was a 6.4-inch caliber bronze smoothbore with a tube that weighed 1920 lb. It fired a 25.6-lb shell up to 1504 yards with a 2.5-lb charge at an elevation of 5 degrees.

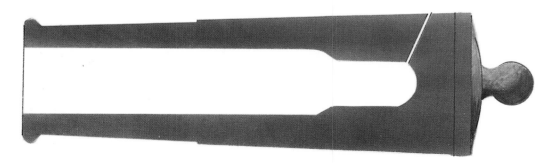

TOP: *12-pdr gun Model 1841*
The 12-pdr gun, rendered obsolete by the Napoleon, weighed 1757 lb, compared to 1227 lb, and was 78 inches long compared to 66 inches. Despite its greater dimensions, its performance was almost identical, firing 12-lb solid shot.

ABOVE (CUTAWAY): *24-pdr field howitzer Model 1819*
Howitzers were designed to fire a relatively large shell using no more powder than standard field guns. Note the small size of the chamber in the breech compared to the width of the bore.

accessories. A gun and caisson formed a platoon commanded by a sergeant and two corporals. Every battery had its own traveling forge for horseshoeing, a vital consideration since a battery at full strength included more horses then men. Other supplies and equipment were borne in the battery wagon. These included carpenters' and saddlers' tools, spare spokes, harness, gunners' implements and so on; the full list ran to 125 items. A fully equipped battery was supposed to have another caisson full of reserve ammunition for each gun, but this was not always achieved.

Artillery battlefield ranges

Like many modern weapons, Civil War artillery was limited more by the lie of the land than its absolute range. At an elevation of 5 degrees a Napoleon's 12-pound shot had a range of 1619 yards. The Parrott rifles reached over 2000 yards and the British Whitworth breachloading 12-pounder could hit targets at 2800 yards. Maximum elevation offered the possibility of very long-range fire – witness the "Swamp Angel" siege gun at Charleston. A Whitworth 12-pounder with its tube cranked up to +35 degrees could fire a solid slug over 10,000 yards. Yet in reality it proved very difficult to exploit these impressive ranges. Some spectacular long-range shooting was recorded when the ground favored it, but gunners accepted that they were restricted by the limit of direct vision. This was typically around 1000 yards' range against infantry. Against cavalry, which presented a larger target, gunners could expect to engage at 1200 yards. If the ground was hard and suitable for exploiting the ricochet effect of cannonballs, 12-pounder Napoleons could fire with some effect at up to a mile.

Artillerists had to be able to estimate ranges accurately or their fire would be ineffective. Experience taught them to rely on the uniform detail of their potential target. At 200 yards every part of a man's body could be observed. As the range neared 500 yards it became harder to make out individual limbs, but the overall division between head, upper and lower body was still clear. Belts and packs were still visible. At 750–800 yards the human body appeared as an elongated form only, although an extended arm could be seen in profile and legs could be distinguished if the men were walking. By 900 yards no uniform detail could be observed and individuals began to merge together, although files were still seen as separate. Between 1100 and 1200 yards a body of infantry appeared as a solid mass. Movement could still be detected.

It took a trained crew 30–40 seconds to fire one round from a 6-pounder smoothbore; to fire a 12-pounder gun took about a minute. If the battery was hard pressed, guns could fire two or even three rounds per minute but this meant taking dangerous short cuts, like not sponging out the barrel between shots. Howitzers took longer to fire – a 24- or 32-pounder required about 90 seconds to reload. It was not the physical process of sponging out the barrel and inserting a fresh round that took the time. The main problem was that Civil War artillery had no recoil system, and the process of aiming

a piece was a matter of delicate judgment. There were no range-finding aids.

The 6-pounder jumped back about 5 feet when it was fired, the 12-pounder a little more. The howitzers were much worse offenders: 24-pounders hurtled back about 10 yards. The little 12-pounder mountain howitzer leapt a foot in the air and up to 12 yards backwards. This could be reduced to as little as 4 yards by using a rope to restrain its wheels. In a sustained action, as the gun crew tired and suffered casualties, the sheer effort in constantly running a gun back into its firing position imposed a serious constraint on their rate of fire. In many battles volunteer infantrymen were employed to help manage the guns.

Gunners throughout history have sacrificed their hearing by long exposure to the literally deafening detonations. Stuffing cotton-waste in the ears could minimize the damage, but few nineteenth-century soldiers appreciated the danger. Repeated firings steadily damaged their hearing and a single error could do a great deal of harm. John Imboden forgot himself at First Bull Run and knelt down beside the muzzle of one of his 6-pounders, keen to observe the first shot. The blast perforated his left eardrum, leaving him with blood tricking down his collar and permanent deafness in that ear.

Artillery ammunition

Cannonballs were fired by pre-ready cloth cartridges containing a measured quantity of black powder. Fixed ammunition was even more convenient; here the cannonball and bag full of powder were supplied as one unit. Solid shot was usually supplied on a wooden sabot, secured to it with tin straps. Spherical shells for smoothbore guns came in a similar way, but the straps and sabot had a hole for the fuse to be inserted. Rifled guns also fired solid shot, sometimes known as bolts. These were the most accurate artillery projectiles of the war and scored several incredible hits, such as the killing of General Polk.

Field artillery fired four types of ammunition: solid shot, common shell, spherical case, and canister. The amount of ammunition carried by a limber depended on the size of the cannon: 50 rounds of 6-pounder ammunition, 32 rounds for a 12-pounder gun, and 23 for a 24-pounder howitzer. According to US Army regulations in force at the beginning of the war, 6-pounder guns had 25 rounds of solid shot, 20 rounds of spherical case, and five rounds of canister. For the 12-pounder the division was 20 solid shot, eight spherical case, and four canister. The old 24-pounder howitzer was provided with 12 shells, eight rounds of spher-

32-pdr field howitzer (cutaway)
The thickness of the metal increased around the breech where the chamber was narrower than the bore. On the 32-pdr part of the tube was removed from the exterior of the breech to save weight.

BELOW: ***Armstrong 3-inch breechloader***
A few examples of this British field gun were imported by the Confederacy. It fired a 12-lb shell to 2100 yards at an elevation of 5 degrees. British-made ammunition was expensive, so locally-made Confederate shells were substituted. Unlike the Whitworth, the Armstrong breechloaders could not be used as muzzleloaders in an emergency.

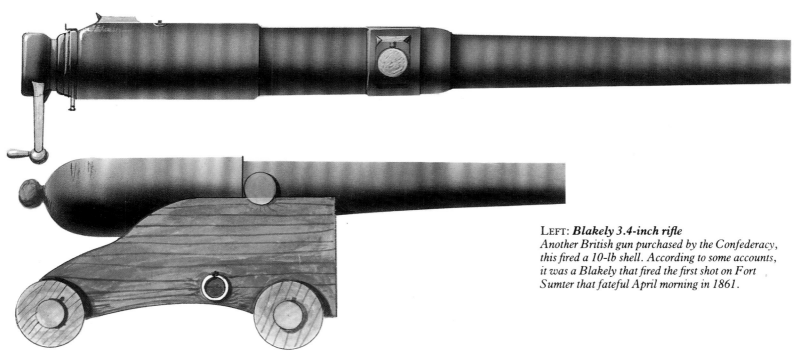

LEFT: ***Blakely 3.4-inch rifle***
Another British gun purchased by the Confederacy, this fired a 10-lb shell. According to some accounts, it was a Blakely that fired the first shot on Fort Sumter that fateful April morning in 1861.

Field Artillery

ical case, and three of canister. The exact ratio of the different ammunition types during the war varied from army to army, with spherical case proving unpopular, so there was rather more canister fired than pre-war artillerists had anticipated.

Spherical case was also known as case shot or shrapnel, named for its British inventor, Captain Henry Shrapnel, although some US sources misspell his name Schrapnell. During the Napoleonic wars he developed a hollow cannonball packed with powder and musket balls and detonated by a time fuse. Early experiments showed that the musket balls could explode the charge by rubbing together at the moment of firing, so Shrapnel embedded them in resin, leaving a central hole into which the gunners inserted a tin tube containing the powder charge. The fuse fitted on top of this.

The charge was not required to fling the musket balls over a 360-degree arc, but just to break open the case and free them. The velocity of the projectile would do the rest, showering them forward against the target. For this reason the gunners had to get the ranges exactly right and explode the shrapnel round just in front of the target. Because of the problem in achieving accurate range, spherical case was not worth firing against enemy troops advancing rapidly toward the battery.

US 12-pounder spherical case rounds contained 78, 58-caliber musket balls anchored in sulphur or asphalt instead of resin. The whole round weighed 13½ pounds. The 6-pounder equivalent contained 38 balls and had a 2½-ounce detonating charge. Union and Confederate case shot rounds reflected the Northern superiority in industrial resources. Union case shot consisted of a spherical casing into which the lead bullets and sulphur or asphalt were poured. When it had set, a hole was drilled out for the bursting charge. By contrast, the Confederacy was suffering a dearth of lead and generally used iron balls inside its case shot. As this was harder to drill, they manufactured their casings with a side filler hole into which the bullets and fixative were poured. The fuse hole was meanwhile occupied by a stick until the mixture had cooled. It was then withdrawn, leaving a chamber for the detonating charge. The filler hole was plugged with a lead, brass, or iron plug.

Spherical case shot would develop into the artillery's primary weapon in the years after the Civil War. By 1914 the rain of shrapnel from quick-firing guns helped make fighting in the open a recipe for monstrous casualty list. But shrapnel did not prove as effective during the Civil War. Dependent on accurate range estimation, it was at its best against a static

target. Unfortunately, static targets tended to be entrenched, which negated the effect of shrapnel. Gunners tended to rely more on the old-fashioned but brutally simple cannonball. Solid shot was made of cast iron formed in copper molds. It remained the best multi-purpose projectile since it could engage fieldworks as well as troops in the open, batteries, or buildings.

Solid shot had several important limitations. Its effect relied on a steady cannonade rather than the accuracy of individual rounds. To strike an enemy gun or wagon with a deliberately aimed round was extremely difficult unless the gunners were using one of the few Whitworth rifled guns. Although solid shot could certainly batter fieldworks and suppress the defenses with a heavy bombardment, it could not inflict major losses on entrenched infantry. Explosive shells could do the job much better and they were the preferred round with which to engage enemy artillery batteries.

The shells carried in the ammunition caissons of Civil War artillery batteries were made of iron filled with a charge of black powder. Detonated by a wide variety of fuse types, these shells tended to break into large chunks rather than a hail of small fragments. They could thus inflict ghastly wounds on men and horse but a single shell's effect was limited. The incendiary

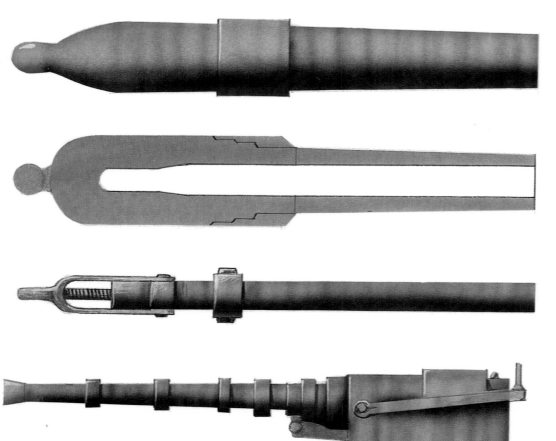

Blakely 2.9-inch rifle
This was a British mountain gun firing a 10-lb shell. The tube was made of iron.

Wiard 4.62-inch 12-pdr (cutaway)
Norman Wiard was employed by the US Department of Ordnance and designed several unusual cannon, including rifles and smoothbores, guns and howitzers. They had cast "semi-steel" tubes and were mounted on carriages that anticipated those of the 1890s.

Confederate 2.75-inch breechloading rifle with straight-type lands and grooves
This measured 61.25 inches overall, excluding the breech block. The chamber was 5.87 inches long and 4.87 inches wide. The weapon was bored out from the wheel-shaft of a river steamer in 1863 at the Columbus Ironworks, later to become the Confederate Naval Ironworks, and was the first breechloader built by that foundry.

Tappey & Lumsden 3.13-inch field gun
The adoption of the revolver principle for working cannon had interested both Union and Confederate inventors. One such design was produced by Henry Pate, a lawyer of Petersburg, Virginia, and two were cast by Tappey & Lumsden. Unfortunately, one burst during tests in May 1861 owing to the light construction which was unable to withstand the stresses of rapid fire in action. These field guns were 5-shot smoothbores firing 4-lb projectiles. Overall length was 70 inches, including the lock-up crank, which forced the 13.5-inch long cylinder against the barrel to minimize gas leaks. The weapon was loaded from the front.

value of shellfire was a useful secondary effect, especially against enemy artillery whose wagons and caissons could be blown up by shells igniting the ammunition.

Shells were cast in molds similar to those used for solid shot but with a core inserted to leave the center hollow. It was crucially important to align this exactly in the center or the shell casing would be uneven. This sand core was broken up and removed, leaving a hole communicating with the hollow interior. This was used for the fuse. After casting, shells and solid shot both required a little work with hammer and chisel to remove excess "flash" around the mold line. They were then placed in a large iron tumbler, which revolved, rubbing the newly cast projectiles together to smooth them. After a final check, those rounds which passed inspection were coated with lacquer.

Civil War fuses

The standard Civil War method for detonating a shell was a paper time fuse held in a metal or wooden fuse plug. The cylindrical paper fuse held a paste of fine black powder and its exterior was marked with graduations. These represented one second of burning time, although the variations in the rate of combustion made this more of a guide than a truly precise measurement. The gunner estimated

6-pdr gun
The Confederate batteries equipped with 6-pdr guns found themselves at a distinct disadvantage once the Union had re-equipped with Napoleons and 3-inch rifles. The Army of Northern Virginia managed to replace its 6-pdrs by the time of the Gettysburg Campaign – there was only one 6-pdr used in the battle – but they continued in service with the Army of the Tennessee well into 1864.

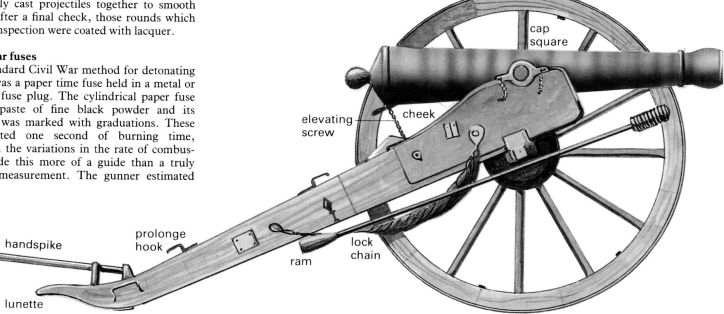

how long it would take the shell to reach its target and cut the fuse down accordingly. The Union gunners had a major advantage in shell supply since their fuses were all produced by the Frankford Arsenal to relatively consistent standards. Confederate fuses were manufactured in several ordnance factories and, as previously noted, earned a poor reputation among some Confederate artillerists.

Shells for the Parrott rifles used a variation on this theme. Their fuses also relied on a soft metal plug screwed into the nose of their elongated shells. Color-coded, conical paper fuses containing fine powder fuse composition were then inserted. Black fuses burned 1 inch in two seconds, red took three seconds, green four, and yellow five seconds. All the fuses were a standard 2 inches long and could obviously be cut down if required.

Federal artillery introduced a new type of fuse for spherical shot. The Borman time fuse was a disc attached to a screw thread which fitted into the shell. Below its pewter or similar semi-soft metal cap lay a ring of powder which looped around the top before descending through the threaded length of the plug to the

bursting charge of the shell. The cap was marked in ¼-second increments from zero to 5½ seconds. To set the time of detonation the gunner pierced the thin metal skin of the cap with a knife after he had affixed the fuse to his shell. When the cannon fired, the flash from the explosion would wash over the shell and ignite the fuse at whichever point it had been pierced. The Borman time fuse proved fairly reliable and became the standard fuse for Union smoothbore projectiles.

Although these fuses relied on the flash produced on firing to ignite them, it was important to keep them facing the muzzle. If the fuse was in direct contact with the main charge, it was likely to explode immediately with potentially catastrophic consequences. This was the reason for the wooden sabots attached to spherical projectiles by iron straps. If the round was loaded with the sabot resting against the powder charge, the fuse faced the front and all was well. So-called "fixed ammunition" was a combination of a projectile, its sabot, and the powder bag all tied together. Since this could be loaded in one movement, it helped gun crew maintain a rapid rate of fire.

Rifled cannon and their ammunition

The development of rifled artillery led to a series of innovations in artillery ammunition. The Civil War was the last major conflict in which muzzleloading guns predominated and it produced many different solutions to the problem of imparting spin to a projectile that was loaded via the muzzle. All the main systems relied on the forced expansion of part of the projectile so it gripped the rifling on its way up the muzzle.

The most successful muzzleloading ammunition was the Parrott shell which sat on a ring made of wrought iron. This did not project much beyond the diameter of the shell and did not impede the round being rammed down the muzzle. When the shell was fired, however, the soft metal was flattened by the pressure and its rim expanded into the barrel rifling. A similar method was to fit a copper ring – the Parrott-Reed shell – which also expanded on firing. The Federal Ordnance Department purchased over a million rounds of this type of ammunition. Other variations on this theme included the Burton shell, which used a lead cup, and the Mullane, which relied on the expansion of a

Field Artillery

copper disc. All four systems tended to shed their discs or cups after firing, which made firing them over the heads of friendly troops disagreeable for the infantrymen in between.

An alternative option was to taper the rear end of the projectile toward the base and fit it with a ring. Benjamin B. Hotchkiss developed an expanding shell which was fabricated in two sections. The front end had a round nose, then tapered to a short stem; the back half fitted around this but a lead ring surrounded the join. When the gas pressure behind the shell acted against the rear of the projectile, it forced the lead outward and into the rifling. This imparted a spin but the battered lead ring tended to fragment in flight, shedding tiny bits of metal and making an eerie noise. The Confederates developed their own version – the Archer shell. Also a two-part projectile, this used a lead driving band between them.

Similar to the Hotchkiss expansion method, the Schenkl shell was another common rifled projectile which used papier-mâché instead of iron. The tapering stem of the shell had a series of ribs around it into which the papier-mâché was compressed when the gun fired. Its primary disadvantage was the vulnerability of the papier-mâché to damp: if it was poorly varnished and exposed to wet or humid conditions, it expanded and became difficult to load.

There were two other systems which were developed for specific types of cannon. Rhode Island militia general Charles T. James produced a 14-pounder cannon design and a 3.8-inch caliber shell to go with it. Manufactured in Chicopee, Massachusetts, between 1861 and 1862, they were delivered to the Union Army. The shells had an iron skirt around the base with slots cut into it and filled with lead. A thin layer of tin covered the whole surface. The gas pressure produced on firing the cannon forced the lead out of the slots, through the tin skin and against the rifling. Still gripped by the iron skirt, the lead transferred the torque to the shell. James died in the fall of 1862, by which time his special projectiles had already proved of questionable value. His guns, which looked very similar to the 3-inch Ordnance rifles, continued in service for a while and Hotchkiss-pattern rifled ammunition was produced for them.

There was obviously no way to anticipate which part of a spherical shot from smoothbore cannon would strike the target first, so designing a percussion fuse was very difficult. But the elongated projectiles fired by rifled guns made it possible to develop a round which could detonate on impact. The standard method was to fit a fulminate cap under the hard nose of the shell with a powder-filled plunger behind it. When the shell struck the target, the plunger would fly forward under inertia and strike the cap. The nose of the shell acted like an anvil. The fulminate would explode, detonating the powder train back to the main charge. Hotchkiss shells worked on this basic principle but had the plunger held back by two safety wires attached to a lead plug. When the shell was fired, the plug dropped back and snapped off the safety wires, freeing the plunger.

Parrott shells had a safety system too. This consisted of a semi-soft metal cylinder around the plunger, which locked it in place until the force of impact sheered the two little lugs that held it on. Some Union gunners distrusted the arrangement and removed the cylinder before firing, relying on the plunger not banging forward before they fired the round. The Schenkl shells described earlier used a similar percussion fuse in which the plunger was held in place by a small screw through the side. Other variations included time-delay fuses in which the shock of impact initiated a time fuse, and one system which employed a glass tube of fulminate that shattered when the shell struck the target.

Close defense of the battery

Artillery batteries were not expected to defeat absolutely anything that came at them. Infantry and cavalry were always posted in support of guns if their position was likely to be attacked. Since infantry advancing at the double could cover 200 yards in 2 minutes, the infantry could afford to get into cover, out of reach of the enemy artillery. Cavalry were often posted in reserve, ready to assist artillery batteries if closely pressed. They could cover 200 yards in little over 30 seconds, so they too could remain out of harm's way until the last moment. However, on the handful of occasions cavalry were rushed forward to cover the withdrawal of a gun line, they sustained serious losses from enemy musketry.

If batteries did have to face a direct attack by enemy troops, they relied on canister. This converted their cannon to massive shotguns, spraying the oncoming enemy with an unselective, but potentially lethal hail of projectiles. As noted earlier, the small number of canister charges carried in the caissons indicates that it was regarded as a last-ditch defensive weapon. Properly deployed, it could beat back an attack, or at least gain the artillerists time to withdraw or have their supports come up to their rescue.

A canister round consisted of a flimsy cylinder of thin iron filled with a quantity of large-caliber balls, generally also of iron. The canister round fired by the 12-pounder Napoleon contained 27 iron balls each 1½ inches across. (They were packed in sawdust to stop them rattling about.) The cylinder was fixed to a wooden plug at one end and crimped over a heavy iron plate at the other. When the cannon fired, the cylinder disintegrated and the shot flew from the muzzle. It dispersed quite rapidly, spreading across a frontage roughly equal to a tenth of the range, so at 200 yards the 27 balls were scattered over approximately 20 yards.

The ideal range for canister was considered to be 300–400 yards against a massed target because at closer ranges the shot was too concentrated for best effect. However, it was normally used for close protection of the battery at ranges of around 200 yards. Hard, dry ground, which allowed the gunners to exploit the ricochet effect, increased the potential range of canister in the same way as it did for round shot. The gargantuan charges fired by larger guns were effective at proportionally

longer ranges. By contrast, the maximum range of canister from the little 12-pounder mountain howitzer was only 300 yards.

Canister proved most effective when fired from smoothbore cannon. It has been said that rifled guns tended to disperse their shot in too erratic a pattern because the rifling affected the passage of the shot. In fact, any reduction in effect may have been due to the nature of the canister rounds themselves. The 3-inch rifle's canister ammunition was fixed since rate of fire was obviously critical. It contained 49 balls to the Napoleon's 27, but they were just under 1 inch across. It may have thrown its shot in too tight a pattern for the full sawn-off shotgun effect to have worked.

Rifled cannon were generally slower to load than smoothbores since most of their ammunition was semi-fixed rather than fixed. In close range action a Napoleon smoothbore was supreme. This bore out some of the arguments used by the diehard exponents of smoothbore guns before the war. In the same way that progress toward breechloading rifles was retarded by the exponents of the muzzleloading rifle, rifled cannon had some powerful opponents to overcome. They argued that it would be impossible to develop expanding projectiles for artillery in the same way as for infantry rifles. Various tests conducted in the 1850s gave them added ammunition as experimental rifles blew their barrels because mechanically fitting shells stuck halfway.

Strengths and weaknesses of rifled guns

Once the problem of designing muzzleloading rifle ammunition had been overcome, the advantages of rifled guns became obvious. For example, the James rifle weighed 918 pounds and used a 12-ounce charge to fire a 14-pound shell to 1700 yards. The 12-pounder Napoleon weighed 309 pounds more and required a 40-ounce charge to fire its lighter projectile to 1600 yards. The future clearly belonged to rifled artillery.

Unfortunately, every silver lining has a cloud. Although rifled artillery was demonstrably superior to smoothbore cannon, it had an Achilles' heel: the barrels could not be made from bronze because experience earlier in the century had shown that rifling wore out too rapidly. The solution was to build guns from cast or wrought iron. The former was the cheapest and easiest answer, but cast iron was dangerously brittle and not well suited to containing the detonation of black powder. Unlike nitrocellulose- and nitroglycerin-based propellants which have been in use now for just over a century, gunpowder detonates rather than burns. It delivers all its energy in one sudden rush so that it is all consumed before the projectile has gone far up the barrel. The smokeless powders introduced in the late 1880s burned more slowly and evenly, generating much lower chamber pressure but still imparting considerably greater muzzle velocity to the projectile.

The pressure created by the explosion of a large black powder charge tended to burst cast-iron cannon barrels. Robert P. Parrott,

Limbers carried the ammunition chest, secured with pins and brackets for rapid removal, and two or three gunners could ride on top of it. The center of

gravity was slightly to the rear of the axletree to counterbalance the weight of the central pole.

Sponge rammer *The rammer pushed the charge and projectile down the barrel. The woolen sponge, soaked in water, extinguished any sparks present before the next round was loaded.*

Worm *This device was used to extract cartridge bags and rags from the bore.*

LEFT: *Trail handspike*
This short pole was used to move the carriage to the right or left.

superintendent of the West Point Foundry, New York, developed a cost-effective solution to the problem. Taking a cast-iron barrel, he added a wrought-iron band around the breech. While still hot, the iron band was forced on to the breech of the tube, which was rotated and cooled with water from the inside. The iron band then cooled, which created a substantially stronger breech without the weight penalty that would have been incurred by using a thick, cast-iron breech.

Parrott's banded rifles became the most common of their type during the war and were copied by the Confederates. Three basic field guns were manufactured: the 10-pounder Model 1861, the 10-pounder Model 1863, and the 20-pounder. The original 10-pounder had a 2.9-inch caliber tube, but since this could not use ammunition fabricated for the 3-inch Ordnance rifle, the design was modified in 1863 and the bore expanded to 3 inches. The 20-pounder was the largest true field gun of the war. At an elevation of 5 degrees it fired its shell just over 2000 yards – not much further than the 10-pounder; it was the greater shell weight that gave it the advantage. Parrott guns were produced in much larger calibers for siege and naval service. The 30-pounder was strictly a siege gun, although some were employed in the field; the Confederates captured one at Bull Run mounted on a field carriage. Since the tube alone weighed over 4000 pounds, it was not really suitable for maneuver across a battlefield.

Parrott's wrought-iron bands did not completely solve the disagreeable tendency of cast-iron tubes to burst. Parrott rifles frequently burst, often just at the end of the band. At Fredericksburg a two-gun battery of 30-pounder Parrotts in Confederate service were shelling the Union positions under the eyes of General Lee himself. On its 39th round one of the guns burst, fortunately without harming the crew, General Lee, or any of his officers who were all nearby. The other Parrott later burst as well, this one on its 54th round. The Confederate gunners were lucky that no one was injured. Perhaps the most notorious instance of the Parrotts' unreliability was the US Navy's bombardment of Fort Fisher in December 1864. The navy lost more men from the explosion of its own 100-pounder Parrott rifles than it did from Confederate return fire. Postwar investigations of the Parrott system revealed frightening examples of gun barrels fracturing in the gun yard – not from firing, but simply from residual stress in the metal.

Imported English breechloaders
The idea of reinforcing the breech of an iron cannon with extra hoops of metal was not unique to Parrott. An English engineer, William Armstrong, had already perfected a technique in which numerous bands were shrunk over a wrought-iron tube. They were even shrunk over each other, giving Armstrong guns a characteristic beer-bottle shape. The Confederates imported a number of his heaviest siege guns, and major defense systems usually incorporated a handful of monstrous 150-pounder Armstrong guns.

Armstrong also introduced a breechloading mechanism for some of his guns. The tube had a removable vent piece, which was lifted out to load the gun. The shell and charge were inserted via the screw-threaded breech and the vent piece was then dropped into place behind the charge. Locked into position by the turn of the screw, it was then fitted with a fuse and fired. Armstrong manufactured his own lead-coated shells which gripped the rifling of the rest of the barrel, which was of a fractionally smaller diameter than the breech. When the charge was fired, it forced the shell into the rifling, sacrificing some velocity for accuracy in the same way as the other expanding projectiles previously described.

The Armstrong system worked effectively but it did have one weakness. The vent pieces were placed under enormous strain and they did occasionally fail. Artillery batteries tried to carry spare vent pieces but they were not always available. Even if an Armstrong gun's crew had managed to obtain one, their troubles were not over. If the vent piece broke up while the gunners were hard pressed by the enemy, they might not have the time to extract the mangled remains of the old one and repair the damage in time. Since the shells were marginally wider than the barrel, they could only be loaded via the breech. It was impossible to feed them backwards into the muzzle if the breech mechanism were broken.

Another English artillery manufacturer, Sir Joseph Whitworth, made much of the fact that his rifled breechloaders could be muzzleloaded in just such as emergency. Both the Union and Confederate armies included a handful of imported Whitworth guns and they were unequal-

Field Artillery

led for long-range accuracy. Whitworth had invented a system quite different from the conventional rifling systems. His pieces employed a hexagonal bore which twisted, imparting spin to a mechanically-fitting hexagonal projectile. The tube had no chamber like the Armstrong and was sealed at the breech by a hinged screw-cap. The shells themselves were sheathed in tin to help prevent gas escape from the breech and a wad of tallow and wax was inserted behind it to lubricate the barrel.

General E.P. Alexander, who commanded the artillery of Longstreet's corps, praised the accuracy of the Whitworth cannon but stated after the war that all six Whitworth breechloading rifles under his command had had problems with their breech mechanisms. The gunners managed to fix all of them, but in the meantime the Whitworths were fired as muzzleloaders. With the breech cap left closed and a copper disc employed to help check the escape of gas, they functioned perfectly well. Like the target and sniper rifles that also employed the Whitworth hexagonal breech system, Whitworth 12-pounder guns tended to foul badly and required diligent maintenance to retain their accuracy. Since the shells carried such a small charge of powder, their explosive effect was not impressive and Whitworths tended to fire their solid shot, often described as a bolt. Actually weighing 12 pounds 12 ounces, this hexagonal iron missile made a distinctive sound in flight, according to some Union sources who were on the receiving end.

How field guns were fired
Field guns were operated by a gunner and seven artillerymen, who were numbered according to their job. On a muzzleloading cannon the drill went as follows. The gunner standing behind the trail gave the order to load. Number 1 sponged the tube using a wooden pole with a water-soaked sponge at one end and an iron rammer at the other. This extinguished any smoldering residue in the barrel and cleaned the bore. Numbers 6 and 7 manned the limber, where they cut fuses and handed shells to Number 5 who carried them to the gun itself. He passed a round to Number 2 who inserted it in the barrel when Number 1 had finished sponging out. Number 1 then rammed the round down the barrel while Number 3, standing to the right of the breech, held his thumb over the vent. Since barrels rapidly became very hot with repeated firing, leather thumb protectors were manufactured. Once the round had been rammed home, Number 3 left the breech and moved to the trail, which he nudged left or right at the direction of the gunner. Number 5 meanwhile headed back to the limber to collect the next round.

Once satisfied that the aiming of the cannon was as accurate as possible, the gunner stepped aside and called "Ready." Numbers 1 and 2 stepped aside from the muzzle. Number 3 pricked the cartridge, while Number 4, who stood on the other side of the breech, hooked a lanyard to the friction primer, which he then inserted into the vent. Number 3 covered the vent with his left hand, while Number 4 moved to

the rear, taking care to keep the lanyard slack.

On the command, "Fire," Number 3 stepped clear of the wheel and Number 4 yanked the lanyard. The primer he put into the vent consisted of two copper tubes soldered together at right angles. The shorter one contained a friction composition with a serrated wire insert. This terminated in a loop to which the lanyard was attached. The longer tube which was pushed into the cannon tube's vent was packed with musket-grade black powder sealed with a wax plug. The whole body of the primer was usually varnished to help keep it waterproof. When Number 4 pulled the lanyard, it drew the serrated wire through the friction composition. This ignited, igniting in turn the musket powder in the tube and then the main charge. Pricking the charge before firing exposed the powder inside to the flash from the primer.

To accelerate the rate of fire Numbers 5 and 7 could alternate, forming a human chain to pass ammunition up to the gun. The distance they had to travel depended on the terrain where the battery had deployed. Under regulations the limber lay just 6 yards behind the gun and the numerous photographs of dead artillery horses, all killed in their traces, testify that this was often done in practice. Artillerymen could sacrifice mobility for protection if they were fighting from prepared positions; ammunition chests could be taken from the caissons and dug in near the cannon, but if a field battery needed to move at a moment's notice, it had to have its horses close by. This exposed them to enemy fire which could obviously be counterproductive. This was another reason why gunners preferred to find a position where they could fire over the crest of a hill, keeping their vulnerable horses, limbers, and caissons under cover. Looking at photographs of Civil War batteries drawn up with the regulation 14 yards between guns, it is immediately obvious that the limbers and the caissons stacked behind the cannon offer a much better target than the guns themselves. Gunners that found themselves coming into action against an entrenched opponent were at a serious disadvantage.

The one-horse gun
The 12 pounder mountain howitzer was a very different weapon, although it did fire the same ammunition as the 12-pounder Napoleon. This 4.62-inch caliber weapon was used during the Mexican War, and after 1865 it became the most widely employed artillery piece in the US Army's campaigns against the Plains Indians. Both sides used the mountain howitzer during the Civil War, but not in the numbers they might have done considering the rugged terrain of many battlefields. The mountain howitzer was a smoothbore, bronze cannon with a tube weighing 220 pounds – less than one sixth the weight of a Napoleon. It was mounted on a carriage just 5 feet 1 inch long, which was drawn by a single mule or horse.

In very broken country the whole gun could be dismantled into three mule-loads. The leading mule carried the 37-inch tube on its back, together with the two shafts which connected the trail to the mule's harness when

the gun was being towed. The center mule carried the two wheels, the carriage, and the gunners' implements, while the third mule carried the ammunition. As the mountain howitzer had no limber, ammunition was supplied in eight-round boxes weighing 112 pounds. A mule carried two, one on either side of a pack saddle. Two more mules were needed to carry the forge and tools plus coal and carriage-maker's kit. A battery at full strength consisted of six howitzers, seven carriages (one was a spare) and 33 pack animals. The regulation ammunition load was 36 boxes, i.e. 288 rounds. At an elevation of 5 degrees the mountain howitzer could lob a shell 900 yards using its 8-ounce charge.

Artillery on the move
Horses or mules can draw roughly seven times as great a load along a good road as they can carry on their backs, hence the significance of good roads during the Civil War and the importance of corduroying bad ones to aid the pack animals. For artillerymen a thorough understanding of horses' capabilities was absolutely essential. Including the weight of the carriage, a horse of medium strength was reckoned capable of drawing a 3000-pound load for 20–23 miles a day over paved road. This fell to 1900 pounds if the road was only macadamized. Over ordinary dirt roads horses could manage 1500–1600 pounds, and as little as 1100 pounds if crossing broken ground. If the team had to traverse a relatively short distance, a skilled wagoner might get 2200-pound loads. Increasing the size of a team was commonly done to get guns and wagons over difficult stretches but doubling the teams did not produce a proportional increase in locomotive power. Teams only achieved maximum efficiency if they were used to working together.

The state of the roads was also critical to the amount of space occupied by a battery on the move. On a good road carriages travelled in single file at 1-yard intervals. Closed up in this manner, they could manage a steady 2½ miles per hour. But on a bad road it was important to leave a good 5 or 6 yards between them, keeping them all to the right-hand side of the track so they could turn around if necessary. The battery would normally stop for 10 minutes every hour to allow the rear elements to catch up.

At a slow trot over good going, an artillery battery could travel at 5 miles per hour for short distances. But in the isolated regions to which some armies were drawn, life was rarely that easy. Brigadier-General George Morgan's Union troops at Cumberland Gap had to move their artillery through a narrow defile with a mountain on one side and the Cumberland River on the other. In May 1862, with some elements of his command already weakened by scurvy, his men dragged 22 guns, including two 20- and two 30-pounder Parrotts, across the steeply sloping Pine and Cumberland Gaps. Multiple teams of horses were used for some, but the heaviest demanded blocks and tackles, with 200 men laboring on a single piece.

Artillery Specifications

Ranges shown here are the maximum for shot (guns) or common shell (howitzers). The charge is that required to reach maximum range. Guns are bronze unless otherwise noted. Howitzers smaller than 8 inches are bronze unless otherwise noted. Large howitzers and Columbiads are iron.

Abbreviations: BLR = Breechloading rifle; MLR = Muzzleloading rifle.

Guns

Type	Bore (inches)	Length (inches)	Weight (pounds)	Charge (pounds)	Range (yards)	Notes
6-pdr M1841	3.67	60	884	1.25	1523	Used during early years. Confederates melted many down to make other cannon.
6-pdr M1841 (rifled)	3.67	60	884	1.25	1700	Standard 6-pdr, rifled using the James system.
6-pdr M1848	3.67	44	462			Cadet gun.
6-pdr M1841 (CSA)	3.67	70	910			Only a few used.
9-pdr M1836	4.2	77				Out of service before 1861.
12-pdr M1841	4.62	74	1757	2.5	1663	Also fired spherical case to maximum range of 1250 yards.
12-pdr M1857	4.62	72	1187			First Napoleon.
12-pdr M1857	4.62	72	1220	2.5	1619	Standard Napoleon field gun. Also fired shell to maximum range of 1300 yards, and spherical case to 1135 yards.
12-pdr (CSA)	4.62	72	1250			Cast-iron version.
18-pdr M1839	5.3	123	4913	4.5	1592	Siege & Garrison gun firing from barbette carriage.
24-pdr M1839	5.82	124	5790	8	1834	Siege & Garrison gun.
32-pdr M1841	6.4	125	7200	10.67	1517	Siege & Garrison gun. Widely used by US Army in defenses of Northern cities.
32-pdr M1845	6.4	106	4761	6	1756	
32-pdr M1846	6.4	125	6384	9	2731	"Long 32-pounder."
42-pdr M1841	7.0	129	8465	14	1915	Firing from barbette carriage.

Field Artillery

Howitzers

Type	Bore (inches)	Length (inches)	Weight (pounds)	Charge (pounds)	Range (yards)	Notes
12-pdr M1841	4.62	53	788	1	1072	Range with spherical case was 1050 yards. Standard model of the war.
12-pdr M1841 (mountain)	4.62	32.9	220	0.5	1005	Also fired spherical case to 800 yards and canister to 250 yards.
24-pdr M1841 (field)	5.82	71	1318	2	1332	1200 yards with spherical case. Made of bronze.
24-pdr M1844 (Siege & Garrison)	5.82	69	1476	2	1322	1200 yards with spherical case.
32-pdr M1844	6.4	82	1920	2.5	1504	800 yards with spherical case.
8-inch M1841 (Siege & Garrison)	8.0	61.5	2614	4	2280	45-lb shell.
8-inch M1841 (seacoast)	8.0	109	5740	8	1800	45-lb shell.
10-inch M1841 (seacoast)	10.0	124	9500	12	1650	90-lb shell.

Columbiads

Type	Bore (inches)	Length (inches)	Weight (pounds)	Charge (pounds)	Range (yards)	Notes
8-inch M1844	8.0	124	9240	15	4468	Fired shot to 4812 yards.
8-inch M1861	8.0	119	8465	10	3873	Fired shot to 3224 yards.
8-inch M1861 (CSA)	8.0	120.5	9020	–	–	Other model weighed 8750 lb.
8-inch M1861 (CSA)	5.82	120.5	–	–	–	Confederate 8-inch re-bored and rifled.
10-inch M1844	10.0	126	15,400	20	5654 4828	With 128-lb shot. With 100-lb shell. Time of flight, 35 seconds.
10-inch M1844 (CSA)	10.0	122.5	13,320	–	–	
10-inch M1844 (CSA)	6.4	122.5	14,850	–	–	Confederate 10-inch re-bored and rifled.
12-inch M1865 (CSA)	12.0	–	–	–	–	Two uncompleted guns found at Tredegar after surrender.
15-inch M1861	15.0	190	49,099	40	5018	First pattern.
15-inch M1861	15.0	192	50,000	40	–	
20-inch M1864	20.0	243.5	115,200	200	8001	Firing solid shot.

Parrott Rifles

Type	Bore (inches)	Length (inches)	Weight (pounds)	Charge (pounds)	Range (yards)	Notes
10-pdr M1861	2.9	78	890	1	2000	At 5° elevation; 3200 yards at 10°; 5000 yards at 20°.
10-pdr M1863	3.0	78	890	1	2000	At 5° elevation; 3000 yards at 10°. M1863 distinguished by lack of muzzle swell.
20-pdr M1861	3.67	89	1750	2	2100	At 5° elevation; 4400 yards at 15°.
30-pdr M1861	4.2	133	4200	3.75	2200	At 5° elevation; 4800 yards at 15°; 6700 yards at 25°.
30-pdr M1861 (Navy)	4.2	112	3550	3.25	4874	At 15° elevation.
100-pdr M1861	6.4	155	9700	10	6820	At 15° elevation, firing 101-lb shell; 8453 yards with 80-lb hollow shot.
100-pdr Navy	6.4	139	9850	–	–	Breechloader.
175-pdr	8.0	162	16,500	16	4272	At 11° elevation.
250-pdr	10.0	173	26,500	25	4290	At 13.5° elevation. Never tried for extreme range.

Dahlgrens and Shell Guns

Type	Bore (inches)	Length (inches)	Weight (pounds)	Charge (pounds)	Range (yards)	Notes
12-pdr boat gun (rifled howitzer)	3.4	63.5	880	1	1770	Bronze.
20-pdr boat gun (rifled howitzer)	4.0	–	–	2	1960	Bronze.
30-pdr rifle	4.2	92	–	–	–	Iron.
12-pdr medium boat howitzer	4.62	63.5	750	1	1085	With spherical case: 1150 yards.
50-pdr rifle	5.1	107	–	–	–	
24-pdr boat gun (rifled howitzer)	5.82	67	1310	2	1270	With spherical case: 1308 yards.
80-pdr rifle	6.0	–	–	–	–	
150-pdr rifle	7.5	140	16,000	–	–	
8-inch M1845	8.0	114.5	6160	7	2600	Naval broadside gun.
8-inch M1864	8.0	115	6500	7	2600	
9-inch Dahlgren	9.0	131.5	9000	13	3450	Standard broadside armament of major US warships.
10-inch Dahlgren	10.0	146	12,000	12.5	3000	Also mounted on broadside and pivot mounts.
10-inch Dahlgren	10.0	–	16,500	40	–	Pivot gun, also known as 125- or 130-pdr Dahlgren.
11-inch Dahlgren	11.0	161	15,700	15	3400	Pivot.
11-inch Dahlgren	11.0	161	15,700	20	3650	Turret.
11-inch re-bored and rifled	8.0	158	17,330	25	–	
15-inch	15.0	162	42,000	35	2100	In *Passaic* class.
15-inch	15.0	178	42,000	35	2100	In *Canonicus* class.

Brooke Rifles

NB The Confederacy never undertook a systematic test of Brooke rifles, so there is limited range data.

Type	Bore	Length (inches)	Weight (pounds)	Charge (pounds)	Range (yards)	Notes
4.62-inch rifle	–	111.5	6170	–	–	Single band.
6.4-inch rifle	–	144	9120	–	–	Single band.
6.4-inch rifle	–	144	10,700	–	–	Double band.
7-inch rifle	–	147	14,800	–	–	Single band.
7-inch rifle	–	148	15,160	23	7900	Double band.
8-inch rifle	–	–	–	–	–	No data available.
11-inch rifle	–	–	24,350	–	–	Seacoast rifle.

Brooke Smoothbores

Type	Bore	Length (inches)	Weight (pounds)	Charge (pounds)	Range (yards)	Notes
8-inch	–	142	10,400	–	–	6.4-inch rifle bored to 8 inches and smoothbored.
10-inch Navy	–	158	21,560	–	–	Double band.
10-inch Seacoast	–	150	21,140	–	–	Double band.
11-inch	–	170	23,612	–	–	Double band.

Field Artillery

British Rifles

Armstrong

NB Ranges where given are for solid shot ("bolts").

Type	Bore (inches)	Length (inches)	Weight (pounds)	Charge (pounds)	Range (yards)	Notes
12-pdr BLR	3.0	83	918	1.75	3961	At 10° elevation.
12-pdr MLR	3.0	76	1009	–	–	British Army field gun.
20-pdr MLR	3.75	96	1882	–	–	
40-pdr MLR	4.75	120	3640	–	3660	1859 pattern.
40-pdr MLR	4.75	120	3640	–	3986	1860 pattern.
70-pdr BLR	6.4	–	6903	9	6903	Many were converted to breechloaders.
110-pdr BLR	7.0	120	9184	–	–	Many were converted to muzzleloaders.
150-pdr MLR	8.0	131	15,737	–	–	
300-pdr MLR	10.0	156	26,880	–	–	
600-pdr MLR	13.3	183	51,296	70	7300	Bolt actually weighed 507lb.

Blakely

Type	Bore (inches)	Length (inches)	Weight (pounds)	Charge (pounds)	Range (yards)	Notes
12-pdr	3.5	84	–	1.5	1760	
12-pdr	3.6	58	–	–	–	
18-pdr	4.0	83	921	–	–	
100-pdr	6.4	96	8000	–	–	
120-pdr	7.0	119	9600	–	–	
150-pdr	7.5	101	–	–	–	
200-pdr	8.0	136	17,000	–	–	
250-pdr	9.0	150	24,000	–	–	
375-pdr	11.0	–	35,000	–	–	
650-pdr	12.75	194	60,480	55	2200	At 2° elevation. Same gun also known as 600-, 700-, or 900-pdr. Shells actually weighed 470 lb. Bolt weighed 650 lb.

Whitworth

Type	Bore (inches)	Length (inches)	Weight (pounds)	Charge (pounds)	Range (yards)	Notes
12-pdr BLR	2.75	104	1092	1.75	2800	At 5° elevation; maximum range, 10,000 yards, at 35°.
12-pdr MLR	2.75	–	1090	1.75	–	
32-pdr MLR	4.14	87	3360	5.25	4800	At 10° elevation.
70-pdr MLR	5.0	134	8580	13	5000	At 10° elevation.
120-pdr MLR	6.4	–	16,660	27	–	

Other Cannon

Type	Bore (inches)	Length (inches)	Weight (pounds)	Charge (pounds)	Range (yards)	Notes
Wiard 6-pdr	2.6	53	725	–	800	At 35° with full charge; maximum range, 7000 yards.
Dyer 9-pdr	2.9	–	–	1	3270	
Ordnance rifle	3.0	73.3	820	1	1835	9-lb shell fired at 5° elevation; 3972 yards at 20°.
CSA rifle	3.0	72	967	–	–	Copy of Ordnance rifle. Several versions made with and without a muzzle swell.
Wiard 12-pdr	3.4	64.5	783	–	–	Fired Hotchkiss shells.
Cameron 14-pdr	3.56	83	1000	–	–	Confederate field gun.
Dyer	3.67	–	880	1.25	–	Fired 14-lb Dyer shells.
Reed (CSA)	3.69	–	1200	1.5	–	Fired Reed 12-lb shells.
James 14-pdr	3.8	65	918	0.75	1700	At 5° elevation. Produced by Ames 1861–2. Fired James shells which did not prove successful.
4.5-inch siege gun	4.5	133	3450	3.25	3265	At 10° elevation. Fired Dyer 25.5-lb shells.
Reed Field Rifle (CSA)	4.6	–	1900	2	–	Fired 15-lb shells.
Reed Siege Rifle	4.8	–	5000	3	–	Fired 22-lb Reed shells.
Ames 50-pdr	5.1	106	5500	3.5	–	Fired 37-lb shot.
Sawyer	5.8	–	8822	5.5	4359	Fired 45-lb Sawyer shell.
Dimick	6.4	–	9300	6	–	Fired 51-lb Dimick shell.
Reed	6.4	–	8500	6	3665	At 11.5° elevation.
Ames 125-pdr	7.0	168	19,400	25	9230	106.5-lb Hotchkiss shell fired at 34.5° elevation.

Mortars

Type	Bore (inches)	Length (inches)	Weight (pounds)	Charge (pounds)	Range (yards)	Notes
24-pdr Coehorn	5.82	16.3	164	0.5	1200	Minimum range 25 yards.
8-inch M1841	–	22.5	930	1	1200	Time of flight 14.5 seconds; 46-lb shell.
8-inch M1861	–	22	1010	2	2225	Minimum range 500 yards.
10-inch M1841 siege	–	28	1852	4	2100	Time of flight 21 seconds; 90-lb shell.
10-inch M1841 seacoast	–	46	5775	10	4250	Time of flight 36 seconds; 98-lb shell.
10-inch M1861 siege	–	28	1900	4	2064	
12-inch seacoast	–	–	–	20	4625	Experimental. Fired 200-lb shell.
13-inch M1841	–	53	11,500	20	4325	200-lb shell.
13-inch M1861	–	53	17,120	20	4325	200-lb shell. Known as "Dictator".
16-inch M1839	–	31.5	1600	1.5	250	Bronze "stone" mortar, fired 120-lb stones.

Railroads

The American Civil War was the first true railroad war. Although Prussian troops had made a strategic railroad move as early as 1842, and the French concentrated their forces on the Italian border by rail in 1859, they had continued their operations on foot. In America strategic concentrations took place by railroad over unprecedented distances throughout the war. For example, for the surprise attack on Grant at Shiloh the Confederates reinforced Johnston's existing force with troops from Columbus, New Orleans, Mobile, and South Carolina. The railroads became vital strategic arteries, supplying vast armies across every theater of war.

In the 10 years before the war the American railroad network extended over 9021 miles; by the end of 1860 this figure had increased to 30,626 miles, of which only 8541 miles were in the seceding states. The North also had another advantage; not only did it have more absolute mileage, but there were more connecting lines and fewer different gauges.

The American railroads of 1860 followed the lie of the land as closely as possible because the locomotives did not have enough power in reserve to tackle any significant gradient. Railroads were laid around hills rather than over them, so the lines tended to curve sharply. The ties were usually of white oak, 10 × 10 inches. They were placed on the bare earth without stone or shingle ballast. T-shaped iron rails ran on top of them, but not all rails were made of solid iron; in the earliest days of the railroads wooden ones had been used with just a thin iron strip fixed to the surface. Although many such

The Confederates were the first to experiment with artillery fired from railroad cars. During the battle of Savage Station on 29 June 1862, the Confederate troops pressing McClellan's rear guard were supported by a railroad gun sent up the line from Richmond. Commanded by Lieutenant Barry, this was a 32-pdr rifled gun mounted on a rail car and protected from enemy fire by a wooden shield covered with iron plates. Allowing the accompanying infantry to advance against the Federals, the railroad gun halted within a mile of Savage Station and engaged Union troops covering the field hospital there.

lines had been replaced by 1861, there were some still in use.

Civil War trains traveled at average speeds of 15–25 miles per hour. The locomotives could pull a maximum load of about 150 tons – typically 15 loaded cars. Confederate locomotives burned wood, which was stockpiled alongside the track. Some Northern locomotives were already burning coal in 1861 and almost all had converted to this more efficient fuel by the end of the war.

The South's smaller rail network was unhelpfully built with three different gauges. Virginia and North Carolina used a 4 feet 8½-inch track, while most of the other lines in the states east of the Mississippi used a 5-feet gauge. There was an important exception in the line from Montgomery, Alabama, that ran to the state line with Georgia; this used the 4 feet 8½-inch gauge. The two lines running through Louisiana west of the Mississippi relied on a 5 feet 6-inch gauge. To travel from Richmond to Mobile involved three changes of gauge. Communications between Virginia and the western Confederacy depended on only two lines: one via Wilmington and Columbia, the other via Knoxville and Chattanooga. In 1861 work was already in progress on a third line that ran between Richmond and Augusta. The Confederates were fortunate that they completed this in May 1864, as the other two routes were cut by Union action.

Confederate armies were concentrated by rail from all over the South on several occasions. The first railroad maneuver was on the eve of First Manassas when Johnston's troops were withdrawn from the Shenandoah via the Manassas Gap Railroad to join Beauregard. This

Confederate rail move was achieved despite the railroad staff, who refused to work overtime, preventing some of Johnston's command reaching the battlefield in time. Confederate forces were subsequently maneuvered by rail at the opening of the Seven Days' Campaign in the Peninsula and again before Shiloh and Chickamauga.

While railroads allowed the Confederate armies to exploit interior lines in the defense of their nation, the Federal armies also carried out major strategic redeployments by rail. Hooker was sent from Virginia to the western theater with XI and XII Corps before the battle of Chattanooga, a deployment that moved some 23,000 Union soldiers 1192 miles in seven days. In 1865 Schofield's 15,000-strong Army of the Ohio journeyed 1400 miles from the Tennessee Valley to Washington in 11 days. These concentrations were carried out over a far wider area than those of the Napoleonic era and represented one of the most important military developments of the nineteenth century. The railroad (and the telegraph alongside) had profoundly changed the pace of military strategy.

Although spectacular troop movements gained the most attention during the war, the railroads' primary function at this time was the simple transport of goods and supplies. The gradual deterioration of the Confederate railroads was the single most important economic factor in their defeat. Southern industry achieved astonishing success given the disadvantages it labored under. But transportation problems mounted. When Catesby ap Jones commanded the naval ordnance facilities at Selma, Alabama, he was frustrated by the knowledge that there was plenty of coal available but too little railroad capacity to deliver enough of it to him. Similarly, the Southern harvests during the war were good, but inadequate transportation left many people hungry while other areas were in surplus.

It is a situation mirrored today in the Soviet Union. In the Confederacy finished products completed at such effort – naval armor plate, cannon or even shoes – were often held up at obscure railroad sidings for week after week. The tracks needed repair, the locomotives had broken down or were simply not available . . . it was an administrative nightmare. The Con-

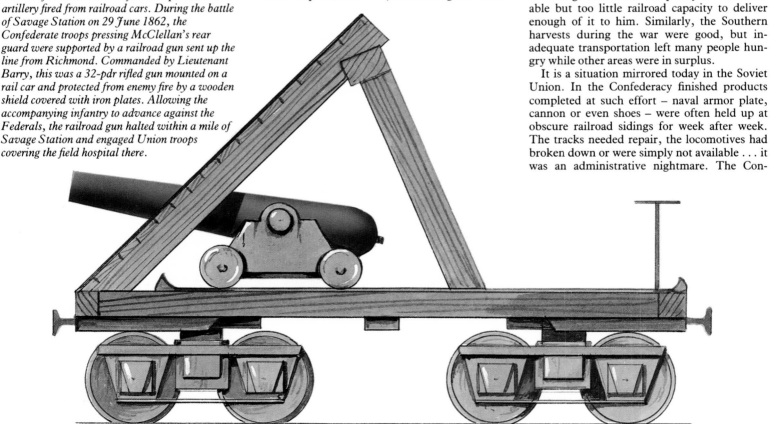

federates made every effort to keep their locomotives in service, but there was a limit to what they could improvise. Captured locomotives were prized indeed; Jackson seized five from the Baltimore & Ohio Railroad early in the war and dragged them up the Shenandoah Valley with his horse teams. They were put back on the rails at Strasburg.

In the later campaigns in the western theater railroads became the object of military operations. As the Union armies penetrated deep into the Confederacy, so they depended on their rail lifelines with the North. Confederate cavalry raiders tied down tens of thousands of Union soldiers posted to protect the railroads. Bridges, generally built of wooden trestles, were an especially vulnerable target and log blockhouses were often built next to them to guard the crossing. However, while these sufficed to repel lightly armed guerrilla groups, the later raiding parties took to bringing horse artillery with them.

Early in the war the Philadelphia & Baltimore Central railroad was patrolled by an armored train but this was not widely copied. The Confederates mounted a field gun on a flat car during the battle of Seven Pines and the Union gunners built an armored siege gun during the operations around Petersburg. But trains were seldom the objective of enemy attack; it was the vulnerable rails themselves that were the target.

Both sides demonstrated equally thorough techniques for the destruction of railroads and their rapid repair. After Hood cut Sherman's

rail communications near Resaca, the Confederates wrecked 35 miles of track. Sterling work by the troop and the Construction Corps saw 25 miles of railroad relaid in a week. The civilian Construction Corps numbered 24,000 men at the peak of its power and it earned an incredible reputation for building bridges in record time. Railroads were laid through broken country with Confederate guerrillas sniping at the work parties. One of their most impressive achievements was the 800-feet long, 100-feet high Chattahoochie bridge, erected in four and a half days from unfelled timber.

Wrecking a railroad was simple: a handful of men could loosen a few rails in a matter of

minutes. But unless such sabotage achieved a catastrophic derailment, it would not block the line for very long. To destroy the line permanently it was necessary to tear up the rails and bend them. The ties were burned in great heaps with the rails heated over the fire until they glowed. A team of men could then bend them around a convenient tree, manipulating the red-hot rail with pincers. However, unless the rail was bent right round like a hairpin it proved possible to straighten it out by similar means. Experienced railroad wreckers learned to twist the rail as well as bend it. There was no field expedient or remedy to this and any rails so treated had to be returned to the rolling mill.

This large-caliber Parrott rifle was mounted on a railroad car by Federal artillerymen during the siege of Petersburg. It followed much the same arrangement as the Confederate rifle at Savage Station. Like the famous mortar "Dictator," the gun could be traversed in a limited fashion by positioning the railroad car on a curve in the track. The sharply sloping frontal armor was intended to deflect incoming projectiles.

In early 1864 the Union forces employed armored railroad cars to protect the Baltimore & Ohio railroad from Confederate raiders. Defensive positions were established at Martinsburg, Cumberland, Grafton, and Clarksburg, while Harper's Ferry was reinforced. Parties of troops were held in readiness to intercept a Confederate attack on the line. Blockhouses were built overlooking the most vulnerable points of the line. The "ironclad railroad cars" each carried a light gun.

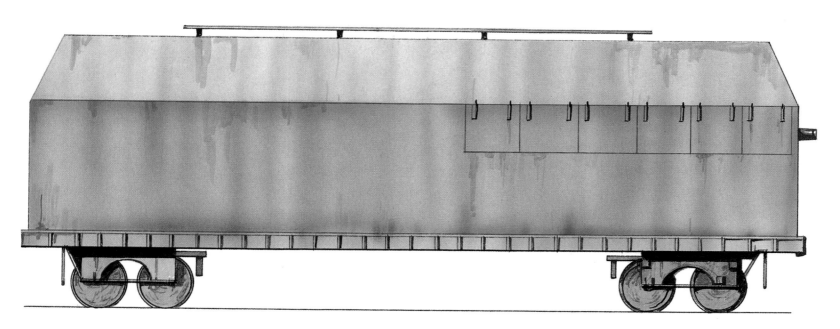

The War in the Air

Union and Confederate balloons

Aerial reconnaissance has been a vital factor in military operations since 1914. Today, most major armies employ helicopters as part of their reconnaissance formations and fixed-wing aircraft can probe deep into enemy territory without crossing the front line. Intelligence can be transmitted by radio and vital information can reach a military commander in an instant.

Nineteenth-century commanders had no such blessings. By modern standards they were all but blind, dependent on cavalry patrols that had to report by sending back couriers. This time-honored means of monitoring enemy movements provided most of a Civil War commander's tactical intelligence. But some generals supplemented their cavalry reports with a new source – aerial observation.

Balloons had been appearing at carnivals for some years before the war. Thadeus S.C. Lowe was a famous pre-war balloonist and he organized a balloon corps for the Union Army in 1861. He and his assistants took to the field with McClellan's forces for the 1862 Peninsula campaign. Seven balloons were used, supported by a mass of wheeled transport that enabled Lowe's men to generate hydrogen gas. Large, box-shaped gas generators were mounted on the chassis of a standard army wagon. Sulphuric acid and iron filings were mixed to produce the gas, which was pumped into the balloons via a pressure regulator. McClellan authorized an extension of the telegraph so the occupants of the basket could signal directly to his headquarters.

Day after day a balloon rose into the air from the balloonists' site near General Fitz John Porter's headquarters. It overlooked the Confederate lines at Yorktown and invariably drew the occasional shot from the Rebel artillery. They never hit one. One day a balloon parted from its moorings and wafted over the lines, to the consternation of its occupants. They were lucky: the wind changed and blew them back to safety. Many senior Union officers, including McClellan, McDowell, and Porter, ascended in a balloon to study the surrounding terrain.

From his lofty position in the balloon *Intrepid*, Lowe observed the battle of Seven Pines from his station north of the Chickahominny. The Confederates had a Whitworth gun south of the river that could engage the balloon while it was below 300 feet. As it rose to its usual observation altitude of 1000 feet, the balloon was out of danger because the Whitworth could not be elevated sufficiently to reach it.

There were obvious limitations to the value of a balloon. While it was a useful observation platform in static warfare, monitoring troop movements and developments in the enemy defenses, in a mobile battle the cumbersome balloon equipment could not be deployed rapidly. The terrain did not help either. Although the Federals had their balloons in service at Chancellorsville, they did not learn much from them since the densely forested landscape denied the occupants a clear view.

The Confederates were not slow to appreciate the potential of observation balloons but they lacked the necessary facilities. Without the means to manufacture hydrogen gas, they hit upon a novel solution. A balloon was made at Richmond from silk dress material – a riotous patchwork of different colors and patterns. Inflated with town gas from the Richmond gas works, it was secured to a locomotive which steamed down the York River railroad to a suitable vantage point.

The Confederate balloon provided useful intelligence during the Seven Days Battles, detecting and reporting the Union reinforcements crossing the Chickahominny during the battle of Gaines Mill. After McClellan withdrew from Malvern Hill, the Confederates fixed the balloon to a little tug, the *Teaser*. Unfortunately for them, the tug ran hard aground on July 4, 1862, just as the tide fell. The crew escaped but Union troops captured the vessel and its bizarre cargo. General Longstreet lamented the loss (the last silk dresses in the Confederacy) as "the meanest trick of the war."

The Union Balloon Corps lasted longer than its Confederate counterpart but was disbanded in 1863. McClellan had first placed it under the command of the Corps of Topographical Engineers. It was transferred to the Quartermasters Department and then to the Corps of Engineers. Eventually, General Hooker transferred the balloons to the Signal Corps, which claimed it lacked the resources to manage this new unit and promptly issued the order to disband.

General E.P. Alexander was critical of the Union decision. As commander of a 26-gun artillery battalion in Longstreet's corps at Gettysburg, he had a tricky task in maneuvering the guns on to the Union flank without being detected by the signal station on Round Top. The need to keep out of sight cost the Confederates valuable time in what became a critical race. The eventual Confederate assault came too late: Union troops had plugged the gap and Meade's left flank held. Alexander observed that the balloons could have performed the same role in other battles. Even if they spotted nothing, they automatically delayed Confederate movement.

A section of the Union Balloon Corps in operation during the Peninsula Campaign. The hydrogen gas generators (far left) feed gas into a pressure regulator to fill the balloon. McClellan's favorite staff officer, Lieutenant George A. Custer, made a series of ascents in a balloon to study the Confederate lines, while rebel sharpshooters took optimistic potshots at him. He was the first to spot Johnston's evacuation of Yorktown.

TOP: *Balloon carried on naval barge serving on the James River.*

85

River Crossing

Many campaigns of the Civil War were shaped by the location and state of the local rivers. Sometimes they were a terrible obstacle obstructing an army's progress; at other times they were a vital supply line or a welcome source of fresh water for drinking and washing. River crossing was a regular feature of military life and several armies became extremely accomplished bridge builders. All four of Sherman's corps were provided with a pontoon train for the March to the Sea, each capable of bridging 900 feet. Yet his soldiers frequently did not wait for the pontoons to arrive, but built improvised bridges from timber along the riverbank. Sherman's men certainly bore out his conviction that a nation of engineers would always defeat one of agriculturalists.

Bridging was, of course, a last resort. If a river or stream could be crossed without resort to any construction, the army could pass over far more quickly. Rivers could be crossed when frozen provided the ice was thick enough. Ice 3 inches thick could be crossed by infantrymen, while cavalry and light guns could pass over provided it was at least 4.3 inches thick. To get field guns over required 6 inches of ice (8 inches for big guns like a 24-pounder). To help horses keep their footing it was usual to cover the crossing point with boards or straw. The ice always creaked as the first men crossed; this was disturbing but did not indicate any weakness in the ice. The critical sign of danger was the appearance of water in surface cracks.

Horses can swim straight over a river, a fact neglected by the US Army before the war. By contrast, the French Army regularly practiced swimming its cavalry regiments across rivers. Infantrymen were able to ford safely up to a depth of 39 inches, although 51 inches was the pre-war army's accepted maximum if the current was very light. Cavalry's maximum fording depth was 51 inches. Artillery could ford only up to 27½ inches because their ammunition boxes were not watertight. If these were waterproofed or raised to keep them clear, artillery could ford up to 40 inches. In any case, it was always important to ford a river on as wide a front as possible and for the leading troops to move rapidly away from the bank so as not to congest the ford.

Troops frequently crossed rivers in locally obtained boats. This called for some important calculations, particularly when cavalry or artillery had to be shipped over. A cubic foot of water was calculated as weighing 62.4 pounds; multiplying the surface area of the boat by 62.4 gave an approximate indication of the potential load that could be crammed into a small boat. To calculate a boat's load it was assumed that an infantryman weighed 145 pounds; fully equipped, he weighed 160 pounds. Three men standing close together occupied one square yard. A horse on its own weighed 1000 pounds, or 1225 with rider and equipment. A cavalryman occupied a space 40 inches by 10 feet.

Where a more permanent crossing was required, armies built bridges. Many were improvised, others were assembled by the engineers from their purpose-made pontoon trains. High banks or marshy areas were avoided wherever possible because they delayed construction considerably. Ideally the bank had to be between 3 and 8 feet above the water level. Successful bridging required the army to be in secure possession of both riverbanks, although there were examples – notably at Fredericksburg – where engineers led an assault river crossing against enemy defenses.

Both armies used pontoon trains based on those in service with the French Army. Flat-bottomed wooden boats traveled on four-wheeled carriages that also contained ropes, oars, boat hooks, and anchors. These were lowered into the water and anchored in a row at the desired crossing point. Five lines of 27-feet long timber balks were laid across the boats. Each balk measured 5 × 5 inches and rested at either end across the full width of a boat. Once these were lashed in place, 13-feet-long chesses were laid across them to form the roadway. This was covered in straw or earth to protect it from the wear and tear of hooves and wheels when the troops crossed.

Pontoon bridges could span impressive distances – US engineers spanned the James with a bridge 2200 feet long in 5½ hours – but they were vulnerable to accidents and enemy action. Wherever possible, military bridges were duplicated with several crossings close by so that the loss of a single bridge was not critical. To prevent the enemy floating tree trunks or other heavy objects downstream to ram the bridge, the best counter-measure was a boom swung across the water. Constructed from large tree trunks connected by heavy chain, it was best placed to block such an attack if placed obliquely across the river at about 22 degrees with the current. Nearer the bridge it was a sensible precaution to post a guard of observation with small boats, grappling hooks, and long cables.

As an alternative to the cumbersome pontoon train, the US Army copied a form of light-weight pontoon bridge in service with the Imperial Russian Army. Instead of relatively heavy wooden boats, the Russians used canvas pontoon boats. These were nothing more than a wooden framework with canvas wrapped around and wetted until it was waterproof. Planks placed along the bottom of the framework allowed the engineers to stand up in the boats. The individual pontoon boats in Federal service were 26 feet long, 5½ feet wide, and 28 inches deep. A 21-feet long version was also employed.

Pontoon bridges were crossed with care. Infantry marched without music at the route-step since the cadence set up a dangerous rocking motion that could upset the bridge. If the structure did begin to sway, the column was halted to let it subside before any further movement was attempted. Cavalry crossed dismounted, horses led by the riders at a slow walk. Mounted crossings were apt to lead to horses jumping off or attempting to trot, which led to broken legs as hooves slipped between the planks. When artillery crossed a pontoon bridge, all but the rear driver dismounted to lead the horses. Guns stuck rigidly to the center of the bridge and maintained at least a 20-yard separation between carriages.

If time was short, rivers or streams could also be crossed by means of a "flying bridge" – a raft or cluster of boats planked over that swung between the two banks on a rope anchored upstream in the center of the channel. The "bridge" was fitted with a rudder. Pushing out from the bank and adjusting the rudder allowed the current to take the raft. It then transcribed a circle, centered on the anchor, and swung over to the opposite bank. Flying bridges demanded a strong current to work successfully; without one it was necessary to rig additional ropes to the banks so that the raft could be pulled over by teams of men or horses. Flying bridges were easy to build: a pre-war manual reckoned 36 men could build one in an hour. Made from six boats, it could transport 250 men, two cannons, or 12 horses.

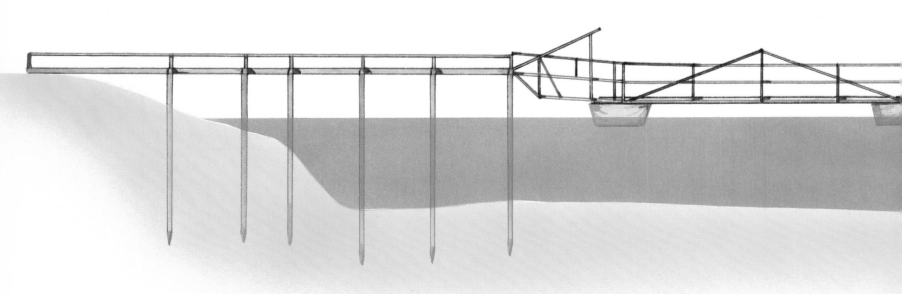

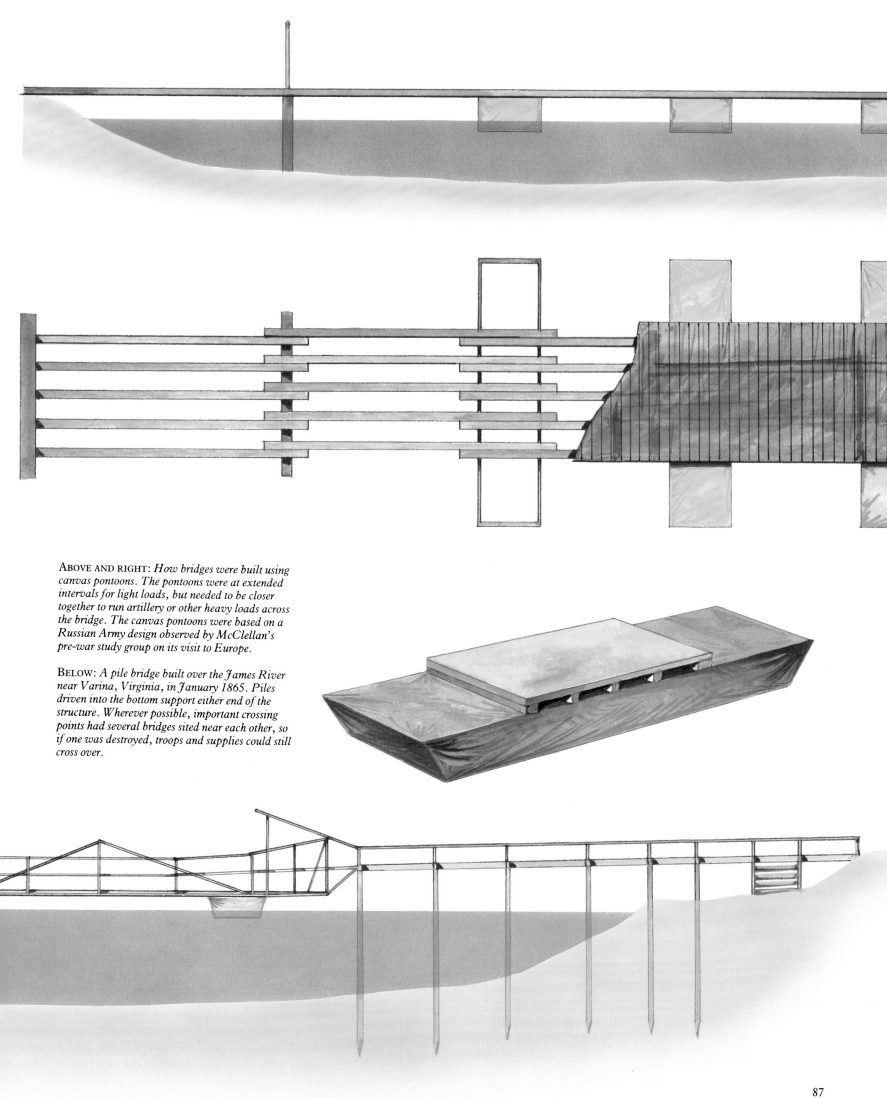

ABOVE AND RIGHT: *How bridges were built using canvas pontoons. The pontoons were at extended intervals for light loads, but needed to be closer together to run artillery or other heavy loads across the bridge. The canvas pontoons were based on a Russian Army design observed by McClellan's pre-war study group on its visit to Europe.*

BELOW: *A pile bridge built over the James River near Varina, Virginia, in January 1865. Piles driven into the bottom support either end of the structure. Wherever possible, important crossing points had several bridges sited near each other, so if one was destroyed, troops and supplies could still cross over.*

Wagon Trains

Supply has always been a vital factor in warfare. As armies through the ages acquired new and more complex weapons, so their dependence on a supply line increased. By the time of the American Civil War, military units could still "live off the land" by foraging for food but they could not improvise a supply of percussion caps for their rifles or ammunition for their cannon. All military units relied on wheeled transport and the roads behind an army were invariably choked with wagons.

Mule-drawn wagons carried all manner of supplies, from ammunition to tents and food. Wagons shuttled to and fro from the nearest railhead, forming an umbilical cord that sustained the army in the field. Should this cord be cut – by enemy action or intentionally by a bold commander – an army could not continue indefinitely. Enterprising officers like Grant, who cut loose from his supply line to win the Vicksburg campaign, were taking a gamble. If they failed to re-open a supply line, their forces were doomed. Sherman's celebrated march to the sea was rather less risky since the Confederacy lacked the military force to stop him.

The length of a wagon-based supply line was equally finite: about 100 miles. This was the maximum distance a wagon could travel before the fodder required by its mules exceeded the load it could deliver. Over poor roads, in adverse weather conditions, the practical distance was much shorter and a lack of fodder compounded the problem by weakening the mules. The appalling 70-mile journey from Bridgeport to Chattanooga cost the lives of over 10,000 mules when Rosecrans's army had to be supplied at all costs.

The standard US Army wagon had a 10-feet long body and a canvas top stretched over six iron loops. Its shape and general construction are familiar from western movies, but during the Civil War the canvas top was seldom left plain. In the Union Army it was marked with the insignia of the unit to which it belonged and a description of the contents. Thus, wagons carrying ammunition had AMMUNITION painted in large letters running almost the length of the wagon. A wagon was usually drawn by six mules – tougher than horses and better able to get by on bad fodder.

Most roads in the Confederacy were unmetalled. Heavy rain or thawing snow could turn them into a quagmire that wagons could only struggle through, with double or triple teams pulling and men putting their shoulders to the wheels. Many armies had their plans disrupted by the weather and its effects on the roads and the wagon trains.

Most campaigns were at least partially affected but the most notorious took place in January 1863. Just over a month after the disaster he had orchestrated at Fredericksburg, General Ambrose E. Burnside ordered the Army of the Potomac to leave its quarters at Fredericksburg and cross the River Rappahannock a few miles upstream. However, the clear, cold weather that had lasted since mid-December vanished in torrential rain the day after the advance began. The whole army became literally bogged down. The wagons remained stuck in the mire, despite teams of 150 men hauling on drag ropes. The three days' rations issued to the troops were consumed in an advance of less than 5 miles! On January 23

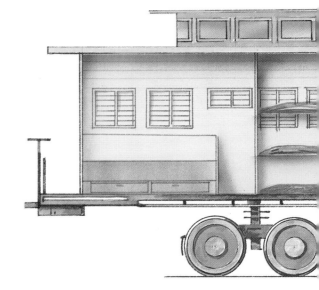

the Army of the Potomac turned around and squelched back to Fredericksburg, its commander demanding the dismissal of many of his senior officers. General Burnside was sacked two days later.

The number of wagons required to supply an army corps of 15–20,000 men varied from 600–800. During Sherman's Georgia campaign each corps fielded 800 wagons, a column that occupied 5 miles of road. To prevent the total loss of supplies, each corps marched using four parallel roads wherever possible.

Other wheeled transport used by the Civil War armies included purpose-built ambulance wagons. By 1863 each division of the Army of the Potomac had 40 four-wheeled ambulances able to take four stretcher cases each. They were manned by two stretcher bearers and a driver. The ambulances were drawn by two horses because they were more steady under fire than mules, which were liable to bolt. Two-wheeled ambulances were also used, particularly in the early years of the war, but they gave an agonizingly bumpy ride for a wounded man and were highly unpopular.

According to the 1860 census, the US horse population was 6,115,458. Of these animals, 1,698,328 were in the South. The armies had a voracious appetite for horses, particularly the Union forces between 1861 and 1862, when many cavalry units were raised from scratch. Inexperienced riders, who had no idea how to care for a horse, got through thousands of animals without meeting the enemy. Even by 1863 the Union armies required 500 new horses every day since the average service life of a horse was but three or four months. Confederate cavalrymen provided their own horses but inadequate fodder and hard campaigning soon killed or invalided many animals. All outfits needed an instant source of horseshoes, so cavalry and artillery formations invariably included mobile forges to produce them. These outfits comprised a limber, ridden by the smiths, and a forge with bellows and firebox.

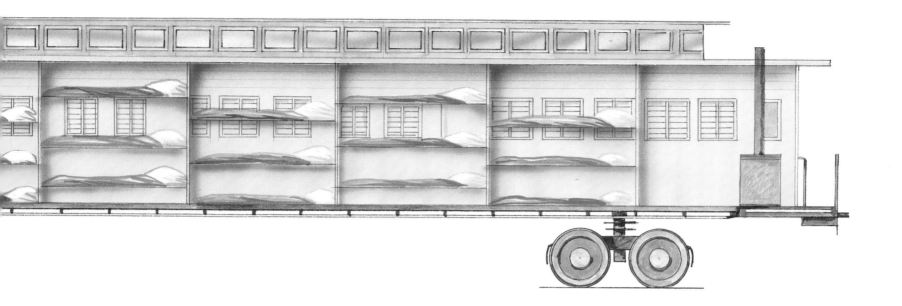

LEFT: *The Rocker ambulance was the most popular of several types of four-wheeled ambulance. Manned by a driver and two stretcher-bearers, it could carry four stretcher cases. By 1863 each division of the Army of the Potomac had 40 such ambulances commanded by a lieutenant. The ambulances were drawn by two horses as mules were too liable to bolt under fire.*

BELOW: *Usually drawn by a team of six mules, the standard US Army wagon was 10 feet long and covered by a canvas top, which was often painted with the insignia of the corps to which the wagon belonged. Good mule teams could be guided by the driver's voice alone – not surprising given their legendary vocabulary.*

ABOVE: *A US Army hospital railroad car as used in the eastern theater. It could accommodate up to 30 stretcher cases, which were suspended by rubber rings to reduce the jolting. The US Sanitary Commission also organized hospital ships and rest homes for soldiers convalescing from their injuries.*

Fort Sumter

Charleston's defenses against attack from the sea had been found wanting during the War of Independence. Fort Moultrie, a battery on the southernmost tip of Sullivan's Island, was open to attack from the landward side and it was by this route that the British took it in 1780. Fort Moultrie had been commanded by Major Richard Anderson. By a strange coincidence, his son Robert was to command Charleston's new defenses in 1860.

In 1829 the War Department began the construction of a large fort in the harbor mouth. Granite rubble was dumped in three fathoms of water at the southern edge of the main shipping channel. No one could accuse the department of haste in its work on the fort, named after the South Carolina revolutionary hero Thomas Sumter. Fifteen years passed before the walls were constructed on the artificial granite island. Thirty-one years after work began Fort Sumter was still incomplete, ungarrisoned, and awaiting full armament.

Built of Carolina gray brick in the standard pentagon shape, Fort Sumter's walls towered 40 feet above the high-water mark. The scarp wall was 5 feet thick but backed by piers and arches of the casemates so that in place it was 10 feet thick. The fort was designed to deal with wooden men of war and had two furnaces for heating solid shot near the northern faces. Its cannon were in three tiers: the lower two in casemates, while the upper battery was mounted *en barbette*, i.e. projecting over the walls with no overhead cover for the gun crew.

Fort Sumter was designed to hold a garrison of 650 men but at the beginning of December 1860 it was empty of troops. The sole occupants were the workmen still laboring at a leisurely pace to finish the defenses. The Union troops in Charleston were limited to nine officers and 65 other ranks stationed at Ford Moultrie. Since this was overlooked by nearby houses and sand had piled against the walls enabling grazing cattle to wander into the defenses, it was clearly untenable if the local secessionists determined on its capture. The commander of Fort Moultrie was a veteran of the war of 1812 and he was replaced by Major Robert Anderson on November 21, 1860. Secretary of War John B. Floyd, soon to be Confederate officer, may well have selected Anderson for his Southern sympathies. If so, he was to be sadly disappointed as Anderson remained obstinately loyal.

Had the bellicose secessionists of Charleston occupied Fort Sumter with militia while it was still empty they would have saved themselves a good deal of trouble. But they were taken by surprise when, on the night of December 26, 1860, Major Anderson rowed his whole command from Ford Moultrie to Fort Sumter. Captain Abner Doubleday led a detachment of troops with fixed bayonets into the fort and ejected the local construction workers.

The newly created Confederacy had demanded the withdrawal of Federal troops from the Charleston defenses. Whereas Fort Moultrie could not be realistically defended, Sumter was a different proposition. Although only part of its armament was operational, an amphibious assault was likely to result in very heavy casualties. Major Anderson sat tight and waited for Washington to support him.

There were 66 cannon in Fort Sumter when the Union garrison occupied it. Only 15 were mounted, and although there was plenty of gunpowder in the magazines, there were few friction primers and hardly any cartridge bags. The heaviest guns were three 10-inch Columbiads found sitting on the parade ground surrounded by carriages, timbers, blocks, paving stones, shot and shell, and other materials.

The rest of the guns were 8-inch Columbiads plus 24-, 32-, and 42-pounder smoothbores, and some seacoast howitzers. With trucks and tackle to hand, Anderson's men soon had the 32- and 42-pounders ready for action on the lower casemates. The main entrance to the fort was bricked up, leaving just a manhole covered by an 8-inch seacoast howitzer loaded with a double charge of canister.

Two of the 10-inch Columbiads were laboriously raised to the top of the walls where they could engage the batteries being built by the Confederates. Hauling the 15,000-pound bulk of these cannon on improvised tackles was no mean achievement and the 128-pound shot for the Columbiads was carried up to the guns by hand. The third Columbiad was left on the parade ground where it was steeply elevated to fire like a mortar on the city itself. An experimental shot with a 2-pound charge nearly landed a shell on the wharves, so the Union gunners were confident of returning the Confederate fire with interest should it come to a shooting match.

barracks

hot shot furnace

sally port

Since the tiny garrison could not repel a simultaneous assault from all sides, the wharf in front of Sumter's main entrance was mined with 5-gallon demijohns filled with powder. The esplanade – a broad promenade extending the length of the gorge wall – was boobytrapped with a giant *fougasse* (a pile of rubble with a charge hidden underneath that would sweep the area with a mass of sharp stones when detonated). Captain Truman Seymour invented what he called the "flying fougasse" – barrels of stones containing a small powder charge that could be dropped over the walls on attacking troops. One was tested to spectacular effect, the Charleston newspapers reporting the mighty explosion at Sumter and speculating on the design of the garrison's "infernal machine."

After the attempt to revictual Fort Sumter from the steamer *Star of the West* had been defeated, the Confederate batteries finally opened fire on Fort Sumter at 4.30 a.m. on April 12, 1861. The Union gunners did not reply to the bombardment until it was light, partly because many guns lacked proper sights and also because Major Anderson was concerned not to hit private property by mistake.

The lack of cartridge bags compelled the gunners to improvise cloth containers from several unlikely sources. Several pairs of Major Anderson's woolen socks were stitched up as powder bags and blasted back at the Confederate guns! After a day and night of firing, Sumter surrendered. Fire had threatened the magazine, the main gate area was blown in, and the supply of cartridge bags and primers was all but exhausted. Sumter's construction had proved sound enough – only one man in the garrison had been wounded by enemy fire.

After over 30 years' construction, Fort Sumter was still incomplete and without a garrison in 1861. Built of bricks laid with mortar and concrete made from cement and pounded oyster shells, the walls rose 40 feet above the water and were between 5 and 10 feet thick. The Federal troops in Charleston were actually based at Fort Moultrie – part of the original eighteenth-century defenses that were open to attack from the landward side. The political leadership in Charleston did not credit Major Anderson with any initiative, possibly because he was expected to be pro-secession. Outwitted by his occupation of the fort, it was only a matter of time before their blockade of Sumter turned into a shooting match and, ultimately, civil war. The small US garrison did not man the barbette guns (top tier) which were exposed to fire from the Confederate batteries.

shell magazine

hospital

traverse

barracks

esplanade

The Defenses of Charleston

After the surrender of Fort Sumter, the Confederates continued to augment the defenses of Charleston, correctly anticipating a Union attack from the sea. Blockade runners slipped in and out of the port but the US Navy's constant presence made this a hazardous enterprise. Union troops were landed along the southern coast of the Confederacy. Known to the US Army as the Military Department of the South, this included South Carolina, Georgia, and Florida. By mid-1863 there were over 10,000 US troops holding 11 small enclaves on the enemy shoreline, each chosen to block Confederate sea-borne communications.

The entrance to Charleston Bay is flanked by two islands: Sullivan's in the north and Morris Island to the south. Both were fortified by the Confederates. Fort Moultrie on Sullivan's Island was given additional guns and new earthworks thrown up either side of the old stone

fortification. On Morris Island batteries were established on the northernmost tip, covering the harbor mouth and the narrow neck of land leading to the rest of the island. Inside the bay other batteries were established alongside the old brickwork defenses of Fort Johnson and Castle Pinckney.

The land batteries were supplemented by a naval squadron consisting of two (ultimately three) ironclad rams, plus several smaller steamers. The commander of the Confederate Department of South Carolina and Georgia, the prickly General P.G.T. Beauregard, was highly critical of the rams. *Chicora* and *Palmetto State* drew too much water to operate with freedom in the confined channels of Charleston harbor and, like most Confederate ironclads, they were chronically underpowered.

The brick monolith of Fort Sumter was the centerpiece of the Charleston defenses. No ship

could pass up to the city without coming within easy range of the heavy cannon the Confederates had shipped over to the fort. The US Navy's South Atlantic Squadron commanded by Rear-Admiral Du Pont made a direct attack on Sumter on April 7, 1863. Nine ironclads attacked and five were disabled after an hour's engagement, while *Keokuk* foundered the following day from damage inflicted by Sumter's and Moultrie's heavy guns. Although Fort Sumter was struck by 11- and 15-inch projectiles from the monitors, its own armament was formidable. The Confederate garrison returned the fire of the US squadron with two 7-inch Brooke rifles, two 9-inch Dahlgrens, four 8- and four 10-inch Columbiads, four 8-inch Navy guns, six 84-pounder James rifles, eight 32-pounder smoothbores, and three 10-inch seacoast mortars. Fort Moultrie was armed with nine 8-inch Columbiads and five 64-

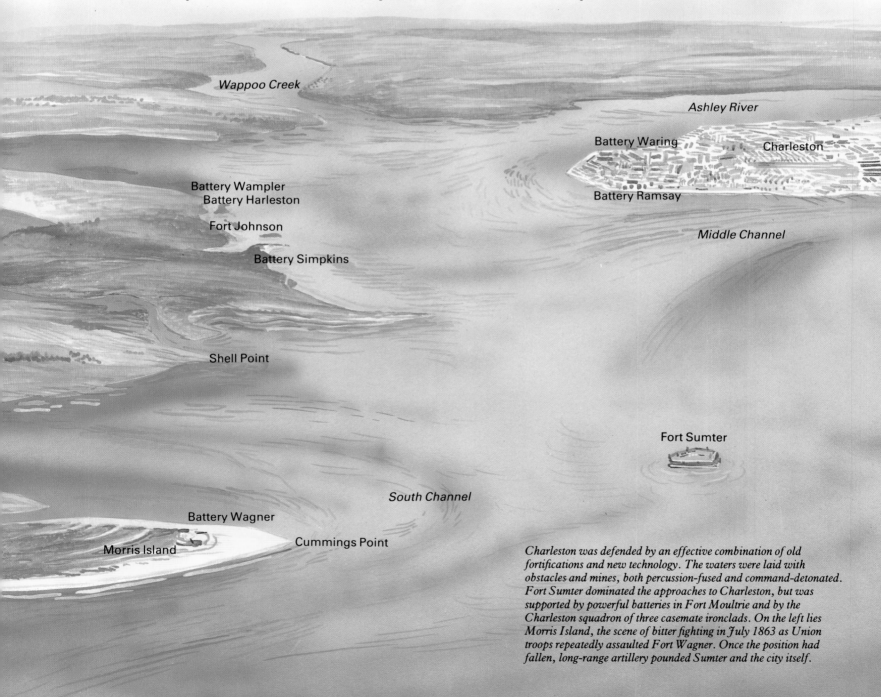

Charleston was defended by an effective combination of old fortifications and new technology. The waters were laid with obstacles and mines, both percussion-fused and command-detonated. Fort Sumter dominated the approaches to Charleston, but was supported by powerful batteries in Fort Moultrie and by the Charleston squadron of three casemate ironclads. On the left lies Morris Island, the scene of bitter fighting in July 1863 as Union troops repeatedly assaulted Fort Wagner. Once the position had fallen, long-range artillery pounded Sumter and the city itself.

pounder James rifles, plus five 32-pounder smoothbores and two 10-inch mortars. The Confederate gunners were able to estimate the range to each US warship with the greatest ease since the channels were dotted with buoys to which the exact distance was known.

The US Navy regarded Fort Sumter as the key to Charleston, but it was determined to make another assault. At a conference in Washington during May 1863 the army was asked to help. Major-General Quincy A. Gillmore, harking back to the lessons of Fort Pulaski, argued that heavy rifled guns placed on Morris Island could reduce Fort Sumter to a pile of rubble. With the relatively small ground forces at his command, he could not hope to press on into Charleston where the defenders could be reinforced rapidly by rail. The plan adopted was for the army to destroy Fort Sumter, then the fleet to steam into the bay,

hugging the southern channel, where the ships would be beyond the effective ranges of Fort Moultrie's cannon.

On July 9 Union troops stormed the southern part of Morris Island, rowing across from Folly Island supported by heavy guns behind them and by the fire of four monitors. Now the defense of Charleston depended on the Confederate earthwork at the northern tip of Morris Island – Fort Wagner.

Fort Wagner was assaulted on July 11 but the narrow stretch of beach that led to it was swept by 32-pounder carronades. Although the leading troops reached the ditch, their supports were mown down by the Confederate gunners and the Union infantry was driven off. From July 16–18 the Federal troops placed 41 guns and siege mortars on Morris Island and bombarded the position from gun emplacements dug between 1300 and 1900 yards away. The

Confederate garrison was about 1000 strong but the fort's bombproof shelter could not accommodate more than 750 of them.

On the evening of July 18 some 5000 Federal infantry attacked Fort Wagner in a desperate battle that forms the climax of the 1989 feature film *Glory*. The assaulting column was commanded by Brigadier-General Truman Seymour who had been a brevet captain in Major Anderson's garrison inside Sumter in 1861. His division consisted of two brigades: that of Brigadier-General George C. Strong leading that of Colonel Haldimand S. Putman. As the infantrymen neared Fort Wagner, they blocked the line of fire of their supporting guns and those of the navy. At the same time the Confederates raced up from their bombproof shelter and opened a devastating fire on the troops negotiating the narrow approaches to their earth rampart and ditch.

The Defenses of Charleston

The result was a massacre. Although some US troops penetrated the southeast bastion, they were driven out again after two hours of bitter fighting. The young Colonel Robert S. Shaw, commanding the 54th Massachusetts (Colored) Volunteers, died at the head of his regiment. Of the other nine regimental commanders involved, one other was killed and three wounded. Of the two bridgade commanders, Putnam was killed and Strong was badly wounded, dying of tetanus several weeks later. Brigadier-General Seymour was wounded too. Altogether 1515 US troops were killed or wounded, while Confederate losses were 174. The defenders of Fort Wagner recorded that they buried some 800 US soldiers in front of their rifle pits over the following days.

At Fort Pulaski rifled guns had inflicted terminal structural damage at the unheard of range of over a mile. Major-General Gillmore was confident that he could destroy Sumter at an even greater distance with the heavier cannon available to his command in 1863. Accordingly, while batteries on Morris Island bombarded Fort Wagner around the clock, others were established for heavy rifles to engage Sumter at ranges of up to 4200 yards.

Fort Sumter received the first of several prolonged bombardments on August 17, 1863. Soon 450 heavy projectiles were hitting the fort daily and large sections of masonry tumbled down. The southeast face was pierced repeatedly, until some shot passed through to strike the northwest face in reverse. The bombardment lasted seven days, at the end of which 5009 rounds had been fired, of which about 50 percent hit. Fort Sumter's walls were smashed almost beyond recognition and only one gun was left operational on August 24.

Sumter was knocked out for over six weeks. The Confederates pulled many of the heavy guns from the ruins of their casemates and withdrew them to batteries in the inner harbor. Meanwhile, Fort Wagner was besieged in a manner that would have been familiar to any eighteenth-century engineer officer. US troops sapped forward under cover of mortars and siege guns. The ironclad *New Ironsides* steamed close inshore to batter the fort with her powerful armament. The Confederates could not stop the trenches creeping ever closer and were hard put to repair the constant damage to

their defenses. US engineers illuminated the fort with calcium lights at night so cannon and snipers could fire on repair parties.

By September 6 the US sap had reached past the south front of the fort and the formidable *cheveux-de-frise* arrangement of sharpened stakes in front of the Confederate ditches had been dismantled. A new assault was scheduled for 9.00 a.m. the next day, when the low tide would expose the widest stretch of beach for the infantry to advance across. The garrison, aware of what was coming and still under constant fire from Union mortars and cannon, withdrew during the night.

Originally known as the "Neck" battery, this earthwork blocked off the eastern end of Morris Island. Heavy cannon mounted on the eastern tip of the island could reach Fort Sumter and Charleston itself, so it was important for the Confederates to retain this position. An infantry assault in July 1863 cost the Union over 1500 casualties, but the Confederates still held on. The garrison was finally withdrawn on September 7 after US troops had sapped very close to the battery and prolonged bombardment had badly damaged the defenses.

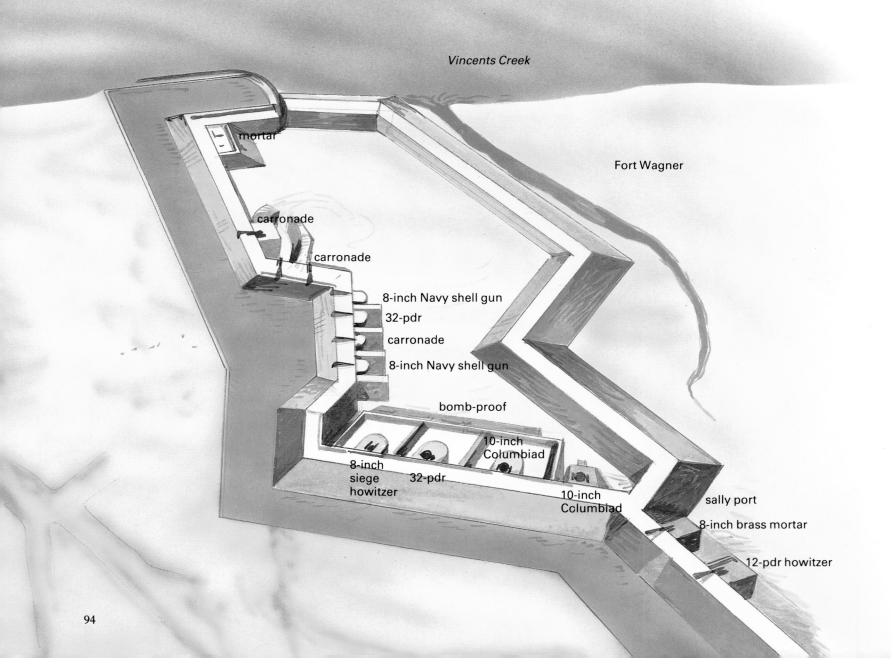

94

The heavily damaged and now silent Fort Sumter invited attack. Accordingly Rear-Admiral Dahlgren organized a boat attack by 400 sailors and marines, apparently in ignorance that the army was preparing a similar assault. Unfortunately for the US Navy, it preceded its attack on Sumter by steaming the monitor *Patapsco* close to the fort to check the channel. The Confederates had also captured a signal book and could interpret some of the signal traffic that took place in full view of observers from the shore. The Sumter garrison was ready for the landing attempt and drove it off with 125 casualties.

The Union heavy artillery that fired on Forts Wagner and Sumter included Parrott rifles of all calibers. No less than 51 of them blew up during the Charleston campaign, a record that did little to endear them to the gunners. Among them was a 200-pounder, 8-inch Parrott dubbed the "Swamp Angel." This gun fired incendiary shells into Charleston itself, some landing up to 5¾ miles away. It had fired just 36 rounds from a redoubt built at enormous effort on the waterlogged sand of Morris Island.

In October Fort Sumter's new commander,

Lieutenant-Colonel Stephen Elliott, mounted two 10-inch Columbiads and a 7-inch Brooke rifle in the northeast casemates. For 40 days and nights, beginning October 26, the US siege guns fired on Fort Sumter with renewed vigor, concentrating on the southeast face until it was little more than a gently sloping pile of rubble leading up from the water's edge.

In December 1863 Fort Sumter was subjected to another furious bombardment and suffered severe damage when a small arms magazine accidentally exploded. The cause of this disaster was never established; the only men who knew were among the 11 dead. Forty-one others were wounded. None the less, the garrison held out, with the fort divided internally by loopholed walls in case another landing managed to establish a lodgement. In effect, Fort Sumter became a large earthwork, the masses of rubble absorbed numerous hits without further consequences and the Confederates found they could maintain a battery of six heavy guns in position. Nightly shipments of sandbags were supplied to the garrison to modify the defensive layout as the rubble shifted under bombardment.

If the breaching of Fort Pulaski had demonstrated the destructive potential of rifled siege cannon, the defense of Fort Sumter revealed their limitations. The guns could smash a practicable breach in brick walls, but unless an infantry assault could be mounted quickly and easily, endless pounding of a position like Sumter could not achieve very much without a fluke hit on a magazine.

A pre-war brick fort on Sullivan's Island, Fort Moultrie was strengthened with earthworks by the Confederate garrison, which consisted of 300 men of the 1st South Carolina Infantry (Regulars). It had 38 guns that ranged from 24-pdr smoothbores to 8-inch Columbiads. By the time of Du Pont's naval assault on Charleston, Fort Moultrie was armed with nine 8-inch Columbiads, five banded and rifled 32-pdrs, five 32-pdr smoothbores, and two 10-inch mortars.

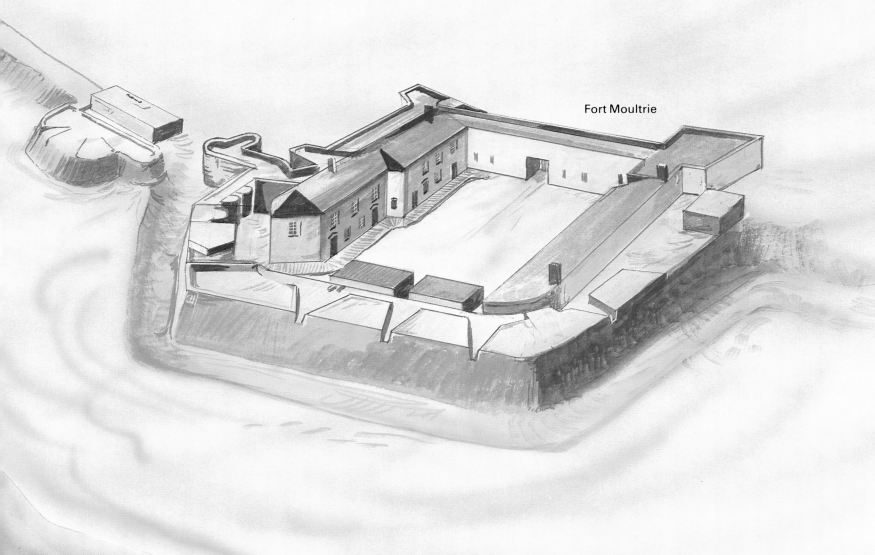

Fort Moultrie

The Siege of Petersburg

In May 1864 the Army of the Potomac returned to the offensive. Directed by Ulysses S. Grant, the first US officer since George Washington to hold the rank of lieutenant-general, 122,000 Federal soldiers crossed the Rapidan River. Northern public opinion demanded that Grant take on Lee. Grant's maneuver around Lee's eastern flank led to a head-on clash in the tangled underbrush of the Wilderness. Despite a 2:1 numerical advantage, the Union Army was emphatically stopped in its tracks in three days of bloody combat.

Grant headed east again but the Confederates marched rapidly and entrenched at Spotsylvania. Lee's veteran troops repulsed another series of assaults beginning on May 10. Grant's forces then made another turning movement around Lee's eastern flank, forcing the Confederates to retreat again. Although the Confederates inflicted another bloody defeat on the Federals at Cold Harbor, the Union Army was less than 9 miles from Richmond by early June.

Grant followed his failure at Cold Harbor by a rapid turning movement against Petersburg. Three railroad lines ran into Petersburg from the south, while another ran directly from Petersburg to Richmond. Their destruction or capture would starve out the capital and compel Lee's army to retreat. But Grant's attack on Petersburg was defeated in three days of fighting, beginning June 15. The Army of the Potomac halted and entrenched its positions, remaining there for the next nine months.

The siege of Petersburg pinned down the Confederacy's finest military formation, the

Battery No. 6 formed part of the main Confederate defensive line and was over 100 feet across at its widest point. The massive ditch was over 20 feet across and 10 feet deep, and would have proved an impossible obstacle to an army making a direct frontal attack.

Army of Northern Virginia. While Grant's siege lines slowly extended, cutting the Weldon railroad in August, Lee's soldiers could do nothing but improve their defenses and await the inevitable assault. The rival trench lines were only a few hundred yards apart and photographs of the siege lines bear more than a passing resemblance to those of the western front in World War I.

One spectacular attempt to break through the Confederate lines was mounted in the summer. On July 30 nearly 4 tons of gunpowder were exploded under a Confederate redoubt called Pegram's or Elliot's Salient. The Confederate position vanished in a monstrous fountain of earth and fire. The resulting crater was 170 feet across and up to 80 feet deep. The Confederates were fortunate that anxieties about committing black soldiers to a potentially costly assault had led the specially trained Negro division to be replaced at the last minute by white troops who had not rehearsed or planned for such an operation. The infantry attack was botched. Thousands of Federal troops swarmed into the smoking crater and the chain of command broke down. While the assault was paralyzed by lack of leadership, the Confederates maneuvered their reserves forward and counter-attacked. Grant was bitterly disappointed and called it "the saddest affair I have witnessed in the war."

The siege dragged on into the fall. Although Lee boldly detached Jubal Early to raid up the Shenandoah in what proved to be a brilliant minor campaign, it could delay, not stop, a Union offensive in the same quarter. Ultimately, 50,000 Federal troops came surging down the valley, outnumbering the Confederates by over 2:1. While the confederates had faced such odds here before, incompetents like Banks had all been replaced. The Union Army was led by the manic Philip H. Sheridan and Early's men were driven out.

Soldiers of both sides preferred the fresher weather of the fall to the debilitating heat and humidity of the summer, but the winter was hard – hardest for the Confederates whose supplies were erratic and for whom the war looked increasingly futile.

While Lee was locked in the Richmond-Petersburg defenses, Atlanta fell, Lincoln was re-elected, and the Army of the Tennessee was smashed at Franklin and Nashville. Sherman led 60,000 US troops on their march through Georgia, a shattering blow to the Confederate railroad network that had a catastrophic effect on Southern morale. Mobile was captured after the US Navy fought its way into the bay and 40,000 Federal troops were landed.

For Lee's soldiers, eking out a meager existence in the trenches, the winter was bad enough, but the continued run of bad news from other fronts sapped their morale. Desertion increased. Lee grew steadily angrier at the complacency of Southern senators who led conspicuously comfortable lives in Richmond while his soldiers starved. The complacency of the capital's senior politicians was only broken in the spring as the siege lines now extended some 37 miles. Stretched so thinly, Lee's army could not guarantee against a breakthrough occurring, nor maneuver to prevent a further turning movement.

In early April Sheridan's command of the cavalry corps and two infantry corps arrived in the rear of the Petersburg defenses after a destructive raid from the Shenandoah through western Virginia. Lee had no choice but to withdraw or face complete encirclement. As he pulled out, so the Army of the Potomac at last launched its final offensive. Union troops broke through the Confederates lines but the Army of Northern Virginia managed, against all odds, to break contact and slip away westward. The heroic defense of Fort Gregg helped to delay the Union entry to Petersburg. Lee evacuated the city on the night of April 2 and headed west on the road to Appomattox.

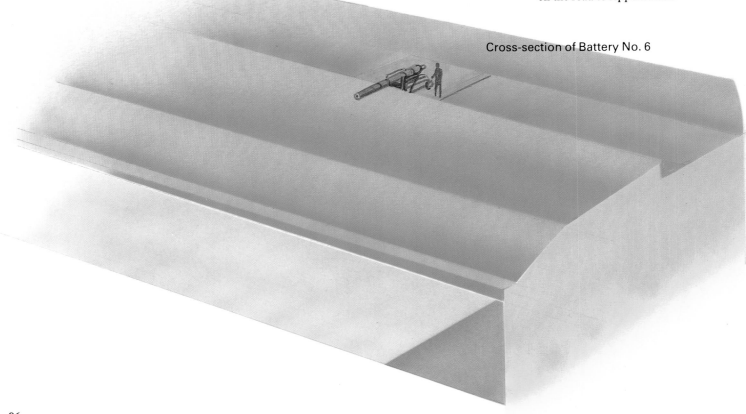

Cross-section of Battery No. 6

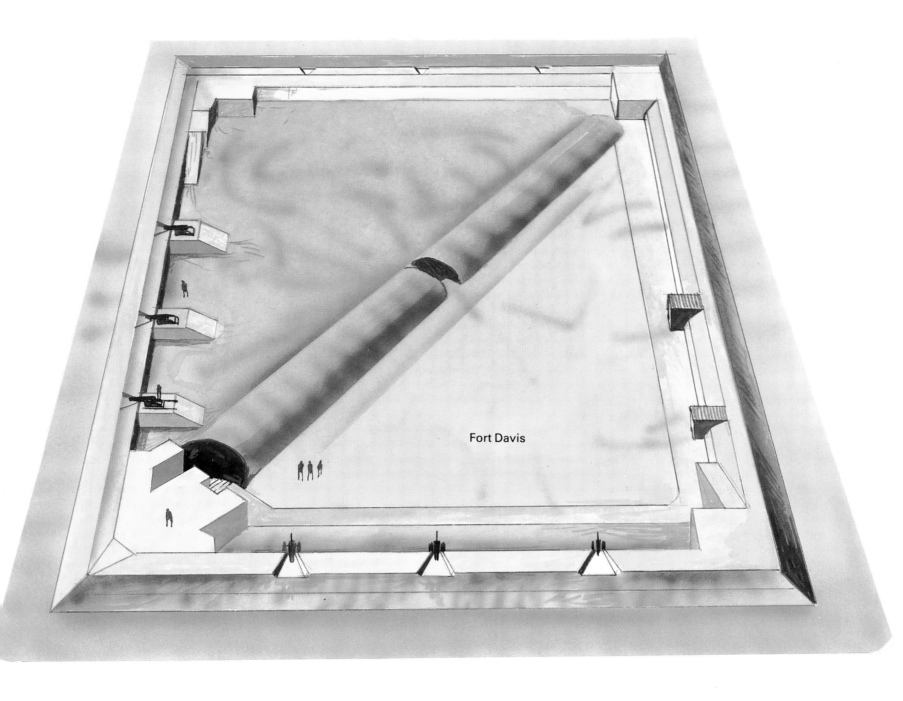

Fort Davis

The defenses of Petersburg were made up of a number of forts linked by a comprehensive system of trenches that stretched for over 36 miles and guarded the approaches to Richmond as well as Petersburg itself. Behind this defensive line, manned with great difficulty by the Confederates owing to the shortage of troops, ran a network of four railroads that endeavored to keep both cities supplied. In front of these lines stood a corresponding line of Union siege works with Fort Davis (cross-section shown right) forming a part.

Cross-section of Fort Davis

Fort Fisher

Wilmington, North Carolina, was the Confederacy's last operational port after the fall of Mobile, Alabama, in August 1864. Despite the close attention of the US Navy's South Atlantic squadron, blockade runners continued to slip in and out of the Cape Fear River. This was protected by a series of batteries dug in along the sandy peninsula between the river and Onslow Bay. The low-lying sandy peninsula was 7 miles long, terminating in what had been called Federal Point, but for the duration of the war inevitably became Confederate Point.

At the tip of the peninsula, where the land hooks around to the west, the Confederates built a large earthwork, the Battery Buchanan. Housing four guns, it had a wharf nearby at the edge of a marsh. The main seaward defenses began half a mile to the northeast, with the 60-feet high Mound Battery. This was separated from Battery Buchanan by a low-lying sandplain that was nowhere more than 3 feet above sea level and vanished beneath the foaming waves during the winter gales. The Mound Battery housed a 6⅜-inch rifle and a 10-inch Columbiad. From their lofty position, these guns could direct a plunging fire on to the decks of ships in the deep-water channel that ran close to the beach inside the bar.

North of the Mound Battery the seaward side of the peninsula was defended by a continuous parapet 12 feet high that ran north for ¾ mile. Heavy guns were emplaced in ones and twos at intervals of 50–100 yards. These seaward defenses consisted of the following cannon: eight 10-inch and five 8-inch Columbiads, plus five 6⅜-inch rifles, two 7-inch and one 8-inch Brooke rifles. In front of the guns was a line of mines fired electrically from inside the fort.

The defenses extended across the neck of the peninsula to protect the sea-facing batteries from a ground assault by troops landed further up the peninsula. Facing this landward side were 24 heavy guns: two 10-inch and one 8-inch Columbiads, three 8-inch smoothbores, nine 6⅜-inch smoothbores, one 7-inch Brooke, and three 6⅜-inch rifles. A 150-pounder Armstrong rifle was placed at the northeast corner of the work. Behind the earthworks were three 8-inch

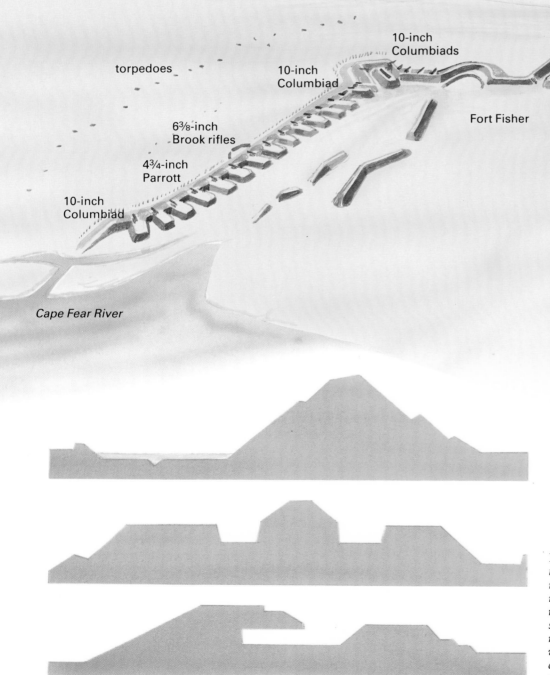

LEFT: *The defenses sectioned. Section A–B shows the high parapet facing the land side; section C–D is cut across the redoubt on the corner, showing how it was divided in two; section E–F shows the re-entrant built into the works. The defenses showed remarkably little damage after the intense naval bombardment. Nevertheless, without weapons capable of driving off the monitors that came close inshore, the garrison was unable to man the parapet.*

sea-coast mortars. The parapet was 20 feet high and 25 feet thick, sloped at 45 degrees, and was covered in marsh grass. The guns were deployed in ones and twos, protected from enfilade fire by enormous revetments that towered another 12 feet above the parapet and ran back 30 feet or more. These revetments alternately housed magazines or bombproof shelters for the gunners. Passageways ran through some of them to enable relief gun-crews to reach the batteries under fire.

The landward defenses had no ditch in front because the shifting sands made it impossible to maintain one. Instead, there was a line of rifle pits and a forward gun battery covering the road to Wilmington that ran along the western side of the peninsula. Some 200 yards from the main gun line was another line of electrically fired mines. Fifty feet from the gun line the Confederates built a 9-feet high palisade of

Major-General Butler cancelled the attack and re-embarked his troops. The withdrawal was hampered by a rising sea and some 700 Union infantry spent an uncomfortable night on shore before being rescued.

General Braxton Bragg had been appointed to command the Confederate forces in the Department of North Carolina in November 1864. He had 6000 troops in Wilmington, in an entrenched camp at the foot of the peninsula some 6 miles from Fort Fisher. These could intervene against a Union landing on the peninsula, compelling any Union force to hold off Bragg while it attacked Fort Fisher. Unfortunately for the Confederacy, Bragg did not stir when the Federal fleet returned on January 12 and landed 8000 men under Major-General Alfred Terry 2 miles above Fort Fisher. The fort was defended by about 1500 men, including 50 Confederate sailors and marines.

The fleet bombarded Fort Fisher again on January 13, detaching its ironclads which closed to within 1200 yards. This was much

The weary battle of Fort Fisher lasted until 10 p.m., when Battery Buchanan surrendered. The sailors and marines were routed, with over 300 killed and wounded. The sailors were from 35 different ships and had no experience of working together in this sort of operation; there had been no rehearsal. Armed with pistols and cutlasses, they were halted by intense musketry which the marines were unable to suppress. The whole force fled back up the beach. Meanwhile, the army assaulting column broke into the western end of Fort Fisher and the battle became a desperate close-quarter fight as groups of infantry struggled for the possession of each gun position. Attack succeeded counter-attack as the Confederates stubbornly resisted. Terry detached one of the three brigades he had held back to face Bragg and sent that in to nourish the Union attack. With the monitors firing into the fort until dark, the defenders were eventually driven back. Union losses were 184 dead, 749 wounded, and 22 missing. The Confederate casualties were reported by General Bragg as 500 killed and wounded, but this may have been an overestimate since over 2000 officers and men were captured.

sharpened logs, loopholed for muskets. This projected more at the ends so an attack on the center would be enfiladed. In the center was a small redoubt guarding a sally-port from which two 12-pounder Napoleon smoothbores could be run out to fire canister into attacking infantry. On the western side of the peninsula the road to Wilmington came into the defenses over a bridge above a muddy slough. This too was commanded by a 12-pounder Napoleon.

On Christmas Eve 1864 60 US warships, including five ironclads, began a two-day bombardment of Fort Fisher. Between them they fired some 20,000 rounds at the Confederate positions – over 600 tons of explosive! But since the fleet made no attempt to cross the bar, the Confederate gunners lay low in their bomb-proof shelters and the formidable bombardment inflicted surprisingly little damage. On Christmas Day 6000 Federal infantry were landed on the peninsula between Fort Fisher and Wilmington, but when they probed towards the fort they discovered the undamaged state of the defenses. Fearing another disaster like the attack on Fort Wagner in July 1863,

closer than they had approached during the Christmas bombardment and their fire was more accurate. The following day the ironclads returned to the same position, while 38 wooden warships, including the most heavily armed steam frigates in the navy, subjected the defenses to concentrated shelling. Each warship was assigned to engage a specific section and the fire was very effective. The Confederate gunners were unable to man their relatively exposed guns without heavy casualties. Had they had some heavy seacoast mortars deployed on the east side, they might have been able to drive back the anchored monitors. But they were helpless. The bombardment continued until 3 p.m. on January 15, when 3000 troops assaulted the landward defenses, breaking in at the western end. The northeastern corner of Fort Fisher was attacked by 1600 sailors landed from the fleet, supported by 400 US marines. Terry left 5000 men entrenched behind him, facing Bragg's men in Wilmington.

ABOVE: *The mile-long line of redoubts linked by breastworks faced the Atlantic Ocean with the Cape Fear River behind. This peninsula was the key to the defense of Wilmington, the great importing depot of the South. Robert E. Lee wrote Colonel Lamb, the commander of Fort Fisher, stressing that the position must be held or he could not supply the Army of Northern Virginia. Five miles up the peninsula was an entrenched camp directly protecting Wilmington, and had Braxton Bragg counter-attacked while the Union assault was delivered against Fort Fisher, the defenses might have held.*

Fort Henry

The geography of northern Tennessee distinctly favored the Union Army. In addition to the Mississippi running down the western border of the state, two other rivers offered good invasion routes. The Tennessee River rises in the east of the state, then runs southwest, passing into Alabama before turning again and flowing almost due north through Tennessee into Kentucky and on to join with the Ohio River. It offered the Federal forces a conveniently straight north-south route through Tennessee and into Alabama.

The Cumberland River rises in eastern Kentucky and flows south and west in a wide bend through northern Tennessee until it passes back into Kentucky only 12 miles to the east of the Tennessee River. The Cumberland provided the Union forces with easy access to the vital industrial center of Nashville. Manufacturing clothing, ammunition, priming caps, and even heavy cannon, Nashville was second only to New Orleans in its importance to the western states of the Confederacy.

In 1860 the Confederates constructed two earthworks to defend these obvious invasion routes. They were close to the Kentucky border on the neck of land between the Cumberland and Tennessee rivers. To the west, guarding the treacherous waters of the Tennessee, was Fort Henry. To the east, overlooking the Cumberland, was Fort Donelson.

Named for Gustavus A. Henry, a Confederate senator from Tennessee, Fort Henry was begun in May 1861. Built where the Kentucky state line west of the river runs a little further south, Fort Henry faced the then neutral state of Kentucky. Under the vigorous direction of Colonel Heiman, the 10th Tennessee Regiment had the first cannon in position by July.

Fort Henry became a strong work during the following months, but a succession of officers commented on its poor location. It was overlooked from the Kentucky side and its low-lying position would be a critical problem in the spring when the river rose. The fort's highest point was below the high-water mark! Concerned at reports from Fort Henry, General Johnston sent his chief engineer to investigate. He recommended occupying the opposite bank but nothing happened during the winter.

The ill-starred Confederate invasion of Kentucky was defeated in January 1862 and it was less than two weeks later that Union forces launched their western offensive. The target,

correctly divined by General Johnston, was Nashville. On several occasions during the fall, US gunboats had ventured within range of Fort Henry to trade shots with the Confederate battery and test the mettle of the defenders.

Fort Henry was built on a bend in the river that allowed an uninterrupted view north for several miles. Five bastions were connected by a parapet in a rough pentagon shape, while rifle pits to the north and east protected the gun positions from the landward side. The garrison consisted of some 4000 infantry who were chronically short of weapons. Most were armed with shotguns or squirrel rifles they had brought along from their farms. The best-equipped regiment was the 10th Tennessee, which was fortunate to have Tower 1812 pattern smoothbore muskets.

On February 4 over 6000 Union infantry began to disembark from Grant's transports, while the US gunboat fleet prepared to bombard the fort. Having manned their trenches throughout the following day, the Confederate infantry were evacuated that night by their jittery commander General Tilghman. Fifty-four men of Company B 1st Tennessee Artillery were left behind to man the guns, and were

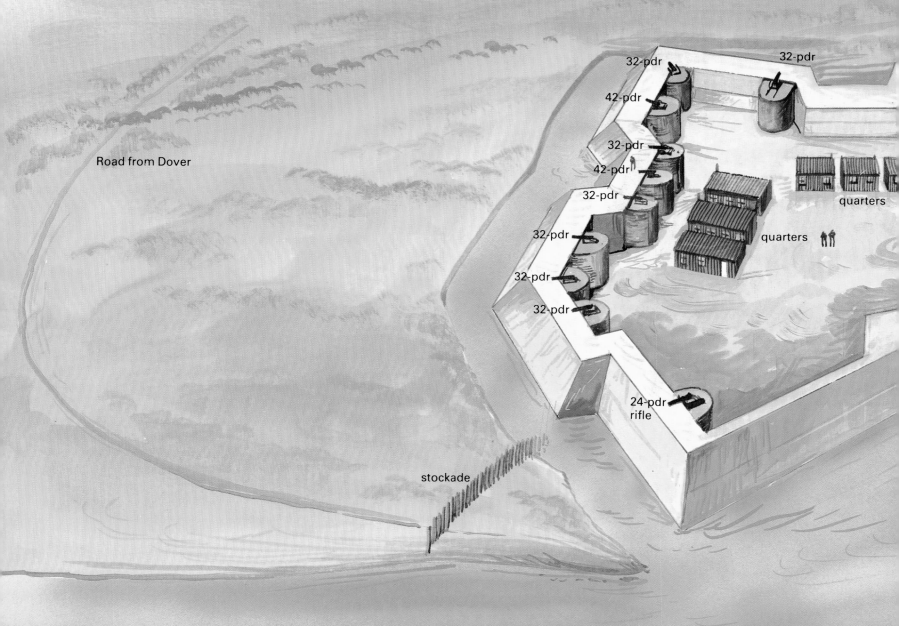

Road from Dover

32-pdr

32-pdr

42-pdr

32-pdr

42-pdr

32-pdr

32-pdr

32-pdr

32-pdr

24-pdr rifle

quarters

quarters

stockade

ordered to hold the fort for at least an hour after daylight to give the infantry a good chance to get away.

Fort Henry's armament consisted of the following cannon: eight 32-pounder smooth-bores, five 18-pounder siege guns, one 6-inch rifle, and one 10-inch Columbiad. In addition, there were two 42-pounders but no shot for them. The powder supplied to the guns was of very poor quality and the Confederates adopted the desperate expedient of adding fast-burning powder to each charge.

The naval attack on Fort Henry was led by *Carondelet*, *Essex*, *St Louis*, and *Cincinnati*. The gunboats opened fire at noon and traded shots with the fort until its surrender at 1.50 p.m. The Confederates fired at a range of about a mile, disabling the *Essex* and inflicting 32 casualties, *St Louis* was struck seven times to no effect, but *Cincinnati* was hit 32 times and had two cannon disabled. One sailor was killed and eight wounded. Fort Henry's 6-inch rifle burst

and the Columbiad was disabled after its priming wire jammed. Two 32-pounders were knocked out by a heavy shell and the Columbiad was dismounted by the end of the bombardment. Five gunners were killed, 11 wounded, and five missing by the time the colors were hauled down.

The level of the Tennessee River had been rising quickly since the beginning of February. By the time Fort Henry surrendered, the US cutter that rowed across from the river fleet was able to pass through the sally port. The Union infantry splashed its way inside during the afternoon. Grant telegraphed Halleck with news of the victory and the newspapers were immediately informed. The next day they trumpeted the news of a Northern victory.

Fort Henry was built on low ground, with nine cannon facing the Tennessee River and five facing inland. Rifle pits were dug on the land side covering the road to Fort Donelson. The fort was at a slight bend in the river, giving a clear view north for several miles. On February 4, 1862 the garrison watched as a long line of riverboats landed the first of Grant's 17,000 Federal infantry at Bailey's Ferry. The Union landing was completed the next day, and General Lloyd Tilghman ordered his garrison to evacuate. Lieutenant Watts of Company B, 1st Tennessee Artillery was left behind with 54 men to gain time for the rest of the men to escape. Watts's men resisted the Union gunboats' bombardment for about two hours before hauling down their colors. Meanwhile, the rising river had all but flooded the position anyway.

2-pdr

24-pdr
siege gun

12-pdr
siege gun

rifle pits

quarters

Three Men and a Fort

The Surrender of Fort Donelson

The unexpected ease with which the Union gunboat flotilla and Grant's small army had overwhelmed Fort Henry came as an icy shock to the Confederates in Tennessee. General Johnston immediately ordered more troops up to Fort Donelson. It was the only fortified position between the Union Army and the undefended city of Nashville.

Fort Donelson was a much stronger position than Fort Henry. The site was selected in 1861 by General Daniel S. Donelson acting under the orders of Governor Harris. Located on bluffs overlooking the Cumberland River, at its highest point the fort was 100 feet above the water. It had a splendid view to the north and two artillery batteries had been constructed facing this direction. The lower battery had nine 32-pounders and one 10-inch Columbiad. About 100 yards further upstream was another Columbiad, bored and rifled, which was covered by two 32-pounder carronades. The guns were protected by revetments of sand in old coffee sacks.

At the summit of the bluffs lay the fort itself. Riflemen posted there could cover the batteries easily. The surrounding terrain was thickly wooded and cut up by deep gullies that had filled with back water. An attacker coming from the landward side would have to pass through this broken country to reach the line of rifle pits with which the Confederates had surrounded the position. After breaking through them, any assault force would have to scale the 80-feet ridge surmounted by the fort.

By February 13 the Confederates had packed 15,000 troops into the defenses, but their supreme commander was not here. In the most controversial decision of his career, Albert S. Johnston turned his back on Donelson and joined Hardee's similar-sized force in its withdrawal toward Nashville. He had one senior critic: General Beauregard, who urged a concentration at Fort Donelson. While the outnumbered Confederate Army in Tennessee could not hope to defend all points against a Union invasion, it might have been able to inflict a major reverse on the Federals by operating on interior lines. But it was not to be.

General Johnston's retreat to Nashville left Fort Donelson in the hands of an undistinguished triumvirate. The senior officer present was John B. Floyd, President Buchanan's secretary of war. Next in line was Gideon J. Pillow, whose combat experience in Mexico had been overshadowed by personal disputes with several other officers, most notably Winfield Scott himself. Brigadier-General Simon B. Buckner was the only one of the three fit to command the defenses but he was outranked and barely on speaking terms with Pillow anyway.

The Confederate garrison made no attempt to interfere with Grant's march from Fort Henry to Fort Donelson. Grant's army arrived on February 12 and the arrival of 10,000 reinforcements with the gunboat flotilla brought the total Union strength to 27,000. That night the first Union batteries were emplaced on the hillsides facing the Confederate lines. During February 13 the Union forces engaged the defenses but made little progress. The ironclad *Carondelet* attacked the water batteries but was disabled and driven back downstream. During the night the unseasonably mild weather vanished in a bitter wind and the temperature sank to 10 degrees. By dawn on February 14 the whole battlefield was coated in 2 inches of snow.

Foote's ironclads attacked the water batteries that morning. Although their shells threw up fountains of earth and battered the defenses out of recognition, they failed to inflict a single casualty on the Confederate gunners. For their part, the Confederates fired as fast as possible to keep their batteries shrouded in thick smoke. Employing ricochet fire, they bounced their 32-pounder shot across the water to strike the ironclads' waterlines. One by one the Union warships were disabled and driven off.

It had been a splendid victory for the Confederacy, but Floyd knew it could not last. Before Grant attacked, he decided to evacuate. The next morning his troops attacked the Union lines. General Grant was not with his troops – he was aboard Foote's flagship discussing future tactics. In his absence he had left strict instructions to his subordinates to stay put. When the Confederates launched their sortie, they stuck to their orders. Although

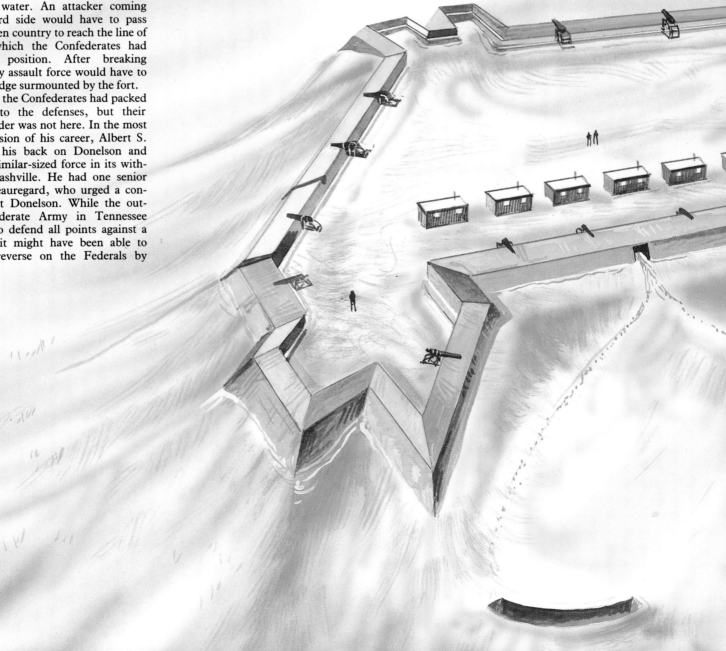

Lew Wallace sent McClernand a brigade on his own responsibility, it was not enough. As the light began to fade on this short winter's day, the Confederates had broken through to the Charlotte road and their escape route was clear.

Having achieved their objective, the Confederates failed to press on. General Pillow rushed off a bombastic telegram to Johnston announcing his victory, then he ordered the army back inside the defenses. Buckner's objections were overruled. Floyd supported Buckner at first, then changed his mind. While the Confederate command was paralyzed by indecision, Grant hastened back to his forces and organized a counter-attack. By dusk the armies were back in their original positions.

As the soldiers huddled around camp fires, the three Confederate officers argued into the night. Once again surrounded and outnumbered, could the troops make another breakthrough in the morning? Floyd and Pillow thought not and proposed negotiating with Grant. Buckner held out for another sortie.

Having maneuvered their command into this disastrous position, Floyd and Pillow then announced that they personally would have to escape. Floyd was under indictment by a grand jury in Washington and Pillow was equally determined not to become a prisoner. In a farcical turn of events, Floyd passed the command to Pillow who handed over to Buckner. Both then made their arrangements to escape while Buckner sent for a bugler and pen and paper to write Grant.

Apprised of the decision, Nathan Bedford Forrest, the commander of the Confederate cavalry, made his own plans. His men rode through the backwaters to freedom, each horseman with an infantryman sitting behind him clinging to his rescuer. Floyd escaped across the Cumberland on a steamer, Pillow in a little scow. Several thousand Confederates simply slipped away through the woods. The exact number of men who surrendered is shrouded in mystery to this day. Buckner had to confess to Grant that he could not provide exact figures. Modern research places the number at around 8000. Whatever the number, it was a disaster for the Confederacy. Nashville was doomed.

Buckner's surrender was, of course, not preceded by any negotiations. Grant's response, "No terms, except unconditional and immediate surrender can be expected," marked him out as an unusually forceful leader. Bedford Forrest's equally determined approach had also been noted.

Fort Donelson stood about 100 feet above the Cumberland River and had a good view to the north (the expected line of attack). Thirteen guns in two batteries faced the river: the rifle and two carronades on top of the bluff, and the water battery of one 10-inch Columbiad and eight 32-pdr smoothbores. The irregular fort itself occupied the summit of the hill and enclosed an area of roughly 15 acres. The garrison lived in log huts inside. The fort was designed to support the batteries covering the river and was not designed to face an assault from the landward side. When such an attack became inevitable, the Confederates surrounded the position with a line of rifle pits stretching for 3 miles.

The Defenses of Nashville

After his catastrophic failure at Franklin, General John B. Hood led the battered Army of the Tennessee to Nashville. Here, ensconced behind formidable entrenchments, lay a substantially larger Union Army commanded by General Thomas. Hood had no chance of taking Nashville. By any military logic he should have fallen back; his invasion of Tennessee was over. But Hood was as hard to drive off as he was to kill. His shattered arm and amputated leg were testimony to his iron determination. The Confederates marched up to the Union Army and began to dig in.

The city they faced was protected by a double line of earthworks. By the time Hood reached it, Nashville's defenses were on a par with those of Washington itself. Immediately south of the city was a 5-mile long line of entrenchments that included 20 artillery batteries. To the south and west lay a line of hills about 1000 yards distant. This was surmounted by another line of defenses where most of the Union forces were deployed.

Nashville had not been fortified when the surrender of the Confederate Army at Fort Donelson left northern Tennessee defenseless against Grant and Buell's armies. Union troops entered the city in August 1862 and immediately entrenched themselves in anticipation of a Confederate counter-offensive. Captain James

St Clair Morton of the US Army Engineers' Corps was dispatched to Nashville to supervise the construction of suitable defenses. Under his instruction, three forts were built covering the southeastern approaches to the city. The largest and most impressive was Fort Negley, since rebuilt to its original form and preserved as a Nashville City Park.

The defenses were not hurried along during 1863 once the Confederate counter-offensive had failed to materialize. The breastworks and redoubts that greeted Hood's Confederates were built in a frenzy of activity that began in November 1864 as the Army of the Tennessee marched inexorably north. General Tower

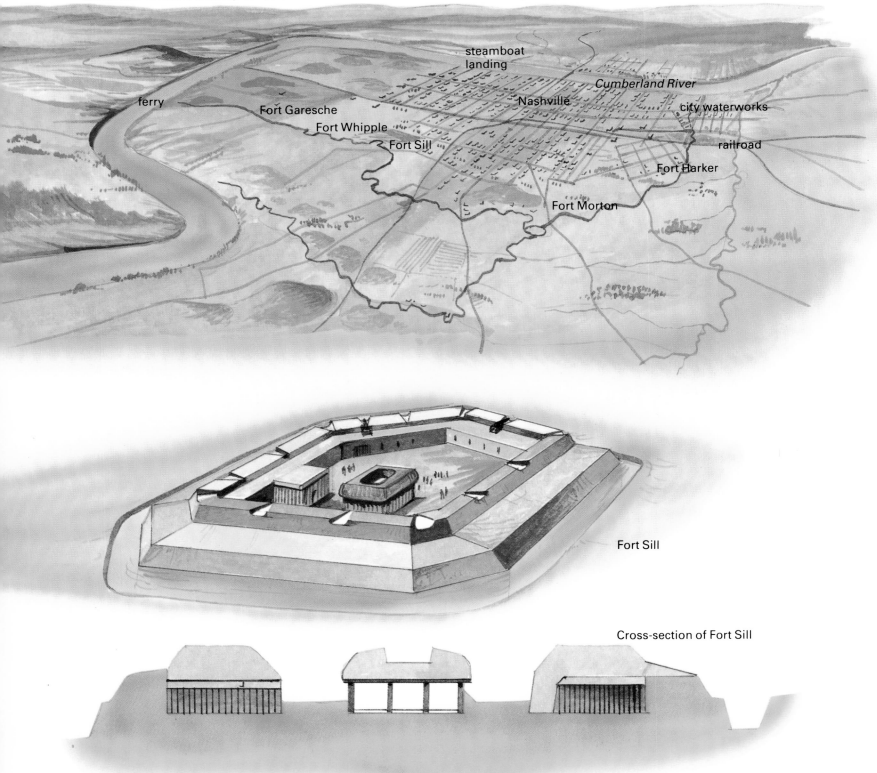

Fort Sill

Cross-section of Fort Sill

supervised this second phase of defenses. The troops were helped by unseasonally mild weather. This vanished as the Confederates appeared before the city and they had to dig their defenses in alternate snow and slush. Thomas concentrated his best fighting troops along the V-shaped line of hills south of the city. The second line was occupied by the men of the quartermaster's corps.

General Thomas commanded approximately 70,000 troops at Nashville. Obligingly deployed before him were the 23–25,000 men with Hood. The Confederate cavalry under Forrest had been ordered off on a raid toward Murfreesboro and they were not present for the battle. The day Hood expended 6000 Confederates at Franklin, he extinguished all hope of bringing his offensive to a victorious conclusion. A speedy withdrawal would have escaped Thomas's army – its pursuit was ponderous enough after Nashville – but it was not to be. Hood dug in opposite Thomas, clinging to the hope that he could repel the inevitable attack when it came. Whether in his wildest dreams he hoped to convert a repulse into a defeat and bounce Thomas out of Nashville is not clear from his account of the campaign.

With his smaller army Hood could not afford to spread his troops across the full frontage occupied by the Union forces. Instead, he entrenched to the southeast of the city, protecting his western flank by a series of redoubts. Redoubt Number 4 was typical: a four-gun battery of 12-pounder Napoleons was deployed on the low hills overlooking the Hillsboro Pike on December 9. The ground was frozen hard and it took five days' labor to produce a 7-feet high breastwork for the battery. The infantry's trenches were only 2 feet deep.

Thomas's army left its defenses on December 15. Hood's intelligence was up to its usual high standard and the Confederates knew about the attack the evening before. Despite their readiness, the sheer weight of numbers all but guaranteed their defeat. Hood's left was overwhelmed by an infantry attack supported by four regiments of dismounted cavalry armed with Spencer carbines. Although reinforcements were hastily ordered from the center, the line was turned and the Confederates were driven south as the short winter day ended. Again, the obvious decision for Hood was to order a withdrawal. Thomas assumed he would and returned to his headquarters in Nashville. General Schofield, who knew Hood at the Military Academy, visited Thomas shortly afterwards with a startling declaration. Hood would not give up however bad the odds.

Nashville was one of the most heavily fortified cities in the western hemisphere by the time John B. Hood led the Army of the Tennessee against it. Union engineers had been constructing defensive works at a leisurely pace since August 1862. As Hood's invasion threatened the city, General Z.B. Tower took charge of the defenses and hurriedly completed the existing forts. Additional positions were created during November 1864 and the entire city was ringed with two strong lines of breastworks that ran from riverbank to riverbank.

The Army of the Tennessee fell back but 2 miles. Hood's weary men dug in as best they could on a December night after a hard-fought battle, but few had any enthusiasm for another defensive action. The soldiers could see the writing on the wall, even if their commander was apparently blind. When the Union attack resumed the next day, the Confederate position collapsed rapidly. There were probably no more than 15,000 Confederates in Hood's frontline. Assailed by 55,000 of Thomas's 70,000, they headed for home. Most of the Confederate artillery was abandoned. Only a gallant rearguard action by Chalmer's cavalry gained enough time for the shattered army to outdistance Thomas's pursuit.

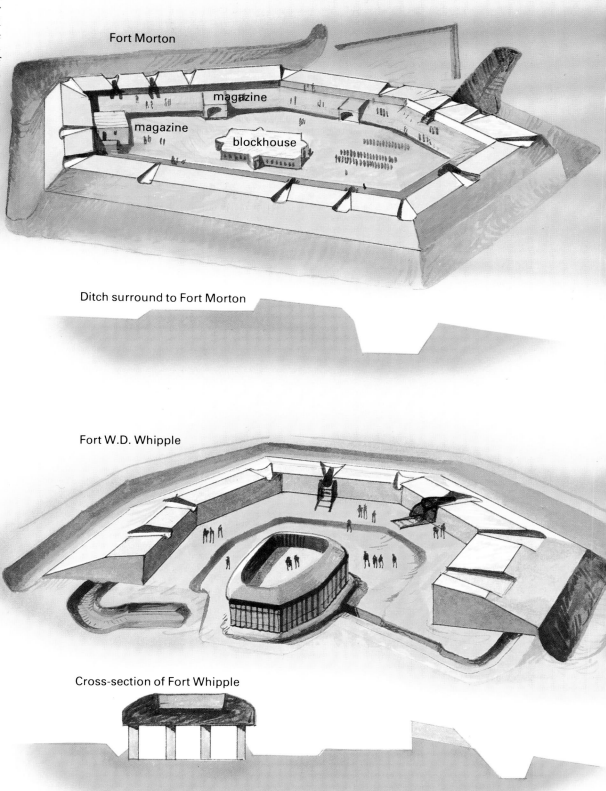

Fort Morton

Ditch surround to Fort Morton

Fort W.D. Whipple

Cross-section of Fort Whipple

105

The Defense of Mobile

Before the war Mobile had been an important cotton-exporting port. By the summer of 1864 Mobile and Wilmington were the Confederacy's last major ports still operational. Admiral Farragut had resumed command of the Western Gulf squadron in January 1864 and had been badgering Washington ever since. He had a powerful fleet based around the screw sloops *Brooklyn*, *Hartford*, and *Richmond*, supported by six smaller steamers and several double-enders. But inside Mobile Bay lurked the CSS *Tennessee*, the most powerful of all the Southern casemate ironclads. Farragut was deeply concerned that the aggressive Admiral Franklin Buchanan would repeat his performance in command of the *Virginia* and sortie as soon as his warship was ready.

Tennessee was more than ready, but her deep draft prevented her from getting over the bar. Farragut's preparations went undisturbed and he duly received four monitors to spearhead his assault on Mobile.

The entrance to Mobile Bay was guarded by two old brick forts: Fort Gaines on Dauphine Island to the west, and Fort Morgan to the east. The harbor defenses of Mobile were not as powerful as those of Charleston or Fort Fisher that guarded the approaches to Wilmington. Together, Forts Morgan and Gaines mounted 104 cannon, mostly old 32- and 42-pounder smoothbores, although a handful of heavy rifles were added. It was not enough to stop a large fleet from running past into the bay itself.

The Confederates were painfully aware of the inadequacy of their forts. They supplemented the old brick defenses with immense stacks of sandbags, and laid an extensive field of torpedoes in the channel. Blocking the center of the deep-water channel, these torpedoes forced the US warships to approach closer to the guns of the forts.

Admiral Farragut spent some time before the attack "wargaming" the battle with wooden blocks, each of which represented one of his ships. Using the models, he planned the order of his attack, calculating the number of heavy guns he could bring to bear on the forts and how long it would take to have his fleet assembled inside the bay. He ordered the attack for the flood tide early in the morning of August 5. The water would be at its deepest, thus helping to protect his ships from the torpedoes, and the tide would carry any disabled vessel past the forts and into the bay.

Farragut's wooden ships went into action with their machinery surrounded by sandbags and anchor chains ranged along their exposed sides. They had sent down their light spars, leaving just lower and top masts standing. The ships' boats were left behind on Sand Island. Each of the big wooden ships had a smaller gunboat lashed alongside. The fleet approached Fort Morgan in line with several gunboats detached to engage from the seaward side. Leading the assault were the monitors *Tecumseh*, *Manhattan*, *Winnebago*, and *Chickasaw*.

Cross-sections of Lunette D, one of the strongest of the defensive positions around Mobile.

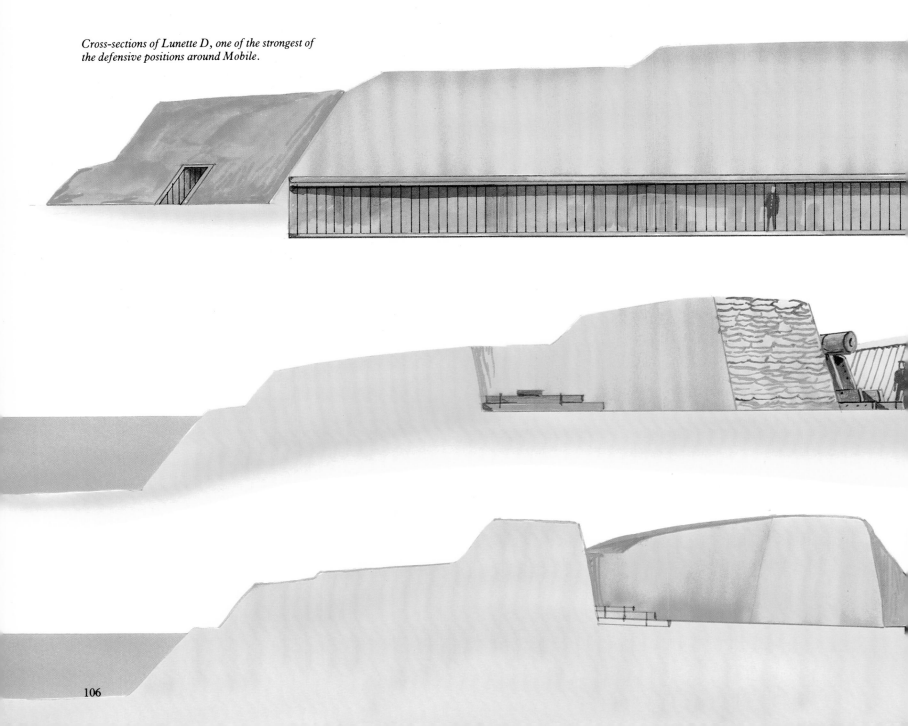

At 6.30 a.m. the monitors opened fire on Fort Morgan. The Confederates did not reply until the Union warships had come into closer range. Firing became general by about 7.00 a.m., the US squadron steaming past Fort Morgan at a range of just under 1000 yards. The guns of Fort Gaines, 2500 yards away, were too far off to threaten Farragut's ships. The Confederate underwater defenses claimed their first and only victim at about 7.30 a.m. when the *Tecumseh* altered course to engage the *Tennessee*, which had lumbered into view from behind Fort Morgan. *Tecumseh* filled rapidly and went down. *Brooklyn*, next astern, stopped her engines. The commander of Fort Morgan immediately concentrated his guns on her, believing the sloop to be Farragut's flagship.

Farragut, bellowing furiously above the roar of the cannon, ordered *Hartford* on. Putting her helm over to starboard, his flagship sheered past the *Brooklyn* and led the fleet into Mobile Bay. Although several US warships struck further torpedoes, none exploded.

The Union fleet kept Fort Morgan under a heavy fire throughout the attack, but the Confederate defenses proved their worth. Only one gunner was killed and three wounded. Fort Morgan's guns fired 491 rounds at Farragut's squadron, ceasing fire after the Union formation passed out of range to the north. *Brooklyn* suffered the most serious damage, with 70 hits. *Oneida*, lashed to the former ironclad *Galena*, had her boiler ruptured, which killed eight and wounded 30 sailors out of a crew of only 186.

With the exception of *Brooklyn*, none of the Union warships was under concentrated fire for any length of time. Thanks to Farragut's instant decision to press home the attack, the fleet presented the Confederate gunners with a moving target, constantly shrouded in smoke as all warships fired as fast as they could. Once past the forts, Farragut had won the battle. *Tennessee* made a gallant last stand, but failed to take any of the US vessels with her. Fort Gaines surrendered to US troops on August 9 and Fort Morgan did likewise on August 23.

Mobile was not as well defended as Charleston and its two forts were not as well placed to stop the US Navy's attack. If the US squadron broke into the bay, it would be practically out of range of the forts' cannon. The defenses had over 100 guns available but only a handful of them were large-caliber rifles that could seriously menace an ironclad. The obstructions and torpedoes (mines) that choked the channel did claim one famous victim – the monitor Tecumseh – but many other US warships bumped into mines that did not detonate. Yet again, a line of warships firing a hail of suppressive grapeshot was able to run past the forts without suffering prohibitive losses.

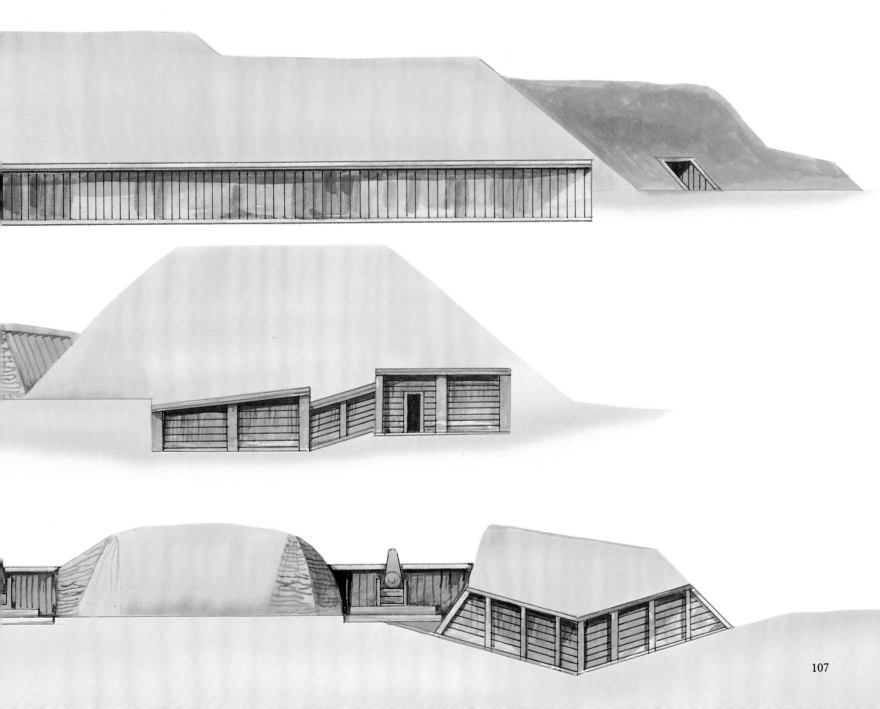

Running the Forts at New Orleans

New Orleans was the Confederacy's most important port and its capture in April 1862 was a serious blow to the Southern economy. It was defended by two forts on opposite banks of the Mississippi, 2 miles east of Bolivar Point. The river was about 1000 yards across and was blocked by a line of hulks covered by the guns of Fort St Philip on the northern bank and Fort Jackson on the southern.

Fort Jackson was a stone fort built in the classic eighteenth-century star shape: a pentagon with diamond-shaped bastions at all five corners. Set back 100 yards from the levee, it seemed to be practically in the river since the Mississippi was running very high at the time of the Federal attack. Fort Jackson was armed with 74 cannon.

In the casemates: ten 24-pounder howitzers and fourteen 24-pounder smoothbores;
In barbette mountings above: three 8-inch and two 10-inch Columbiads, one 7-inch Brooke rifle, two 8-inch mortars, six 42-pounder, fifteen 32-pounder and eleven 24-pounder smoothbores, one 7.4-inch howitzer, and one 8-inch howitzer;
Parade: one 6-pounder smoothbore and one 12-pounder howitzer;
Water battery: one 10-inch and two 8-inch Columbiads, one 10-inch seacoast mortar, and two 64-pounder James rifles.

The bombproof shelters and other key areas of the fort had the additional protection of sandbags.

Fort St Philip was about a ½ mile upstream from Fort Jackson. A less formal affair, its 52 guns were all mounted *en barbette* rather than casemates. The line of cannon projected over a brick wall, were covered with turf, and divided into an upper and lower battery. Total armament was as follows:

Face: four 8-inch Columbiads;
Salient: one 24-pounder;
On the covered way: one 8-inch and one 10-inch mortar, and one 13-inch seacoast mortar;
Upper battery: sixteen 24-pounder smoothbores;
Lower battery: one 7-inch Brooke rifle, one 8-inch Columbiad, six 42-pounder, nine 32-pounder, and four 24-pounder smoothbores;
Field works ("northeast battery"): four 10-inch seacoast mortars;
On parade: one 6-pounder and one 12-pounder smoothbore, plus one 24-pounder howitzer.

Traditional naval thinking rated a gun in a fort as worth five similar weapons mounted in a wooden ship. However, this assumed the ship was going to slug it out with the fort to the finish; Farragut planned to run his vessels past the fort under cover of darkness. Leading the assault were five powerful warships: *Hartford*, *Brooklyn*, *Richmond*, *Pensacola*, and *Mississippi*. Twelve gunboats supported them. Together these vessels carried 192 guns and howitzers and the fleet was completed by another 19 mortar schooners each armed with a single 13-inch seacoast mortar and a pair of 32-pounders. Since the vast majority of the Confederate cannon were 32-pounder smoothbores or smaller, the US fleet had a considerably heavier armament.

The mortar schooners subjected the forts to five days and nights of bombardment, firing some 7500 rounds into Fort Jackson. But the garrison took cover in the bombproofs and the spectacular shelling dismounted only seven of the two forts' combined total of 126 guns. Only Fort St Philip had a gun able to bear on the mortar schooners' firing position – its 7-inch Brooke rifle. To the gunners' dismay it was destroyed by a shell exploding prematurely in the breach, so that the rest of the bombardment had to be endured without effective reply.

With the Confederate ironclads *Louisiana* and *Mississippi* unready for action, it fell to their little fleet of tugs and river steamers to bear the brunt of the naval action on April 24. Mounting a total of 40 guns, this flotilla was defeated without difficulty by Farragut's vastly more powerful squadron.

Attacking at just after 4.00 a.m., the US warships presented a poor target as they steamed past, firing full broadsides into the forts. The veritable hail of grapeshot from so many heavy cannon prevented the Confederates from firing accurately, if at all. After the battle the forts were littered with the wooden "lamp-posts" – the frames on which a stand of grapeshot was arranged. It proved very difficult

for the gunners in either fort to identify ships in the darkness. Giant flashes stabbed out of the murk as warships discharged their broadsides and accurately judging the range of a vessel proved almost impossible. Fort St Philip fired at least 75 rounds at the Confederate ram *Manassas* by mistake. They all missed.

The Confederates were further hampered by the quality of their powder which proved to be very poor, reducing effective range and muzzle velocity. The gunners on the water battery were even under attack from both sides as CSS *McRae* fired over their heads with her six 32-pounders and single 9-inch gun, showering the intervening Confederates with the sabots from her projectiles.

The action lasted about 70 minutes. *Manassas* was sunk, the Confederate gunboats driven off, and the Union fleet safely established above the forts. Farragut had proved that his warships could run past powerful defenses without serious damage.

The defeat of the Confederate river defenses at New Orleans showed that old-fashioned forts could not stop well-handled modern warships from running past. The forts might have won a stand-up fight if the fleet had stopped to shoot it out, but Admiral Farragut had no need to risk his warships on such a hazardous undertaking. By breaking past the defenses and destroying the improvised Confederate gunboat squadron, Farragut had won the battle.

The Bombardment of Fort Pulaski

Fort Pulaski was built on Cockspur Island at the mouth of the Savannah River in 1829 and is preserved today as a national monument. It still bears the scars of the bombardment that compelled its surrender. The fall of Fort Pulaski marked a turning point in the history of siege warfare because it was the first occasion that rifled cannon demonstrated a clear superiority over the large-caliber smoothbores which were traditionally employed to breach the walls of a fortress.

Captain (later Brigadier-General) Quincy A. Gillmore, chief engineer of the Union expeditionary force under Brigadier-General Thomas Sherman, conducted a personal reconnaissance of the area on November 30, 1861. Union troops occupied Big Tybee Island a few days later. Like all the islands along this Georgia coastline, Tybee was mostly mud marsh but did have some hummocks of firm ground. The Union guns and their stores were landed on the northeastern tip of the island and it was a laborious business hauling them 2½ miles across the marshes to establish them in batteries facing Fort Pulaski.

Manned by 385 officers and men, Fort Pulaski was built in the shape of a pentagon; the brick walls were 7½ feet thick and stood 25 feet above the water, with one tier of cannon in casemates and another above *en barbette*. The fort could mount up to 140 guns, although at the time it was attacked it had 48. Of these, only 19 bore on Tybee Island.

Barbette guns: five 8-inch Columbiads, four 10-inch Columbiads, one 24-pounder Blakely rifle, and two 10-inch seacoast mortars;
Casemates guns: one 8-inch Columbiad, four 32-pounder smoothbores;
In batteries outside the fort: one 10-inch and one 12-inch seacoast mortar.

The union troops constructed a causeway on fascines and brushwood between the landing point and the intended sites of the batteries. Entirely under cover of darkness, the troops laid the causeway and built batteries and bombproof shelters opposite Fort Pulaski.

Heavy cannon and mortars were positioned and painstakingly camouflaged, so the Confederates were unaware of their location. It took 250 men to maneuver a single mortar on a sling cart across the swampy pathway and, as the Confederates were less than a mile away, all work had to be done without bellowed words of command. The men were forbidden to raise their voices above a whisper and were guided by the notes of a whistle.

Eleven batteries were completed by April 9. Stretching across 2500 yards of shoreline, they mounted the following armaments:

Twelve 13-inch heavy mortars
Four 10-inch mortars
Six 10-inch Columbiads
Seven 8-inch Columbiads
Five 30-pounder Parrott rifles
One 48-pounder James rifle
Two 64-pounder James rifles
Two 84-pounder James rifles

The mortars and guns were to be fired by detachments of infantrymen under the supervision of the engineers. The bombardment began at 8.15 a.m. on April 10, with the Columbiads and mortars firing one round every 10 minutes. The crews were ordered to increase their rate of fire to one round every 6–8 minutes once they

were sure of the correct elevation. The faster firing 30-pounder Parrotts and the 48-pounder James concentrated on the Confederate barbette guns which had immediately returned the Union fire.

The Union gunners soon learned to duck when they saw a shot coming and although the Confederate gunnery produced showers of earth and mud, it inflicted just one casualty in 1½ days of firing. By 1 p.m. observers from the Union batteries could see through their telescopes that Fort Pulaski's walls were being honeycombed. It was immediately evident that the rifled guns were penetrating deeply. The only negative observation was that the fire of the 13-inch mortars was highly erratic. Less than one shot in 10 was landing inside the fort. Since none of the gunners had ever fired a mortar before and had only trained for 10 days, this was perhaps not surprising. Weather conditions were not conductive to accurate mortar fire anyway; there was a stiff, easterly wind blowing across the gun line throughout the bombardment.

Overnight most of the guns fell silent, with just a couple of cannon firing at 20-minute intervals. The bombardment opened with renewed vigor on the morning of the 11th, quickly dismounting almost all the Confederate guns trained on Tybee Island. By noon the first two casemates on the southeast face were blown open and it was obvious that a few hours' more shooting would create a breach too wide for the garrison to defend. Fort Pulaski's commandant, Colonel Ormstead, surrendered to avoid further bloodshed.

When the Union engineers examined the fort they discovered just how effective the rifled guns had been. At a mean range of 1700 yards the rifles had breeched the 7½-feet thick wall with the expenditure of 2293 rounds. The 84-pounder James had proved able to penetrate 25 inches of brickwork, while the 64-pounder James penetrated 20 inches. By comparison, the enormous 10-inch Columbiad smoothbores penetrated only 13 inches. Although their large, solid shot was excellent at battering the masonry after it had been penetrated by the

rifles, Gillmore concluded that the time and effort required to assemble these large smoothbores in battery was not worth while. A small number of rifled guns could destroy a brick fort from a mile away.

The ease with which Fort Pulaski succumbed to rifled artillery came as a nasty surprise to the Confederates, who had had considerable confidence in the position. It was clear that the old-style brick forts were now obsolete.

Three centuries of military engineering came to an end at Fort Pulaski, Georgia. Since siege cannon entered widespread service in the sixteenth century, massive stone and brick defenses had always been able to sustain a long bombardment. So many bombardments had been undertaken by heavy smoothbore guns that the duration of a siege could be calculated with some precision. Such operations had always lasted for weeks or months, but at Fort Pulaski the Union artillery opened fire with modern rifled guns. They breached the walls in a morning's work, rendering old-fashioned forts and traditional siege guns equally obsolete.

The Defenses of Washington

The defenses of the capital were begun in a panic; no one had anticipated a Confederate victory at Bull Run. When General McClellan reached Washington on July 26, 1861 he found a city in chaos, streets choked with demoralized soldiery, and few units deployed to defend it. It was fortunate for President Lincoln that the Confederates were equally disorganized by their victory and were still adopting a defensive posture.

Although some troops occupied entrenchments on the Virginia bank of the Potomac, Washington was not defended on the Maryland side. McClellan took charge and under his energetic leadership the capital was soon surrounded by earthworks. By the early fall, Washington's defenses consisted of a series of earth forts sited so that they could support one another with their guns. The ground between them was defended with entrenchments for infantry and smaller redoubts for artillery.

These early war defenses were never tested. The Confederates remained in Virginia awaiting the next Union invasion. But this was by no means a unanimous decision. General Beauregard was locked in a bitter wrangle with Jefferson Davis, demanding that the Confederacy concentrate its forces for a knock-out blow against Washington. He planned to cross the Potomac upstream and advance on the capital from Maryland, compelling McClellan to fight a battle. To sustain this offensive strategy, he argued that the scattered groups of Confederate troops posted along the Virginia coast be concentrated with the main field army.

McClellan's defenses were not designed to hold off a large army indefinitely. His objective was to create a defensive position sufficiently strong to survive a hasty assault by a large field army. To take Washington the Confederates would have to commence a regular siege, committing their greatest body of troops to weeks or months of static operations. McClellan estimated that 34,000 troops and 40 guns was the maximum force required.

From 1862 through 1864 the defenses south of Washington extended in an arc from Occoquan on the lower Potomac to Centerville, to the Falls of the Upper Potomac. The incessant guerrilla raids led by John S. Mosby made the US War Department retain at least a full cavalry division with the Washington defenses, partly to ensure communications with the Army of the Potomac and partly to prevent any daring raids into the capital itself. The embarrassing capture of Brigadier-General Stoughton was not quickly forgotten. In the spring of 1863 the planks on the Chain Bridge over the Potomac were taken up each night in case of a guerrilla attack.

The trees that surrounded Washington were rapidly felled to provide the heavy artillery with a clear field of fire. Volunteer artillery regiments provided a garrison artillery force until Grant's 1864 campaign. Confident of his immense numerical superiority over Lee, Grant ordered these artillerymen into the field with the Army of the Potomac. This had the ironic effect that they were absent when, at last, a Confederate force marched to within rifle shot of the defenses.

Jubal Early's brilliant campaign in the Shenandoah culminated in his dramatic arrival north of Washington on July 11, 1864. Although the sight of Confederate battle flags just four miles north of Georgetown caused some jitters, Early's small army had been reduced to little more than 10,000 men. One look at the defenses told him that an assault would be futile.

The Confederates approached with the infantry on the 7th Street pike that ran by Silver Springs into Washington. Early's cavalry were on the Georgetown pike. Rock Creek then ran through a deep ravine that the Federals had blocked with fallen timber. A few hundred yards east of the creek lay Fort Stevens, a heavy artillery position. Every prominent point at intervals of 800–1000 yards was crowned with a fully enclosed gun position. Infantry trenches with room for two ranks of riflemen ran between them. The defenses were so sited that reserves could be shuttled around behind the frontline, sheltered from enemy fire. Large-caliber rifled guns were positioned to engage likely sites for Confederate field guns should the rebels attempt a concentrated bombardment of one sector.

The heavy artillerymen taken away by Grant more than made up for their spell in a quiet posting. These large, 12-company regiments bore the brunt of several assaults. The 1st Maine Heavy Artillery holds the distinction of suffering the most fatal casualties of any unit in one battle during the Civil War. Attacking a Confederate redoubt at Petersburg on June 18, 1864, the regiment sustained 210 dead. Second place in this grisly league is the 8th New York Heavy Artillery. They suffered 207 dead during the attack at Cold Harbor a week earlier.

The Washington defenses were never seriously tested. Yet although they absorbed thousands of troops and a considerable number of heavy guns, the forts and rifle trenches were a sound investment. The consequences of a victorious Confederate assault on the capital were incalculable. Although it would have been all but impossible for a Confederate Army to have held Washington long, the political damage would have been tremendous, perhaps even fatal to the Union cause.

Washington was the most important political target of the war. Had the Confederacy ever managed to storm the Northern capital, the international consequences could have been enormous. The tantalizing prospect of European recognition led several Southern commanders to press for an assault on Washington after the battle of Bull Run. Later in the war, Confederate forces did make feint attacks toward the capital on several occasions, all designed to reduce the pressure on Lee's army, but they never managed to launch a full-scale assault. Washington remained a sensitive nerve throughout the war; very large bodies of troops were retained for its defense when there was no realistic prospect of a Confederate attack.

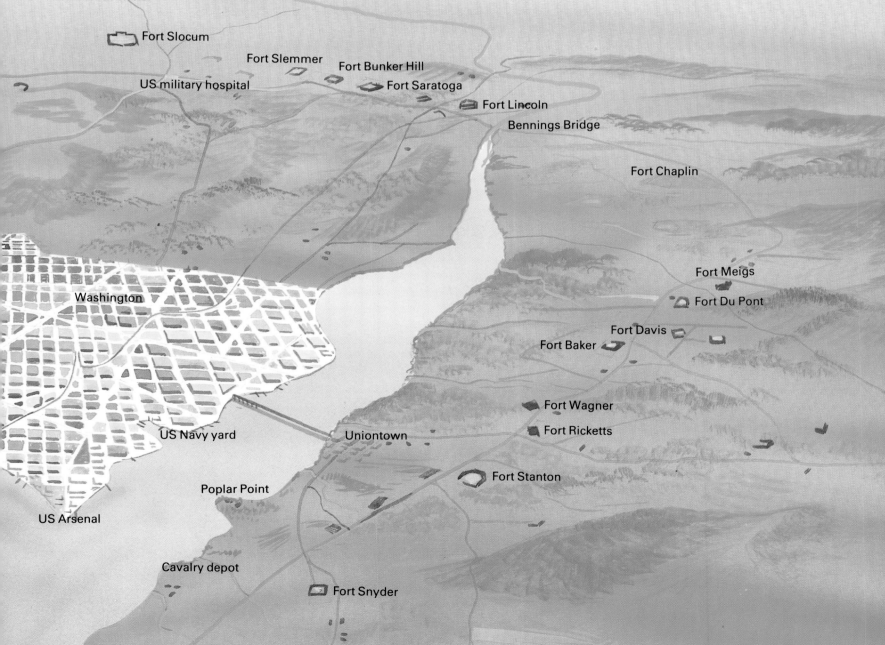

Siege Artillery

Siege artillery has a longer history than field artillery. The first cannon were better at bombarding fortifications than attempting to maneuver in the field. The distinction between mobile cannon suitable for field operations and heavier guns intended for a more static role was maintained from the seventeenth century to World War II.

During the Civil War the siege artillery was in the same state of transition as small arms and lighter artillery. The large smoothbore guns used for generations were being replaced by more powerful rifled weapons. The rifles offered longer range, better penetration against fortifications, and much greater accuracy. A few of the biggest smoothbores did soldier on, but many of their smaller brethren were converted to rifles.

The heaviest land-based cannon were divided into two categories: siege or garrison artillery, and seacoast artillery. The distinction was primarily one of weight. Siege guns could be moved by road and were intended to follow in the wake of an army. If a formal assault had to be made against a fortified position, the heavy guns would be assembled to bombard it and pave the way for the infantry. It was a science all of its own, perfected in Europe 200 years earlier. Seacoast artillery had a purely static role: the defense of coastal positions against warships. Intended to stay where they were installed, they could afford to be as big as manufacturers could make them. During the Civil War the distinction between siege and garrison artillery became blurred as some seacoast weapons, such as the 13-inch mortar or the heaviest Parrott rifles, were brought forward to tackle enemy fortifications. Here we will concentrate on the cannon and mortars that were used in the siege operations during the war, whatever their original classification.

The original siege guns serving with the US Army in 1860 were the 4.5-inch Ordnance rifle; the 30-pounder Parrott; 12-, 18-, and 24-pounder smoothbores; and the 8-inch smoothbore that fired a 50½-pound shell. The intermediate-caliber smoothbores saw little service in siege operations and, as we shall see, the 8-inch weapon was completely eclipsed by the rifles. The heaviest of these guns was the 24-pounder smoothbore model 1839 and it was the largest cannon that could be moved by road. Limbered up and ready to move, it weighed more than 10,000 pounds and took a

10-horse team to draw it. At 100 yards' range it could drive its shot through 8½ feet of earthen parapet, 3 feet of brick, or 2 feet of stone. When it was built this sort of close-range pounding was perfectly feasible, but when the infantry acquired rifles, no siege gun was likely to last long within 100 yards of enemy trenches.

Seacoast artillery included 32- and 42-pounder smoothbores, the monstrous Columbiad and Rodman cannon, plus 100-, 200-, and 300-pounder Parrott rifles, and the imported Whitworth and Armstrong guns.

The first full-scale siege train employed during the Civil War was assembled by the Union to besiege Yorktown. The Confederates wisely withdrew rather than stand against overwhelming force. In 23 days the following weapons were established in battery against the Southern lines:

Two 200-pounder Parrotts
Five 100-pounder Parrotts
Five 30-pounder Parrotts
Ten 4.5-inch Ordnance rifles
Ten 13-inch Model 1861 seacoast mortars
Sixteen 10-inch Model 1841 seacoast mortars

More guns were in reserve but were not deployed since the Confederates evacuated just as the massed guns were preparing to begin their bombardment.

The heavy Parrott rifles were produced in three calibers: 6.4 inch (100 pounder); 8 inch (200 pounder); and 10 inch (300 pounder). All earned a worse reputation for bursting than the Parrott field artillery, yet with maximum ranges of over 8000 yards and enormous penetration, their occasional failures were tolerated. The Union gunners learned to treat them with caution, keeping the bores scrupulously clean with bristle sponges and frequent washing. Since any obstruction in the bore had the potential to lead to a burst, dust caps were employed when the gun was not in action. Fuse plugs were checked most carefully and projectiles were greased to ease their passage along the barrel. The guns were gently run into battery so as not to start the round forward in the bore. Some army gunners believed that this was very important, and the inability of their navy colleagues to ensure this was the reason for the Parrott's poor record aboard warships.

Parrott himself was painfully aware of the deficiencies and studied the failure of his guns

very thoroughly. He noted that premature explosions – where the shell detonated in the barrel – were a key factor. They certainly weakened the tube and sometimes the evidence was there for all to see. The "Swamp Angel" at Charleston suffered several premature explosions and displayed several dangerous symptoms, such as enlargement of the bore, before it finally burst. Parrott discounted the danger from a gap developing between the charge and the projectile, perhaps by the motion of a ship. His experiments showed that this did not necessarily damage the gun, but it did seem to reduce the range. However, he did note that chamber pressures rose to alarming levels in the larger rifled guns – much higher than in smoothbores, which dissipated some of the force because of their looser fitting rounds. When a 6.4-inch Parrott fired its 100-pound shell using a 10-pound powder charge, the pressure in the chamber reached 3.1 pounds per square inch. By contrast, a 15-inch Columbiad smoothbore firing a 428-pound shot with 40 pounds of powder generated 2.7 pounds per square inch.

The expanding part of the Parrott projectile impacted against the same part of the bore with every round. This hammering was another source of weakness that could not be avoided. The root of the problem was that individual Parrott rifles varied. One that Parrott studied closely fired over 1000 rounds, including 11 that exploded in the barrel, yet showed no damage. The same 30-pounders that nearly killed General Lee by their failures at Fredericksburg impressed the Union artillerymen later in the war. One fired 4606 rounds during the operations against Charleston, many at an elevation of 40 degrees and was still firing accurately without serious wear at the end. Of the twenty 30-pounder Parrotts firing from the Union lines around Richmond and Petersburg between 1864 and 1865, only one was damaged; a shell detonated when the gun was fired and the explosion blew 12 inches off the muzzle. The artillerymen worked at it with a cold chisel, cut it smooth, and returned it to action. To their delight it fired perfectly well with the foreshortened barrel.

The 4.5-inch Ordnance rifle Model 1861 looked similar to the 3-inch Ordnance rifle but was mounted on a siege carriage and was manufactured from cast, rather than wrought, iron. By comparison, its tube weighed 3450 pounds as opposed to 816, and it fired shells weighing 30 rather than 10 pounds. It was

24-pdr model 1839 siege gun
Designed to batter enemy defenses from within a few hundred yards, the 24-pdr smoothbore was obsolete by the 1850s when infantry began to acquire rifles capable of picking off the gun crew. The 24-pdr fired either solid shot or a shell containing a 1-lb bursting charge. Grapeshot and canister rounds were also provided.

Caliber: *5.82 inches.* **Length:** *124 inches.*
Weight: *5790 lb.* **Maximum range:** *1834 yards using solid shot, 8-lb charge at an elevation of 5 degrees.* **Powder charge:** *6 or 8 lb.*

regarded with suspicion at the beginning of the war because it was not fully tested before the army went ahead and ordered it. The trial gun had burst after 800 rounds. Experience showed that after more than 500 rounds the vent holes on the 4.5-inch guns displayed signs of enlargement, the telltale warning of an overstressed barrel liable to burst.

In practice the 4.5-inch gun proved quite successful and was even used in the field. Two companies of the 1st Connecticut Artillery were attached to the Army of the Potomac in December 1861. Each equipped with four guns towed by 10-horse teams, they were provided with one caisson per gun with 48 rounds of ammunition. The officers, sergeants, and buglers were mounted and the men handed in their rifled muskets to serve like field artillery rather than siege gunners. They were in action at Fredericksburg but the suspicion of some staff officers about the 4.5-inch guns' mobility led them to be kept in the rear at Gettysburg. It was feared that in a battle of maneuver they might hamper the army. However, they confounded the critics by coming into action at Kelly's Ford at the gallop in November 1863. After that they entered winter quarters and were eventually absorbed into the siege train which accompanied the Army of the Potomac in the spring of 1864. While serving as field artillery they traveled over 500 miles, sometimes covering as much as 30 miles a day, and never failed to keep up. Indeed, they proved more mobile than the 20-pounder Parrotts because these concentrated all their weight on the rear axle which made them harder to shift over soft ground.

The greatest concentration of siege artillery during the war took place at the siege of Richmond and Petersburg. The siege train was assembled in April 1864 and consisted of the following:

Six 100-pounder Parrotts with 500 rounds of ammunition each
Forty 4.5-inch Ordnance rifles with 1000 rounds
Forty 30-pounder Parrotts with 1000 rounds
Ten 10-inch mortars with 600 rounds each
Twenty 8-inch mortars with 600 rounds each

Thirty-three mortar platforms were provided (a 10 percent margin to allow for damage) and 44 siege gun platforms. The load of stores accompanying the siege train included 30,000 sandbags, 100 globe lanterns, and 2000 pounds of grease. To move this siege train by road would have been a transport officer's nightmare. Fortunately, the artillery could move by sea. The army chartered 10 schooners for a fee of $10,500 per month. With an average burden of 165 tons, the guns were loaded as follows: one took the 100-pounders, one the 10-inch mortars, and another four carried the 4.5-inch and 30-pounders. The 8-inch mortars were split between two schooners that also carried 20 Coehorn mortars plus wagons and stores. Another carried miscellaneous equipment. Two further vessels were kept well clear of everything else; one had the ammunition (some

fixed), while the second was loaded with powder. Note that this deliberate separation of weapons and ammunition is at complete variance with modern practice – lose one ship and the whole force is harmless. This was forced on the gunners by the tremendous danger inherent in black powder.

By April 2, 1865 the siege train had swollen substantially. The Confederate lines were faced by 31 earthworks, some called forts and others batteries, although this did not affect their armament. In position were:

Eight 8-inch smoothbore siege guns
Sixteen Coehorn mortars
Sixteen 8-inch mortars
Four 10-inch siege mortars
Three 10-inch seacoast mortars
One 13-inch seacoast mortar ("Dictator")
One 30-pounder Brooke rifle
Seven 4.5-inch Ordnance rifles
Twelve 100-pounder Parrott rifles

There were another 73 weapons in reserve, including 20 Coehorn mortars and another 24 30-pounder Parrotts. To reduce the wear on barrels, individual guns were constantly moved among the batteries so those positions which saw the heaviest action regularly changed cannon. These heavy guns and mortars were supported by field guns placed within the batteries to defend them against Confederate infantry attack. Although they fired mighty

TOP: *24-pdr siege and garrison howitzer*
This was designed for use in the forward trenches during a siege, or as part of the armament of a permanent fortification. This type of 24-pdr howitzer was usually stationed in the flank casemates of the coastal forts.

Caliber: *5.82 inches.* **Length:** *69 inches.*
Weight: *1476 lb.* **Powder charge:** *3 lb.*

CENTER AND BOTTOM: *8-inch siege howitzer*
A very short piece, the 8-inch siege howitzer was loaded by hand. Because it was intended for close-range action against enemy defenses, it was designed not to use a sabot. Sabots were always prone to disintegrate and they would endanger friendly troops in the front-line trenches. The chamber was spherical, allowing the shell to sit close over the mouth. The breech of the siege howitzer was weighted to keep the center of gravity well to the rear, so that when firing from inside a fort the barrel could project as far as possible from the embrasure. It fired a 45-lb shell.

Caliber: *8 inches.* **Length:** *61½ inches.* **Weight:** *2614 lb.* **Maximum range:** *2280 yards at an elevation of 12½ degrees.* **Powder charge:** *4 lb.*

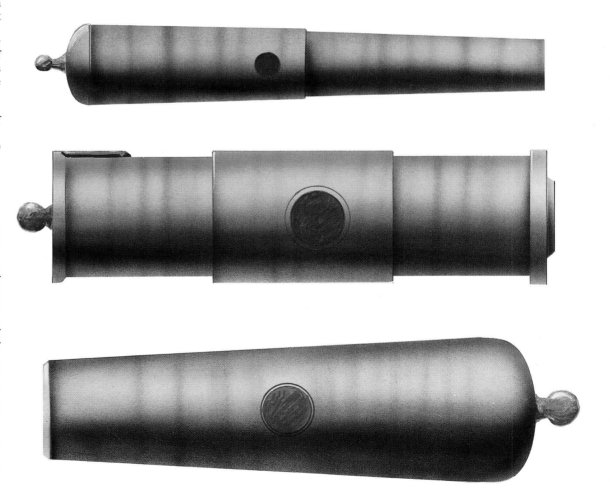

Siege Artillery

projectiles, their rate of fire was too slow to defeat determined infantry. Entrenched alongside the siege guns were:

Eleven 12-pounder Napoleons
Eight 12-pounder howitzers
One 24-pounder howitzer
Two 32-pounder howitzers
Nine 20-pounder Parrott rifles
Four 3-inch Ordnance rifles
Four 3-inch Parrott guns
One 6-pounder Sawyer gun

Union gunners praised the old 24- and 32-pounder howitzers for their close-range defensive firepower. The 32-pounder was equal in bore size to the 100-pounder Parrott and threw a massive canister charge. Being relatively light, they could be kept out of danger from enemy artillery fire, yet run into position in time to defeat an infantry attack. It was the fire of two howitzers that mowed down the 22nd South Carolina Infantry Regiment when it rushed a Union redoubt at Bermuda Hundred on June 2, 1864. The defending company of the 1st Connecticut Artillery drove off the Confederates, killing their commander.

The eight 8-inch smoothbore siege guns were brought along with a view to exploiting their ricochet effect and heavy shell weight, but they did not prove worthwhile. The era of the smoothbore artillery train was truly over. The Confederates too made little use of smoothbore siege guns, relying instead on 8-inch Brooke rifles weighing 22,000 pounds and 7-inch Brookes weighing 14,500 pounds. These were designed by John M. Brooke, one of the best Southern naval officers and a vital force behind the Confederate ironclad warship program. The first were cast at Tredegar in the fall of 1861 to become the fore and aft armament of the *Merrimack*, later renamed CSS *Virginia*. The use of heavy naval ordnance on land was by no means new and the Brooke rifles served as well ashore as they did aboard the Confederacy's river squadrons. The US Navy insisted that Parrott make minor changes to every one of his guns it adopted, although the subsequent "naval pattern" Parrotts did not differ in any major respect. The Confederacy could not afford such cosmetic changes.

Other Confederate heavy ordnance included the old 32-pounder smoothbores which were banded and rifled to produce 8000-pound, 6.4-caliber weapons. They also employed 4.62- and 4.2-inch rifles. Even monsters like the 10-inch Columbiads were banded and rifled on occasion – one was in position at Fort Johnson, Charleston. In the Confederate service the dividing line between siege, seacoast, and naval ordnance meant little. In many cases the same cannon served in all three roles.

BELOW LEFT: *13-inch mortar* (*cutaway*)
The 13-inch iron mortar had a 26-inch bore. The chamber was 7¼ inches in diameter at the bottom and 9½ inches across at the bottom of the shell. It weighed 11,500 lb.

BOTTOM LEFT: *10-inch siege mortar M1819*
Until the introduction of the 13-inch seacoast mortar, this was the standard heavy mortar for both offensive and defensive siege work.

BELOW RIGHT: *10-inch siege mortar M1861*
There were two iron 10-inch siege mortars. This is the "heavy" model – a 5775-lb monster with a 25-inch bore. With a 4-lb charge it could throw a 90-lb shell 2100 yards.

BOTTOM RIGHT: *Stone mortar*
The 16-inch bronze mortar was built to fire a hail of stone shot or small shells into the breach just before a storming party launched its assault. In defense it was used in the same way, cutting down the attacking infantry in a hail of splinters. As it fired a charge of shot rather than a solid projectile, it did not need the great strength of other mortars, hence the different shape where a large proportion of metal at the rear of the mortar is omitted. It weighed 1500 lb and had a 19.8-inch bore.

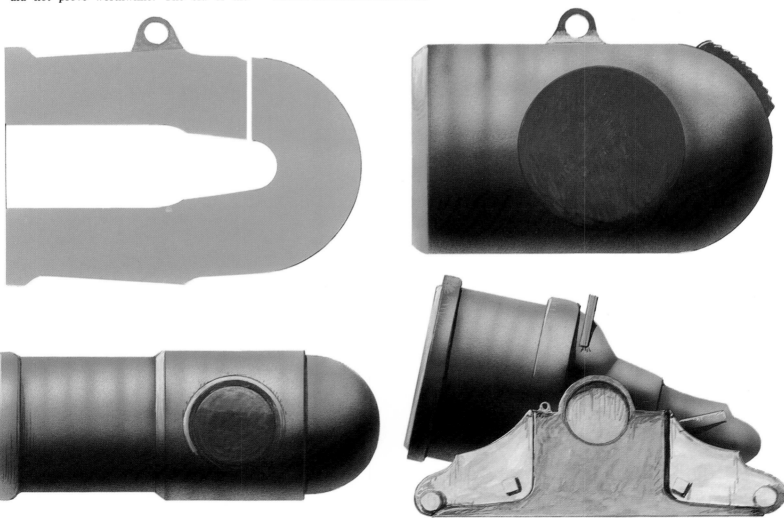

All major Federal siege guns employed the same sort of rifling with equal lands and grooves so that they could equally well fire round shot or shells. With the rejection of the James system, the US Artillery settled on three main types of ammunition: the Parrott, the Schenkl, and the Hotchkiss pattern. The Parrott shells were for Parrott guns; the Schenkl and Hotchkiss ammunition were used by Ordnance-pattern cannon. All three systems offered a choice of case shot or shell but Schenkl-pattern solid shot were also manufactured.

The heavy Parrott projectiles were of the same pattern as those fired by the 10- and 20-pounder field guns. Toward the end of the war the wrought-iron cups at the base of the shells were replaced by brass rings, which gunners learned to chip with a cold chisel in three or four places to help them take the rifling. This was the key to the success of a rifled projectile. None of the expansion systems were infallible; sometimes a shell would manage to fly up the barrel with the cup or sabot failing to grip the rifling. The result was at best an erratic trajectory; at worst it meant a hopelessly tumbling round as likely to land base-first as on its nose. This was both embarrassing and disheartening for a gun crew.

Parrott shells took the rifling 95 percent of the time, which was better than any other. They had only two significant drawbacks. First of all the brass ring at the base frequently detached itself from the rest of the projectile, endangering friendly troops forward of the gun. This did not endear the gunners to the infantry protecting the battery from a sudden rush by an enemy storming party. Parrott himself blamed variations in the powder charges for the problem, but given the less-than-uniform standard of the rifles themselves, it may have been due to variations in the ammunition.

The second problem was the number of premature explosions which, as described earlier, did much to shorten the barrel life of the larger Parrotts. These were sometimes due to weakness in the base of the shell that allowed the flash from the propellant charge to enter the projectile. But the interior surfaces of some Parrott shells were found to be very rough – possibly rough enough to fire the charge by friction alone when the shell was fired. The designer's solution which he offered to the US Artillery was to mix common bar soap, tallow, and resin in the ratio (by weight) 32:12:10. This was poured inside and the shell rolled around to coat its insides. It was drained before filling with powder.

The Schenkl projectiles relied on a papier-mâché sabot which, as already noted, failed to satisfy the field artillery because it was vulnerable to damp. Larger cannon had exactly the same problem, despite Schenkl coating the rounds with zinc. When it worked, it worked very well, delivering pleasing accuracy and posing no threat to friendly troops because it

lacked any metal sabot. If the papier-mâché was in good condition, Schenkl-pattern ammunition was better than the Parrott projectiles because the elastic toughness of the sabot allowed it to begin its spinning motion immediately and consistently shot after shot. Parrott shells were affected by variations in the powder because the exact distance from the seat of the charge determined at what point the brass ring gripped the rifling.

Schenkl projectiles seem to have deteriorated in quality toward the end of the war, at least for larger caliber guns. Much of the 30-pounder Schenkl ammunition issued in 1864 proved to be defective. Schenkl 4.5-inch shells for the Ordnance rifles had excessively solid papier-mâché – hard instead of fibrous, and almost impossible to load. Gunners who had favored the Schenkl as a result of test firing from the heavy batteries surrounding Washington were disappointed in their ammunition when the time came to use it against the defenses of the

Confederate capital. After the death of the inventor, some 21,000 sabots were condemned and even the replacements were little better. About 20 percent of them failed to stabilize the shells which led them to tumble dangerously, threatening to land in the Union front line instead. The dubious character of late-war Schenkl siege artillery ammunition and the greater strain it imposed on the barrels led artillerymen to prefer Parrott ammunition.

Hotchkiss-pattern shells also seem to have imposed a greater strain on cannon than Parrott projectiles, and they were preferred as a field artillery round. Their reliability when fired from the 3-inch Ordnance field gun was extremely good.

BELOW: *30-pdr Parrott rifles*
These demonstrated their superiority over smoothbore siege guns at the siege of Fort Pulaski. They penetrated the brick walls of the defenses at the unprecedented range of 1670 yards.

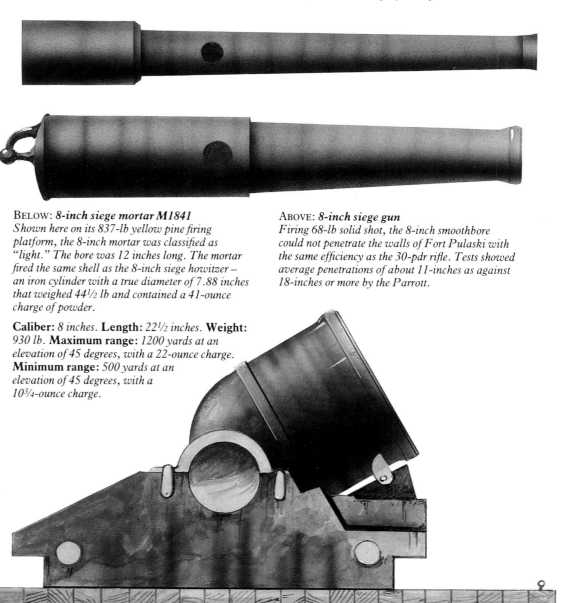

BELOW: *8-inch siege mortar M1841*
Shown here on its 837-lb yellow pine firing platform, the 8-inch mortar was classified as "light." The bore was 12 inches long. The mortar fired the same shell as the 8-inch siege howitzer – an iron cylinder with a true diameter of 7.88 inches that weighed 44½ lb and contained a 41-ounce charge of powder.

Caliber: *8 inches.* **Length:** *22½ inches.* **Weight:** *930 lb.* **Maximum range:** *1200 yards at an elevation of 45 degrees, with a 22-ounce charge.* **Minimum range:** *500 yards at an elevation of 45 degrees, with a 10¾-ounce charge.*

ABOVE: *8-inch siege gun*
Firing 68-lb solid shot, the 8-inch smoothbore could not penetrate the walls of Fort Pulaski with the same efficiency as the 30-pdr rifle. Tests showed average penetrations of about 11-inches as against 18-inches or more by the Parrott.

Siege Artillery

Several other types of ammunition were employed by siege artillery. The Dyer pattern was used for both solid shot and shell, and some 168,000 of these rounds were produced in calibers up to 8 inch. A lead-cupped sabot cast around the base and rear half of the shell was forced into the rifling. The whole round was grooved and covered in fine wire. They did not prove an overwhelming success, especially for the 4.5-inch rifle, with a significant proportion failing to take the rifling. The sabot tended to fragment, showering friendly troops ahead with dangerous shards of lead.

The Absterdam-pattern shells had a lead sabot and two lead rings which gripped the lands in the rifling – at least, in theory they did. Fired from Union 4.5-inch Ordnance rifles, they proved a humiliating failure. In a sample 239 firings from three separate Union batteries, 60 percent tumbled and only 27 percent took the rifling. It was uncertain whether the others did take the rifling or landed on target by chance. Worse still, 12 percent exploded at the muzzle and 26 percent never exploded at all.

Field trials in 1864 meant exactly that for two experimental Sawyer guns which the inventor supplied to the Union Army. Sawyer 3.75-inch rifles were used in limited numbers – only 24,000 rounds of ammunition were ever ordered – but he did supply a heavy 5.8-inch rifle for use as a siege gun. Using a mechanically fitting round, it was tested at Fort Monroe, then sent to join the siege train before Richmond. There, it exploded on its eleventh shot. The tube from the trunnions to the muzzle remained on the carriage but the bottom of the bore fell between the cheeks of the carriage and the top split into two from the vent. One half lodged on top of the parapet and the other was blown clean out of the battery. On examination, the vent proved to be enlarged with a double cavity at the lower end. Fortunately, the artillerymen had had the sense to fire it by quick match rather than friction primer, and were out of harm's way when the gun burst.

A detailed record of siege artillery firing on Richmond and Petersburg showed the following percentage of "serviceable" rounds fired.

Gun	Projectile	% Serviceable
100-pounder Parrott	Parrott	96
30-pounder Parrott	Parrott	96
30-pounder Parrott	Schenkl	57
20-pounder Parrott	Parrott	86
20-pounder Parrott	Schenkl	93
4.5-inch Ordnance	Schenkl	82
4.5-inch Ordnance	Dyer	80
4.5-inch Ordnance	Absterdam	31
3-inch Ordnance	Hotchkiss	95

These were all standard rounds, primarily common shell with some rounds of spherical case. But Union artillerymen experimented with several varieties of incendiary ammunition during the war. During the operations against Charleston they fired a number of projectiles filled with experimental incendiary mixtures, which were tried again at Petersburg. Using a Parrott shell with its cavity divided by a thin diaphragm, the Fleming and Birney incendiary shells had a small bursting charge in the nose of the shell and an inflammable mixture in the rear. The different inventors tried hard to keep their incendiary recipes secret but curious gunners experimented with them, interested to see what was inside.

Birney projectiles were fired from a 6.4-inch 100-pounder Parrott from Fort Brady north of the James River in October 1864. Each shell held 6 pints of incendiary fluid poured into cotton wadding packed inside the back, the round and the hole then sealed with a copper plug. Their target was a cluster of wooden houses 2500 yards away inside the Confederate lines. Six buildings were burned down after an expenditure of 29 rounds. Whenever a shell exploded inside a house, a fierce conflagration occurred. The gunners found that if they poured a little of the Birney mixture on the ground and ignited it, it burned for about five minutes with a clear flame. They concluded that it was based on petroleum and turpentine.

Firing such ammunition from smaller caliber guns did not seem to work because the shells held insufficient incendiary material. The Fleming mixture was tried in March 1865 against a wooden pallisade and abatis about 300 yards from a 30-pounder Parrott. Each shell contained about 1 pint of fluid and it consistently failed to set the dry underbrush alight.

Confederate siege artillery
The Confederate siege cannon and the heavy naval ordnance mentioned above used 10 separate rifling systems, including the saw-type developed by Brooke, another invented by Commander Scott, and the British Armstrong, Whitworth, and Blakely guns all had their own systems. Scott and Blakely both used three deep grooves in the barrel with corresponding flanges on the projectiles. The Confederates also produced a version of the Hotchkiss ammunition which had fine wire wrapped around it, imparting a curious sound to the shell in flight. They also copied the Schenkl.

As the Union forces encountered new varieties of Confederate ammunition, samples were taken for examination by the Ordnance Department. Neither side exactly copied the

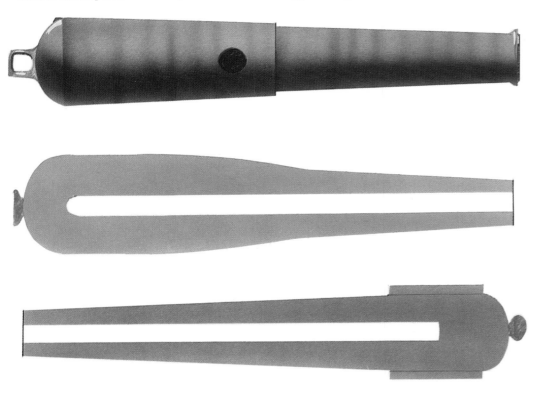

TOP: *Sawyer 5.8-inch siege gun*
This was given to the US Army by its inventor for evaluation in the field at the siege of Richmond. It fired a mechanically-fitting projectile with flanges that engaged the grooves in the barrel. The shell was lead-coated to reduce the wear on the barrel. It was successfully test fired at Fort Monroe before joining the siege train, where it made good practice with its first 10 rounds. Unfortunately, it exploded at its 11th shot, blowing the barrel into four pieces.

MIDDLE: *Confederate 4.62-inch siege gun*
Confederate industry supplied the Southern forces with a wide variety of heavy ordnance, but many types of gun were manufactured only in small quantities. Ten different systems of rifling were used. Confederate rifled guns were often much heavier than Union weapons. This one weighed 6170 lb – almost 50 percent heavier than the comparable 4.2-inch, 30-pdr Parrott.

BOTTOM: *Brooke 4.62-inch siege rifle*
James M. Brooke's rifled guns were the standard armament of Confederate ironclads, and the same system was used for a series of rifled muzzleloaders used to arm Southern forts and coastal batteries. The defenses of Richmond included 16 Brooke rifles, ranging in size from 4.2- to 8-inch caliber. Two other 8-inch rifles had been smoothbored to 10-inch caliber.

other's methods but the rounds employed did bear a strong general resemblance. Confederate heavy shell was manufactured differently to standard Union projectiles; where the US factories smoothed the shell over its whole length by forcing it through a die, the Confederates simply turned two rings on the shells and left the rest of the surface rough.

Some US Artillery officers rated the Confederate Reed shells as better than their own Parrott ammunition. Reed projectiles were similar, Reed having worked with Parrott before the war. They used an expanding ring of wrought iron, copper, or lead but not brass. Reed shells proved less likely to shed their metal sabot in flight and so posed less of a threat to friendly troops. However, they did seem to fail to take the rifling rather more often than the Parrott ammunition. Since Reed ammunition was produced in several calibers used by Federal gunners, it was occasionally fired back against its former owners after Confederate stockpiles had been captured.

Precise figures for the performance of Confederate ordnance are not widely available. One survey was conducted on the orders of Major-General Warren, commander of the US V Corps, who demanded an analysis of unexploded Confederate artillery rounds within his lines. This revealed that of 57 unexploded shells, 24 (i.e. 52 percent) displayed grooves along their cases, showing that they had taken the rifling properly; four (or 8.7 percent) had lost their metal sabot or ring; while 12 (21 percent) showed evidence of iron chipped away from their base.

The Confederates used curved copper plates secured by screws or dowels to grip the rifling on their largest cannon. This required between 6 and 8 pounds of expensive copper per shell but remained the most common expansion system until the end of the war. The plate frequently separated on firing, endangering anyone in front. The large Brooke rifles tended to use a ratchet or "Tennessee" sabot – a cupped copper plate secured by seven or so grooves in its base. One type of Confederate ammunition, however, remained unique. The ironworks at Tredegar manufactured some shells from coiled bars of wrought iron with a built-in groove. This was first compressed and then expanded to fit the rifling when the shell was fired.

The Confederates' English Whitworth cannon were employed in siege operations where their long range and great penetration enabled them to sweep a large proportion of a trench line. Union heavy artillerymen reported the morale-lowering effect produced by the eerie sound of a Whitworth bolt in flight and the way the subsequent explosion mangled men and horses. The Confederates supplemented their supply of finely made British ammunition with some homemade Whitworth bolts. Although crude by comparison with the imported bolts, they worked effectively. Confederates attempts to copy the Whitworth shell were rather less successful; they had little powder inside and broke into only two or three large fragments when they detonated.

TOP: *24-pdr siege gun on carriage*
The 24-pdr siege gun's carriage weighed 2522 lb without implements. The total weight of the gun, carriage, and limber was 10,155 lb and it required a 10-horse team to pull it. The wheels were 60 inches in diameter and the limbered-up carriage was 23 ft 5 inches long.

ABOVE: *10-inch siege mortar on carriage*
Mortars could not be mounted on wheeled carriages. The violent recoil of a mortar fired at an elevation of 45 degrees would have snapped the axles. Mortars were transported on special wagons which had a windlass at the front to winch the mortar on board.

Mortars

The massed siege guns at Petersburg and Richmond were never used to batter away at the Confederate lines in the manner of a World War I preparatory bombardment. It was recognized that nothing less than a 100-pound shell could inflict any real damage on earth parapets, and even these were ineffective if the defenders were able to keep repairing the damage. Instead, the heavy rifled guns were employed in direct support of Union assaults or to suppress Confederate artillery. Long-range fire against the Petersburg bridges was also conducted but there was to be no attempt at levelling the defenses by shellfire alone.

Only one weapon could continue to inflict casualties on an army sheltering in stoutly constructed earthworks with overhead cover: the siege mortar. In size and appearance little different from the first medieval bombards, Civil War mortars were able to lob very powerful explosive shells directly into enemy positions. Like the heavy cannon, they were divided into "siege" and "seacoast" classes for the same reason. The latter were larger and much heavier weapons designed to occupy a shore battery permanently, while the siege mortars were just light enough to be carried by wagon and maneuvered into position against enemy fieldworks.

The lightest and most widely used mortar of the war was the Coehorn. Named after its seventeenth-century Dutch inventor, this was a stubby 16.3-inch bronze tube with a caliber of 5.82 inches. Designated a 24-pounder, it actually fired 17-pound shells containing a 1-pound bursting charge. Whereas the Confederacy did not inherit many larger mortars in 1860, it did manufacture its own Coehorns in both 12- and 24-pounder varieties. Confederate ammunition was considered superior in one respect: they added little "ears" to the rounds near the fuse hole. These allowed the gunners to lower the shell into the tube with hooks, ensuring that the fuse faced away from the charge and thus preventing premature explosions. The 24-pounder Coehorn's tube weighed 165 pounds and it was fired from a 131-pound wooden bed. The whole 269-pound burden could be moved and fired by a four-man crew. Its range of 1200 yards allowed it to reach into enemy defenses but it was usually fired from near the front line to maximize its accuracy. The Army of the Potomac brought eight Coehorns with it for the campaign of 1864 and they were used in the field during the battle of Cold Harbor.

The 8- and 10-inch siege mortars were made of iron and fired 44.5- and 87.5-pound shells respectively. Maximum ranges were 1200 and

Siege Artillery

2100 yards. The 10-inch seacoast mortar was much larger, weighing 5775 pounds compared to the 1852 pounds of the siege weapon of the same caliber. Its tube was 46 instead of 28 inches long and used a 10-pound instead of a 4-pound charge of propellant. Although it also fired an 87.5-pound shell, its maximum range was 4250 yards. Its primary purpose was to land its shells on the decks of enemy warships and the range was needed to match the ever-increasing range of naval ordnance.

The famous mortar "Dictator", used by the Federals during the Petersburg campaign, was an 1861 model, 13-inch seacoast mortar. This was the largest mortar used during the war and Union forces employed handfuls of them in several siege operations. Although three times the weight of the 10-inch seacoast, it was much better designed and easier to maneuver into position. Its first appearance was in the lines before Yorktown in 1862. Firing shells weighing up to 220 pounds using a 20-pound charge of propellant, it could lob them to 4350 yards when elevated to 45 degrees.

Mortars were employed by both sides during the operations around Yorktown in early 1862. The Union siege guns were established in position under constant harassing fire from an 8-inch siege mortar in Confederate hands. The Union gunners found the experience very disagreeable and the morale effect of mortar fire was to be demonstrated in several subsequent siege operations. The Confederates found themselves in a serious dilemma when the armies dug in around Petersburg with just a few hundred yards between the trenches. The proximity of numerically superior forces compelled them to concentrate their infantry in or near the front line, but the Union artillery deployed their siege mortars as rapidly as they could and opened fire. Shells landed with deadly effect inside the crowded defenses. Major Abbot of the US Army Engineers observed a Confederate soldier blown clean out of the parapet. His body lay in no man's land, clothing on fire, while Union snipers prevented any possibility of retrieving the body.

The digging of the canal at Dutch Gap led Union and Confederate mortars to exchange a heavy fire. The Confederates certainly had a good target and rained a steady stream of large-caliber mortar shells on to the works. But heavy counter-battery fire from the Union siege mortars drove the Confederates to move their mortars behind clumps of trees on the low-lying right bank of the James River. This protected them from Union shelling but deprived them of a direct line of sight to the digging. Without a

clear view of the target they were compelled to fire blind. Although they got the bearing exactly right, they misjudged the range and landed almost all their shells short.

The Confederate shelling of the Dutch Gap was mainly the work of four or five mortars at a time, mostly the diminutive Coehorns. The Union response included both 8- and 10-inch siege and seacoast mortars with their fire directed from the high signal tower at Crows Nest. Field guns fired spherical case and shell into likely areas where Confederate observers were spotting for their mortars.

The iron mortars were solid and reliable weapons which proved capable of protracted firing with no sign of damage to the vent. At Petersburg some of the 8-inch mortars fired over 2000 rounds without difficulty and not a single one burst.

The 1861 model mortars demonstrated a marked superiority over the older weapons. Elevating bars working from a fixed fulcrum on a ratchet replaced the quoins formerly used and allowed much finer adjustment of the elevation. A reshaped chamber enabled them to reach much longer ranges.

The high trajectory and relatively low velocity of the mortar rounds meant they took some time to reach their targets and the large shells could be seen in flight. The 10-inch seacoast mortar's 98-pound shell took 36 seconds to reach its maximum range of 4250 yards while the 10-inch siege mortar's 90-pound shell took 21 seconds to reach 2100 yards. With the tubes elevated to 45 degrees the gunners altered the range by reducing the propellant charge. The 10-inch siege mortar required a 1-pound charge to lob a shell to its minimum range of 300 yards. The charge increased in 8-ounce increments for ranges of 700, 1000, 1300, 1600, 1800, and 2100 yards.

The diminutive Coehorn could cut its range to as little as 25 yards by using a ½-ounce charge to fire the 17-pound shell. This increased to a maximum of 8 pounds to reach 1200 yards.

Artillerymen on both sides lamented the fact that whereas the better rifled muskets came equipped with excellent adjustable sights, large cannon were still provided with the crudest sighting devices imaginable. For the mortar crews there was an added complication. It was essential to get the mortar's platform exactly level: if it canted even slightly, accuracy suffered badly. Getting the weapon level was a painstaking business, which would have been easier if an exact mark had been provided on the mortar base itself. In the absence of such a mark the artillerymen had to use a level and mark the mortar with a chalk line.

Although slow match was still used by the siege artillery – and was a sensible precaution when firing suspect cannon liable to burst – friction primers were normally preferred because they were safer, easier to use, and did not illuminate the battery position at night. Unfortunately, even the 1861 model siege mortars were not equipped to take friction primers. There was no guide provided to keep the lanyard perpendicular to the vent and no cap to prevent the metallic cap of the primer flying off when it fired. The enterprising US gunners rigged wires to the mortar bed to allow the use of the lanyard, but there was no way of stopping the primer cap. One Union officer lost an eye during the operations against Richmond and several other artillerymen suffered cuts. The Ordnance Department belatedly approved changes but they did not take place until the war was over.

The 10-inch seacoast mortar's tube weighed 5775 pounds but the most famous siege weapon

Siege guns were placed in some difficult firing positions during the war, but the "Swamp Angel" was in one of the toughest. This 200-pdr Parrott rifle was dragged through the swamp on Morris Island by 450 soldiers. Its firing platform was built by ramming logs 20 feet down into the mud to reach solid ground. Some 800 tons of earth in 13,000 sandbags furnished a battery position able to take the weight of the gun. After all this effort, the gun exploded after shelling Charleston for a day.

of the war, the 13-inch seacoast, weighed an incredible 17,120 pounds. This was not thought to be a problem when it was designed since it was intended for a purely static role. The one named "Dictator" was in action at Petersburg for several months and fired from several positions, finishing its brief service near the captured Confederate Battery No. 5. Although maneuvering this immense weapon did not prove to be as difficult as might have been anticipated, the Union artillerymen hit upon a novel idea for a mobile firing platform. The mortar was placed on an ordinary eight-wheel railroad platform car strengthened with beams and iron rods. When hoisted on board, the mortar stood 9 feet above the track.

Run down the Petersburg and City Point Railroad to a spot near the Union front line, it was positioned on a curve in the track. By moving it back and forth the artillerymen could traverse it far more easily than with a siege mortar sitting on a conventional platform. Firing its shell with a 14-pound charge of powder, it recoiled about 24 inches on the car, which was driven 10–12 feet back up the track. The gunners were pleased to discover that even with a full 20-pound charge the axles were able to take the strain without any sign of damage.

Dictator's shells were able to crush and bury a dug-out like no other weapon. Its fire was credited with stopping Confederate batteries on the Chesterfield Heights, shelling the right end of the Union lines. During the Battle of the Crater one shell was observed to score a direct hit on a Confederate gun position, blowing the entire gun and its carriage out of its parapet from a range of 3600 yards.

At the beginning of the war mortars were equipped solely with common shell exploded by time or percussion fuses. But in 1863 Major Henry L. Abbot, US Corps of Engineers, applied to the commander of the Washington Arsenal to experiment with spherical case rounds. A series of test firings were arranged during the fall at Fort Scott, part of the capital's defenses south of the Potomac. An 1861 model 10-inch siege mortar fired standard mortar shells filled with the 27 cast-iron balls from a 12-pounder canister round, plus a 2½-pound bursting charge. The shell itself weighed 90 pounds and each canister ball averaged 0.43 pounds to produce a total weight of 104 pounds. Fired with a 22-ounce charge, the round took 13 seconds to reach the target, which lay 850 yards away and some 150 feet lower than the firing platform.

The bursting charge was just sufficient to shatter the metal casing, blowing the canister balls out in a cone-shaped pattern to impact in a circle. The diameter of the circle was found approximately to equal the height at which the shell detonated. This was in sharp contrast to a spherical case round from a field gun which sprayed its contents forward, missing completely if it exploded even a little way beyond the target. The canister balls proved to have enough force to penetrate 3–7 inches of turf. Their velocity was calculated to be 200 feet per second – enough to inflict serious injury on a human target. As the mortar was able to lob its

spherical case rounds with such precision, it was recognized that it would be better than spherical case shell at striking enemy troops behind breastworks or in batteries.

The experiments were judged to be successful and the spherical case mortar shells were employed in action for the first time during the Battle of the Crater. A battery of 10 10-inch mortars fired on a Confederate artillery battery 800 yards distant that was able to lay its guns against the flanks of the assaulting columns. As soon as the mortars found the exact charge that exploded their shells directly above the target, the Confederate gunners were compelled to cease fire. With 10 mortars firing, the Union artillerymen could explode a shell over them every 30 seconds, so the battery was silenced.

The spherical case mortar rounds continued to be used after the Battle of the Crater, but with further experience the artillerymen found them disagreeably prone to premature explosions. Many gunners attributed these to the concussion of firing acting on the filling of loose gunpowder and iron balls. However, it may well have been due to the long fuse plug jolting loose and firing the bursting charge immediately. The obvious answer was to manufacture them properly by fixing the iron balls as in conventional spherical case shot instead of making them up in the field. Experiments with smaller caliber mortar rounds did not prove successful – they lacked interior space for enough powder and balls to be effective. Filling the Coehorn shell with powder and musket balls was tried by both sides but did not work. Union gunners were sometimes struck by small iron balls from Confederate 12-pounder spherical case shot that lacked enough velocity to cause more than a bruise. Unless the individual balls weighed 6 ounces or more, they were unlikely to inflict much damage.

Both Union and Confederate artillerymen introduced new mortar ammunition. The Federals tried the Pevey patent mortar shell, which consisted of a single casting making two concentric shells connected by studs. The center was filled with the bursting charge, the outer with small iron balls. They were fired by 8- and 10-inch mortars and worked well with no premature explosions, even when a 10-inch seacoast let one go with a 7-pound charge behind it. Pevey shells exploded with much greater fragmentation effect than common shell, although they were not as lethal as the spherical case rounds.

The most bizarre siege mortar round was McIntyre's repeating shell. Also tried by the Union gunners, this consisted of two or three concentric shells so arranged that the explosion of one fired a fuse to detonate the next and the next. McIntyre used a modified time fuse which managed to achieve the desired effect. A few rounds were test-fired by the siege train at Yorktown after the Confederate evacuation and the double detonation effect recommended the projectile as a potentially useful way of penetrating and destroying enemy powder magazines. McIntyre supplied some double-bursting 24-pounder shells and some triple-bursting 10-inch ammunition which arrived in the

Union lines before Petersburg just before the end of the war. Only a few rounds seem to have been fired but they did work as advertised.

Confederate innovation did not end with the ears they added to their mortar shells in place of the tin straps used by Union gunners. The Confederates manufactured their mortar shells with the interior surface forming a polyhedron instead of a sphere. When the bursting charge detonated, the casing fractured along the edges, producing a much better fragmentation effect than Union shells, which often split into a few large chunks rather than the desired hail of fragments. Two patterns were used, the first a dodecahedron, the second two pentagons connected by 10 even-sized trapezoids. Both types were supposed to shatter into 12 fragments, but the latter did not work so well because the trapezoids tended to split off in pairs.

The Union Army anticipated Confederate night attacks on their siege lines. A daring sortie which captured a battery even for a few minutes could put it out of action for days or weeks by spiking the guns or exploding charges to blow them from their carriages. To help deal with the threat, the mortars were supplied with illumination rounds. Fired from 8-inch siege mortars, these 12¼-pound projectiles burned for about 10 minutes. Applying the usual rule of thumb for propellant charges – one 25th the weight of the ball – the gunners employed an 8-ounce charge to lob the incendiary ball 350 yards. However, they discovered that its range was limited to 250 yards because when it was fired any further it broke up on impact and did not burn properly.

Tests of accuracy showed that a 10-inch mortar could drop 60 percent of its rounds within 40 yards of a target half a mile away. At the same range an 8-inch mortar landed 50 percent within 50 yards and a Coehorn scored 50 percent within 80 yards, although this range was known to be a little too far for it. These figures were determined by careful firing from batteries of the Washington defenses.

The long flight-time of mortar shells rendered them vulnerable to the influence of the wind, which made it hard to judge exactly how long to cut the fuse. Mortar fire during the siege of Pulaski was frustrated by a stiff crosswind that blew the shells off target. This difficulty and the lack of proper sights made it essential for Civil War mortars to be fired *en masse* if they were to achieve their full potential. The Confederate bombardment of Fort Sumter involved about 20 10-inch mortars firing from ranges of between 1000 and 1900 yards. After six to eight hours of steady firing, they were able to judge the range exactly and landed two out of three shells right inside the fort, bursting them at the level of the upper tier and preventing Sumter's barbette batteries from replying.

The key to accurate mortar firing, as with any form of shooting, was to eliminate as many sources of variation as possible. Mortars did not use fixed ammunition (it was considered dangerous to have live rounds in close proximity to them), so the shell casings were stored outside the battery magazine and filled with powder when required.

Siege Artillery

Smoothbore siege gun ammunition
RIGHT: *Solid shot fired by Civil War siege artillery shown here in proportion.*

BELOW: *Mortar and artillery shells (same scale).*

Smoothbore siege guns were designed to batter down the brick and stone walls of early nineteenth-century fortifications. Firing as close as possible – ideally from within 200 yards – their solid shot would steadily crumble the walls until an infantry assault was possible. Their performance under service conditions (rather than test firing) was measured during the siege of Fort Pulaski: 8-inch Columbiad smoothbores penetrated 11 inches into the brick walls at a range of 1740 yards, while the 10-inch Columbiad penetrated 13 inches. This compared poorly with the rifled guns: Parrott 30-pdrs penetrated 18 inches, while old 42-pdrs banded and rifled put their 84-lb James rifle shot through 26 inches of wall. The calculations for breaching fort walls were a precise science perfected by years of siege operations. British studies from the Peninsular War estimated that a rubble wall backed by earth required 254,400 lb of solid shot for every 100 feet of breach. This assumed the use of 24-pdr cannon at 500 yards.

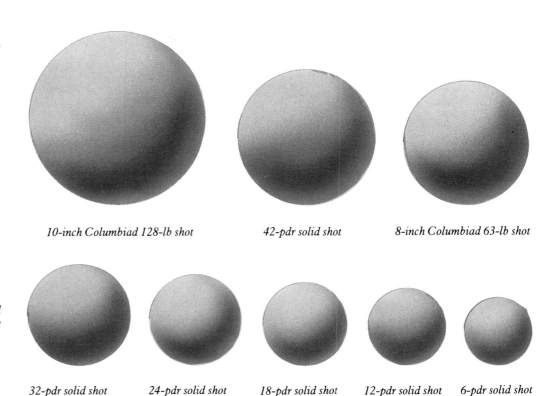

10-inch Columbiad 128-lb shot   *42-pdr solid shot*   *8-inch Columbiad 63-lb shot*

32-pdr solid shot   *24-pdr solid shot*   *18-pdr solid shot*   *12-pdr solid shot*   *6-pdr solid shot*

*8-inch mortar shell
(weight: 44.5 lb; diameter: 7.9 inches)*

*10-inch mortar shell
(weight: 88 lb; diameter: 9.9 inches)*

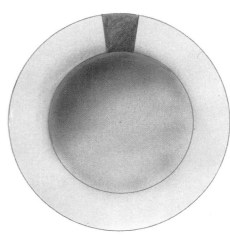

*13-inch mortar shell
(weight: 197 lb; diameter: 12.9 inches)*

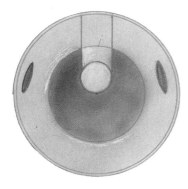

*10-inch carcass
(an incendiary round primed with
quick match at the additional holes
in the casing)*

10-inch Columbiad shell (101 lb)

32-pdr howitzer shell (22.5 lb)

*32-pdr spherical case (16 lb).
Note the thinner walls:
at their thickest they were
0.65 inches, as opposed to
1 inch in a conventional shell.*

Shells and grapeshot

Smoothbore guns had no way of ensuring which side of the projectile landed first, so percussion fuses were out of the question. The shells fired from smoothbores relied on time fuses. The canister and grapeshot rounds illustrated were used during siege operations to suppress the fire of hostile batteries and to hamper working parties trying to repair damage. In defense a fort would reserve its canister ammunition to stop an infantry assault in a hail of fire. This is where light 12-pdr guns were valuable; the defenders could maneuver them within the position to repel an assault that had broken through the first line.

Individual shell casings always varied slightly in weight, so the experienced mortar crews weighed them first and added bullets or gravel to make them up to a uniform weight. To ensure the powder was similarly standardized, all the powder needed for the day was poured on to a clean surface, mixed thoroughly, and measured into the shells. Here the Confederates had another advantage because their powder measures, unlike Federal-issue ones, allowed for the density of the powder to vary and were graduated in ounces for fine adjustment. Union powder measures were fixed-size containers with no graduations marked. As they measured only the volume, not the exact weight, loose powder would produce an undercharge and compact powder would overcharge. The error could be as much as 12 percent either way.

Accurate mortar fire required a view of the target but a view serves both parties and some targets fired back. Siege guns were sometimes shrouded in screens so hostile sharpshooters could not see individual gunners to pick them off. The standard method of aiming a mortar relied on the use of a cord and plummet with stakes hammered into the top of the parapet for the gunners to take their mark from. Since planting stakes was impossible under sniper

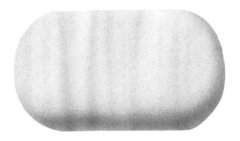

25-lb wrought-iron elongated shot.

8-inch, 102-lb projectile.

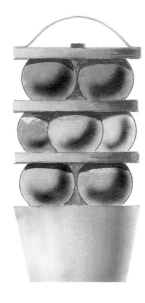

8-inch canister round for seacoast howitzer. Standing 25 inches high, this weighed 54.5 lb and contained 48 shot.

8-inch grapeshot round for the seacoast howitzer. Grape was similar to canister but usually consisted of nine balls stacked in three tiers. Their size depended on the caliber of the gun. A "stand" of grape had iron plates at top and bottom and two iron rings holding the balls in, all secured with a nut and bolt. It was widely used by naval guns for suppressing the fire of coastal batteries.

211-lb wrought-iron elongated projectile for 10-inch Columbiad.

8-inch 100-lb solid shot.

10-inch Columbiad shell with sabot strapped on. This keeps the fuse pointing down the barrel, not next to the powder charge.

32-pdr field howitzer shell with sabot.

12-pdr fixed ammunition. A complete round with powder charge attached behind the sabot. Although impractical for larger cannon, it was very useful for the lighter guns.

12-pdr canister round, consisting of 27 1.5-inch diameter iron shot packed in sawdust inside a tinned iron cylinder. The cylinder is nailed to a wooden sabot at the back. At the front it is crimped around an iron disk.

Siege Artillery

fire, some Union gunners ·developed a novel solution. They drilled two holes about 5 feet apart in a board and put sticks into them. Laying the board on the parapet, they adjusted it until the two sticks were aligned on target. Drawing a line backwards, they located another stake at the rear and placed the mortar exactly in the center. The rear stake could then be replaced by a low fence along the rear of the mortar platform with notches marked on it to show the necessary traverse needed to engage known targets. By recording the exact bearing of different enemy batteries, the mortar crew could even fire blind if necessary with reasonable hope of hitting the target.

Rifled ammunition was manufactured in an astonishing number of styles during the Civil War. Since almost all rifled cannon were loaded from the muzzle, the shells had to slip easily down the tube during loading. But unless they gripped the rifling tightly on the way back up, their accuracy would be poor. No one ever produced the ideal solution, although the war spawned a variety of methods. The Confederates alone had 10 different systems of rifling, and the search for the best continued throughout the war. Most rifling systems were variations on the same theme: a cup or sabot of brass or wrought iron fitted to the base of the shell expanded when the powder charge fired and pressed into the rifling, imparting a spin to the projectile. Sometimes the sabot would fail to expand properly and the shell would not take the rifling. Sabots often detached themselves from the shell as it exited the muzzle – a dangerous menace for friendly troops in front of the battery.

30-pdr Parrott shell
A copper or zinc fuse plug fitted in the nose. Note the sabot attached to the base.

30-pdr Parrott incendiary
Several incendiary compositions were tried but the 30-pdr shell could hold only about a pint of fluid, which was insufficient to start a good blaze.

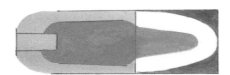

4.2-inch Reed-Parrott shell
Used by both sides in 30-pdr Parrott rifles.

4.5-inch shell
Used by the US 4.5-inch M1861 siege gun. Shown here with a lead sabot to grip the rifling.

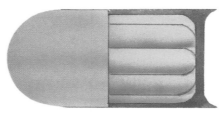

4.5-inch solid shot
This is a Dyer pattern "bolt."

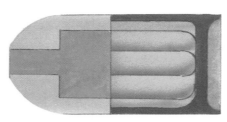

4.5-inch Dyer-pattern shell
Fitted with lead sabot.

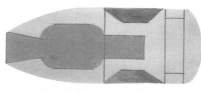

4.5-inch Absterdam shell
Absterdam shells had a hollowed lead base and two lead rings that gripped the rifling.

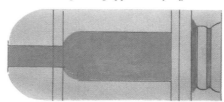

3.67-inch shell
Fired by 20-pdr Parrott rifles.

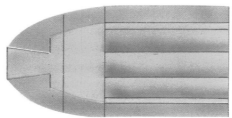

Sawyer 5.8-inch shell
This mechanically-fitting projectile was fired by the US Sawyer siege gun that exploded during the siege of Richmond.

Sawyer 3.67-inch shell
This was coated with lead, which expanded into the rifling when fired.

Stafford sub-caliber bolt
This fired an iron bolt from a wooden sabot in the same manner as modern tank guns fire high-velocity armor-piercing rounds.

Reed shell
Reed designed shells similar to the Parrott pattern for the Confederacy. They used an expanding ring of lead or copper to grip the rifling.

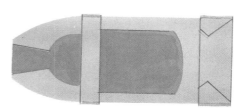

3-inch Reed shell
This has a copper rim to engage the rifling.

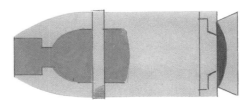

3-inch Reed-pattern shell
This has a sabot fitted. Copper screws were used to secure it to the shell.

Reed 7-inch shell
Reed-pattern shells were used for the heaviest siege guns, as well as field artillery.

Reed 3.7-inch shell
Fired by 20-pdr Parrot rifles in Confederate service.

Reed 3.67-inch shell
Fitted with a wrought-iron cup to engage the rifling.

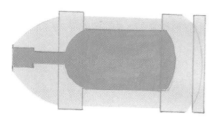

Reed 6.4-inch shell
Wrought-iron cup and wooden fuse plug.

Reed 3.67-inch shot
Also fitted with a wrought-iron cup.

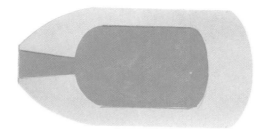

Reed 6.4-inch shell
Wrought-iron cup on the base and a threaded brass ring in the nose to receive the fuse plug.

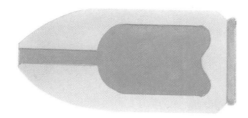

Parrott 8-inch shell
The heaviest of the siege guns used on land, some captured and copied by the Confederacy.

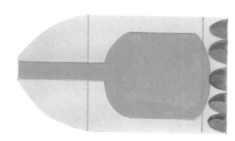

Parrott 8-inch shell (CSA)
A Confederate version manufactured at Tredegar, fitted with a copper ring.

Parrott 8-inch bolt
Primarily used by seacoast batteries or naval guns to batter the armor of ironclad warships.

Parrott 4.2-inch shell
The most successful type of rifled shell. In the siege of Richmond 96 percent of Parrott 30-pdr shells took the rifling properly.

Canister was frequently used against infantry at a quarter of a mile range with deadly effect, especially in the type of country, often wooded, in which many civil war battles were fought. Unfortunately, canister could not be fired over the heads of friendly troops as the canister would discharge lethal shot over its own infantry. The Wiard canister (below) was one way of overcoming this problem.

Wiard's canister for field artillery 1863
As well as using Hotchkiss shot, shell, and case for his rifled guns, Wiard developed a unique canister, which did not scatter too early in flight. The projectile was made up of a cast-iron case divided into a maximum of 10 sections, loaded with shot and held together with wire. Small holes in the base let discharged gas pass into the projectile, forcing the canister to stretch along its length, so allowing pressure to drop along its sides, which reduced the tendency to expand the rifling, a common fault with canister fired rifled ordnance.

Siege Artillery

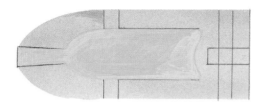

Confederate Mullane 4.62-inch shell

Mullane 7-inch bolt

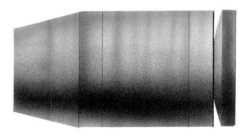

Mullane 8-inch bolt

Mullane 5.8-inch shell

Mullane 7-inch bolt

Brooke 8-inch bolt

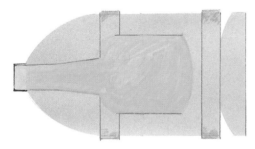

Mullane 6.4-inch bolt

Mullane 7-inch shell

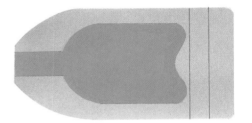

Brooke 7-inch case
This could also be used as a shell.

Mullane 6.4-inch shell

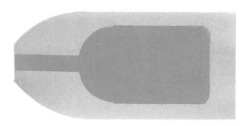

Mullane 6.4-inch shell

Brooke 7-inch shell

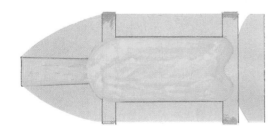

Mullane 6.4-inch shell

Mullane 4.62-inch shell
Conventional Mullane projectiles had heavy copper cups, up to 8lb in the heavier rounds.

Brooke 7-inch shell
Note side fuse and heavy weight of nose cap. These shells were used against ironclads.

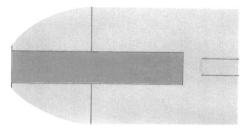

Brooke 7-inch case
Tin tube with bursting charge was soldered direct to fuse plug.

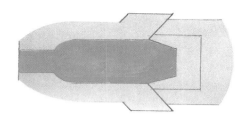

Hotchkiss 3-inch shell with lead bands
8-inch wrought-iron bolt

8-inch wrought-iron bolt

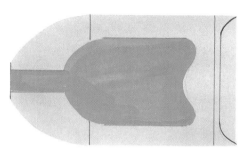

Brooke 8-inch shell

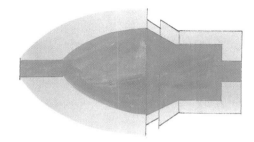

Hotchkiss 5.3-inch shell

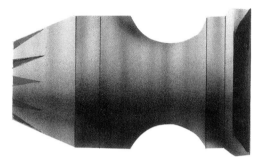

6.4-inch curved bolt

Brooke 4.2-inch shell

Quinlivan 7-inch wrought-iron shot

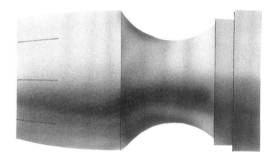

6.4-inch curved bolt

Brooke 4.2-inch shell

6.4-inch wrought-iron bolt

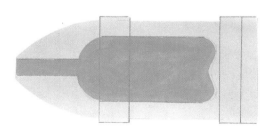

Brooke 7-inch shell

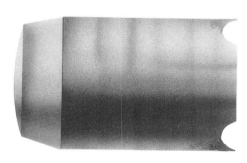

7-inch wrought-iron bolt
Used by Confederate fleet in James River with some success.

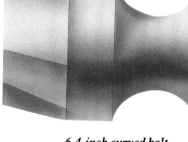

6.4-inch curved bolt

Seacoast and Naval Ordnance

Since 1811 the US Army had defended the American coast with Columbiad smoothbore cannon. Over the years new versions were developed until, by the time of the Civil War, there were seven different types in service. The 1844 pattern 8-inch and 10-inch Columbiads were complemented by 1858 pattern weapons in the same caliber. The former were in widespread service in the Southern states and many were subsequently rifled and banded by the Confederates.

Columbiads of the 1861 pattern were often referred to as "Rodmans" for the US ordnance lieutenant (later brigadier-general) Thomas Jefferson Rodman who invented a new system of casting them to give greater strength. Casting very large barrels had proved difficult since the outside cooled quickly while the inside remained hot. The dramatic difference in temperature imposed enormous stress which could crack the tube. Rodman's solution was to cast the tube around an air-and-water-cooled core. With their flat breeches and smoother lines, his guns are easily distinguished from the round, bottle-shaped Columbiads.

The Confederates acquired some Rodmans but also copied them in both 8-inch and 10-inch calibers. The War Department asked Rodman to develop a 15-inch gun in 1860, and the quest for greater power against an armored warship eventually led to a demand for a 20-inch cannon. But here the designers encountered enormous problems. Casting such huge barrels – the 15-inch Rodman tube weighed 25 tons – was still very difficult. Eventually, Rodman succeeded in casting a 20-inch caliber cannon which fired four test rounds from Fort Hamilton in New York harbor before the end of the war. The tube itself weighed 58.5 tons and its solid shot projectile weighed 1080 pounds. Fired again in 1867, ultimately using a 200-pound charge of gunpowder, it proved able to reach 8000 yards at 25 degrees' elevation. By comparison, the 15-inch Rodman could fire its 300-pound shell to 4680 yards using a 50-pound charge.

Seacoast mortars were employed against land defenses from ashore, as described earlier, but also from mortar boats. Heavily-built, flat-bottomed craft with boiler-plate sides to keep out rifle bullets, the "bummers," as they were

ABOVE: *Columbiad smoothbore cannon: 50-pdr, 10-inch (cutaway), and 10-inch mounted on wooden barbette carriage. Introduced in 1811, these were the standard seacoast defense guns until the Civil War. Using an 18-lb charge, the 10-inch Columbiad could fire its 128-lb solid shot to 1800 yards at an elevation of 5 degrees. The tube itself weighed 15,400-lb. Some of the 1844 pattern 8- and 10-inch Columbiads in the South were banded and rifled by the Confederacy. The bore was 99 inches long on the 1844 pattern. The 1861 Rodmans increased this to 101 inches and reduced overall weight by 400 lb.*

BELOW: *The largest seacoast gun was the Blakely 12.75-inch muzzleloading rifle. It weighed 54,000 lb and fired a 700-pound projectile using a 50-lb powder charge. This particular piece was used by the Confederates at Charleston. The ammunition was manufactured with studs along the sides, which engaged in six deep grooves in the tube.*

ABOVE: *Ames Navy 5.1-inch rifle*
The Ames company developed several wrought-iron rifles, but wrought-iron barrels cost nearly 10 times more than cast-iron barrels. This 5.1-inch 50-pdr weighed 5500 lb.

Ames 7-inch seacoast
Tested in the fall of 1864, this 125-pdr won high praise from the normally critical Army Board. Elevated to 30 degrees, it reached a maximum range of 8960 yards, but welding techniques of the 1860s could not guarantee consistent performance, so ultimately only a handful of these expensive guns were ordered.

In 1840 Daniel Treadwell developed a method of construction which involved building up a series of wrought-iron rings welded together and reinforced by bands. It took three years to set up the furnaces before construction of light guns could commence, but his weapons, although completely successful in tests, were thought too expensive by the authorities. In 1863 Treadwell lost a suit for damages filed against Parrott, whom he accused of copying his ideas, and he lost interest in further work on weapons. The 6.4-inch smoothbore shown fired a 32-lb projectile.

Attick 7-inch seacoast
This was mounted in the Stevens Battery. A 42-pdr rifled and banded, it was tested with 14- and 16-lb charges firing 100-pdr James projectiles. It burst after a brief period of test firing.

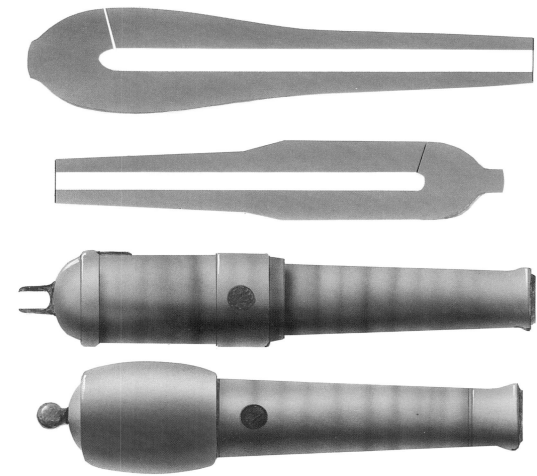

known to the Union fleet, were widely used to reduce Confederate river forts. Armed with a single 10- or 13-inch mortar, these craft could manage about one round every 10 minutes. The recoil was so severe that the crew stood aft with their mouths open every time it fired. The black powder spread everywhere until the crew looked like coal miners emerging from a long shift underground.

The vertical fire of mortars was designed to destroy ships by crashing a shell through the deck. They had the added advantage that it was

very difficult for a warship to suppress a mortar battery. Whereas a large warship could steam past a fort, raking the parapet with grapeshot to keep the gunners from their pieces, a mortar could still be fired over the parapet. The US Army engineer Colonel Abbot argued that Fort Fisher might have beaten off the final US attack had the Confederates had enough mortars. They could have prevented the US Navy anchoring monitors close offshore and sweeping the Confederates off their parapet.

To land a mortar round on a moving ship

(even a large one moving slowly) proved exceedingly difficult. The range had to be judged exactly. Even firing against a large fort, the mortars would miss more times than they hit during the opening stages of a bombardment. Provided the wind did not change dramatically, the gunners would eventually be able to adjust their charge sufficiently and then shell after shell could drop on to the target. Although Union ironclads sometimes added heaps of sandbags to their upper decks when engaging Confederate shore batteries, they did

BELOW: *The 15-inch Rodman was the ultimate Columbiad-type to be produced in quantity. Lieutenant Thomas J. Rodman invented a new method of casting cannon that gave the iron barrels greater strength. Columbiad guns built to his design were entering service in 1861 in 8-, 10-, and 15-inch calibers.*

The 15-inch Rodman fired a 428-lb shot, but it is unlikely that they were ever fired in anger; these monstrous guns were depolyed to defend Northern ports, and in the defenses of Washington and Alexandria. The Rodman is illustrated here on the wrought-iron, center-pintle barbette carriages widely used in the North. The Confederates produced their own Rodmans, but only in 8- and 10-inch calibers.

Seacoast and Naval Ordnance

not run foul of Rebel mortars. In fact, it was the Confederate gunboat *Drewry* (also spelt *Drury* in some accounts) that demonstrated the disagreeable effect of a mortar hit. During the James River squadrons operations in January 1865, she ran aground and was fired on by several Union batteries. A mortar shell, which smashed through her deck, penetrated to her magazine and blew up the whole ship with terrific force.

River and coastal batteries were also equipped with 6.4-inch caliber 32-pounder and 7-inch 42-pounder seacoast guns. Many of the forts surrounding Washington D.C. were equipped with 32-pounders on wooden bar-

bette carriages. The 1829 model featured a breeching loop on the cascable so that it could be used aboard a ship. Both these cast-iron smoothbore cannon saw a great deal of action in Confederate service. At an elevation of 5 degrees they could reach a range of 1922 and 1955 yards respectively. With their enthusiasm for rifled artillery, the Confederates banded and rifled these guns using the James rifling. Instead of 32-pound spherical shot, the 32-pounder could then fire 64-pound projectiles. The 42-pounder became the James 84-pounder.

In addition to these American guns, the Confederates imported a small number of Armstrong muzzle loading rifles. The 8.5-inch

caliber 150-pounder demonstrated the advantage of a rifle. At 15,737 pounds, it was just over 300 pounds heavier than the 10-inch Columbiad, but it fired a heavier shell to a much greater velocity with a similar charge. The giant smoothbores used by the US Army and Navy were not efficient at penetrating armor, despite their enormous weight. By the end of the war, the British Royal Navy was arming its warships with 9-inch Armstrong rifles able to penetrate over 11 inches of wrought-iron armor. The US Navy's 15-inch Dahlgrens were the last and greatest of the smoothbore guns taken to sea, but they could not match the performance of the large-caliber rifles that were appearing during the 1860s.

Dahlgrens were the US Navy's standard cannon by 1860. Rear-Admiral John A. Dahlgren joined the navy in 1826 and ultimately commanded the South Atlantic Blockading Squadron during the war. In 1847 he commanded the Ordnance Workshop in the Washington Navy Yard and began working on improved guns capable of firing either shot or shell. By the 1850s 9-inch smoothbore guns of his design were the standard broadside gun in the navy. These were soon supplemented by 10- and 11-inch weapons.

What might have happened had Dahlgren's 11-inch guns on *Monitor* been allowed to fire with full 30-pound charges when she engaged *Virginia* remains one of the war's unanswerable questions. The apparent failure of the 11-inch Dahlgren in Hampton Roads was an added spur to the development of the 15-inch gun. Rodman was already working on a land pattern weapon; Dahlgren soon developed an enlarged smoothbore of his own, but he too encountered great difficulties in casting such large tubes and the rate of production of 15-inch Dahlgren naval guns was slower than anticipated. The *Passaic*-class monitors ended up with only one 15-inch gun instead of the planned two and had to substitute 11-inch Dahlgrens or 8-inch Parrott rifles.

The screw frigate USS *Merrimack* steamed to Norfolk, Virginia, in 1860 for an urgently needed refit. She was armed with two 10-inch, 24 9-inch, and 14 8-inch Dahlgren smoothbores. When the Confederates converted her to the ironclad *Virginia*, they retained some of the 9-inch guns they had captured, shipping six on either broadside. But in her bow and stern they mounted specially designed rifled guns. The Confederate Navy Department, led by the highly capable Stephen R. Mallory, asked Brooke to produce 7-inch caliber rifled cannon for *Virginia* and in due course the Tredegar Ironworks cast six of them. Brooke then designed a 6.4-inch rifle and a contract for 12 of these went to Tredegar as well. His later designs included 8-inch rifles, as well as 11- and 12-inch smoothbores.

Unlike the US Navy, which concentrated on ever-larger smoothbore guns, the Confederates recognised the advantages of rifled cannon, and the 6.4- and 7-inch rifles became practically the standard armament of Confederate casemate ironclads. This was a conscious decision, not

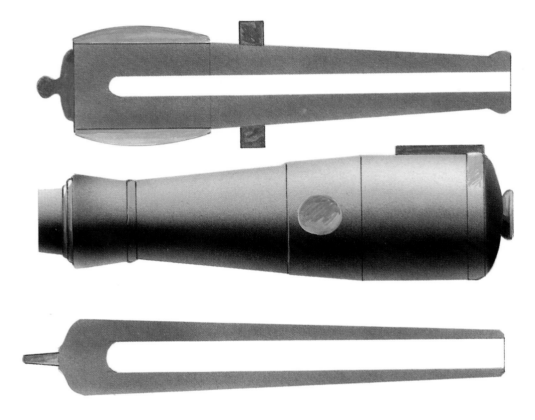

TOP (CUTAWAY): *Attick seacoast 7-inch*
The Attick's composition was a trade secret, but the band was believed to be made of bronze, forced on by hydrostatic pressure. Later methods of banding and rifling 42-pdrs proved more successful.

CENTER: *Bomford 12-inch seacoast*
Colonel George Bomford, inventor of the Columbiad cannon, also designed this monstrous cast-iron smoothbore. Cast in Boston during 1846, it weighed 25,500 lb and fired a 181-lb shot to 5800 yards using a 28-lb powder charge. It was not adopted for service, although it was reinforced with a 1-inch iron band in 1861.

ABOVE (CUTAWAY): *Stockton 12-inch Navy*
Commodore Robert F. Stockton designed this wrought-iron smoothbore. Only three were made: the first and third in England, the second in the USA. The US-made one exploded aboard USS Princeton *in 1844, nearly killing President John Tyler. The third gun was built in 1845, but the navy was now set against wrought-iron weapons, believing them to be fatally flawed. Welding was not consistent enough: one gun might be perfect, but the next one could explode after a couple of shots.*

one born of necessity. When Union forces abandoned the Norfolk Navy Yard with precipitate haste, they left some 300 Dahlgren naval guns behind. These were employed all over the Confederacy, but the Confederate Navy preferred muzzleloading rifles.

Brooke's rifles proved effective weapons in service. At 300 yards the 8-inch rifle could penetrate 3 inches of iron armor plate inclined at 60 degrees and travel another 5 inches into the wooden backing behind. Against wooden ships they were deadly, although poor ammunition saved several Union ships. *Hartford* was struck by a shell from *Tennessee* that hit one of her masts butt first and failed to detonate. Crew

TOP RIGHT: ***Blakely seacoast 12.75-inch***
The biggest rifled guns in the Confederacy, two of these English cannon were brought across the Atlantic standing upright because they were too large for the steamer's cargo hold. Built of cast iron with a bronze air chamber in the breech, they also had a steel band over the powder chamber. At an elevation of 2 degrees it fired 470-lb shells over 2000 yards. Unfortunately, the ammunition proved unreliable, and these enormous and expensive (£10,000 each) weapons were never fired in anger. Both were blown up by the Confederates when Charleston was evacuated.

RIGHT: ***Dahlgren guns*** (*in proportion*)
Lieutenant John A. Dahlgren began testing naval guns at the Washington Navy Yard in 1847. Carefully measuring barrel pressures when guns were fired, he soon designed his own cannon. The first model was cast in 1850: a large smoothbore capable of firing shot or shell. The first gun was a 9-inch caliber weapon weighing 9080 lb. It proved successful but Dahlgren modified the design, installing two firing vents each with a hammer lock for friction tubes. His guns were adopted as the main armament of larger US warships before the war. Dahlgren was promoted to captain and his 11- and later 15-inch guns were used to arm the monitors.

Although an acknowledged ordnance expert, Dahlgren was anxious for a major command but was held back by the regulation that only officers voted the thanks of Congress could be promoted to rear-admiral. In February 1863 he was given the thanks of Congress for his work and Lincoln promoted him and sent him to take over command of the South Atlantic Squadron.

BOTTOM RIGHT: ***Whitworth 5-inch rifle***
Two of these British steel rifles were captured by Union forces from a blockade runner off Charleston. Installed in the "naval battery" on Morris Island, they were used in the bombardment of Fort Sumter. One was disabled at the 111th round, when the inner cylinder slipped backward through the outer jacket and blocked the vent.

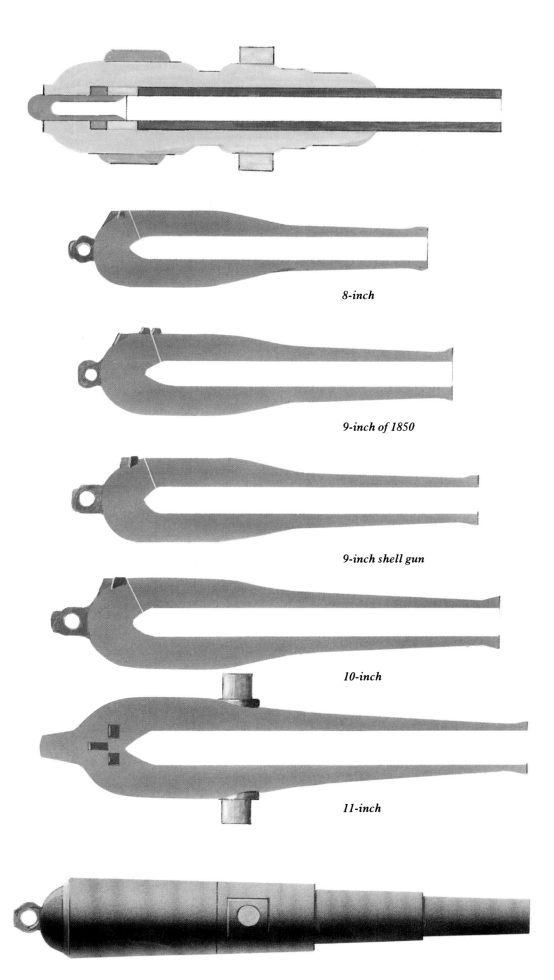

8-inch

9-inch of 1850

9-inch shell gun

10-inch

11-inch

Seacoast and Naval Ordnance

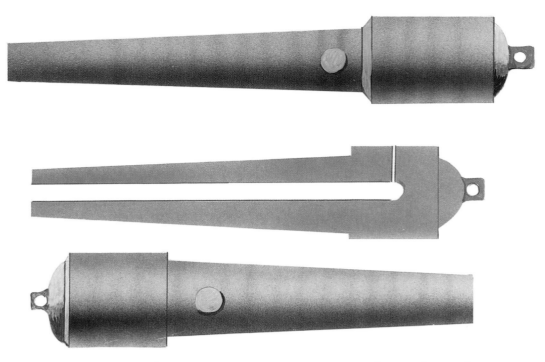

TOP: *6.4-inch Parrott rifle*
Widely used by the navy, these 100-pdr rifles had a bad reputation for bursting. The army's 6.4-inch rifles were 151 inches long, but navy ones were 20 inches shorter to enable them to be worked on a narrow deck. Navy Parrotts have an anchor instead of "US" on the tube between the trunnions.

CENTER: *8-inch Parrott rifle*
Over 50 Parrott rifles burst during the Union bombardments of the defenses of Charleston. Most of the 8-inch Parrotts broke at the vent.

ABOVE: *10-inch Parrott rifle*
Only three of these saw action, all at Morris Island off Charleston. The first one to arrive fired several 300-lb shells, then blew 18 inches off its own muzzle. However, it was chipped smooth and went on to fire 370 times at Fort Sumter from a range of 4290 yards.

error was another weakness; the gunners aboard *Louisiana* forgot to remove the lead patch from the fuse of a shell that penetrated *Brooklyn*'s bow 12 inches above the waterline. It penetrated 3 feet of timber and, had it detonated, *Brooklyn* would have lost her bows and undoubtedly foundered.

Brooke rifles were manufactured from cast iron with a wrought-iron hoop shrunk over the breech like a Parrott rifle. But whereas Parrott's field and seacoast cannon used one iron band, Brooke used double and sometimes triple bands to maximize their strength. Brooke's guns were considerably heavier for equivalent caliber; his 8-inch rifles weighed 11 tons to the 8¼ tons of an 8-inch Parrott. Despite this extra strength, Brooke's guns did burst on occasion. Two of the 7-inch rifles at Fort Fisher exploded during the battle on Christmas Day, 1864, wounding

several gunners. Shot and shell weights varied, the shot for his 6-inch rifles as mounted on CSS *Tennessee* weighed 95–110 pounds.

The US Navy did turn to rifled guns to supplement its Dahlgren smoothbores, but the Parrott guns it adopted were a constant source of anxiety for the men who used them. As already noted, Parrott rifles had an unfortunate tendency to burst, and while this was serious enough ashore, it could be catastrophic in the confined space of a ship's gun deck. During the first attack on Fort Fisher, more Union sailors were injured by the explosion of 100-pounder Parrott rifles than by Confederate fire.

The US Navy used 4.2-inch caliber 30-pounder Parrotts, 5.3-inch 60-pounder Parrotts, 6.4-inch 100-pounder Parrotts, and 8-inch 150-pounder Parrotts. Navy-pattern Parrott rifles were lighter than their army equivalents and had shorter barrels to make them easier to load on a gun deck where space was always at a premium.

Naval guns were fired from four main types of mounting. Cannon mounted on the broadside were either on traditional four-wheeled wooden gun carriages, or the new Marsilly carriages that dispensed with the two rear wheels. Guns were also mounted on pivots and trained on an arc of overlapping rails. Using such a system, Confederate casemate ironclads and Union warships alike often mounted a single heavy gun at bow and stern that could be trained on either beam.

The old-style, four-wheeled gun trucks shot backwards the moment the cannon was fired. A breeching rope, which passed through the hole in the gun's cascable, was attached to the ship's side and looped through a block. This helped contain the recoil, but with the increasing size of smoothbore guns it was not enough. The US Navy's solution was the Marsilly carriage, which rested its rear directly on deck. It was maneuvered on a roller in the end of a handspike, and several burly sailors leaning on the handspike could lift the rear of the carriage just enough to get it moving. Firing a large

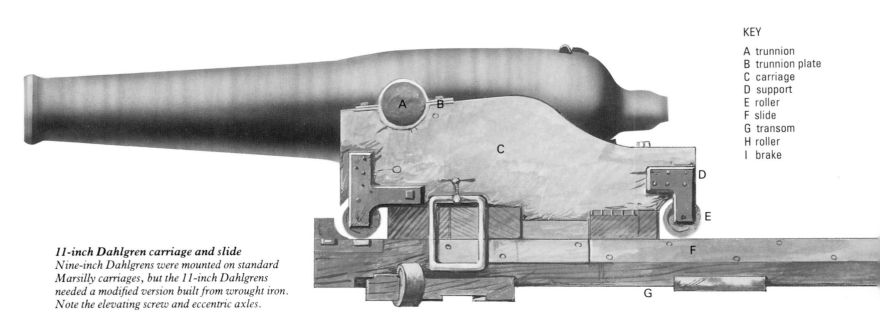

KEY
A trunnion
B trunnion plate
C carriage
D support
E roller
F slide
G transom
H roller
I brake

11-inch Dahlgren carriage and slide
Nine-inch Dahlgrens were mounted on standard Marsilly carriages, but the 11-inch Dahlgrens needed a modified version built from wrought iron. Note the elevating screw and eccentric axles.

cannon on a Marsilly carriage did not do much for the deck, especially as sand and grit were spread around to increase friction.

The guns in the turrets of the monitors used a different system. They were fixed on sliding mounts which revolved with the turret. When the guns were run in for reloading, large, wrought-iron port stoppers closed protectively over the gun port worked by a pendulum system. Getting them open again was a major physical effort, so the turret was sometimes rotated to the disengaged side.

Aiming naval guns was frequently very difficult, which is why the theoretically long ranges of heavy ordnance were seldom achieved in action. If a ship's captain wanted to inflict damage, he closed to within a few hundred yards – warships frequently fought it out practically hull to hull. Away from the sea and on the calmer waters of the great rivers, naval gunnery could take place at longer ranges. The union ironclads engaging Fort Donelson opened fire at over 2000 yards and scored hits regularly as they continued to close. Ironically, their shooting was better at a mile or so than it was when they reached 200 yards because they consistently overshot the target at that range.

When Du Pont led his squadron against Charleston, *New Ironsides* fired at Fort Sumter with her broadside-mounted, 11-inch Dahlgrens at 1700 yards. The ill-fated *Keokuk* pressed her attack home to within 900 yards, where the Confederate Brooke and James rifles regularly penetrated her 2-inch armor. The Union ironclads fired most of their shots from 1300–1400 yards. Colonel Rhett, Fort Sumter's commander, observed that their shooting was

not very accurate, as some rounds flew over and others landed either side. Some of the rounds fired from a mile or so did not reach the target at all. The Union gunners took advantage of the millpond calmness of the water to employ ricochet fire – bouncing iron solid shot across the surface of the water, just like skimming a stone. This technique was a favorite with smoothbore guns since it made the exact range to the target and the elevation of the gun less critical in scoring a hit. Firing from a ship, it was not possible to judge either with the precision possible ashore. If the gunners could ricochet their shot across the water, they only needed to adjust their aim right or left.

The ironclads fired about 150 shots at Fort Sumter and scored 55 hits. Their target was over 350 feet across, three stories high, and

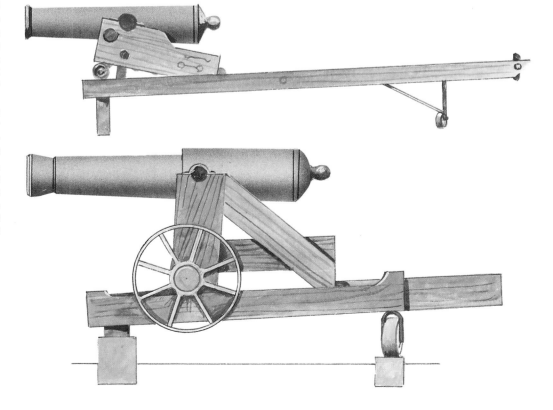

Seacoast and Naval Ordnance

RIGHT: *Abraham Bloodgood of New York designed this circular, revolving armored floating battery in 1807.*

BELOW: *A cross-section of Theodore Timby's revolving battery designed in 1847. This elaborate structure was intended for service on land or water, and was meant to turn on roller bearings like the later Coles' turret. The center column was surmounted by a dome, which housed the control center and observation post.*

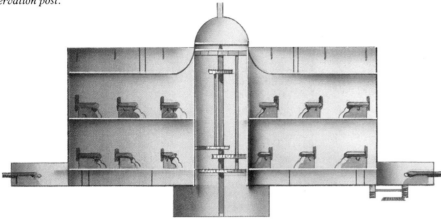

LEFT: *The initial design for Ericsson's turret, showing how the gun was mounted in a revolving dome resting on a central spindle. When Ericsson first presented his revolutionary design to the Ironclad Board in 1861, he claimed that the idea had already been presented to the French emperor, Napoleon III. But extensive research in the French Ministry of Marine archives failed to produce any evidence of such a scheme.*

Captain Cowper Coles of the Royal Navy was already working on designs for warships carrying eight or 10 turrets, but his plans were rejected by the British Admiralty. It would be several years before Coles' turrets were fitted on warships, and then only in the coast defense role.

(obviously) stationary. Lest Colonel Rhett's judgment seem harsh – only one shot in three hitting such an easy target – it is worth remembering that smoothbore gunnery in Napoleonic battles was certainly less accurate. Over 50 years later, when the great dreadnoughts clashed during World War I, accuracy at their engagement ranges was seldom greater than 5 percent. Where the monitors had a problem, it was their rate of fire; the ironclads had 33 heavy guns between them and took nearly 2½ hours to fire their 150 shots. During the same time Fort Sumter's 30 guns and three 10-inch mortars fired 810 shots in return. Fort Sumter's armament consisted of Brooke rifles, rifled and banded 42-pounders, plus Dahlgrens and Columbiads, none of which were known for especially rapid fire. The fastest firing cannon were the eight 32-pounder smoothbores which could be reloaded in under 90 seconds by a skilled crew. However, this was not a performance that could be sustained all afternoon. Even allowing that these smoothbores could unbalance the figures by their much faster rate of fire, the shore-based, large-caliber guns were firing four to five times as many rounds as those aboard the monitors.

The sights were as crude as those of land-based cannon but the movement of the ship sometimes confounded even their use. It was very much a matter of experience. Naval guns were not fired with the same friction primers as used by the army. Firstly, the caps tended to fragment and fly in all directions unless covered – hence the injuries suffered by some mortar crews when they used them on weapons not designed for them. On a crowded gun deck this was unacceptable. Secondly, when a friction primer fired, the gunner was left with the serrated wire on the end of his lanyard. In the field he simply dropped it to the ground and

BELOW LEFT: *Captain Cowper Coles, vigorously supported by the press, strenuously lobbied the British Admiralty to build a seagoing ironclad carrying turrets. Several smaller ironclads, including the Rolf Krake for Denmark and the Prinz Hendrick for Holland, had already been built carrying his turrets, and had proved highly successful in service.*

Coles's turret was an armored cylinder which rose about 4½ feet above the weather deck and was supported at its base by a roller bearing which ran on a metal ring laid on the deck below. In this way the weight of the turret was evenly distributed and better able to withstand the shock of striking projectiles. The turret was entered from the lower deck via a central spindle. Training the turret in early examples was achieved by using a rack and pinion, plus hand spikes from the lower deck. Later, steam power was used. The gun carriage ran upon a slide the width of the turret instead of upon tracks, and the elevation was controlled by screws at each end of the slide. Basically, this is the system used in the battleships and cruisers that served in the two world wars, and is still applicable in today's modern warships.

carried on, but scattering sections of sharp wire over the deck was hardly practical. Instead, the navies employed a gun lock which fired a similar tube filled with fine powder. The lock was designed to clear the vent after striking to prevent the hammer being flung back by the rush of escaping gas.

The priming tubes worked well throughout the war but they were a source of some difficulty, particularly with inexperienced or exhausted gun crew. When the Union gunboats attacked Fort Henry, the Confederates' most effective gun was their single 10-inch Columbiad but it disabled itself almost immediately when the priming wire jammed in the vent. Clearing it would have been fiddly work taking several hours – time that Fort Henry did not have. Fort Donelson's sole large-caliber rifle had fired only a handful of its 128-pound solid shot at the US ironclads when a careless gunner neglected to remove the spent primer tube before another man rammed home a cartridge. The tube bent, rendering the gun useless for the rest of the action. Temporary problems with primers aboard CSS *Tennessee* saved *Hartford* from a full broadside at point-blank range – only one gun was able to fire.

Although warships generally fired solid shot or shells at each other, they did rely on grapeshot, and in some cases shrapnel, to deal with other targets. Many river defense batteries mounted their guns *en barbette*, i.e. pointing

RIGHT: *John Ericsson's turret differed from that of Coles in that it revolved around a single central spindle, which also supported its not inconsiderable weight. The spindle usually rested upon the lower deck when not in use, and before turning was possible, it had to be jacked up by rack and pinion. Steam was then used to turn the turret. A conning tower was mounted on top of the turret and this turned with it. The voice pipe and steering chains ran down from the conning tower via the central spindle. Heavy, solid iron port shutters, which hung from the roof like pendulums, closed the ports when the guns were run in. When the turret was keyed up in the firing position, a small gap appeared at main deck level into which debris could fall and jam the turret.*

Ericsson's turrets were the most common carried by Union warships built during the Civil War, and enabled small vessels to carry a powerful armament securely protected. Monitors made economical and efficient coast defense vessels and appealed to small nations who did not have overseas possessions. They caused the United Kingdom to reconsider its foreign squadrons, where it was likely that such units would be met, resulting in armored vessels being added to those squadrons, especially those serving on the South American Station.

The larger US monitors of the Miantonomoh *class, together with the huge* Dictator, *also influenced UK thinking. As a result of the former class, the UK embarked on a building program that ended up with the* Devastation, *while the* Dictator *clearly influenced the design of the* Glatton.

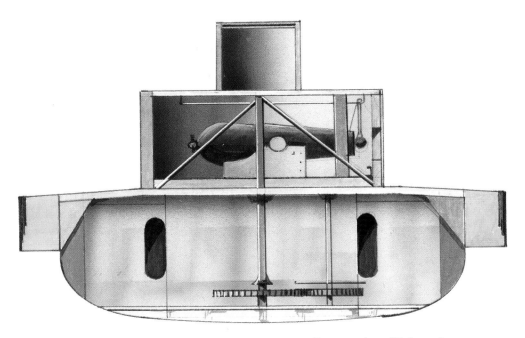

Cross-section of Ericsson's turret including hull

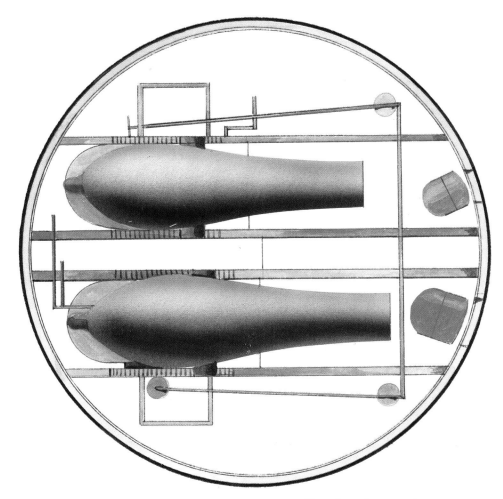

Top view of turret only

Seacoast and Naval Ordnance

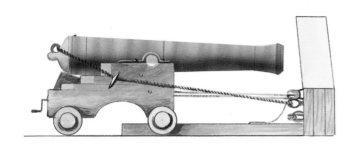

their barrels above a wall rather than firing through a gun port. To land a shell on a shore battery while running past was very difficult, and to hit a gun port next to impossible. Instead, the US Navy relied heavily on unselective grapeshot. This hail of suppressive fire could keep the gunners' heads down long enough for the ships to break through.

Grape was also the standard answer to enemy boarders. As the enemy vessel drew alongside, her deck crammed with sailors and/or troops ready to board, a charge of grape from large-caliber naval guns could inflict monstrous casualties. One Union warship fired shrapnel with one-second fuses in a successful defense against Confederate boarders.

Although the warships of the Civil War were often innovative and anticipated later developments in naval warfare, naval ordnance was in some ways stuck between two generations of weaponry. The massive Dahlgrens and Columbiads were developed throughout the war from 10- to 11- and then 15-inch caliber. After prodigious effort, the 20-inch smoothbore was ready by 1864. But although they were impressive triumphs for the designers and the iron foundries, the guns themselves were a technological dead end. As warships protected themselves with coats of iron, naval guns had to penetrate this new defense to destroy their target. This demanded heavy projectiles traveling at high velocity, but smoothbore guns were automatically limited – they could fire only spherical shot. There was no way of increasing its weight so the designers simply built ever larger guns. Since even these could not penetrate more than a couple of inches of iron armor, "racking" was the only tactic left against a warship like the *Tennessee*.

TOP: ***Ward's "Novelty carriage"***
This four-truck gun mount was devised by Commander James H. Ward. The four trucks remained off the deck, except when maneuvering the gun. Thus the recoil was reduced by the friction of the whole carriage sliding back.

CENTER: ***32-pdr on navy carriage***
This iron carriage was developed for the 8- and 9-inch Dahlgrens. Adapted from the wooden Marsilly carriage, it employed screw elevation. There were no trucks on the rear, so the friction of the carriage would reduce the distance it recoiled when fired.

ABOVE: ***Brooke 7-inch rifle on iron carriage***
This Brooke rifle is still to be seen at Charleston, South Carolina, and it bears the initials of Catesby ap Rhys Jones. Manufactured at Selma in 1864, it survived the evacuation of Charleston when the Confederates destroyed many of the big guns they were forced to abandon.

BELOW: ***Brooke 6.4-inch rifle***
Brooke double-banded rifles were the Confederacy's equivalent of the Union's Parrott guns. Used on many Confederate ironclads, they were employed on carriages like that illustrated when deployed ashore. The Battery Dantzler on the James River below Richmond used several Brooke rifles like this.

Battering away at a warship's armor did have appalling consequences for the men inside, but it was a desperately slow way to overcome an enemy, and it did rather assume a healthy numerical superiority. What was needed was a reliable rifled gun that could fire a heavy iron projectile fast enough to punch clean through. Unfortunately, the US Navy could not trust the Parrott rifles to do this reliably without blowing themselves up in the process. Thus, the monitors were armed with them only when there was a shortage of 15-inch Dahlgrens. By choice, the navy preferred its big smoothbores. Ironically, it was the Confederate Navy that forged ahead with the weapon of the future. The Brooke muzzleloading rifles may not have had the performance of the latest Armstrongs appearing in Britain, but they were along the right lines.

TOP RIGHT: *13-inch mortar mounted on a raft. These mortar boats, nicknamed "bummers," carried a single mortar and were often protected by a high wall of boiler plate to prevent Confederate snipers picking off the crews. The boats had to be heavily constructed to survive the monstrous blast of the big seacoast mortars. They were either towed into position or rowed with sweeps. Mortars were also mounted in schooners, which fired from near the riverbank with their masts concealed in the trees. Observers positioned up in the mast could spot the fall of shot.*

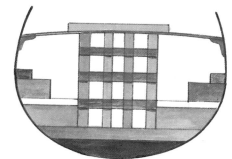

LEFT: *Cross-section of a mortar boat showing how the heavy timbers were fitted together to bear the strain. These were filthy and smelly boats to serve on, as the powder smoke thickly coated men and equipment alike.*

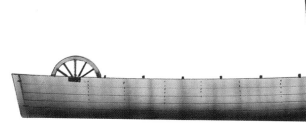

ABOVE AND ABOVE RIGHT: *12-pdr boat howitzer* This fitted into the bows of a frigate's launch and could be traversed 360 degrees on its boat carriage. In the stern of the launch is the field carriage that could be run to the bow once the launch neared the shore. In tests a boat crew could fire the howitzer, mount it on its field carriage, run it ashore, and fire it again in under two minutes!

RIGHT: *The four-truck carriage design dated from the eighteenth century. As guns grew larger, it became difficult to control the recoil forces, so the Marsilly carriage was developed instead.*

The US Navy at the Outbreak of War

On April 19, 1861 President Lincoln proclaimed a blockade of the Southern states. The South's economy depended heavily on its cotton exports, while its military forces desperately needed to import weapons, ammunition, and machinery. If the US Navy could isolate the Confederacy from Europe, the Southern military effort would be severely hampered. Yet the declaration of a blockade was a calculated gamble – albeit not very well calculated in the view of Gideon Welles, secretary of the navy.

Declaring a blockade was tantamount to recognition of Southern independence – nations can close their own ports, but they can only blockade those of other countries with which they are at war. Worse, a blockade had to be seen as effective if it was to have any force under international law. Great Britain declared itself neutral, thus protecting the 30 or so British merchant ships then in New Orleans and several million dollars' worth of British-owned goods. Other European nations followed suit, gaining the protection of neutrals' rights for their merchantmen. But this state of affairs could last only while the US Navy was seen to impose a blockade. Unfortunately, it was not well equipped to do so. Only the complete absence of Confederate naval forces would enable the US Navy to claim it was blockading the Southern ports during 1861.

For a nation with over 5 million tons of merchant shipping, nearly half of which was ocean going, the United States had spent surprisingly little money on its naval forces. Steam power and shell-firing naval guns were affecting a revolution in naval construction but American participation was limited. The capital ships of the 1850s were wooden two- or three-decked ships of the line, propelled by steam and sail, and externally very similar to those of the turn of the century. In 1860 the British Royal Navy had 56 in service, the French 33, the Russians 9, and the US none.

The US Navy's most powerful warships were the six screw frigates built between 1855 and 1856: *Niagara*, *Roanoke*, *Colorado*, *Merrimack*, *Minnesota*, and *Wabash*. Armed with two 10-inch, 28 9-inch, and 14 8-inch Dahlgren smoothbores, they were capable of 9–10 knots, which was relatively slow by contemporary standards. When the US Navy announced its building program in 1854, the British had immediately retaliated with six similar ships of their own. The British frigates were of similar size, mounted 20 10-inch and 10 6.4-inch smoothbore muzzleloaders and were capable of 12–13 knots. The US frigates were slightly larger than their British would-be rivals, but this was more due to ominous political developments than any intentions of the builders.

Southern senators wanted to be sure that these new warships would draw too much water to enter Southern harbors.

In the years up to 1853 only 18 steamers had been built for the US Navy. But over the next six years, 30 more were added. The most useful vessels for the navy during the Civil War were the 12 screw sloops built between 1858 and 1859. The five vessels in the first batch included *Hartford*, *Brooklyn*, and *Richmond*, ships that would see a great deal of action far from their intended stations.

At the outbreak of war the US Navy had 90 ships, of which 40 were steamers. The bankruptcy of the Buchanan administration meant that of the big screw frigates, only one was in service. Seventeen warships were on foreign stations and no orders were issued for their recall until war broke out. In addition to the home squadron, which consisted of *Brooklyn*, *Wyandotte*, and six small steamers, there were five other squadrons. The Mediterranean squadron had just a handful of sailing sloops. The Africa squadron, formed to suppress the slave trade, had the screw sloop *San Jacinto* and the 24-gun sailing sloop *Constellation*. The Pacific squadron included the screw sloops *Lancaster* (flagship), *Powhatan*, and *Wyoming*. *Hartford* began the war as the flagship of the East India squadron; *Mississippi* was off China. The Brazilian squadron flagship was the sailing sloop *Congress*, destined to be destroyed by the ironclad CSS *Virginia*.

Admiral Nelson once remarked that "men fight, not ships." Service aboard US warships was as hard as in any other nineteenth-century navy and many sailors were foreign born. The bounties offered to recruit soldiers tempted

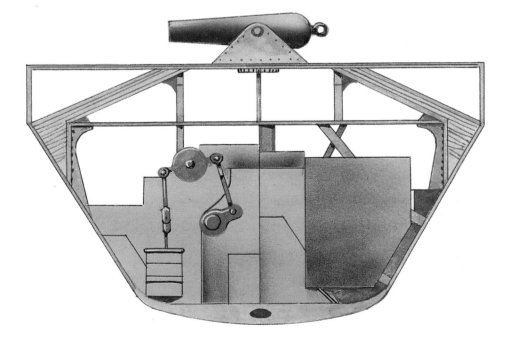

LEFT AND BELOW: *The Stevens Battery was the US Navy's first attempt at an ironclad warship. First authorized in 1842, it was laid down in 1854, but was still incomplete by the beginning of the Civil War. Measuring 250 feet long and protected by 6¾ inches of armor, Robert Stevens' design was the first ironclad to be ordered by any navy. Its armament was ultimately intended to be two 10-inch rifles and five 15-inch smoothbores. Stevens died in 1856, and although his brothers offered to complete the vessel at their own expense in 1861, their offer was refused. When Edwin Stevens died, the vessel was left to the state of New Jersey. Some more work was carried out from 1869 to 1870, but the project was abandoned and the ship broken up in 1881.*

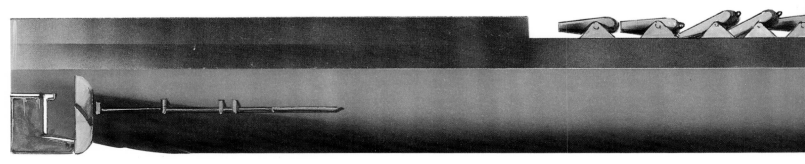

many American sailors into the army in 1861. But although some naval officers resigned to follow the fortunes of their home states, no serving US captain surrendered the vessel he commanded. The US Navy had shown itself to be a progressive and active force in the years before the war, with scientific and exploratory voyages around the world. The Naval Academy at Annapolis, Maryland, ran a four-year course for US officers.

As a professional service, the US Navy held little attraction for those politicians who wanted military rank as a political favor. There was to be no nautical equivalent of the "political generals" who caused so many problems ashore. The US Navy's only serious personnel weakness was similar to that of the peacetime army: an aging officer corps. Until 1862 there was no rank higher than captain. Those commanding squadrons were called "flag officers" and entitled to fly a personal flag; although often referred to as commanders, this was not an official rank. In 1861 the US Navy's most senior officer was a 75-year-old captain who had held that rank for 30 years. A naval retirement board had been instituted in 1855 which endeavored to remove 201 officers as unfit for sea duty. Unfortunately, there was too much vested interest at stake here and the captains combined to block the law. In the end, it was so diluted that it had little impact. However, it is worth noting that age alone did not always mean unfitness for combat. Commander Cooke, the future captain of the CSS *Albemarle*, had been a captain in the US Navy from 1828 to 1861! In the service of the Confederacy he proved an inspiring leader full of initiative.

If the US Navy was lagging behind its traditional European rivals in wooden warships, it was being outpaced even further in the latest class of vessel. At the beginning of 1860 France had six ironclad warships under construction and Great Britain had four. The US Navy had just one, and its construction had been suspended for the second and final time. This was the ironclad steamship built by Robert L. Stevens, authorized as long ago as 1842 and still incomplete when he died in 1856. Congressional parsimony and indecision had frustrated the project from the outset. On the evidence of this performance, there was no indication that the US Navy would soon be relying heavily on a fleet of ironclads to spearhead the naval war against the Confederacy.

TOP: *The Union 3765-ton cruiser* Powhatan *as she appeared in the early 1860s. She was 250 feet long and measured nearly 70 feet over the paddle boxes. Laid down in July 1847 and completed in September 1852,* Powhatan *was typical of large cruisers of this period that relied heavily on sail power because their engines were uneconomic. Although outdated by newer vessels built during the war,* Powhatan *gave long and reliable service. She survived a fierce cyclone off Hatteras that forced the cruiser's fore yardarm into the sea. Not scrapped until 1887,* Powhatan's *career spanned over 30 years – testimony to the quality of American shipbuilding.*

ABOVE: *The powerfully armed, 2150-ton wooden sloop USS* San Jacinto *as she appeared on completion in 1852, 5½ years after she was laid down. By 1862 she was armed with one 11-inch Dahlgren and 10 9-inch smoothbore guns. It was the* San Jacinto, *commanded by Captain Wilkes, that seized the English mail steamer* Trent *on which Confederate commissioners Slidell and Mason were traveling to Europe in 1861. This almost led to war with England. Later in the war* San Jacinto's *crew suffered two serious outbreaks of yellow fever. The luckless vessel struck a reef on New Year's Day 1865 at No Name Key, Great Abaco Island, and rapidly filled with water. All efforts to save her failed and she sank. The wreck was not disposed of until 1871.*

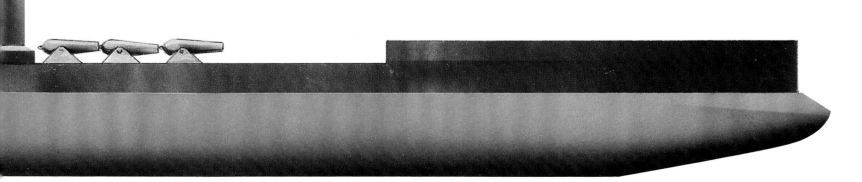

Naval Warfare During the Civil War

Naval battles shaped the course of the Civil War in two ways. First of all the Confederate states' economy was heavily dependent on foreign trade. Indeed, it was widely anticipated that when the US Navy blockaded Confederate ports and halted the export of Southern cotton, Britain would be compelled to intervene on the Confederate side to protect its own industry. This was a grave misjudgment; the Lancashire mill-owners had considerable political influence but Britain was not about to go to war over under-employed cotton mills. However, the Confederacy's lopsided economy required the Southern states to import all manner of goods from Europe that had formerly come from the North. Above all, the South desperately needed modern weapons and machinery and the US Navy stood squarely in the way.

The second way in which naval action influenced the war was the strategic importance of the major rivers. From the beginning of the war, when Scott outlined the "Anaconda" plan, it was obvious that if the Union could control the Mississippi, the Confederate states of Arkansas and Texas would wither on the vine. As Union forces advanced into the Confederacy, rivers assumed still greater importance. River transport was more reliable than rail and could carry heavier loads further and more cheaply. Unlike supply lines that ran by road or rail, river-borne traffic was far harder for Confederate raiders to intercept – despite the episode of "Bedford Forrest's Navy."

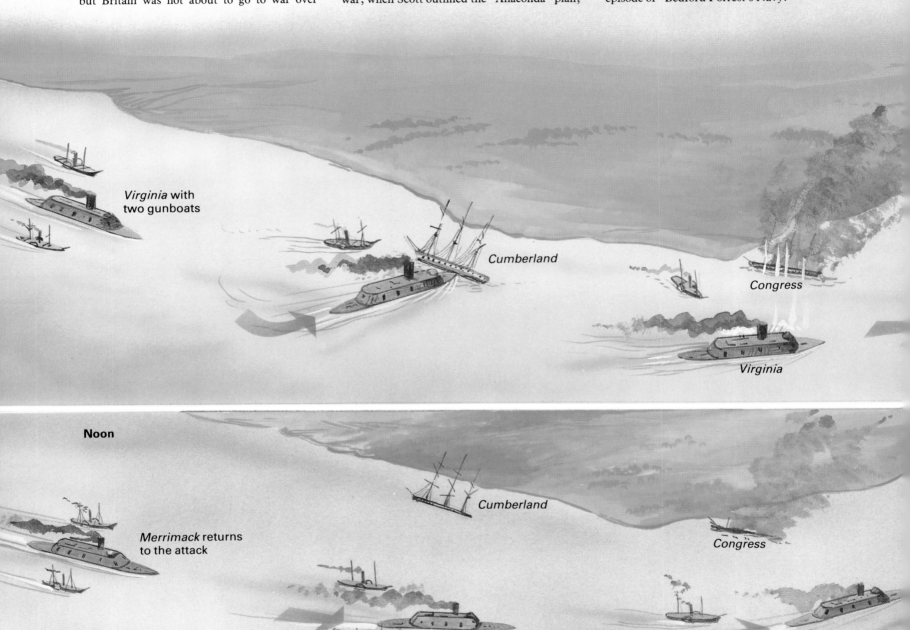

Virginia with two gunboats

Cumberland

Congress

Virginia

Noon

Cumberland

Congress

Merrimack returns to the attack

Monitor tries to ram stern

Merrimack retires

Warships

The Union and Confederate navies fought their battles with an astonishing variety of warships. From graceful sailing ships to bizarre converted riverboats, the rival fleets used every vessel they could lay their hands on. Radically different ships mounted a wide range of armament from conventional cannon to rams, torpedoes, and mortars. They fought in narrow bayous and treacherous coastal waters, among Arctic ice floes and off the shores of France.

Civil War naval battles were a dramatic mixture of the old and the new. Although sails were still used for cruising at sea, steam-powered engines had replaced sail power for tactical maneuver. Naval guns now fired shells, as well as the traditional mixture of cannon-balls, grapeshot, and canister. They were much larger, longer-ranged and more powerful than anything seen in the Napoleonic wars. The effect of explosive shells on wooden warships had been demonstrated with chilling finality in

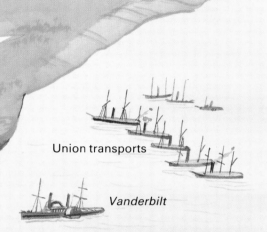

Union transports

Vanderbilt

Roanoke runs aground

St Lawrence runs aground

Minnesota aground

Virginia breaks off action

Saturday, March 8, 1862 dawned bright and clear, a beautiful day that anticipated the spring. A faint breeze blowing from the northwest left just a ripple across the surface of the water. At about 11.00 a.m. the workmen were ordered off Merrimack, *now renamed* Virginia, *and the ironclad got underway. The tide was at half flood, just enough to accommodate the ironclad's 22-foot draft. Hundreds of people lined the riverbank at Norfolk and Portsmouth to see her off. Most witnesses, including all but a handful of officers on*

board, thought this was a trial run. But Admiral Buchanan's idea of a test was an all-out assault on the US warships in Hampton Roads. Virginia *took two hours to make the 10-mile journey from her berth. Accompanied by* Beaufort *and* Raleigh, *she attacked, opening fire at about 2.00 p.m. at 1500 yards. In five hours' action, she sank* Cumberland *and* Congress, *and damaged* Minnesota. *The ironclad retired at dusk, ready to finish the battle the next day.*

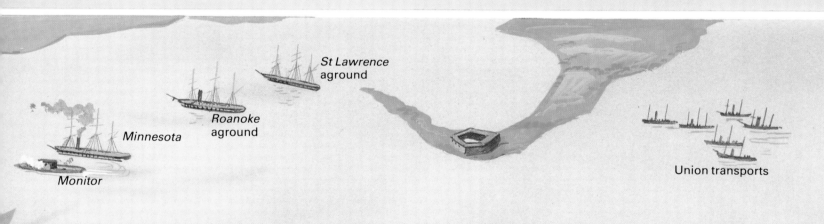

St Lawrence aground

Roanoke aground

Minnesota

Monitor

Union transports

Monitor retires to reload

Virginia *headed back downstream at 6.00 a.m. on March 9. Large crowds assembled around the natural amphitheater of Hampton Roads. But as* Virginia *headed for the stranded* Minnesota, *she was challenged by the Union's new ironclad* Monitor. *The US ironclad consistently outmaneuvered the ponderous* Virginia. *For four hours the rival ironclads fired at each other at*

ranges of less than 100 yards, but Monitor's *guns were firing half-charges, and* Virginia *had run out of solid shot and had to employ shell. Neither could inflict a mortal blow and* Virginia's *ram was useless against an opponent still able to maneuver. As the tide began to fall, the* Virginia *returned to Sewell's Point.*

Naval Warfare During the Civil War

1853 when six Russian battleships attacked seven Turkish frigates at Sinop on the central northern shore of the Black Sea. A ferocious two-hour action set all the Turkish vessels on fire, killing 3000 of the 4500 sailors aboard.

The answer was armor. The French Navy launched *Gloire* in 1860, the Royal Navy replied with HMS *Warrior* in 1861. Both were large, ocean-going warships carrying large-caliber guns and protected by over 4 inches of iron plate. They rendered the three-deck ships of the line obsolete at a stroke. But while European attention was drawn to the bitter rivalry between these traditional naval enemies, the potential of armored warships was to be demonstrated most convincingly in America.

The two battles in Hampton Roads on March 8 and 9, 1862 became one of the most famous episodes in naval history. In the first action the newly commissioned ironclad *Virginia* attacked two wooden sailing ships, catching them at anchor. The first victim was the 1726-ton, 24-gun wooden frigate *Cumberland*. Anchored with her bow outward, 800 yards from shore, only a few of her 9-inch Dahlgren smoothbores would bear. Those that did failed to make any significant impression on the lumbering ironclad that slowly maneuvered itself into position for a ram attack. *Virginia*'s bow rifles fired shells into *Cumberland* from 1500 yards away,

then the ram worked up to full speed and struck the hapless sailing ship, tearing a gaping hole in her side.

Cumberland immediately began to settle in the water and *Virginia* was stuck for an embarrassing moment, her iron prow wedged firmly inside her enemy's hull. Then it snapped off and *Virginia* managed to back away. *Cumberland* continued firing at a range of about 100 yards. One shot knocked the muzzle off one of the ironclad's guns but otherwise there was no apparent effect on her. But *Cumberland* was clearly doomed; her firing slackened and she eventually sank at 3.30 p.m., colors flying.

Virginia's next victim was the 1876-ton,

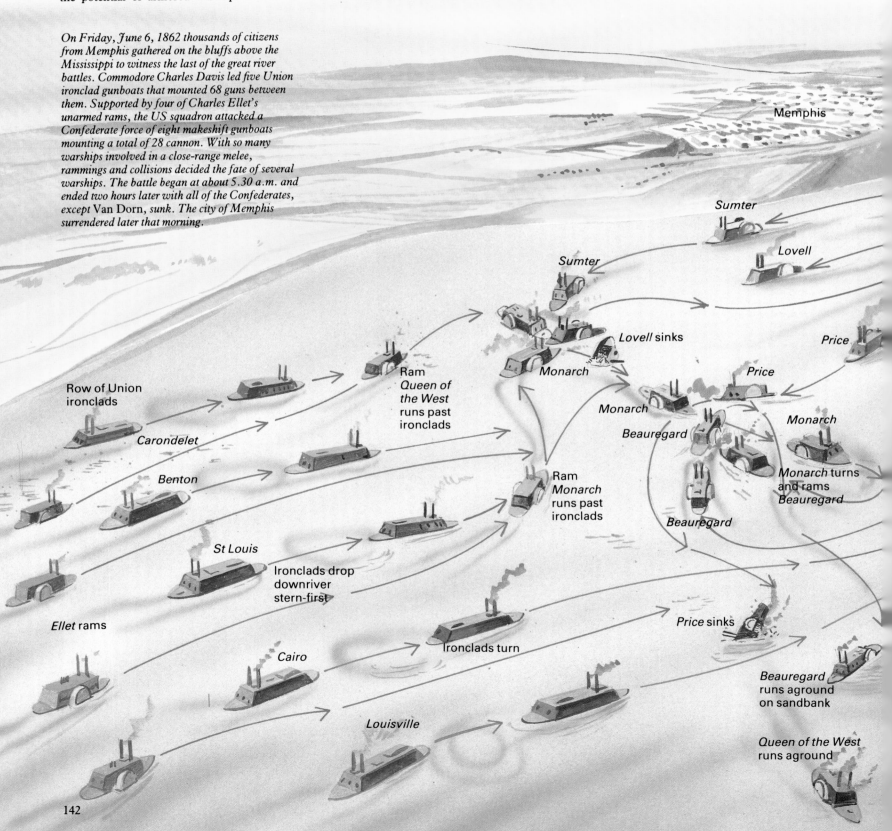

On Friday, June 6, 1862 thousands of citizens from Memphis gathered on the bluffs above the Mississippi to witness the last of the great river battles. Commodore Charles Davis led five Union ironclad gunboats that mounted 68 guns between them. Supported by four of Charles Ellet's unarmed rams, the US squadron attacked a Confederate force of eight makeshift gunboats mounting a total of 28 cannon. With so many warships involved in a close-range melee, rammings and collisions decided the fate of several warships. The battle began at about 5.30 a.m. and ended two hours later with all of the Confederates, except Van Dorn, sunk. The city of Memphis surrendered later that morning.

Memphis

Sumter

Sumter

Lovell

Lovell sinks

Price

Price

Monarch

Monarch

Monarch

Row of Union
ironclads

Carondelet

Benton

Ram
*Queen of
the West*
runs past
ironclads

Beauregard

Monarch turns
and rams
Beauregard

Ram
Monarch
runs past
ironclads

Beauregard

St Louis

Ironclads drop
downriver
stern-first

Ellet rams

Cairo

Ironclads turn

Price sinks

Louisville

Beauregard
runs aground
on sandbank

Queen of the West
runs aground

44-gun frigate *Congress*. She had managed to set her top sails and jib in a frantic effort to escape. Slipping down to the protection of the batteries at Signal Point, she ran aground. Unfortunately, the current swung her seaward, so only two of her guns could bear. Although she carried many more guns than *Cumberland*, she was even less able to defend herself: 42 of her cannon were 32-pounders.

Virginia had displaced over 4600 tons as originally built and she drew 22 feet of water – far too much to let her close with the *Congress*. Under fire from ashore as well as the frigate, *Virginia* maneuvered to within 100 yards and opened fire. The shells from her Brooke rifles and 9-inch Dahlgrens burst inside *Congress* and killed or wounded over 100 of her 480 crew in a few bloody minutes. The battering continued for an hour before *Congress* struck her colors. The shelling had started numerous fires which were by then out of control. She burned into the night, finally vanishing in a huge fireball when the flames reached her magazine.

Wooden warships were desperately vulnerable to shellfire. Only a few minutes' firing could start enough fires to doom a vessel to destruction, although a gallant crew could keep a ship in action for a short period, provided the fire-fighting parties did not suffer too many casualties from enemy action. By contrast, the *Virginia*'s metal skin made her almost invulnerable. The following day she was struck by a full broadside from USS *Minnesota*. The *Minnesota* was one of the six steam frigates that were the most powerful warships in US service; displacing over 3000 tons, she carried one 10-inch gun, 28 9-inch smoothbores and 14 8-inch. "I opened with all my broadside guns and a 10-inch pivot gun; a broadside that would have blown out of the water any timber-built ship in the world," recalled her captain. But it had no effect on the ironclad.

USS *Richmond* fired three 11-gun broadsides of 9-inch solid shot into *Tennessee*'s armored casemate during the battle for Mobile Bay.

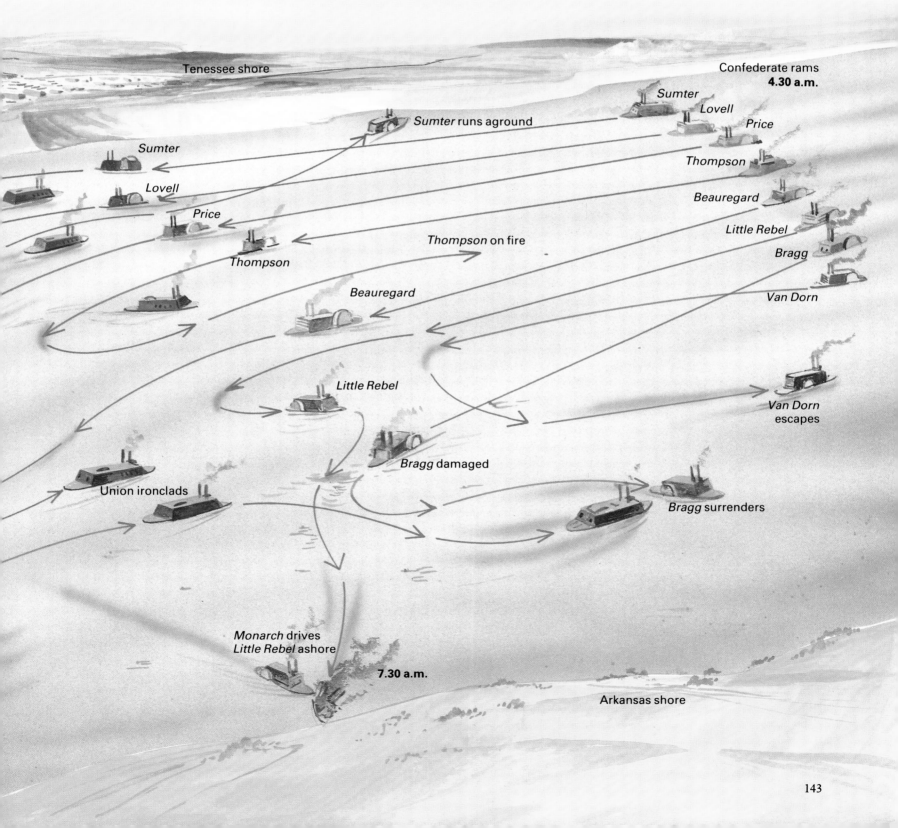

Naval Warfare During the Civil War

When the ram was examined the next day there was barely a scratch to show the effect of a salvo that would have crushed the sides of a wooden warship. *Monongahela*'s captain rammed *Tennessee* and bumped alongside before firing an 11-inch solid shot to equally little effect. *Hartford*, too, fired a full broadside while hull to hull. No lasting damage was inflicted and the frigate was very fortunate that all but one of *Tennessee*'s guns were temporarily disabled by tube primers stuck in their vents.

Although armor plate conferred many advantages, it did not guarantee immediate or overwhelming success. *Virginia* had started life as a steam frigate, as had *Minnesota*, and she carried a formidable battery that could overwhelm a large wooden ship in under an hour. But smaller ironclads did not enjoy such clear-cut superiority. *Albemarle* carried two 8-inch

Brooke rifles – formidable weapons – but since they took a good five minutes or so to load and fire, she could not destroy a wooden ship very quickly. On May 5, 1864 she engaged four Union "double-ender" riverboats. Three displaced over 1000 tons and each carried two 100-pounder Parrotts and four 9-inch Dahlgrens. The *Miami* was slightly smaller and carried one 80-pounder Parrott and three 9-inch Dahlgrens. The battle lasted two hours and *Albemarle* scored hits on three out of four opponents. But although *Miami* and *Sassacus* ended the fight with riddled smokestacks and a few wrecked cabins, they survived a series of hits from their opponent's 8-inch guns without significant damage. The worst hit was on *Sassacus*; a shell hit her starboard boiler, which exploded, scalding 15 crew with steam. Four later died of their burns.

Albemarle's duel with the double-enders finished in a long-range cannonade as the faster Union gunboats kept themselves at a reasonable distance from the ironclad. If any of them had been disabled, *Albemarle* could have used her specially strengthened prow to ram them. At the end of the action, *Albemarle* was only just able to stem the current as her smokestack was so riddled. The crew put bacon fat on the fire to increase steam pressure and get her home. The stern gun had its muzzle shot off, the steering was erratic and several armor plates had fallen off under the impact of enemy shot and shell. Her armor had allowed her to take on four ships carrying a total of 22 heavy guns to her two, but it did not ensure victory on its own.

Virginia, on the other hand, had the size and strength to inspire terror in Washington and wild optimism in Richmond. Even Mallory

The Confederate ironclad Atlanta *was converted from an English steamer in Savannah. Unlike most Southern ironclads, she had sound, modern engines and was potentially one of the more effective Confederate warships. She sortied in the early hours of June 17, 1863, heading down the Wilmington River for Wassaw Sound. Here she found two Union monitors waiting for her. The US Army had been tipped off by a deserter.* Atlanta *carried a spar torpedo with which her captain planned to strike one of the monitors, then shoot it out with the other. Opening fire at over 2500 yards,* Atlanta *suddenly ran aground. She backed free but failed to respond to the helm, and was forced aground again, listing so her guns could not bear.* Weehawken *closed to 300 yards and slammed four rounds into this helpless target.* Atlanta *had no choice but to surrender.*

5.30 a.m. *Atlanta* opens fire on waiting monitors

Atlanta runs aground but backs off

Shallow water forces *Atlanta* aground once more

Weehawken fires at close range, forcing *Atlanta* to surrender

Nahant

Weehawken holds fire

Nahant follows in wake as no pilot available

Nahant

talked of a raid on New York by this armored leviathan, impervious to enemy weapons. On March 9 she engaged the *Monitor* for over three hours at a range that seldom exceeded 100 yards and the *Virginia* shrugged off hit after hit. So did her opponent, so *Virginia* spent nearly an hour trying to ram her but *Monitor* was a much handier vessel. When the ram finally managed to contact, *Monitor* was already turning away and the blow was only a glancing one. As the two warships bumped alongside, *Virginia*'s men ready to board, *Monitor* fired an 11-inch solid shot. Fortunately for the Confederates, the US Navy Department had insisted that the *Monitor*'s guns be restricted to using 15-pound charges rather than the full 30-pound charge because the guns had not been proofed. *Virginia*'s armor was dented and the concussion left everybody near the point of impact with blood streaming from their ears and noses.

When *Virginia* was examined after the two-day battle, she had been struck 97 times. Lieutenant Brooke found evidence of 20 hits from *Monitor*'s guns. *Monitor* had fired 55 times during the battle, taking 6–8 minutes to reload her guns. Given the very close range and relatively large target, this gives a useful indication of the relative accuracy of naval cannon during the Civil War. *Virginia*'s shooting was less accurate, partly because the gunners were aiming at a smaller target and they had been ordered to concentrate on the little pilot house near the bow. Exactly how many rounds she fired is unknown, but she had ten guns to *Monitor*'s two and the 9-inch Dahlgrens were certainly faster to load. She scored 24 hits on her opponent; the pilot house was hit, blinding *Monitor*'s captain, and hits on the turret sent bolts flying around the interior. As *Monitor* was hampered by having to use half charges for her guns, so *Virginia* was frustrated by running out of solid shot. Almost all the projectiles she fired at the Union ironclad were shells, which were less effective against an armored target.

Ironclads could still suffer damage, even when their metal skin kept out the worst effects of a projectile. *Passaic* was struck 34 times by Confederate shot from Fort McAllister during Du Pont's attack on March 3, 1863. Many of the turret crew were injured as bolts sheered off and struck the gunners. Worse was to come. On April 6, Du Pont led his ironclads against Charleston and shot it out with the forts for two hours before withdrawing at 5.00 p.m. He planned to renew the attack the next day, until he saw the damage reports.

3 a.m. *Atlanta* heads downriver

Weehawken

Naval Warfare During the Civil War

Although none of the monitors had taken serious hull damage, their turrets were badly battered. *Nahant*'s turret was jammed; a hit on her pilot house failed to penetrate but it dislodged a 78-pound chunk of iron that crushed the pilot and quartermaster, leaving the captain alone with the broken steering gear. *Patapsco*'s turret was temporarily jammed and her 150-pounder Parrott was disabled after five rounds. *Nantucket* could only traverse her turret with difficulty, and a hit on her 15-inch gun's portstopper prevented that gun from firing. All the monitors had their turret floors awash with bolts and many officers believed that if they were exposed to another pounding without repair, they stood a serious risk of collapsing. At least they were luckier than the experimental ironclad *Keokuk*. She was struck 90 times, 19 hits being on the water line, and she foundered in the rising sea the next day.

It was unusual for a Civil War ironclad's armor to be penetrated by shot or shell. *Monitor*'s reduced charge shot did bulge *Virginia*'s armor, but after the action Brooke found that only six plates needed replacing. The second layer underneath was undamaged and the wooden backing unmarked.

In her epic last stand against the Union fleet at Mobile Bay, *Tennessee* received an incredible pounding from some of the most powerful warships in the US Navy. She was subdued after an hour, the monitor *Chickasaw* clinging to her stern, hammering away with her 11-inch guns. Large screw sloops and monitors made at least four ramming attacks and hits near gunports steadily jammed the Confederate ship's shutters. Then *Manhattan* arrived. The 2100-ton monitor was a sister ship of the ill-fated *Tecumseh* that *Tennessee* had enticed to her destruction on the minefield.

Manhattan came alongside the Confederate ironclad and fired one of her 15-inch Dahlgrens. A 440-pound solid iron shot with no less than 60 pounds of powder behind it smashed into *Tennessee*'s port side, penetrating her 5-inch armor plate and the 2 feet of wood backing. It was the only shot to penetrate *Tennessee* during the battle.

Fleet anchored

Ram struck by *Hartford*

Ram struck by *Lackawanna*

Ram struck by *Monongahela*

Tennessee surrenders

Hartford

Dauphine Bay

Dauphine Island

Fort Gaines

Pelican Bay

piles

lookout station

Pelican Island

At 7.00 a.m. on August 5, 1864 Fort Morgan opened fire on the USS Brooklyn as Admiral Farragut's squadron attacked Mobile Bay. The channel was covered by Confederate land batteries and partially blocked by mines and obstructions. Behind these formidable defenses lurked one of the South's most powerful casemate ironclads, CSS Tennessee.

The US squadron approached the forts rapidly, firing broadsides of grapeshot to suppress the enemy fire. The monitor Tecumseh steered straight for the Tennessee, struck a torpedo, and sank like a stone; 93 of the 114 men aboard her were drowned. Farragut's famous cry, "Damn the torpedoes, full speed ahead!" was not actually attributed to him until 1878, but whatever he actually shouted from the rigging, USS Hartford immediately passed by Brooklyn and led the fleet into the bay. Several other US warships struck torpedoes, but they were lucky: the charges had gotten damp or the fuses failed.

By about 8.30 a.m. the US squadron was anchored about 4 miles inside the bay. Tennessee remained under the guns of Fort Morgan. Farragut set about planning a night attack with his monitors to settle the account with Tennessee, but Admiral Buchanan saved him the trouble. At about 8.45 a.m. Tennessee got up steam and headed straight for the US squadron. There followed an hour of desperate fighting before the ironclad succumbed to the overwhelming odds and struck her colors.

It was another 15-inch Dahlgren that forced the unfortunate *Atlanta* to surrender. *Weehawken* bombarded the grounded ram at 300 yards, striking her with four out of five shots. A 15-inch solid shot fired with a full 30-pound charge struck *Atlanta*'s starboard casemate and went through 4 inches of iron and 18 inches of wooden backing. It showered the gun deck with fragments, wounding 15 and concussing 40 crew. The achievements of these 15-inch guns certainly vindicated the Union decision to persevere with them, despite the difficulties of casting such colossal weapons.

Although the armor of Civil War warships could defeat even the heaviest cannon, it could not do so indefinitely. This was recognized at the time and the term "racking" was coined to describe the destruction of a vessel's armor by repeated blows from solid shot. *Tennessee*'s armor was examined after her capture and the rear of her casemate, although never penetrated by *Chickasaw* and *Winnebago*'s 11-inch guns, was found to be in a very shaky condition. Under a rain of blows, the relatively brittle iron armor fragmented. The Union monitor *Weehawken* suffered 53 hits during Du Pont's attack on Charleston, many of them against her side armor. After the battle her armor was so shattered by hits in the same area that chunks of armor could be picked off by hand.

Racking, or a point-blank shot from a 15-inch gun, was the only way to defeat the armor of the heaviest ironclads. But smaller armored vessels did not enjoy the prolonged immunity of warships like *Tennessee*. CSS *Arkansas* suffered a penetrative hit from one of *Hartford*'s 9-inch Dahlgrens during her daring run through the Federal river fleet to Vicksburg. But her armor was an improvised mixture of boiler plate and railroad T-irons. It kept out the 32-pounder rounds from *Tyler* during the long chase along the Yazoo River, the steep slope of the casemate front deflecting many shots over the top. But it did not offer the same protection as the layers of rolled iron fitted to the larger ironclads. One of *Hartford*'s shells penetrated the armor and passed through a cotton bale and 20 inches of wood backing before exploding inside, killing four men on *Arkansas*'s 32-pounder broadside gun. A 168-pound, wrought-iron bolt – probably from a 150-pounder Parrott – penetrated her side, entered the engine-room and passed through the woodwork on the other side.

Arkansas's armor again penetrated by *Essex*'s 10- and 11-inch Dahlgrens when Commander William "Wild Bill" Porter took the Union gunboat close to the Confederate shore batteries in a determined effort to sink the elusive ironclad. One of *Essex*'s rounds smashed clean through *Arkansas*'s shield, traveled diagonally across the gundeck and upended one of the broadside guns. Another shattered a gunport, breaking off chunks of the railroad iron. Both rounds were fired at such close range that the Confederates suffered powder burns. Porter's plan failed when *Essex* ran aground and he withdrew after 10 hectic minutes, during which the Confederate shore batteries and *Arkansas* fired for all they were worth. *Essex* was struck 42 times but suffered only one fatal casualty and two men wounded. Her fighting efficiency was hardly impaired – testimony to the strength of her construction.

The Union river fleet ironclads were not all fully protected. Like the *Arkansas*, they had their share of penetrative hits. *Benton*'s armor was holed several times during the action against Confederate land batteries at Grand Gulf. *Arkansas*'s two forward 8-inch, 64-pounder rifles smashed through *Carondelet*'s armor before the Union ironclad ran aground. Most of these shots were from astern, but *Carondelet*'s 2½-inch casemate had been penetrated squarely through its front at Fort Donelson. Most of the Fort's weapons were 32-pounders which were unable to penetrate her 2½-inch armored casemate. But after nearly three hours' shooting, the Fort's single 10-inch Columbiad scored a hit on the ironclad's port

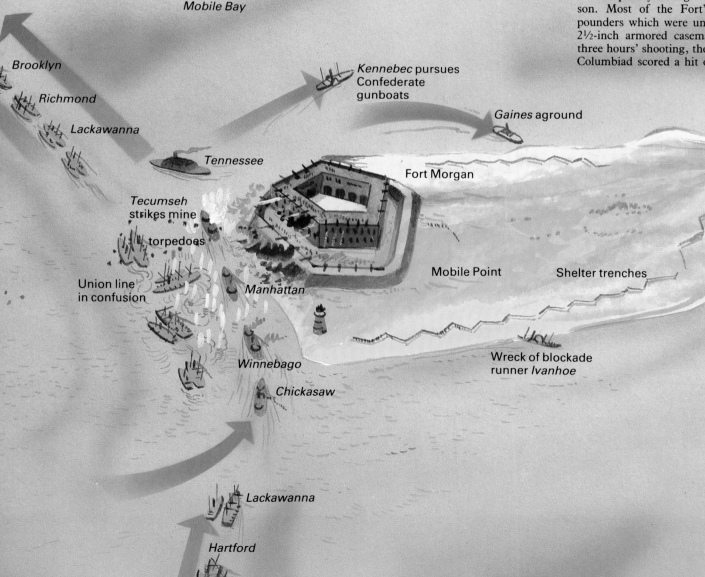

Mobile Bay

Brooklyn

Richmond

Lackawanna

Kennebec pursues Confederate gunboats

Gaines aground

Tennessee

Fort Morgan

Tecumseh strikes mine

torpedoes

Union line in confusion

Manhattan

Mobile Point

Shelter trenches

Winnebago

Wreck of blockade runner *Ivanhoe*

Chickasaw

Lackawanna

Hartford

Naval Warfare During the Civil War

side. The 128-pound solid shot penetrated the armor and badly wounded seven crew members. The impact sent a hail of iron splinters flying across the gun deck. Some were so sharp and so fine that men only knew they had been hit when they felt their shoes filling with blood.

Rams

Steam power had finally liberated ships from the tyranny of the wind. Naval battles were no longer dominated by the strength and direction of the wind, so traditional tactics were abandoned. This new-found ability to maneuver at will led to the revival of the ancient naval tactic: ramming. The discovery that armor plate could keep out almost any projectile made the idea of a ram still more attractive. On several occasions Union warships, despairing of damaging a

Confederate ironclad with their guns, would ram the vessel instead, even if they were not equipped with the necessarily strengthened prow. *Sassacus* worked up to a furious speed to ram *Albemarle* and tilted the Confederate sharply. But the impact did little harm to the ironclad and shattered *Sassacus*'s bow. The screw sloops that cannoned into *Tennessee* in Mobile Bay harmed only themselves.

It was a different story when the ship was properly equipped as a ram, but ramming was still dangerous to the attacker. We have seen how *Virginia* inflicted a mortal wound on *Cumberland* but lost her iron ram in the process. *Albemarle* rammed USS *Southfield*, a 750-ton sidewheel steamer, and sank her, but the ironclad's prow remained stuck fast inside the rapidly sinking ship. *Southfield* sank to the bottom of the Roanoke River, dragging *Albemarle* down with her, so water raced in through the gun ports. Fortunately for the Confederates, the bow broke free and the ironclad bobbed back.

The diminutive ram *Manassas* led the attack on the Union blockading squadron in the Heads of the Passes off New Orleans. Unlike *Albemarle* or *Virginia* she was a small vessel, converted from a tug boat and displacing less than 400 tons. She attacked the screw sloop *Richmond*, which could offer a broadside of 10 9-inch Dahlgrens, plus one 80-pound and one 100-pound rifle. Fortunately, her low profile prevented the Union sailors from seeing her until it was too late. But *Manassas* lacked not only size – she also lacked velocity. Her engines were overdue for the scrap heap and could manage only about 6 knots on a good day. Nevertheless, the force of the impact broke her ram bow and collapsed her smokestack, filling her with fumes and cutting the draft to her boilers. One of her two engines broke down immediately and she drifted ashore. *Richmond* was not badly damaged, but grounded as she headed for the open sea, badly spooked by fireships that had accompanied the surprise ramming attack.

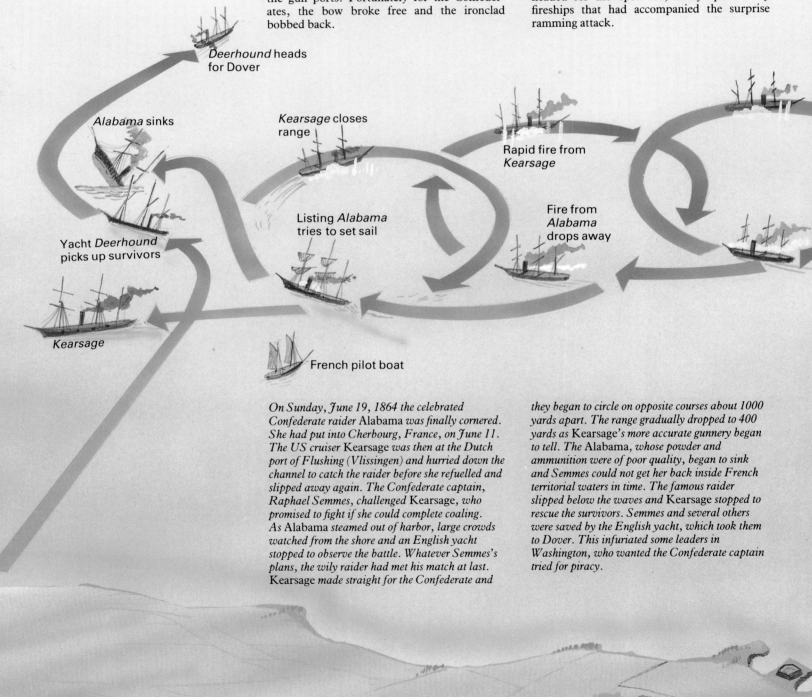

Deerhound heads for Dover

Alabama sinks

Kearsage closes range

Rapid fire from *Kearsage*

Yacht *Deerhound* picks up survivors

Listing *Alabama* tries to set sail

Fire from *Alabama* drops away

Kearsage

French pilot boat

On Sunday, June 19, 1864 the celebrated Confederate raider Alabama *was finally cornered. She had put into Cherbourg, France, on June 11. The US cruiser* Kearsage *was then at the Dutch port of Flushing (Vlissingen) and hurried down the channel to catch the raider before she refuelled and slipped away again. The Confederate captain, Raphael Semmes, challenged* Kearsage, *who promised to fight if she could complete coaling. As* Alabama *steamed out of harbor, large crowds watched from the shore and an English yacht stopped to observe the battle. Whatever Semmes's plans, the wily raider had met his match at last.* Kearsage *made straight for the Confederate and*

they began to circle on opposite courses about 1000 yards apart. The range gradually dropped to 400 yards as Kearsage's *more accurate gunnery began to tell. The* Alabama, *whose powder and ammunition were of poor quality, began to sink and Semmes could not get her back inside French territorial waters in time. The famous raider slipped below the waves and* Kearsage *stopped to rescue the survivors. Semmes and several others were saved by the English yacht, which took them to Dover. This infuriated some leaders in Washington, who wanted the Confederate captain tried for piracy.*

Manassas's ram was repaired and was effective enough during the battle of New Orleans, ripping a 7 × 4 feet section of solid timber from the hull of the sidewheeler *Mississippi*. But the *Mississippi* was already turning and the ram could manage only a glancing blow. *Manassas* then selected another huge opponent: USS *Brooklyn*. Throwing resin in the furnace to make more steam, she ran at the big sloop and managed a direct hit. *Brooklyn* was lucky to survive. The 1½-inch thick chain cables slung along *Brooklyn*'s hull as improvised armor were driven into her side and a 5-feet section of planking was crushed in. It was her coal that saved her. By good fortune the ram had struck a full coal bunker and the extent of the damage did not become apparent until a few days later when the coal was consumed. *Brooklyn* then leaked so badly that she had to head straight for repair at Pensacola.

It proved relatively easy for a ship to avoid being rammed, provided she was still under way and the steering was undamaged. But it was much harder to avoid several rams at once. The first mass ram attack took place on May 10, 1862, when eight Confederate river steamers attacked the Union mortar boats bombarding Fort Pillow on the Mississippi. The mortar boats were defended by one of the Eads' gunboats, *Cincinnati*. She was rammed by a steamer twice her size, the *General Bragg*, and a Confederate sharpshooter shot *Cincinnati*'s captain. The Union gunboat drove off *General Bragg* by shooting away her tiller ropes, but was promptly rammed by *General Sterling Price*, pushed around and struck again by *General Sumter*. The rest of the Union river fleet arrived after about an hour and the Confederates

withdrew rather than shoot it out with armored ships. But *Cincinnati* was in a sinking condition and had to be run ashore.

These Confederate gunboats were lightly armed, typically carrying a couple of 32-pounder guns and a detachment of riflemen. The ram was their main weapon and they relied on their superior speed to break off action with the Union ironclad rams should the situation no longer appear favorable.

Two could play at this. Pittsburgh engineer Charles Ellet figured that a squadron of fast steamers with strengthened prows could demolish the *Virginia* where hours of pounding from the *Monitor*'s guns had failed. He bought nine

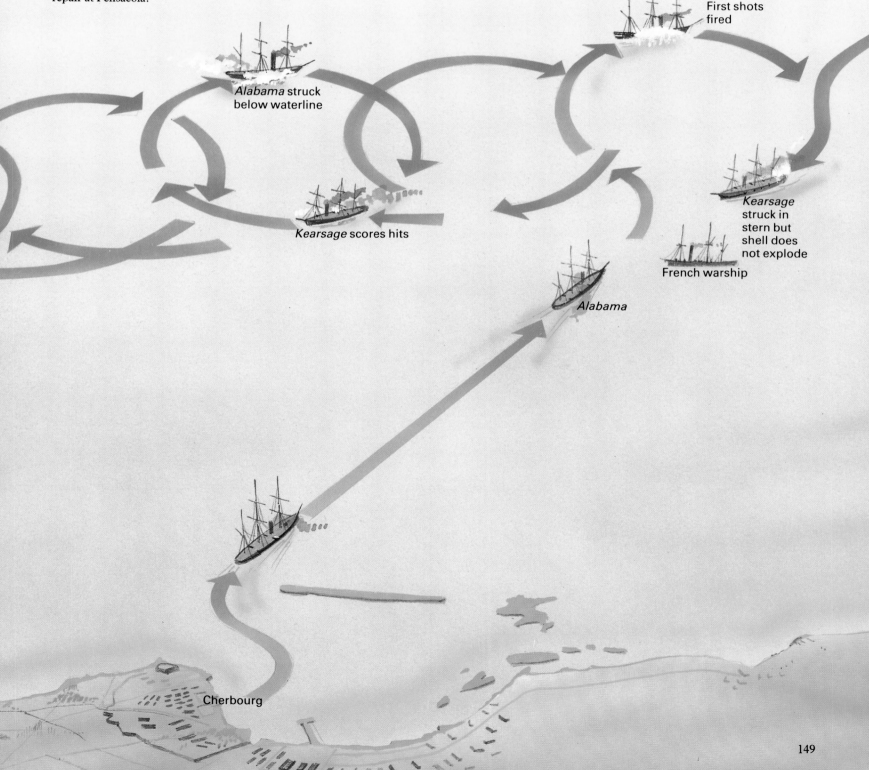

10.57 a.m.
First shots fired

Alabama struck below waterline

Kearsage scores hits

Kearsage struck in stern but shell does not explode

French warship

Alabama

Cherbourg

Naval Warfare During the Civil War

of the fastest steamers he could find on the Ohio and added heavy longitudinal timbers to bolster them against the anticipated impact. By the time his squadron was finished, *Virginia* had been burned, so Ellet's rams were sent down the Mississippi. There they were to operate with the Union fleet against the Confederate river squadron based at Memphis.

The Union attack was opened by the Eads' gunboats, but Ellet soon led two of his rams past the ironclads and headed for the Rebel fleet. None of his ships carried any armament. The only firearms aboard belonged to a small detachment of infantry shipped on board as sharpshooters. Ellet's theory worked; although the Confederates were undamaged and therefore not the easiest of targets, both *Queen of the West* and *Monarch* bore in and rammed *Colonel Lovell* and *General Beauregard*. Gunfire from the ironclads dealt with *Little Rebel* and the Confederates fled. Their ships were pursued down the Mississippi for 10 miles until all but the fastest, *General Earl van Dorn*, had been overhauled and destroyed. Although there was some disagreement afterward as to whether *General Beauregard* was sunk by a Union vessel

or accidently crippled by a collision with another Confederate, there was no doubt that Ellet's rams had achieved the desired result.

Ellet's unarmored and unarmed rams suffered only one casualty: Ellet himself. A Confederate shot him in the leg with a revolver. The wound became infected and he died 15 days later aboard the *Switzerland*.

Ellet's vessel, *Queen of the West*, was a 400-ton river boat; the ship she sank displaced nearer to 500 tons. *Colonel Lovell* sank rapidly but *Queen of the West* sustained considerable damage herself, despite the specially reinforced bow.

Ramming was an attractive tactic because it offered an immediate and decisive result. To sink a ship by gunfire usually took a considerable time unless a vessel was the target of an overwhelming number of heavy cannon. However, Civil War warships did have a few vulnerable points, even the ironclads.

Onboard casualties

The shallow draft of many vessels serving in the rival river fleets was essential if they were not to be restricted to all but the deepest channels of the major waterways. But this left the ships'

boilers dangerously exposed. If the boilers were penetrated by an incoming round, the results were horrific: the crew were engulfed in pressurized steam.

Mound City suffered a catastrophic boiler hit while attacking a Confederate battery in the White River, Arkansas. She had been under fire for 30 minutes at a range of 600 yards when a shot from a 32-pounder banded rifle struck her port casemate just forward of her 2½-inch armor. This lucky hit killed eight men at one of her guns before passing straight through the steam drum. The gun deck was immediately filled with scalding steam that cooked the unfortunate crew alive. Some jumped overboard to escape. Of the 175 officers and men on board at the time, the only survivors were the 23 men and boys in the shell room and magazine; 82 died inside the casemate, 43 drowned, and 25 were severely wounded.

The Union ram *Lancaster* steamed toward *Arkansas* to block the Confederates' retreat to Vicksburg, but *Arkansas* scored several hits with her cannon just in time. "His steam went into the air and his crew into the river," remembered one Confederate officer. USS *Sas-*

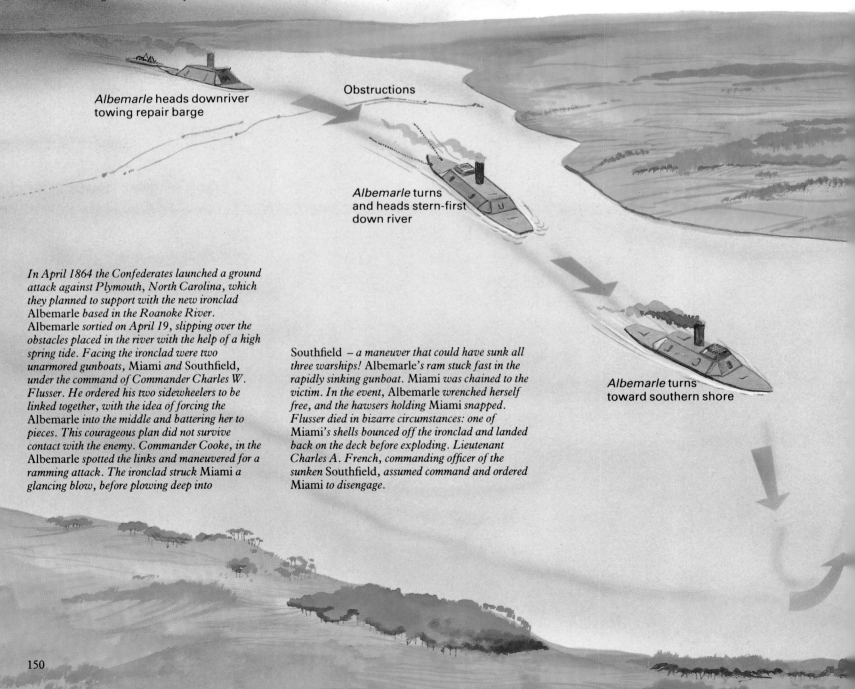

Albemarle heads downriver
towing repair barge

Obstructions

Albemarle turns
and heads stern-first
down river

Albemarle turns
toward southern shore

In April 1864 the Confederates launched a ground attack against Plymouth, North Carolina, which they planned to support with the new ironclad Albemarle *based in the Roanoke River.* Albemarle *sortied on April 19, slipping over the obstacles placed in the river with the help of a high spring tide. Facing the ironclad were two unarmored gunboats,* Miami *and* Southfield, *under the command of Commander Charles W. Flusser. He ordered his two sidewheelers to be linked together, with the idea of forcing the* Albemarle *into the middle and battering her to pieces. This courageous plan did not survive contact with the enemy. Commander Cooke, in the* Albemarle *spotted the links and maneuvered for a ramming attack. The ironclad struck* Miami *a glancing blow, before plowing deep into*

Southfield – *a maneuver that could have sunk all three warships!* Albemarle's *ram stuck fast in the rapidly sinking gunboat.* Miami *was chained to the victim. In the event,* Albemarle *wrenched herself free, and the hawsers holding* Miami *snapped. Flusser died in bizarre circumstances: one of* Miami's *shells bounced off the ironclad and landed back on the deck before exploding. Lieutenant Charles A. French, commanding officer of the sunken* Southfield, *assumed command and ordered* Miami *to disengage.*

sacus received a similar hit from the Confederate ironclad *Albemarle*: her starboard boiler was exploded by a direct hit, scalding 15 men, four of whom later died. The Union steamer *Mercedita* surrendered to the ram *Palmetto State* after filling with steam following a boiler hit. There was little anyone could do if a steam pipe or boiler fractured. The only defense was to surround the most vulnerable points with some sort of protection, hence the chain cables used at New Orleans, Mobile Bay and by USS *Kearsage* in her fight with the *Alabama*. *Brooklyn* entered the battle for New Orleans with her steam drum packed around with sandbags for good measure.

Casualties aboard Civil War warships varied enormously from battle to battle. On some occasions the crew of an ironclad might suffer no serious injuries at all, as their armor protected them from enemy fire. At other times a catastrophic hit on a steam drum or the explosion of a mine might kill half the crew in a matter of minutes. This may have been the dawn of a new era in naval warfare, but the crews of these early armored warships still had to put sand or cinders from the ashpans on their gun decks and stairways to stop people slipping on the blood.

The impact of massive projectiles against an armored casemate could be fatal, even if the armor held. One of *Tennessee*'s machinists was trying to free a jammed gun-port cover when an 11-inch solid shot struck its edge. He was smashed into a pulp; his remains had to be shovelled into a bucket and thrown overboard. This same shot sprayed metal splinters inside, killing another seaman and breaking Admiral Buchanan's leg.

Of the 93 men and boys aboard the Louisiana State Navy steamer *Governor Moore*, 57 were killed and 17 wounded during her last three-hour fight at New Orleans. With only improvised sandbag and cotton-bale protection, she was fired on by some of the largest warships in the US Navy. She was finally crippled by a full broadside from USS *Pensacola*: a salvo of 10 9-inch smoothbores against an unarmored vessel at close range.

Carondelet was left to receive the undivided attention of Fort Donelson during the bombardment on St Valentine's Day, 1862. *St Louis*, *Louisville*, and *Pittsburgh* had been com-

pelled to withdraw by heavy and accurate Confederate fire. The Confederate gunners began to fire low with their 32-pounders, skipping the shot across the water to strike the ironclad's water line. Some entered through the *Carondelet*'s wide gun ports and the gun crew learned to dive on to the deck when they saw incoming rounds. But three men either failed to hear the warning shout or stayed standing out of sheer bravado when the next round hissed through the gun port. "Three sharp splats and a heavy bang told the fate of three brave comrades," one witness recalled. The men had been beheaded.

The larger crews of major warships were not immune. At Mobile Bay several US sailors aboard the steam sloops were cut in half by cannonballs. One unfortunate man lost his legs to one shot and threw his arms up, only to have them taken off by the next round. *Hartford* and *Brooklyn* each lost a sixth of their crews at Mobile Bay. *Oneida* lost one man in five.

Perhaps the most dangerous job aboard an ironclad was that of the pilot. Although thickly armored, the pilot houses were often targeted by enemy gunners in the hope of disabling the

Miami and *Southfield*

Miami and *Southfield* sight *Albemarle*

Albemarle rams *Southfield*

Naval Warfare During the Civil War

vessel's steering. Commanders shared the danger – indeed, they were often more exposed to enemy fire. To see more clearly through the smoke and fire, it was often necessary to brave the deck. Commander Issac Brown of the *Arkansas* was shot in the head by a sharpshooter on *Tyler* during the run toward Vicksburg. Luckily for him it was only a grazing blow and he survived. *Tennessee*'s pilot opened the trap-door on top of the pilot house to get a better view, but a shot slammed the door shut on his head, killing him.

Navigational problems
Fighting in rivers and coastal waters meant that many naval battles were as influenced by the terrain as battles on land. *Virginia*'s inability to close with USS *Congress* was the first of many frustrating experiences for Civil War naval officers. Both navies developed shallow-draft warships to fight on the waterways but, as seen above, this design exposed their boilers to enemy gunfire.

River depths dictated the course of many battles. In 1864 the Red River nearly wiped out a major US river squadron by failing to rise fully, then falling unexpectedly early. The *Atlanta* was potentially the South's most effective ironclad ram. Unlike most of the others,

she had relatively new machinery and was probably the only one that could have steamed in the open sea, but she ran aground just before engaging the Union monitors *Nahant* and *Weehawken*. The unlucky ironclad fired seven shots, which all missed; she lay at such an angle on the sand bar that her guns could not bear on her opponents. She had no alternative but to surrender. CSS *Raleigh* was another victim, running hard aground after her futile night sortie from Cape Fear. Her keel was broken and she was abandoned.

The Union sidewheeler *Mississippi* ran aground in the worst possible place – under the guns of Port Hudson during Farragut's attempt to run past the guns on March 14, 1863. *Richmond* had been driven back by a hit on her steam line, while *Monongahela* had her bridge shot away and her captain wounded. An overheated bearing forced her to turn back, so only *Hartford* made it through. *Mississippi* was the last in line and she ran aground within sight

of safety. For 35 minutes her desperate crew struggled to get her off, while three Confederate batteries bombarded this unexpectedly static target. Escape was impossible, so she had to be abandoned and set on fire.

Armament
Working on the leading edge of contemporary technology, the Civil War navies found themselves using some unfamiliar weapons in unanticipated circumstances. No one really knew what to expect when *Virginia* steamed down the Elizabeth River on March 8, 1862. It was not just her first operation, it was the first time she had moved at all. Most people expected a simple trial run to test her machinery, but Admiral Buchanan had other ideas.

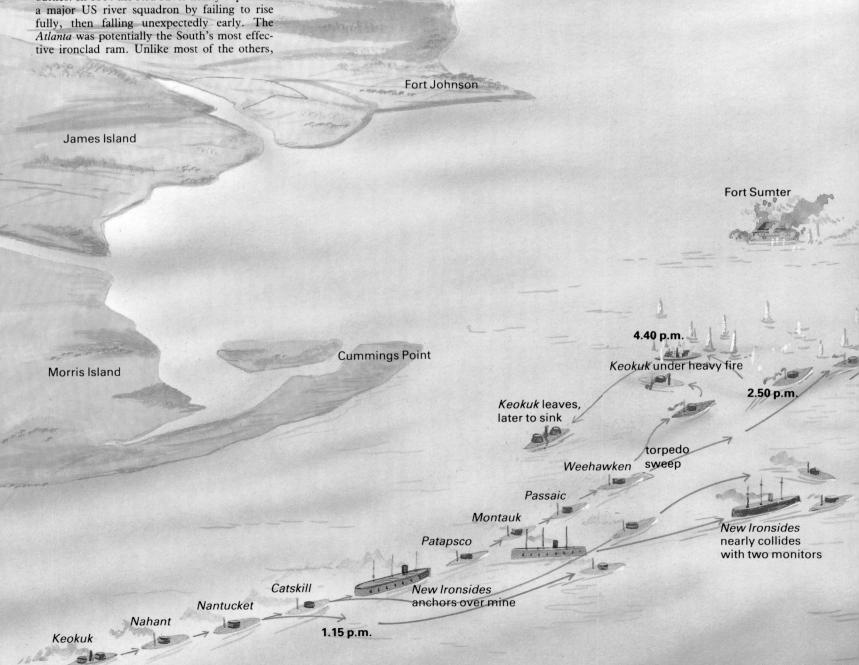

Fort Johnson

James Island

Fort Sumter

Morris Island

Cummings Point

4.40 p.m.

Keokuk under heavy fire

2.50 p.m.

Keokuk leaves, later to sink

torpedo sweep

Weehawken

Passaic

New Ironsides nearly collides with two monitors

Montauk

Patapsco

New Ironsides anchors over mine

Catskill

Nantucket

Keokuk

Nahant

1.15 p.m.

Many of the subsequent naval actions were experimental: untested ships in new situations. For example, no one knew how the appearance of ironclad warships and shell-firing cannon would alter the balance of power between ships and forts. In the eighteenth and early nineteenth centuries land batteries had had all the advantages. They could heat shot to set fire to their wooden opponents. Stone masonry and earthworks were far better able to resist iron cannonballs than the stoutest sail of the line.

The first engagements between Civil War warships and land batteries were all victories for the US Navy. Warships easily overcame Confederate batteries during operations against Hatteras Inlet and Roanoke Island.

Next came the attack on Fort Henry by four Union ironclads. After just under two hours' firing, the Confederates surrendered, with seven of their 11 cannon out of action. Of the nine guns that the fort could bring to bear on the ironclads, only one was capable of inflicting major damage – a 10-inch Columbiad. Unfortunately, this jammed itself with its own priming wire and the second most effective gun, a 6-inch rifle, burst. Although the Confederates managed to land one good hit on *Cincinnati* that penetrated her 2½-inch forward casemate killing one man, they were outgunned and defeated. One of the officers of the 1st Tennessee Artillery observed how the ironclads' large-caliber guns penetrated the earthworks "as

readily as a ball from a Navy Colt would pierce a pine board."

The success at Fort Henry gave heart to the Union ironclad squadron. It seemed that the advantage now lay with them. But subsequent bombardments of Confederate land batteries were not as one-sided. Fort Donelson drove off the ironclads, inflicting damage on all of them. To tackle Island No. 10 and Fort Pillow the Union squadron relied more heavily on its "bummers" – unwieldy schooners mounting 10- and 13-inch seacoast mortars.

The mortar boats were effective, but not the key to instant success that David Porter claimed. He boasted that he could reduce Forts Jackson and St Philip in 48 hours, but the

Charleston

Drum Island

Cooper River

Hog Island

Battery

torpedoes

Mount Pleasant

obstructions

Fort Moultrie

Patapsco

Sullivan's Island

Admiral Du Pont led the US North Atlantic squadron against Charleston on April 7, 1863. Tidal conditions postponed his attack until early afternoon, but by 1.15 p.m. his squadron was heading up the channel to engage the northwest face of Fort Sumter. The US warships found a line of obstructions between Forts Sumter and Moultrie, which forced the leading vessels to veer off. New Ironsides had problems with the shallow water, so anchored – right over a 2000-lb command-detonated mine. Luckily for the crew, the mine failed to explode.

The Confederates opened fire at about 3.00 p.m. and the action lasted two hours, during which the

ironclads were hit repeatedly. The Confederates were able to bounce their shot across the still water, striking the monitors on their turrets. Many officers feared that if the action was renewed their weakened turrets would collapse. By the time the US squadron retreated, Fort Sumter was damaged but most guns were still in action. Only one man

died in the shore batteries – a flagstaff was knocked down by a shell and fell on him.

With Keokuk foundering the next day and the rest of his ships damaged, Du Pont concluded that there was no prospect of taking Charleston by naval action alone.

Naval Warfare During the Civil War

Confederate batteries were still in business after five days' bombardment. Further battles between ships and forts showed that the new weapons had not altered the balance too far. Forts could still be protected more heavily than a warship and the fate of Du Pont's assault on Charleston proved the limitations of the Civil War ironclads.

Civil War naval battles involved warships of radically different capabilities. Some proved hopelessly one-sided; others were surprisingly indecisive. They were dominated by the new business of guns against armor. Rapid and accurate gunnery was no longer enough. The Union monitor *Montauk* was struck 154 times, mostly by solid shot from 10-inch Columbiads, during the battles with the Charleston defenses from July through September 1863. Her armor was never penetrated. The monitors *Weehaw-*

ken, *Patapso*, *Montauk*, *Passaic*, *Nahant*, and *Catskill* engaged the Charleston batteries an average of 10 times each during that period. Together they suffered a total of 629 hits, none of which penetrated.

The Civil War naval actions witnessed the beginning of a struggle between guns and armor that was to be the key feature of naval warfare for the next 80 years or so. The ram was to become a major naval weapon again, but here the lessons of the Civil War were misleading. Although the spectacular ramming and disabling of the *Re d'Italia* during the Battle of Lissa in 1866 helped stampede the world's navies into a ram race, the technique was not as easy as it looked.

Ramming occurred frequently during the Civil War, but two factors made it much easier. First of all, it took place in relatively narrow

waters; the Mississippi off Memphis, for example, was a crowded place during the battles of the rams. At New Orleans the Mississippi was little over 1000 yards across opposite Forts St Philip and Jackson. Collisions between ships of the same side were common enough as they maneuvered in a relatively confined space. Secondly, some ships were remarkably slow. *Manassas*'s commander wisely ran her aground as she had no hope of avoiding being run down once her engines failed. *Tennessee*'s tortoise-like progress across Mobile Bay allowed the far handier Union warships to ram her again and again.

The Civil War was a unique era in naval warfare, a period of engineering genius and incredible improvisation. Above all, the sheer courage to steam into battle in such untried warships must command our deepest respect.

Ebb tide aids submarine

Hunley sighted at 100 yards

Cushing runs in close to examine enemy position

Launch swamped by explosion

BELOW: *The USS* Housatonic *had the unfortunate distinction of being the first warship to be sunk by a submarine. On February 17, 1864 the* Housatonic *was on duty off Charleston when an officer spotted something in the water. It was 8.45 p.m. on a moonlit night. Moments later a powerful explosive charge detonated against the sloop's hull and she sank rapidly. She was in only 27 feet of water, so all but five of her crew clambered into the rigging and survived.*

The attackers were not so lucky. Lieutenant George A. Dixon and his gallant eight-man crew died inside the CSS Hunley, *a cigar-shaped, hand-propelled submarine armed with a spar torpedo containing a 90-lb charge. Thirty-three men had already died in* Hunley's *trials, but more brave volunteers took their place until the patrol that ended with the attack on* Housatonic.

BOTTOM: Albemarle *was the only Confederate ironclad to be destroyed by enemy action. Of the 22 ironclads completed by the South, four surrendered and all others, apart from* Albemarle, *were blown up or burned to prevent their capture. After defeating the* Miami *and* Southfield *in May 1864,* Albemarle *stayed in the Roanoke River, supporting the garrison of Plymouth.*

The US Navy considered many schemes for attacking her and eventually settled on a steamboat fitted with an explosive charge. Commanded by Lieutenant William B. Cushing, the 15-man launch headed upstream on the murky night of October 26/27. At about 3.00 a.m. they spotted the Albemarle *and charged at full speed. The launch crashed over the log barrier, which was slippery after long immersion. Under heavy fire at point-blank range, Cushing lowered the explosive charge against* Albemarle's *hull and fired it. The ironclad sank in 8 feet of water.*

This striking success led the Confederates to practically immobilize their squadron on the James, *surrounding them with obstructions and torpedoes.*

Hunley explodes mine under *Housatonic*

Cutter tows launch

Sunken wreck of *Southfield*

Cushing passes anchored schooner at 2 a.m.

11.30 p.m. start

Cutter is cast off

Cushing turns in to attack

...ushing turns away in wide ...eep to build up speed

Warships of the US and Confederate Navies

The US Navy's blockade of the Confederacy had been in force for only a few weeks when Stephen R. Mallory, the Confederate secretary of the navy, urged his government to buy ironclad warships from Europe. At the same time, the fledgling Confederate Navy was casting around for material to construct ironclads at home, ready to break out and challenge the blockading squadrons. By early July the decision had been taken to rebuild the partially destroyed *Merrimack* (captured at Norfolk Navy Yard) as an ironclad.

Mallory's opposite number in Washington, Gideon Welles, lobbied Congress for funds to retaliate in kind. He was painfully aware that $500,000 had been frittered away on the Steven's Battery but succeeded in extracting $1.5 million for the construction of ironclad warships. The Ironclad Board examined 18 designs submitted by contractors of widely varying competence. Three warships were proceeded with. Two were conventionally designed: wooden hulls protected with iron armor plate, they shipped masts and mounted their guns in broadside batteries. One was very different and has subsequently given its name to a whole class of warship.

John Ericsson's *Monitor* was an iron raft attached to a slab-sided iron hull, which it overlapped by 14 feet at the bow and 32 feet at the stern. The US Navy's Bureau of Construction and Repair had already examined similar designs and, indeed, preferred the idea of a low freeboard ironclad with two turrets built according to the system perfected by the British inventor Captain Cowper Coles. But Ericsson could offer one vital point in his favor: time. He promised to deliver a completed warship in under 100 days.

Monitor's freeboard was only 14–18 inches when fully laden and waves washed freely over her deck. With so little hull to protect, the armor could be concentrated on her turret. This was of Ericsson's own design, pivoting on a central spindle instead of the roller race used on Coles' turrets. In practice the Ericsson turret did not prove a success. It was difficult to traverse accurately and it was vulnerable to being jammed by hits at its base. The Coles turret proved more reliable and his system formed the basis for the turrets fitted to warships in the later nineteenth century.

Monitor was designed to have a speed of 8 knots but only ever managed 6 or 7 knots. The majority of Civil War ironclads that followed her would also fail to meet the speed specified in their contracts. It should be emphasized that although some cannon and small arms were manufactured with standardized, interchangeable parts, this was not the case for marine engines. They were still built individually and spare parts were rarely interchangeable. The exact power of an engine was unknown until it was finished and tested. The large margin of error led to inevitable problems when shipyards started to build the first ironclads.

Nowhere in the North had the facility to forge heavy, wrought-iron plate of the sort fitted to British ironclads, so *Monitor*'s armor, although 8 inches thick on her turret, was actually eight 1-inch plates bolted together and therefore not as strong as one-piece forging.

However, the Confederates were in the same situation and *Monitor* had almost twice as much

protection on her turret as *Virginia* had along her casemate. Although in her celebrated action against *Virginia*, *Monitor*'s offensive power was limited because her two 11-inch guns were firing only half charges, it must be remembered that the Confederate ironclad had its own problems. *Virginia* had no solid shot left and could engage *Monitor* only with shells. These proved ineffective against armor throughout the war; the wrought-iron shells simply shattered on impact.

Monitor was an uncomfortable ship by any standards. She was ventilated by a blower drawing from two pipes, but these proved to be too low and it was not safe to open them in a seaway. (In the summer of 1862 the temperature in the engine-room once reached 178 degrees.) In December *Monitor* was ordered to join the squadron off Charleston but on the night of December 31 she was caught in a storm. Force 7 winds sent 30-foot waves

BELOW: *The French* Gloire *was the first armored battleship, and her completion in August 1860 began a new era in warship construction. Five other ironclads were nearing completion. Although the US Navy had started work on an armored warship in 1842, work had been abandoned in 1856 with the vessel incomplete. France's revolutionary warships were soon in evidence near American waters;* Gloire's *sister-ship* Normandie *was part of the French naval squadron off Mexico in July 1862.*

RIGHT: Re d'Italia *was one of two broadside ironclads built by Webb in New York for the Italian Navy. Laid down in November 1861 and completed in September 1864, she was sunk at the battle of Lissa in 1866. She was wooden-hulled and therefore had no watertight compartments, but was protected by 4.75 inches of iron. Displacing 5869 tons at full load, she carried six 8-inch 72-pdrs and 21 6.45-inch guns. The fact that Northern yards had enough excess capacity to take on major orders for foreign powers at a time when the South was straining to build small, river-going ironclads illustrates the vast disparity between Confederate and Union industrial power.*

Comparison of warship armor protection

The New Ironsides' *4-inch armor was rolled in one thickness and kept out a storm of Confederate fire during the US Navy's assault on Charleston.* Gloire's *4.75 inches of armor was backed by 26 inches of oak. HMS* Warrior's *protection was similar: 4½ inches of iron with 18-inch backing. On the British ship the armor belt consisted of 4-ton plates measuring 15 × 3 feet, tongued and grooved to support each other.*

BELOW: Warrior *displaced over 9000 tons and in 1860 she was the fastest and most heavily armed battleship in the world. The US Navy would not seek to challenge British naval strength until the end of the century. The collapse of the US merchant marine during the Civil War was followed by two very lean decades for the US Navy.*

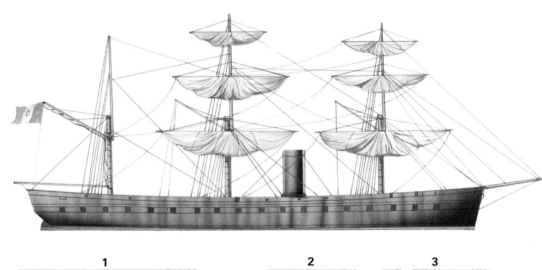

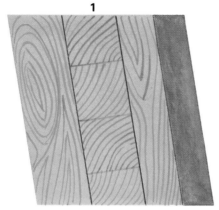  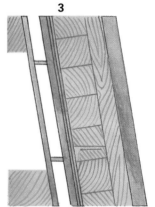

| 1 | 2 | 3 |

A section of USS New Ironsides' *armor.*   *An equivalent slice of* Gloire.   *A section from* Warrior.

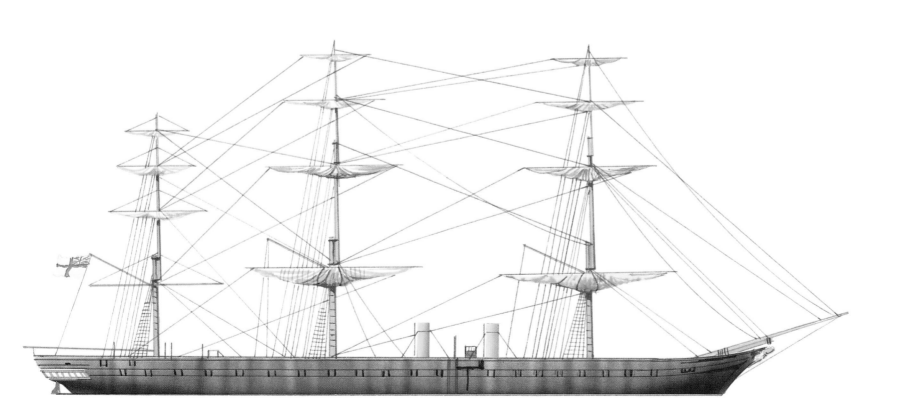

Warships of the US and Confederate Navies

crashing over her, partially flooding the turret. She was being towed by *Rhode Island* into a head sea. Water entered the coal bunkers, wetting the coal so badly that the steam pressure fell from 80 to 20 pounds. As power failed, *Monitor* was in danger of being towed under. Two sailors gallantly made their way across the deck to the bow where they cut the rope before being swept away to their deaths.

Forty-nine of *Monitor*'s crew were rescued by a boat from *Rhode Island* in two exhausting journeys, but when the rowboat set out on its third perilous mission, the red signal light on the foundering ironclad's turret suddenly vanished in the darkness. Four officers and 12 men still aboard were lost. *Monitor*'s loss was widely attributed to water forcing the lower part of the hull away from the upper. Ericsson was understandably unhappy with this explanation and vigorously asserted that the flooding was due to oakum being inserted between the turret and the deck during the ironclad's refit. This was supposed to guarantee a watertight join between the two but Ericsson claimed it had just the opposite effect.

The true reason for the loss of the *Monitor* may yet be established, since her wreck has been located off Cape Hatteras. The little vessel lies upside down, resting on her turret. The iron is probably too badly rusted to survive an attempt at raising her so the vessel is being minutely photographed.

USS *New Ironsides*, completed six months later, displaced over 4000 tons compared to the 987-ton *Monitor*. Bark-rigged and wooden-hulled, she carried a far greater armament: two 150-pounder Parrott rifles, two 50-pounder Dahlgren rifles, and 14 11-inch Dahlgren smoothbores. Her hull was protected by 4 inches of armor in strips 15 feet × 2 feet 4 inches hammered from scrap iron. Despite its dubious provenance, her armor proved tough enough and she survived numerous shore

bombardment operations without sustaining serious damage. Indeed, she survived an attack by a Confederate torpedo boat of Charleston; a 70-pound charge was exploded abreast the engine-room and her wooden sides were sprung for a length of 40 feet.

New Ironsides had a designed speed of 9½ knots but proved unable to reach 7 knots, even with all sails set and engines at full power. Although flat-bottomed and shallow-drafted by European standards, she still drew too much water to maneuver with freedom in the shallow waters of Charleston harbor where she flew the flag of Admiral Du Pont during his unsuccessful fight with the Confederate forts. However, she was more than a match for the much smaller casemate ironclads assembled in Charleston and would have made short work of the Confederate Charleston squadron had it ever seriously challenged the blockade.

The third US ironclad, *Galena*, was a schooner-rigged, wooden-hulled steamer displacing 738 tons. Interlocking bars of iron armor 3–4 inches thick protected her sides and increased her displacement to 950 tons. Armed with four 9-inch Dahlgrens and two 6.4-inch 100-pounder Parrott rifles, she was completed on April 21, 1862.

The US ironclads were in action within weeks of completion. *Monitor* arrived in Hampton Roads in the nick of time to prevent *Virginia* inflicting further destruction against the wooden ships of the blockading squadron. Meanwhile, the successes of the river ironclads against Forts Henry and Donelson implied that armored warships had the advantage over land batteries. On May 15, 1862 *Galena* and *Monitor* attacked the Confederate shore batteries at Drewry's Bluff on the James River. *Galena* fired for nearly four hours before running out of ammunition. Her sides had a pronounced tumble home (i.e. sloped inwards from the water line to the deck) and this 45-degree slope

increased the thickness of armor an incoming projectile would have to penetrate. Unfortunately, the Confederate guns on the James were 200 feet above the river. Engaging at about 800 yards, she was struck by 28 projectiles, of which 18 penetrated. Her armor was later removed in favor of increased armament and she subsequently saw action at Mobile Bay.

The US Senate approved a 21-ship ironclad program in February 1862. The first class to follow the *Monitor* were bigger versions of Ericsson's design. This *Passaic* class consisted of 10 monitors displacing 1875 tons. Most were launched in the fall of 1862. The pilot house was mounted on top of the turret but did not rotate with it. This made gun-laying easier; on the original *Monitor* the guns could not fire directly ahead because of the blast effect on the pilot house which was sited forward. Communication between *Monitor*'s pilot house and her turret had proved very difficult and much confusion had resulted during the engagement with *Virginia*.

The *Passaic* class armament varied. In general they carried one 11-inch Dahlgren and one 15-inch Dahlgren, although an 8-inch Parrott was sometimes substituted for the larger smoothbore. Unfortunately, since the barrel of the 15-inch Dahlgren was about 2 inches shorter than that of an 11-inch Dahlgren, it did not project through the gun port properly. To avoid the appalling consequences of firing it with the muzzle inside the turret, a smoke box was built around it to vent all the smoke and blast outside. This, of course, blocked any view through the gun port, so the 15-inch gun had to be aimed through the other gun port. The *Passaic* class comprised *Camanche*, *Catskill*, *Lehigh*, *Montauk*, *Nahant*, *Nantucket*, *Passaic*, *Patapsco*, *Sangamon*, and *Weehawken*. The last-named foundered by mistake off Charleston while taking on stores. The only other war loss was *Patapsco*, mined off Charleston on

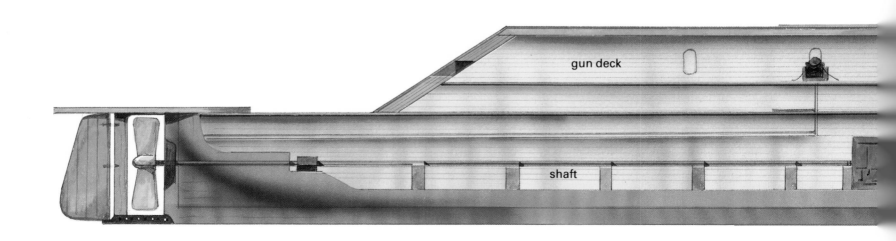

The table (right) shows the rapid growth in warship construction during the period up to the US Civil War and during it. In the 10-year period from 1848 to 1858 the United Kingdom built 33 sailing ships of the line, several of 130 guns, but with the introduction of the ironclad, the existing wooden battleships became obsolete. The Confederate States were quick to realize the importance of the ironclad and laid down several in 1861 in an organized building program, while the US Navy left it to the Army to commence an ironclad fleet for river service.

By 1865 the massive industrial might of the Union had 50 ironclads in service, with many more building, while the ever-failing resources of the South left them with a dwindling fleet of vessels, many with faults through hasty construction and lack of proper facilities.

In 1861 Europe had seven ironclads at sea, and by 1865 there were 66 in service worldwide, including small but powerful units for Brazil and Peru.

Merrimack, *renamed* Virginia, *was planned as an ocean-going warship capable of smashing the Union squadron blockading Virginia and the Carolinas, and possibly sailing north to attack New York. Admiral Buchanan believed she would have foundered had the plan been attempted. Fortunately for her crew,* Merrimack's *seaworthiness was never tested. Protected by 2 inches of iron armor, she carried two 7-inch Brooke rifles forward; two 6-inch Brookes aft; and three 9-inch Dahlgren smoothbores on either side.*

Major Warships, 1859

UNITED STATES
10 sailing ships of the line: *Pennsylvania* 120 guns; *Columbus* 80 guns; *Ohio* 84 guns; *North Carolina* 84 guns; *Delaware* 84 guns; *Alabama* 84 guns; *Virginia* 84 guns; *Vermont* 84 guns; *New York* 84 guns; *New Orleans* 84 guns.

11 sailing frigates: *Independence* 56 guns; *United States, Constitution, Potomac, Brandywine, Columbia, Congress, Raritan, Sautee, Sabine, St Lawrence,* all 50 guns.

There were no screw line of battleships in the US Navy. Of the **10** vessels listed, **4** were still building, and **3** acted as receiving ships.

UNITED KINGDOM
6 screw three-decker ships of the line; **30** screw two-decker ships of the line, plus **12** building; **19** screw frigates, plus **7** building; **43** sailing ships of the line, **4** to be rebuilt as steamships.

FRANCE
9 screw ships of the line, plus **24** vessels converting to steam; **6** screw frigates; **14** sailing ships of the line; **28** sailing frigates.

RUSSIA
7 screw ships of the line; **12** sailing ships of the line.

SWEDEN **2** screw ships of the line.	DENMARK **4** sailing ships of the line.
HOLLAND **4** sailing ships of the line.	SPAIN **2** sailing ships of the line.
AUSTRIA **1** screw ship of the line.	PORTUGAL **1** sailing ship of the line.
TURKEY **7** sailing ships of the line.	

Ironclads, 1861
UNITED STATES **9** ordered by the US Army.   CONFEDERATE STATES **5**.

1865
UNITED STATES **50**: 4 *Winnebago,* 5 *Cairo, Benton, Essex,* 8 *Passaic,* 9 *Canonicus, New Ironsides, Onondaga, Roanoke,* 8 *Casco, Galena, Choctaw, Lafayette, Tuscumbria,* 2 *Osage, Ozark, Dictator, Miantonomah, Dunderberg, Tennessee,* captured from the Confederates.
CONFEDERATE STATES **14**: *Texas,* 2 *Huntsville, Neuse, Richmond, Baltic, Nashville,* 2 *Chicora, Charleston, Columbia, Missouri, Stonewall, Fredericksburg.* In 1865 the US Navy also had another **22** ironclads under construction, including 4 5600-ton ocean-going monitors of the *Kalamazoo* class.

Europe, 1861
UNITED KINGDOM **2**; FRANCE **3**; AUSTRIA **2**.

World total, 1865
UNITED KINGDOM **14**; FRANCE **16**; RUSSIA **4**; ITALY **10**; SPAIN **3**; JAPAN **1**; AUSTRIA **5**; DENMARK **4**; BRAZIL **2**; GERMANY **1**; PERU **2**; TURKEY **4**.

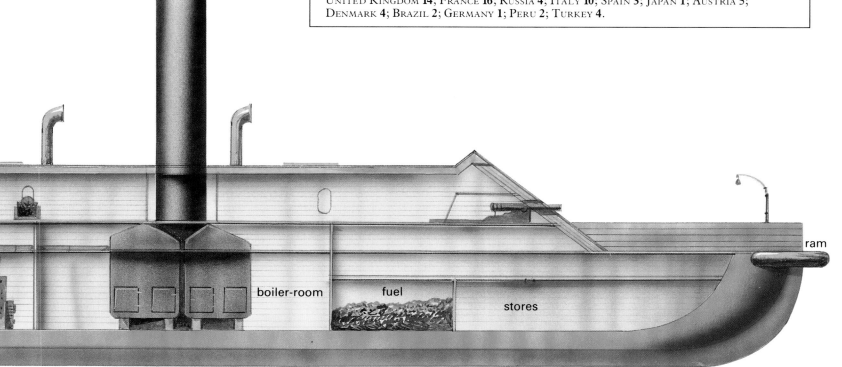

boiler-room   fuel   stores   ram

Warships of the US and Confederate Navies

January 15, 1865. Monitors had very little reserve buoyancy and *Patapsco* sank like a stone, vanishing from view in less than 30 seconds from the detonation of the 60-pound charge. Over half the 105 men on board her were killed.

The armament of the *Passaic* class was altered during the war. Several mounted a pair of 12-pounder smoothbore howitzers on a field carriage. Fired from the deck, it provided the ship with a capacity for rapid fire against targets ashore. Since the gun crews were unprotected, it was of no value against a warship. The mixed armament in the turrets had resulted from a shortage of 15-inch Dahlgrens. As further weapons became available, the rifled guns or 11-inch smoothbores were replaced. By the end of the war all surviving *Passaic*-class monitors were armed with two 15-inch guns.

The ironclad program of 1862 also included another nine monitors of the *Canonicus* class. *Canonicus* was launched in August 1863 and commissioned in April 1864. *Tecumseh*, *Mahopac*, and *Saugus* followed but *Catawba*, *Manayunk*, *Oneota*, and *Tippecanoe* were not completed until 1865 and were never commissioned. They were armed with two 15-inch Dahlgrens, the guns and the turrets modified so that the muzzles did project through the gun ports. Ventilation was improved – it had been so bad on the original *Monitor* that temperatures of 120 degrees fahrenheit were recorded on the berth deck. They never achieved the hoped-for speed of 13 knots, averaging 8 knots instead. *Manhattan* engaged *Tennessee* during the battle in Mobile Bay, finally penetrating the Confederate's armor with point-blank shots. *Tecumseh* was mined at the beginning of the

same battle, again sinking in about 20 seconds with most of her crew.

The *Canonicus*-class monitors displaced 2100 tons. Their sides were protected by five 1-inch layers of armor, while turret armor was increased to 10 inches, again built up in layers. The pilot house above it was similarly protected. *Oneota* and *Catawba* were sold to Peru in 1868 and were both lost during the 1879–81 war with Chile. *Catawba*, renamed *Atahualpa*, was raised and served as a hulk until just before World War I.

The first double-turreted monitor to enter service with the US Navy was the *Onondaga*, which differed from Ericsson's vessels in that she had a conventional iron hull rather than a raft attached to a lower hull. Each turret had one 15-inch Dahlgren and one 8-inch 150-pounder Parrott rifle. They were protected by 11 inches of iron built up from 1-inch plates. Her speed was designed to be 9 knots but she could realize only about 7. *Onondaga* served on the James River and had one brief encounter with the Confederate James River squadron, when they made their unsuccessful sortie in 1865.

Merrimack was not the only one of the 1855 screw frigates to end her days as an ironclad. The US Navy also decided to convert one of them, cutting *Roanoke* down to her battery deck. The original plan for her conversion anticipated much later warships: she was to have eight 15-inch guns in four turrets, but the ship could not stand the weight of four, so three turrets were fitted instead. Her construction was delayed so her 4½-inch armored sides could be assembled from single plates rather than 1-inch plates bolted together. Her forward and aft turrets each had one 15-inch Dahlgren

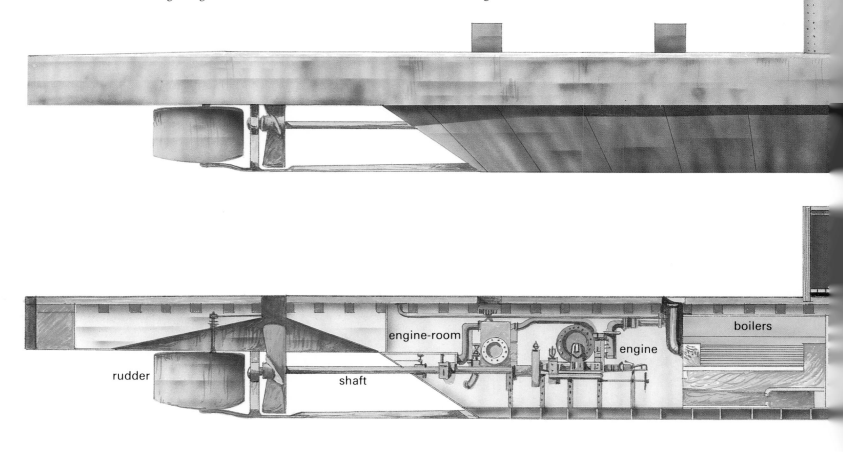

rudder   shaft   engine-room   engine   boilers

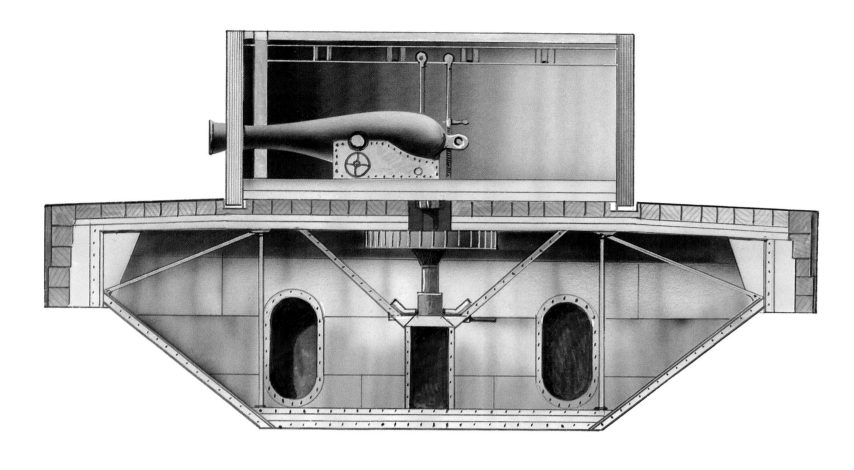

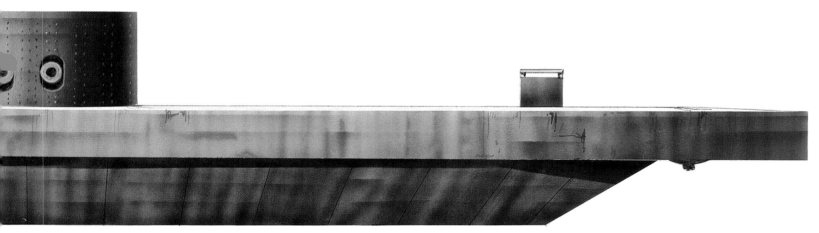

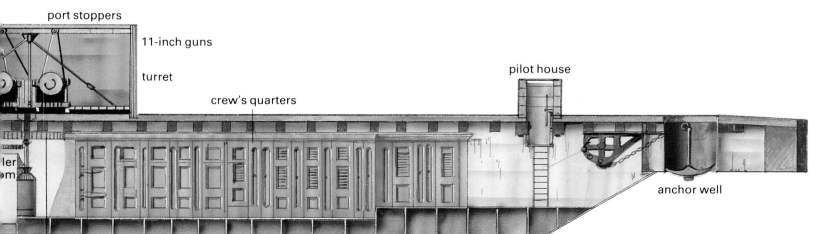

port stoppers

11-inch guns

turret

pilot house

crew's quarters

anchor well

ler
m

turret traversing gear

Warships of the US and Confederate Navies

and one 8-inch Parrott rifle. The center turret housed one 15-inch and one 11-inch Dahlgren. Unfortunately, the combined weight was still too much and her stern was damaged on launch. The hull sagged ominously and she rolled excessively. As a result, *Roanoke* spent her war guarding Hampton Roads.

All the above ironclads were laid down or converted in private yards. The US Navy Yards at Portsmouth, New York, Boston, and Philadelphia each laid down a double-turreted monitor in 1862. The *Miantonomah* class had wooden rather than iron hulls, which was the cause of their ultimate downfall. They deteriorated rapidly and were broken up after less than 10 years' service. Armed with four 15-inch Dahlgrens, they had slightly more freeboard

BELOW: *The* Passaic *class monitors were enlarged and improved versions of* Monitor. *Note the pilot house on top of the turret (this did not rotate with the turret). It was protected by 8 inches of armor plate, the turret by 11 inches. Armed with one 11-inch and one 15-inch Dahlgren smoothbores, the* Passaics *led the attack on Charleston, where they suffered a terrible assault from Confederate shore batteries. Their armor protection was later increased, but it did illustrate the problem of building up armor by successive layers of 1-inch plate.*

than the earlier monitors (24 inches), but their decks were invariably awash. Only *Monadnock*, commissioned in October 1864, saw any service. After the war *Miantonomah* crossed the Atlantic, although she was towed part of the way by a sidewheel steamer.

Ericsson was aware that his first monitors were really limited to coastal and riverine waters. Although the *Passaic*-class monitor *Lehigh* survived a gale off Cape Hatteras during which the sea was 4 feet above her deck, such craft were unsuitable for combat in open waters. Ericsson was keen to show that his monitor-type warships could be taken to sea and he badgered the Navy Department with several designs for enlarged monitors in 1862. The navy ordered two. *Dictator* was laid down in August 1862. Displacing 4438 tons, she had a 500-ton turret protected by 15 inches of armor and housing two 15-inch Dahlgrens. She was designed to make the exceptional speed of 16 knots but in practice managed a maximum of only 9 – in fact, 6 knots was more usual. She was launched in December 1864 and commissioned in time to join the fleet assembled for the attack on Fort Fisher. Unfortunately, her main shaft bearings were too short and the shaft showed signs of heavy wear after just 20 miles, forcing her to turn back.

Puritan was an even larger monitor, displacing 4912 tons. Launched in July 1864 but never

completed, she was to have carried two 20-inch smoothbores, but the difficulty in producing these mammoth weapons was one of many problems attending her construction. Work was suspended in 1865 and she was broken up in 1874.

The Union 1862 ironclad program also included two warships quite different from the monitors. The little *Keokuk* was designed by one of Ericsson's partners. Displacing 677 tons, she was armored with iron strips alternating with oak. She had two gun houses each with three gun ports for the single 11-inch Dahlgren inside. She carried a spur ram and was capable of 9 knots. Laid down in April 1862, she was completed by the end of the year and commissioned in March 1863 in time for the attack on Charleston. Here she suffered 90 hits, 19 penetrating her near the water line, and she foundered in shallow water the next day, leaving just the tops of her funnels above the waves. Two weeks of clandestine work by night allowed the Confederates to remove her armament from the wreck, one of the most enterprising salvage operations of the war. They also recovered her signal book which allowed the Charleston garrison to decode Union signals and learn of the boat attack to be made on Fort Sumter. Armed with this intelligence, the defenders laid on a deadly welcome for the Union sailors and marines.

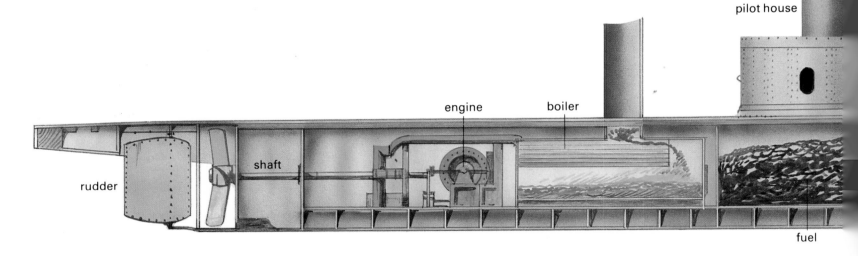

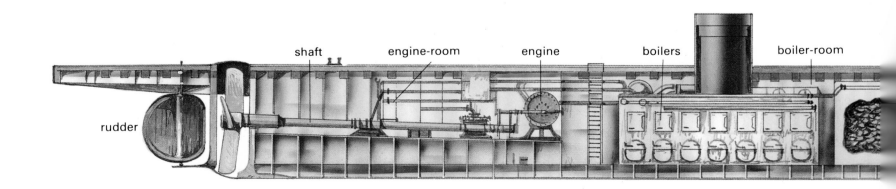

The second US ironclad laid down in 1862 that was not designed as a monitor was the *Dunderberg*. She was the only Union warship to follow the casemate design favored by the Confederates. Far larger than even Ericsson's final monitors – at 7800 tons she displaced twice as much water as the 1855 screw frigates – the *Dunderberg* was constructed partly from unseasoned timber which led her to deteriorate rapidly. Carrying 1000 tons of armor, she was armed with four 15-inch and 12 11-inch Dahlgrens but her construction was bedevilled by shortages. Her builder, W.H. Webb, eventually took her back in 1865, refunding over $1 million to the navy and selling her to France in 1867. Commissioned briefly during the Franco-Prussian War, she was stricken in 1872.

Given the sea-going pretensions of the first monitors, it is ironic that perhaps the best warships of this type were designed by James B. Eads. He built the first Union river ironclads that spearheaded the Union penetration down the Mississippi. In May 1862 he was contracted by the Navy Department to build four shallow-draft warships of the monitor type. They proved so successful that they ultimately served with the West Gulf blockading squadron and two of them fought at Mobile Bay. *Winnebago* was launched in July 1863 and completed in

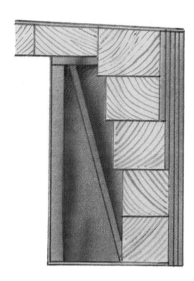

The Passaic's *laminated side armor: 1-inch plates of iron built up to a thickness of 3–4 inches. The armor was brittle and continued impacts from Confederate solid shot at Charleston fractured their deck armor. After the battle another 50 tons of armor was added to the decks, protecting the machinery and magazines.*

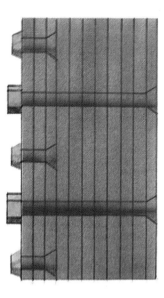

Passaic's *turret armor was also laminated and bolted together. The action at Charleston knocked out so many bolts on the turrets that they threatened to collapse if exposed to further damage.*

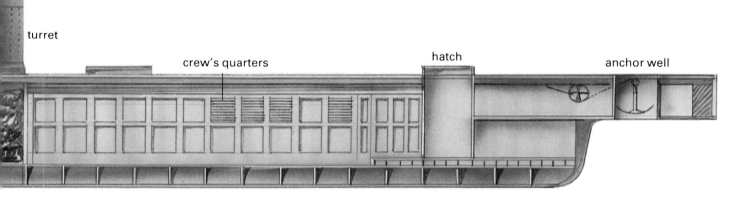

turret

crew's quarters

hatch

anchor well

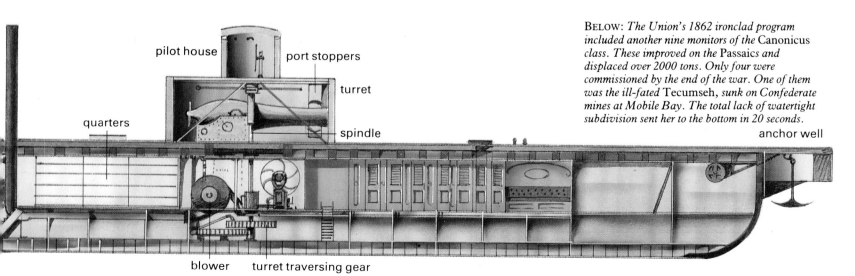

pilot house

port stoppers

turret

spindle

quarters

blower   turret traversing gear

BELOW: *The Union's 1862 ironclad program included another nine monitors of the* Canonicus *class. These improved on the* Passaics *and displaced over 2000 tons. Only four were commissioned by the end of the war. One of them was the ill-fated* Tecumseh, *sunk on Confederate mines at Mobile Bay. The total lack of watertight subdivision sent her to the bottom in 20 seconds.*

anchor well

Warships of the US and Confederate Navies

April 1864 followed by *Milwaukee*, *Chickasaw*, and *Kickapoo*. Displacing 1300 tons, they were double-turreted and turtle-backed. Their hulls were protected by 3 inches of iron in one plate rather than several bolted together. The aft turret was to Ericsson's design, while the forward one was invented by Eads. Both were protected by 8 inches of armor and contained a pair of 11-inch Dahlgrens.

Unlike most of their contemporaries, Eads' monitors actually made their designed speed of 9 knots. They also appear to have been better designed internally with much more subdivision. *Milwaukee* struck a mine in the Blakely River, Mobile Bay, on March 28, 1865. It exploded on her port side abaft the after turret some 40 feet from her stern. Her crew did not share the fate of the men aboard *Tecumseh* or *Patapsco*. Although *Milwaukee*'s stern sank in a few minutes, the rest of the hull remained

above water for another hour and everyone on board was able to scramble to safety.

During the summer of 1862 the Navy Department recognized that the Confederates were determined to defend the Mississippi and other rivers with a combination of shore batteries and ironclads of their own. Many of the waterways could be penetrated only by very light-draft vessels and the monitors then under construction would be unable to tackle them. To support the fleet of converted river boats the Navy Department drew up specifications for a monitor-type ironclad with an exceptionally shallow draft. Ericsson was approached to design these warships and no less than 20 were ordered between March and July 1863. The *Casco* class was designed to have a single turret mounting two 11-inch Dahlgrens. Speed was to be 9 knots and it was to draw just 4 feet of water compared to *Monitor*'s and *Passaic*'s 10½ feet.

Unfortunately, Ericsson's original design was modified by chief engineer Alban B. Stimers and further altered in the light of the *Passaic* class's experience at Charleston. The Navy Department introduced several mutually incompatible requirements: internal ballast tanks to submerge the craft partially when in action and heavier protection for the turret, while still retaining the designed draft. The camel has been described as a horse designed by a committee; the story of the $14-million *Casco*

BELOW: *USS* Milwaukee *was one of four river monitors designed by James B. Eads, builder of the Union's first river ironclads. These turtle-backed, iron-hulled monitors were probably the best of their type to see service in the Civil War. They proved so capable that they later operated in the coastal waters of the western Gulf, and* Winnebago *and* Chickasaw *fought at Mobile Bay.*

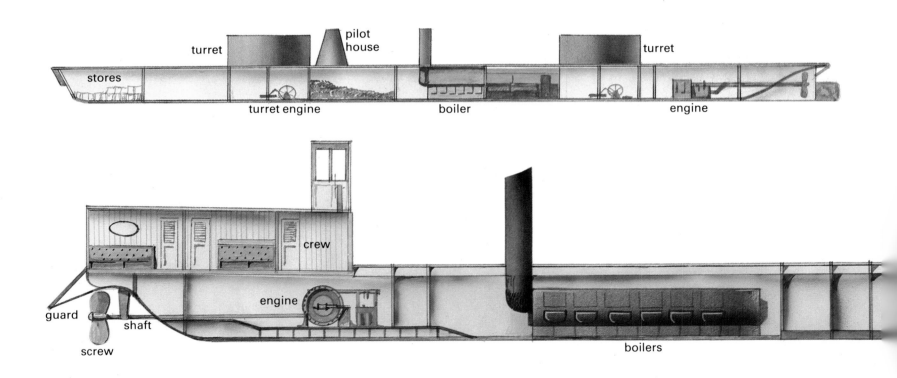

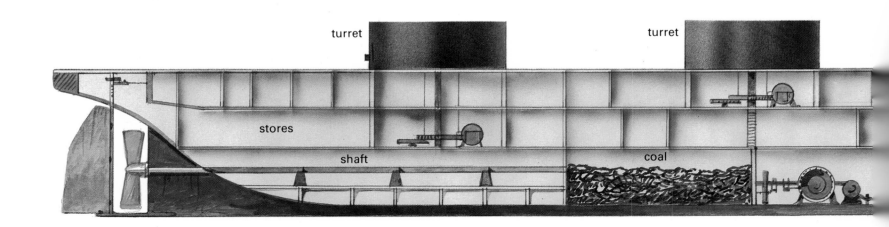

class is a nautical illustration of the same point. Ericsson and Stimers fell out over the design and ceased to cooperate. Unseasoned timber was used but Stimers' team failed to modify the design to reflect its greater weight. When the first of the class, the *Chimo* was launched, she had a freeboard of just 3 inches instead of the planned 15. (This was without stores, ammunition, or the turret!)

The confusion attending their construction did nothing to accelerate building work. Only eight *Cascos* were finished by the end of the war, seven of them arriving as late as 1865.

Casco, *Chimo*, *Modoc*, *Napa*, and *Naubuc* were completed as spar torpedo vessels with no turret. Instead, they carried an 11-inch Dahlgren (an 8-inch 200-pounder Parrott rifle on *Chimo*) in an exposed pivot mounting. To strike another warship with a spar torpedo demanded speed and maneuverability, so it was doubly unfortunate that the *Cascos* never made their designed speed. Capable of only 5 knots, they were of very little value.

The major warships in the Union's 1863 ironclad program were the four *Kalamazoo*-class double-turreted monitors. Essentially an improved version of the *Miantonomahs*, they were to displace 5600 tons and to be armed with four 15-inch Dahlgrens. Intended to be truly ocean going, they were laid down in the fall of 1863 but were still incomplete at the end of the war and construction was finally abandoned in November 1865.

The river flotillas

The US Navy's ironclad program described so far followed a reasonably coherent pattern of development with successive classes of warship following each other. But this is only half the

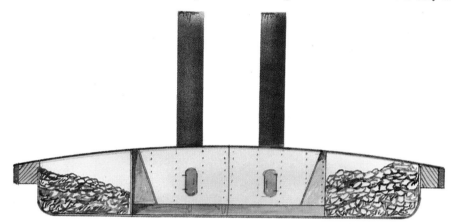

BELOW AND RIGHT: *USS* Sandusky *was a diminutive river monitor displacing only 479 tons and armed with two 11-inch Dahlgren smoothbores. Although ordered in May 1862, she was not completed until 1865 and did not commission until after the war was over.*

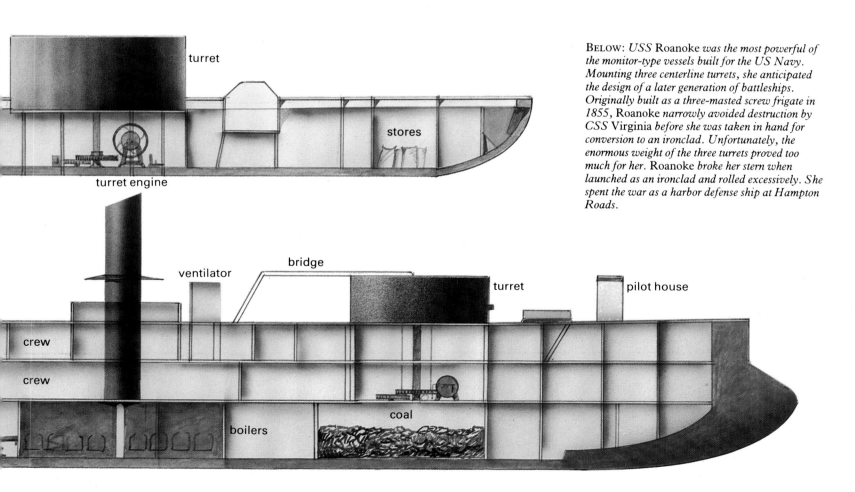

turret

turret engine

stores

BELOW: *USS* Roanoke *was the most powerful of the monitor-type vessels built for the US Navy. Mounting three centerline turrets, she anticipated the design of a later generation of battleships. Originally built as a three-masted screw frigate in 1855,* Roanoke *narrowly avoided destruction by CSS* Virginia *before she was taken in hand for conversion to an ironclad. Unfortunately, the enormous weight of the three turrets proved too much for her.* Roanoke *broke her stern when launched as an ironclad and rolled excessively. She spent the war as a harbor defense ship at Hampton Roads.*

ventilator

bridge

turret

pilot house

crew

crew

boilers

coal

Warships of the US and Confederate Navies

story. Far inland on the great waterways of North America another fleet was in action throughout the war with both armored and unarmored boats. The founding of the Union Mississippi flotilla was actually the work of the army. Under the direction of General McClellan, Commander Rodgers bought three river steamers which became *Lexington*, *Conestoga*, and *Tyler*. They were assembled at Cairo, Illinois, and armed for combat on the Mississippi and Ohio rivers. The unwelcome interest in the flotilla displayed by General Frémont in St

Louis led Secretary of the Navy Welles to dispatch Captain Andrew Foote to command operations on the western rivers under the direction of the War Department. The first product of this unified command was the contract with James B. Eads of St Louis for seven ironclad river gunboats.

On October 12, 1861 the *St Louis*, later renamed *De Kalb*, was launched at Carondelet near St Louis. The six others which followed shortly were *Cincinnati*, *Carondelet*, *Louisville*, *Mound City*, *Cairo*, and *Pittsburgh*. Displacing

888 tons, these ungainly-looking craft drew only 6 feet of water but carried three 7-inch 42-pounder rifles; three 8-inch 64-pounder smoothbores; six 32-pounder smoothbores; and one 30-pounder Parrott rifle. They were partially armored, protection being concentrated around the boilers and single stern paddle-wheel, as well as the forward part of the casemate. Additional armor was fitted after the action against Fort Pillow.

The Eads' ironclad gunboats were supplemented by the *Essex*, originally a river

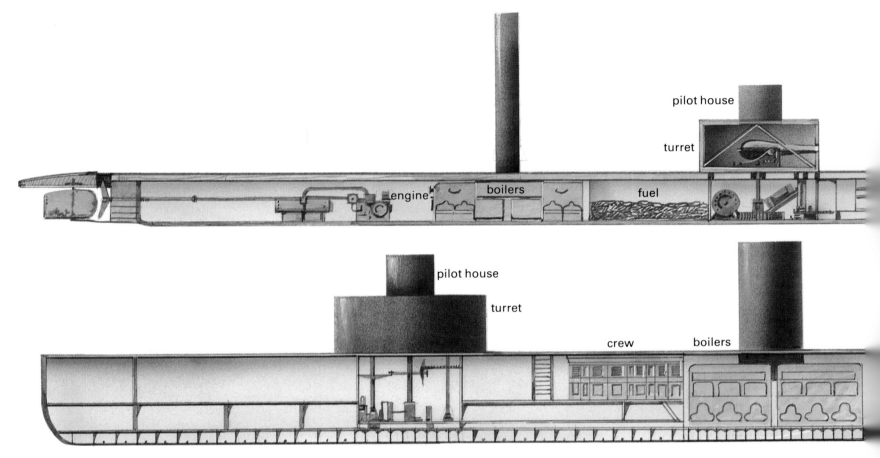

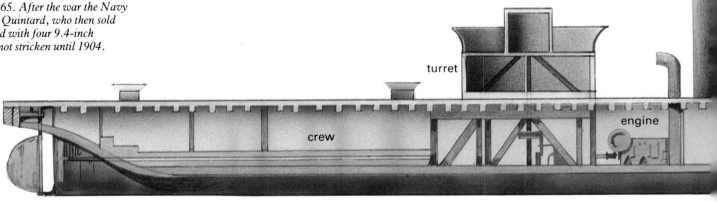

ABOVE: *USS* Onondaga *was the first double-turreted monitor to enter service with the US Navy. Built by George Quintard, she differed from the Ericsson monitors in having a conventional iron hull. Launched in July 1863, she was commissioned in March 1864 and joined the James River squadron. She had one action against the Confederate ironclads when they made their unsuccessful sortie in 1865. After the war the Navy sold* Onondaga *back to Quintard, who then sold her to France. Re-armed with four 9.4-inch breechloaders, she was not stricken until 1904.*

TOP LEFT: *USS* Koka *was one of the 20 shallow-draft monitors ordered by the Navy Department in early 1863 because few of the existing ironclads could penetrate the very shallow waterways inside the Confederacy. Designed to draw just 4 feet of water, compared to the* Passaic's *10½ feet, the Casco class vessels were supposed to have internal ballast tanks to further reduce their draft. Miscalculations when building left the first of the class, USS Chimo, with only 3 inches of freeboard, and this was without stores, ammunition, or the turret!*

BELOW: *View through the engine-room of USS* Koka. *The cylinders are lying on their sides, almost horizontally, in order to save depth.*

steamer called the *New Era*. She was purchased by the US Government and supplied to Eads for conversion to a gunboat. Her armament varied during her long and successful career but it included three 11-inch Dahlgrens and one 10-inch Dahlgren at the beginning of 1862.

The toughest of the river flotilla was the catamaran-hulled snag boat *Submarine No.7*, converted to an ironclad by James B. Eads and renamed *Benton*. She was flagship of the Mississippi flotilla for a time and took part in most of the actions from Island No.10 to the great battle at Memphis. Capable of about 5 knots and protected by up to 3½ inches of armor, she may have been a squat and ugly vessel but she was extremely successful.

The first test for the river flotilla was the

attack on Fort Henry in February 1862. Foote flew his flag on *Cincinnati* and led *Carondelet*, *St Louis*, and *Essex* up the Tennessee River to within 600 yards of the Confederate position. *Conestoga*, *Tyler*, and *Lexington* followed the ironclads. The surrender of the Confederates after about 40 minutes' shelling was the first step of the long campaign that would win Union control of the western waterways and sever Texas and Arkansas from the rest of the Confederacy.

The appearance of the Union river fleet was no surprise to the South. By the summer of 1862 dark rumors of warship construction at St Louis had turned into hard intelligence and the Tennessee State Legislate demanded $250,000 for river defense. The New Orleans press

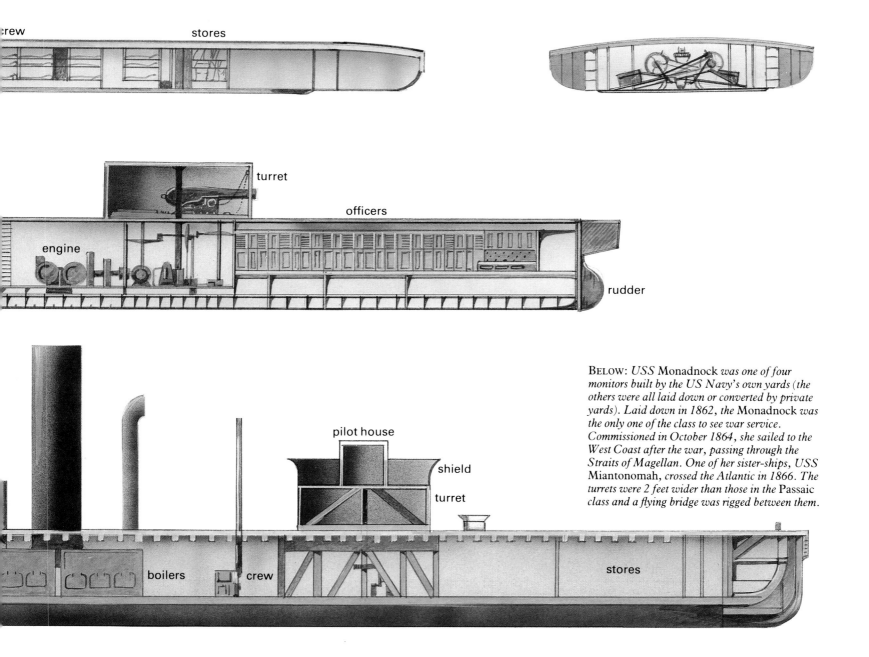

crew   stores

turret

officers

engine

rudder

pilot house

shield

turret

boilers   crew

stores

BELOW: *USS* Monadnock *was one of four monitors built by the US Navy's own yards (the others were all laid down or converted by private yards). Laid down in 1862, the Monadnock was the only one of the class to see war service. Commissioned in October 1864, she sailed to the West Coast after the war, passing through the Straits of Magellan. One of her sister-ships, USS Miantonomah, crossed the Atlantic in 1866. The turrets were 2 feet wider than those in the* Passaic *class and a flying bridge was rigged between them.*

Warships of the US and Confederate Navies

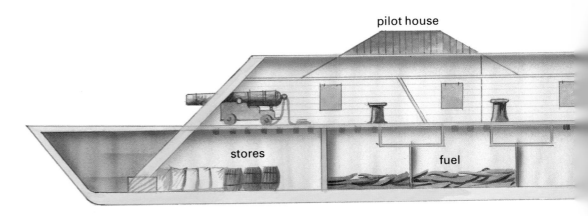

argued vociferously for Confederate warships to meet the challenge and the city authorities voted $800,000 to build them. Thanks partially to pressure from a Confederate congressman from Memphis sitting on the House naval committee, a Memphis contractor won a government order for two ironclad warships.

Less than half the US Navy's pre-war officers came from the South and by no means all of them resigned to join their states. Some 300 officers decided to serve the Confederacy but the Southern navy had no pool of indigenous seamen to call upon. The development of the Confederate Navy was not helped by the creation of several state navies. With only one real shipyard – New Orleans – and one major iron foundry – Tredegar at Richmond – the Confederate response to the Union river fleet was severely hampered. Virginia's entry into the Confederate States brought the greatest prize: the Gosport Navy Yard with over 1000 cannon and the hulk of the *Merrimack*.

The Confederate ironclad program was inspired by two different motives. First, there was the immediate threat of a Union gunboat fleet heading down the Mississippi. This led to a flurry of naval construction in the west that was destined to be just too late to be effective. In the east Secretary of the Navy Mallory was optimistic that *Merrimack* could be converted into an ocean-going warship capable of smashing the Union blockading squadrons. The Confederacy had no facility for building large screw sloops or frigates like those of the US Navy. The only solution was to make a technological jump ahead of the existing Union fleet by building, or buying, armored warships. Hence the contracts with British and French shipyards for ironclads that would cross the Atlantic and sweep the Confederate coastline.

The Confederate Navy Bureau of Ordnance and Hydrography started from scratch but rapidly established facilities to manufacture naval guns and their ammunition at the Tredegar and Bellona ironworks in Richmond and at Selma, Alabama, where over 200 cannon were cast between July 1863 and December 1864. Thanks also to the capture of the Norfolk Navy Yard, the South had sufficient heavy guns to arm its warships by the fall of 1862.

There was some talk of rebuilding *Merrimack* in her original form as not everyone was convinced of the radical proposals for ironclad warships that found favor with the Navy Department. But Secretary Mallory knew the way to the heart of a congressman. He stated that it would cost $400,000 to repair *Merrimack* to her former state, but only $172,523 to cut her down into a very different warship indeed. Joseph R. Anderson, president of the Tredegar Ironworks, contracted to provide the armor: iron plates 8 feet long and 1 inch thick, but then managed to roll 2-inch plates instead. These had to have the holes drilled in them rather than punched, which took longer, but the extra protection was well worth it. She was armed with six 9-inch Dahlgrens on either side with two 7-inch Brooke rifles in the bow and two 6.4-inch Brooke rifles astern.

Unfortunately, the new warship had an Achilles' heel that was to be a common feature of almost all Confederate ironclads. The engines of the new *Virginia* were the same as those condemned the previous year and which had caused the *Merrimack* to be in Norfolk in the first place. Capable of only 6–8 knots, her steerage was dreadful and it took 30–40 minutes to bring her around 180 degrees! She drew 22 feet of water, which severely restricted her freedom of action in Hampton Roads. Despite this, she still rode too high in the water, exposing her unarmored lower hull unless ballasted further. Yet for all these

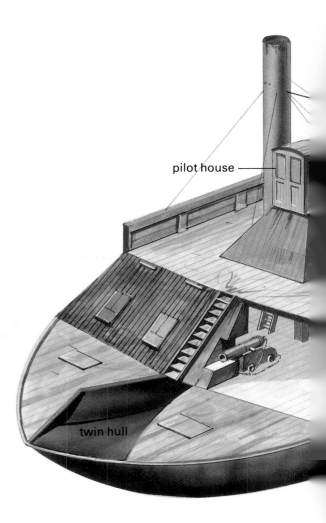

LEFT: *A cross-section of* Benton *clearly illustrates the width and shallow draft of the vessel. The steampipes and funnels run through the gun deck where most of the 120 crew were stationed in action.*

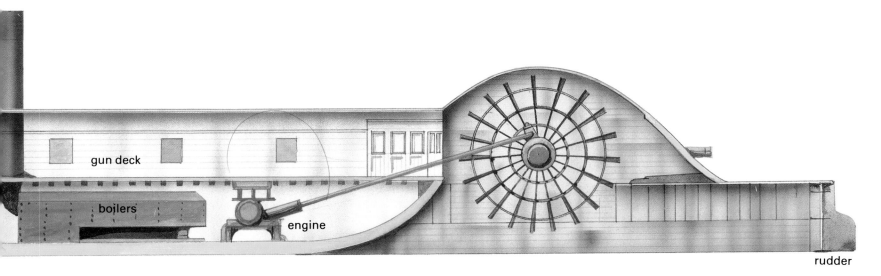

gun deck

boilers

engine

rudder

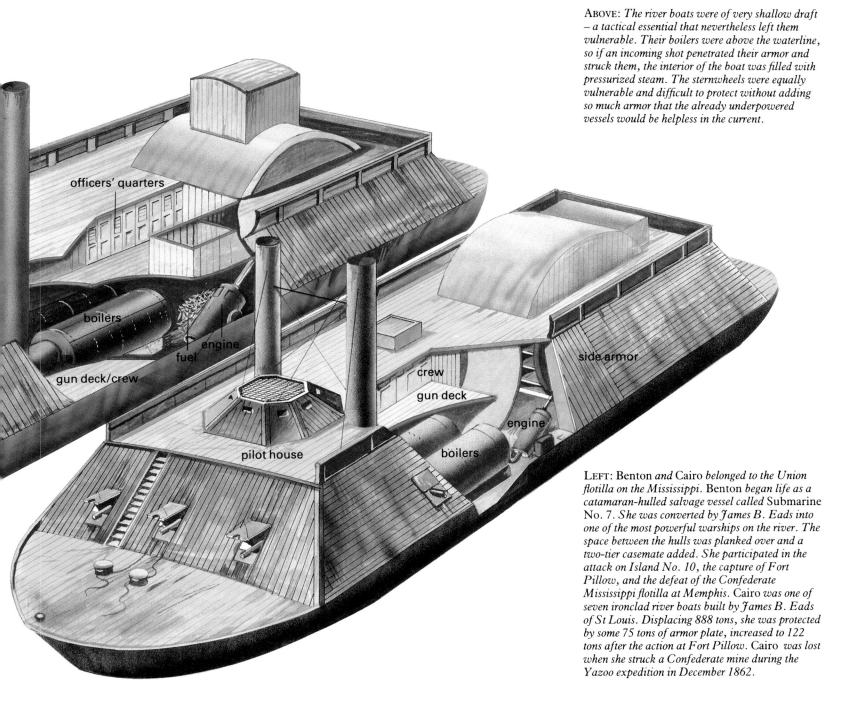

officers' quarters

boilers

engine
fuel

gun deck/crew

side armor

crew

gun deck

engine

pilot house

boilers

Warships of the US and Confederate Navies

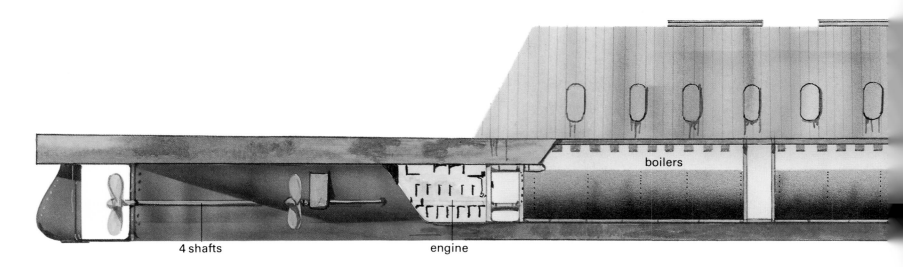

4 shafts   engine   boilers

problems, she made short work of the wooden warships she encountered on March 8, 1862.

Virginia caused panic enough in Washington but the idea, briefly entertained in Richmond, that she could break out into the Atlantic and raid New York was never feasible. Buchanan replied to Mallory's suggestion that *Virginia* would founder in an Atlantic gale and he seriously doubted whether she could survive in a heavy swell. *Virginia's* deep draft ultimately doomed her: she was unable to withdraw upstream to safety and was destroyed by her crew. As events would prove, this was another unfortunate precedent set by the first Confederate ironclad.

As already noted, the Union gunboat and ironclad program in the west began very quickly. Like the Union river squadron, the Confederate gunboats assembled to defend the Tennessee and Cumberland rivers were begun by the army. General Polk purchased the river steamer *Eastport* in October 1861 and work began after Christmas to arm and armor her for service. Another four vessels had been acquired before the fall of Forts Henry and Donelson compelled the Confederates to withdraw. *Eastport* was captured and completed as an armored river gunboat by the Union.

New Orleans was the South's most important port. Five shipyards with 12 docks were in operation in 1861 and by April 1862 they had converted or built 30 small warships. In October 1861 two ironclads were laid down at new facilities at Jefferson City just north of New Orleans. *Mississippi* was designed by men with no experience of naval construction, who tried to allow for the limitations of their equally green workforce. There were to be no complicated curves, just a box-like structure that house-carpenters could tackle with their existing skills. She was almost as long as *Virginia* and it is doubtful whether she could have stemmed the current had she been completed. The Virginia and Shreveport Railroad supplied 500 tons of railroad iron for her armor. An Atlanta iron mill later supplied 1½-inch armor

plates. Construction was frustrated by shortages of every material. No ironworks in the Confederacy could cast the 44-feet center shaft required, so one was salvaged from a wreck in the James River and modified at Tredegar. It was transported to New Orleans on a specially converted railroad car.

Louisiana was of similar size. Her machinery came from a river steamer, the *Ingomar*, but forging her shafts took a long time and they were installed only a few days before her destruction. Her propulsion proved a failure anyway: a combination of two central paddle-wheels and two screws, it could not handle the vessel. The chief engineer described how the wheels formed an eddy around the rudder, making her unmanageable.

Mississippi was launched on April 19, just four days before Federal forces overran New Orleans. She could not be withdrawn upstream and was burned. Unable to maneuver under her own power, *Louisiana* remained anchored during the battle of New Orleans. Her armor protected her inexperienced crew from the most powerful warships of the US Navy. *Brooklyn* fired a full broadside of 11 9-inch Dahlgrens at point blank range but the 70-pound solid shot struck the 45-degree slope of *Louisiana's* casemate and flew into the air. *Louisiana* survived the battle but was blown up by her crew to prevent her capture after the fall of New Orleans.

The one Confederate ironclad able to fight with some freedom during the battle for New Orleans was a bizarre warship indeed. Built by a $100,000 subscription organized by the New Orleans Benevolent Association, she was to be a privateer, rewarding her investors by capturing Union ships. The *Manassas* was a river towboat fitted with a 20-foot long ram. Her upperworks were removed and she was covered in a curved oak frame protected by 1½ inches of armor. Resembling a half-sunken iron cigar, she was seized at pistol point in October 1861 by Lieutenant Warley, CSN, who led a volunteer

Mississippi was one of two enormous casemate ironclads laid down at an improvised building yard just outside New Orleans. Designed and built by men with no previous experience of naval construction, it was an over-ambitious project which was constantly frustrated by material shortages. Timber had to be brought from the other side of Lake Pontchartrain, iron was already in short supply, and armor plate was even rarer. No local foundry could deliver wrought-iron armor, so 500 tons of railroad iron was purchased from the Vicksburg and Shreveport railroad.

Mississippi was designed to have a massive power-plant consisting of three engines and 16 boilers. The wing shafts were obtained locally but the 44-foot center shaft was too long for any Southern foundry to forge. Luckily, one was salvaged from a wreck in the James River and transported to New Orleans on a specially modified railroad car. Construction was further delayed when many workers, who were in the militia, were mobilized in early 1862. The ship was only launched after several hundred Negroes were borrowed from nearby plantations, and 24-hour shifts were needed before the incomplete vessel was in the water. Finally launched on 19 April, the Mississippi was burned four days later when Union forces captured New Orleans.

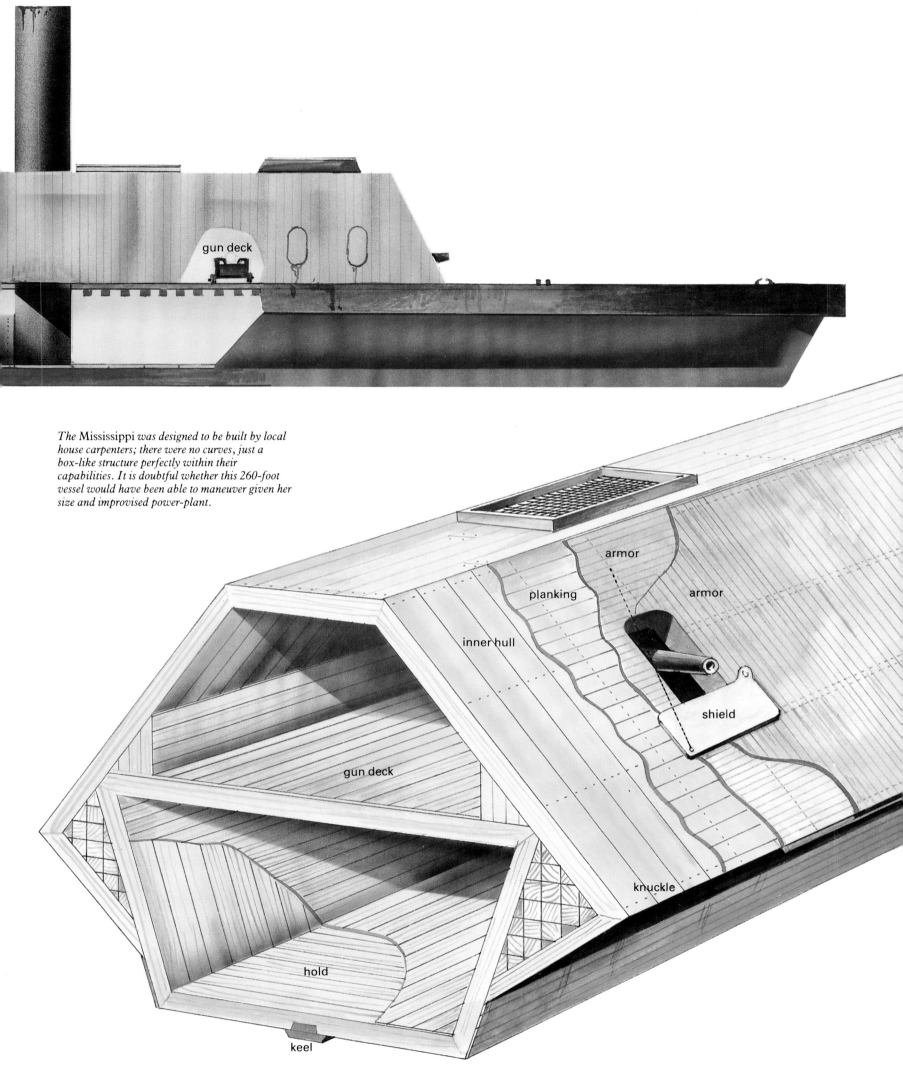

gun deck

The Mississippi was designed to be built by local house carpenters; there were no curves, just a box-like structure perfectly within their capabilities. It is doubtful whether this 260-foot vessel would have been able to maneuver given her size and improvised power-plant.

armor

planking

inner hull

armor

shield

gun deck

knuckle

hold

keel

Warships of the US and Confederate Navies

BELOW: *The intrepid Confederate agent James D. Bulloch came within an ace of spiriting two powerful ironclads out of Europe and across the Atlantic. CSS* Mississippi *and* North Carolina *were laid down at Birkenhead, England, in April 1862 and launched in July 1863. Shallow-draft 2750-ton vessels, they were capable of operating up the Mississippi and their armament of four 9-inch Armstrong muzzleloading rifles made them a dangerous proposition to most US warships. Under great pressure from Washington, the British government blocked the sale. Bulloch circumvented the restriction by arranging for them to be sold to Egypt, only to be resold as soon as they put to sea. This plan too was frustrated when the British bought the vessels for the Royal Navy.*

crew in an attack on the blockading squadron. *Manassas* was destroyed during the battle for New Orleans after a heroic fight. As ever, she was betrayed by her engines which were overdue for the scrap heap. Her thin armor was repeatedly penetrated. She boasted one interesting defensive feature that was, fortunately, never tested: she could vent boiler steam over her hull to scald would-be boarders and drive them off.

While New Orleans was the center of the Confederate ironclad program in the west, further ironclads were under construction at Memphis. However, the chronic shortage of materials and skilled labor led their builder to abandon temporarily one of two ships then being built in the hope of completing the other by the end of 1861. He failed, but the *Arkansas* was nearly ready by the fall of New Orleans. She was evacuated from Memphis and completed at Yazoo City. Measuring 165 feet long and protected by 3 inches of railroad iron, she

had 18 inches of wooden backing at either end and 12 inches along the side of the casemate. She was armed with two 8-inch 64-pounders in the bow, two rifled and banded 32-pounders in the stern, and two 100-pounder Columbiad smoothbores and a 6-inch naval gun on the broadside.

The decision to move the incomplete *Arkansas* from Memphis was taken after the fall of New Orleans. Ironically, the Union forces took another month to capture Memphis; in the meantime, work on the *Arkansas* could not continue. She lay unfinished at Greenwood, Mississippi, until Lieutenant Brown took over command on May 29. He took her down to Yazoo City and had the construction crew working 24 hours a day, seven days a week to get the ironclad finished. After the completion of the *Arkansas* the Confederates laid down three more warships in their improvised shipyard at Yazoo City, although they were never launched.

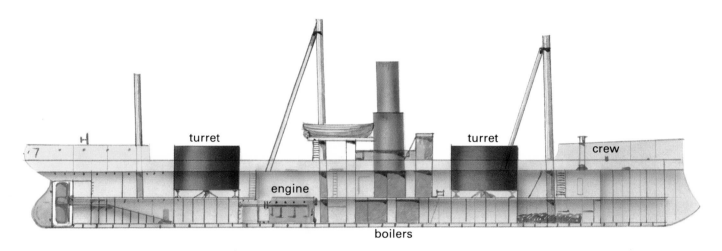

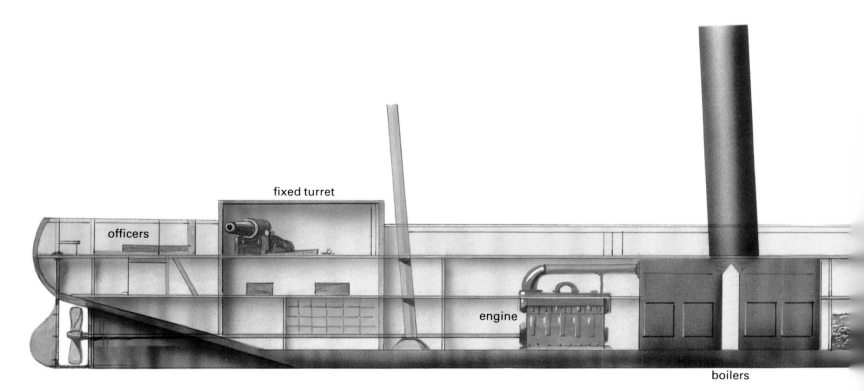

The Yazoo River flows into the Mississippi some 12 miles above Vicksburg. *Arkansas* fought her way past one naval patrol, forcing the Union river ironclad *Carondelet* ashore, then ran through the whole of Farragut's fleet to reach the protection of the Confederate batteries. Attacked again that night by the Union warships and shortly afterwards by "Wild Bill" Porter's *Essex*, *Arkansas* survived and was repaired to head south after the Union fleet went downriver. Unfortunately, *Arkansas* was then betrayed by her typically awful Confederate engines. Steaming to support a Confederate Army operation near Baton Rouge, *Arkansas*'s engines broke down just as she ran into *Essex*, *Gayuga*, *Kineo*, and *Katahdin*. She was blown up by her crew.

In the fall of 1862 the Confederacy laid down an astonishing total of 18 ironclads. Mostly in primitive yards on creeks or riverbanks, they prepared to defend the waterways and in some cases, to sortie into the Atlantic and break the blockade. Three were built at Charleston: the *Palmetto State*, *Chicora* and *Charleston*. The first two did make one brief foray outside the harbor, but they could not challenge the likes of *New Ironsides* cruising off the South Carolina coast. Copious donations from private sources

BELOW: *The nearest the Confederacy came to obtaining a battleship was the 4747-ton broadside ironclad commissioned by Lieutenant North from the British builders Thompson. Known variously as* Glasgow *or* Santa Maria, *this fully rigged, iron-hulled frigate was launched in February 1864, but the British were not allowing their shipyards to supply ships to the Confederacy, so she was sold to Denmark.*

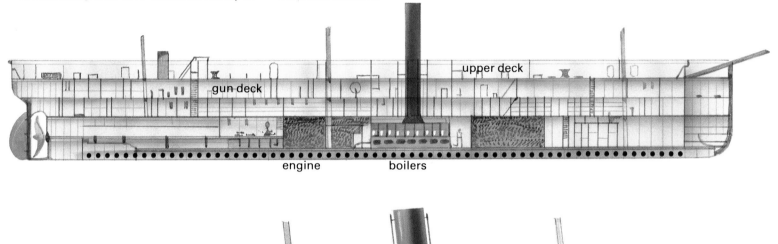

gun deck

upper deck

engine

boilers

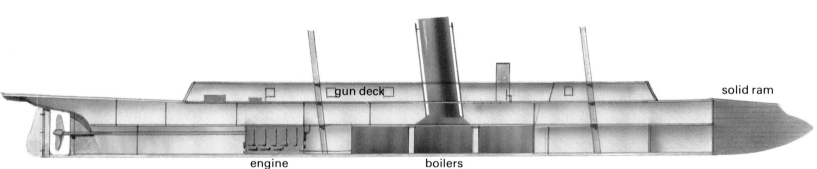

gun deck

solid ram

engine

boilers

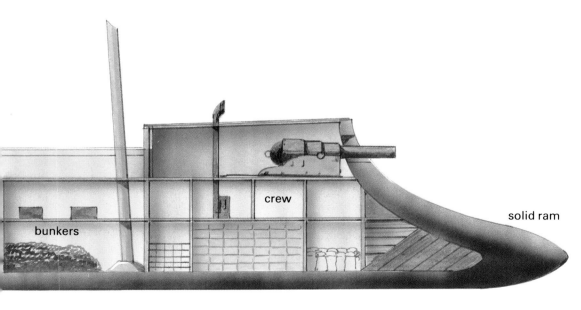

crew

bunkers

solid ram

ABOVE: *USS* Dunderberg *was the only Union warship to follow the center casemate design favored by the Confederacy. Built from green timber – the supply of seasoned wood was rapidly exhausted – she was laid down in October 1862 and launched in July 1865, by which time her value to the Navy was minimal. With a double bottom, collision bulkhead, and a 50-foot oak ram, she was built for survival. Unfortunately, the green wood proved her undoing. Sold to France in 1867, she was broken up only five years later.*

LEFT: *CSS* Stonewall *was the only one of the Confederate ironclads ordered from England that actually made it to American waters. Acquired in great secrecy from Denmark after sale to the South had been blocked by the British government, she broke out into the Atlantic in January 1865.* Stonewall *offered battle to two US warships off the coast of Spain, and reached Cuba in May where her captain learned that the Confederate cause was now lost.*

Warships of the US and Confederate Navies

had funded most of this building program. Several ironclads had been known as "The Ladies' Gunboat" after energetic fund-raising efforts by the ladies of Charleston and other cities. But the money that had poured in, especially after the spectacular success of *Virginia*'s first action, was soon spent. The fall of Norfolk, New Orleans, and Memphis, and the loss of four of the five ironclads built in 1861, discredited the Confederate ironclad program and few private donations were offered in 1863. The unusual iron warships had aroused unrealistically high expectations; since the secretary of the navy himself hoped they would break the blockade, this is hardly surprising. But the dismal record of the first ironclads was a tremendous disappointment. Despite all the hard work, they had proved a failure.

One of the leading opponents of the ironclad

program was General Beauregard. Commanding the defenses of Charleston in 1863, he observed the obvious defects of the ironclads there. Slow, unseaworthy, and drawing too much water to navigate upstream, they were unable to resist close-range fire from 15-inch Dahlgrens. Their own armament could not be elevated more than 5 or 6 degrees, so they could not employ the maximum range of their cannon. The ships were also unhealthy – hot and badly ventilated – so the crews slept ashore and could not stay long on board without their efficiency suffering badly. In the general's opinion, they were an expensive investment that would show no return.

Beauregard was probably correct in his assesment of the Charleston squadron at least. Although they won the reputation of the smartest of the Confederate ironclads, all three

BELOW: *The US Navy spread its patrols in lines surrounding the ports of Wilmington, Charleston, and Mobile. In June 1864 the Navy belatedly established a patrol line several hours steaming from Wilmington. Fast warships stationed there were well placed to catch blockade runners at dawn as they ran for Bermuda, but they were difficult vessels to catch, being fast and with a low silhouette. Like today's drug smugglers, the men breaking the blockade could accept the loss of a vessel with surprising equanimity. The cargoes were so valuable that a specially built ship recouped the owners' outlay and turned a profit after just a few voyages.*

BELOW: Hope *was an English-built steel blockade runner caught by USS* Eolus *off Wilmington in October 1864. Displacing 1700 tons, she was 281 feet long and capable of 16 knots. The turtle-back foredeck anticipated those of some early twentieth-century destroyers – designed to protect the fore part of the vessel while steaming at high speed in heavy seas.*

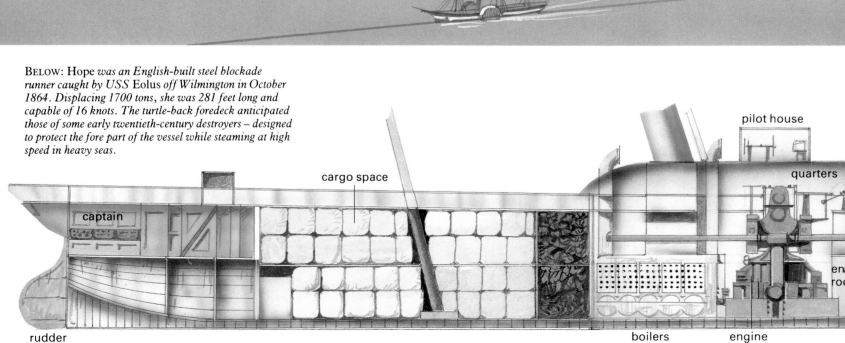

captain

cargo space

pilot house

quarters

rudder

boilers

engine

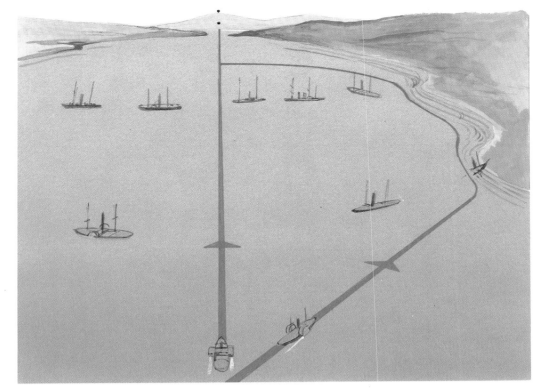

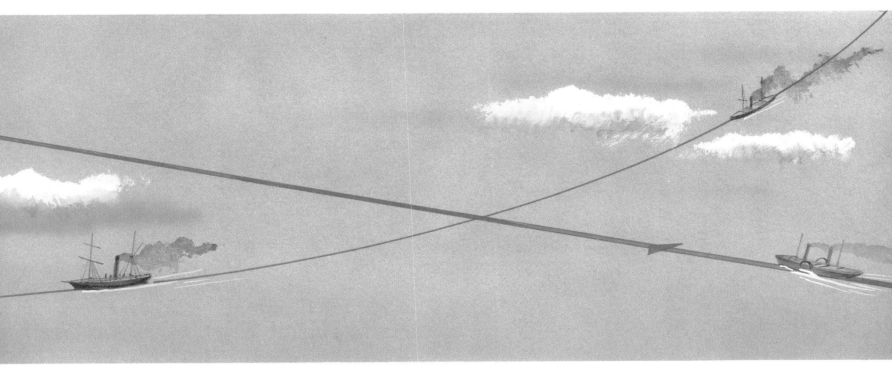

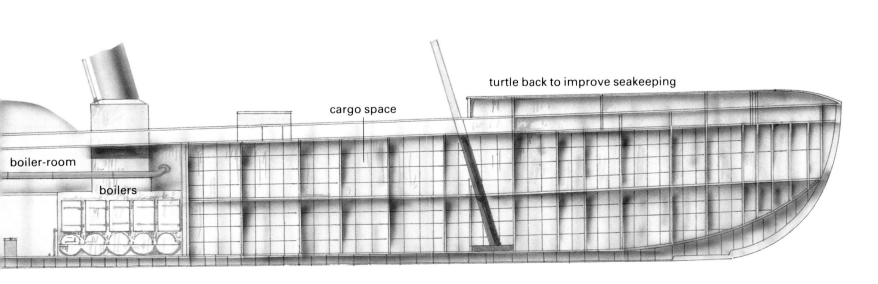

turtle back to improve seakeeping

cargo space

boiler-room

boilers

Warships of the US and Confederate Navies

were powered by engines taken from small steamers. Designed to make 7 or 8 knots, they had trouble making 5 and *Chicora* once had to anchor, unable to stem the ebb tide, while between Forts Sumter and Moultrie. With her engines running at full steam she was dragging on her cables against a 2-knot current! *Chicora* and *Palmetto State* finally attacked the blockading squadron just as it was reinforced with *New Ironsides*, *Passaic*, and *Montauk*. Although Beauregard blustered that they had broken the blockade, this was an empty claim. With Du Pont's squadron off Charleston, there was little the ironclads could do.

Of all the Confederate ironclads built in the Confederacy, only *Atlanta* was likely to have been able to steam in the open sea. Converted from the blockade runner *Fingal*, she had

relatively new British engines. Potentially the best of the Confederate rams, she completed in Savannah in early 1863. Steaming down Wassaw Sound on June 17, 1863, she found the monitors *Weehawken* and *Nahant* waiting for her thanks to advance warning from a deserter. *Atlanta* opened fire with her forward pair of 7-inch Brooke rifles at 3000 yards but then ran hard aground. Heeled over against the sand bar, she could not bring her guns to bear. *Weehawken* commenced a leisurely bombardment from 300 yards and *Atlanta* surrendered. She was later employed by the US Navy as part of its James River Squadron.

The dwindling Confederate river fleet in the west was outnumbered still further before the fall of Vicksburg. Inspired by the success of James Eads' first nine gunboats, another series

of Union river warships was under construction during 1862 and they began to appear on the Mississippi in early 1863. *Choctaw* and her near sister ship *Lafayette* were 1000-ton stern-wheeled river boats with 1-inch armor plate over 1 inch of rubber backing. Both were slow, able to manage only 2–4 knots against the river current. *Tuscumbia* displaced about 900 tons but was significantly faster. The armament of this second-generation river squadron varied during the 2–3 years they were in service but included 4–8 heavy guns (100-pounder Parrotts or 9- or 11-inch Dahlgrens). They all suffered from trying to carry too great a weight of armor, which led to warping, and the rubber backing behind the armor perished quickly. All three served in the Vicksburg campaign and remained in action until the end of the war.

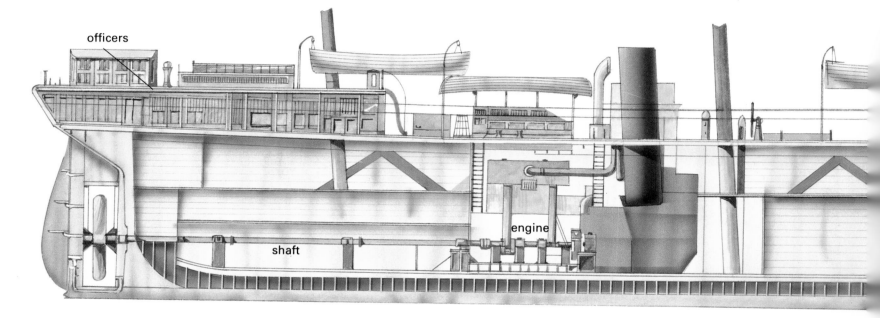

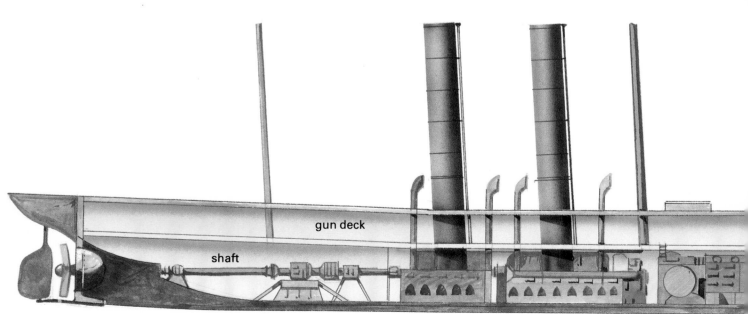

The 1862 Union gunboat program included two less successful river warships. The *Indianola* was a 500-ton sternwheeler that was attacked by the Confederate ram *Queen of the West* and two boats crammed with soldiers. Rammed and sunk near Vicksburg, she had only been in service a matter of months. *Chillicothe* was another small sternwheeler weighed down by too much armor. From design to completion took only nine months.

James B. Eads added two more monstrously ugly vessels to the Union river fleet in 1863. Inspired by the same demand for light-draft warships that led to the massive *Casco* monitor program, *Osage* and *Neosho* drew only 3½ feet of water. A turtle-backed deck ran the length of the 180-foot monitor-like hull. A single turret near the bow housed two 11-inch Dahlgrens

and had a 300-degree arc of fire. The stern was dominated by a towering iron structure resembling an upturned bucket. This housed a single stern wheel that drove them through smooth water at just over 7 knots. They joined the Union river fleet in late 1863 and took part in the Red River and Washita expeditions. *Osage* was sunk by one of the innumerable mines off Mobile in March 1865, but although she went down rapidly, all but two of her crew managed to escape.

The Union river fleet acquired another monitor-like warship in 1863 – the *Ozark*. Screw-driven, she was 180 feet long and displaced just under 600 tons. A single turret housed two 11-inch Dahlgrens and she was capable of only 2½ knots. *Ozark* acquired more cannon in open mountings as the danger from

BELOW: *The last Confederate in arms: the raider* Shenandoah *fired the final shots of the Civil War against the US whaling fleet in the Bering Sea in June 1865. Purchased in London, this sleek raider was originally a merchantman chartered by the British as an army transport. She was spirited out of England and armed at Madeira in the fall of 1864. Snapping up Union merchant ships as she went,* Shenandoah *rounded the Cape of Good Hope and reached Australia in January 1865. She sailed north across the Pacific and her commander, Lieutenant Waddell, took a grave risk in taking his vessel into the ice floes. Learning of the fall of the Confederacy from a passing British ship, he returned to England, completing a 58,000-mile voyage during which he had destroyed over $2,000,000 of American merchant shipping.*

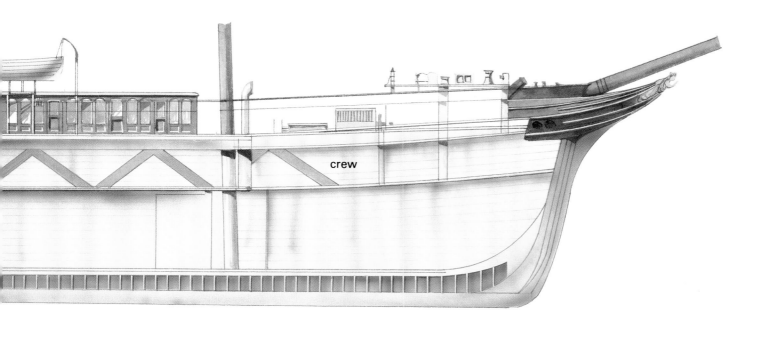

crew

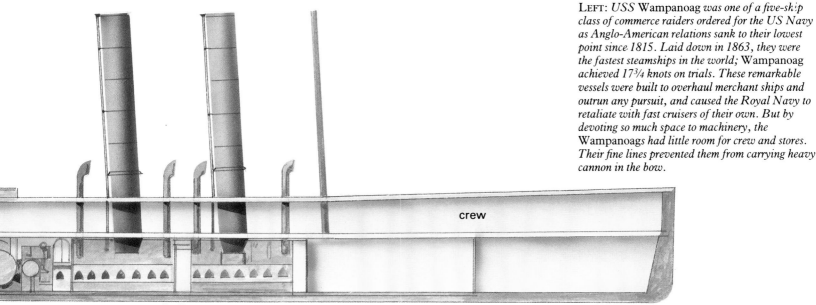

LEFT: *USS* Wampanoag *was one of a five-ship class of commerce raiders ordered for the US Navy as Anglo-American relations sank to their lowest point since 1815. Laid down in 1863, they were the fastest steamships in the world;* Wampanoag *achieved 17¾ knots on trials. These remarkable vessels were built to overhaul merchant ships and outrun any pursuit, and caused the Royal Navy to retaliate with fast cruisers of their own. But by devoting so much space to machinery, the* Wampanoags *had little room for crew and stores. Their fine lines prevented them from carrying heavy cannon in the bow.*

crew

boilers

Warships of the US and Confederate Navies

Confederate warships diminished. By the summer of 1864 she had three 9-inch and one 10-inch Dahlgren smoothbores on pivot mountings. With her light draft she could maneuver down shallow rivers to support Union troops ashore. Two similar river monitors, *Sandusky* and *Marietta*, were ordered in May 1862 but their construction proceeded at a torpid pace and they were not launched until 1865.

In both the US and Confederate navies the ironclad warships were supported by a much larger fleet of wooden vessels. On the rivers both navies took over whatever shipping was available, fitted them with whatever cannon they would take, and sent them into action. The Confederates had some 14 riverboats converted to lightly armed rams during 1862. Although the Union operated even more converted river craft, US shipyards augmented these with a formidable building program to which the Confederacy had no answer. In 1861 12 double-enders of the *Octorara* class were laid down; shallow-draft, wooden paddle-steamers, they had no rounded stern. Instead, they tapered to a bow at both ends (like a canoe) and had a rudder at bow and stern. This allowed them to operate in very confined waters since they never had to turn around. Excellent in rivers and coastal waters, they were not well suited to the open sea.

The double-enders proved so successful that 28 slightly larger ones were ordered in 1862. Built to a standard design (although one was iron-hulled), *Sassacus* was the first of the class, launched in December 1862. *Sassacus*, *Eutaw*, and *Mendota* entered service during 1863, while the rest were completed during 1864. The sheer scale of the US shipbuilding program led to shortages of labor and materials; the supply of machinery was a serious problem with the later vessels of this type and three were never finished. The standard of construction varied, with some ships distinctly jerry-built, but with their boilers and steam lines surrounded by sandbags and cotton bales, these wooden riverboats were in action for the rest of the war. As action on the rivers petered out, so more were employed on blockade duties, but their 9–10 knot speed was insufficient to catch a nimble blockade runner and their performance in a seaway was most unsatisfactory.

One of the most celebrated actions of the double-enders was the fight with the Confederate ironclad *Albemarle* in May 1864. *Sassacus*, *Mattabesett*, and *Wyaslung*, plus the smaller *Miami*, engaged the ironclad which had already rammed and sunk the sidewheel steamer *Southfield* in its first action. The double-enders all survived the engagement, *Sassacus* badly damaging herself by ramming the Confederate. The Union vessels were lucky they were facing a relatively small ironclad that carried only two heavy guns.

Another seven double-enders were ordered during 1863 but only *Suwanee* and *Muscoota* were completed before the end of the war. The armament of the various double-enders varied from ship to ship and from season to season. A typical mixture was two 6.4-inch 100-pounder Parrott rifles, plus four 9-inch Dahlgren smoothbores, and a couple of 24-pounder smoothbore howitzers. Both pilot houses and the masthead lookouts were protected with boiler plate and sandbags to keep out musket fire. Constantly close to the riverbanks these vessels were the target of frequent attack by parties of Confederate sharpshooters.

The Confederate ironclad program eventually ran to 50 ironclads planned or laid down in the Confederacy; 22 were actually commissioned. By 1864 there were four operational squadrons: Savannah, Charleston, Mobile, and the James River.

The first five Confederate ironclads were all over 200 feet long with reasonably high freeboards and were intended to operate in coastal waters, as well as harbors and rivers. Subsequent ironclads that were built from scratch mainly followed the hull form introduced on the *Richmond*. Based on constructor John Porter's 1846 design that had been submitted to Mallory in 1862, *Richmond* was 150 feet long and drew 11–12 feet of water. She mounted four Brooke rifles and two smoothbores. The hull was flat-bottomed with a tapered stern and stem.

The *Richmond*'s hull form was followed by most of the later Confederate ironclads. The Charleston squadron (*Charleston*, *Chicora*, and *Palmetto State*) were all of this type. *Savannah*, *North Carolina*, *Virginia II*, *Columbia*, *Texas*, and *Tennessee* all followed the same form, although exact dimensions varied. Significant exceptions to this hull form were the *Neuse* and *Albemarle*. These two warships were designed to operate in only 6 feet of water and had flared sides rather than a built-on knuckle where the armor shield joined with the side of the hull to form an angle.

The first Confederate ironclads were all large vessels (over 200 feet long) intended to operate in coastal waters as well as rivers. These vessels had little in common beside the general idea of a central casemate. However, with the building of Richmond, *laid down in 1862 at the Norfolk Navy Yard, the Confederate Navy settled on a basic hull design for its new ironclads. The design dated from Constructor Porter's 1846 plan for an armored warship. The original dimensions were 150 × 34 × 11 feet, although some of the ironclads would be larger. Basic features were a flat bottom, with a tapered stem and stern, and the ships were built on "knuckle" (where the hull side met the sloping side of the armor shield, forming an angle).*

Richmond, Chicora, Raleigh, Palmetto State, North Carolina, *and* Savannah *were all 150-foot casemate ironclads built to this design. Some, like* Virginia II *and* Tennessee, *followed the same scheme, but were substantially longer. However, not all the ironclads followed this arrangement.* Albemarle *and* Neuse, *which had to operate in only a few feet of water, adopted a different arrangement. Instead of the "knuckle," these had a flared side as illustrated, which gave them a distinctive diamond shape.*

BELOW: Atlanta *began life as the British steamer* Fingal, *so the armored casemate was installed above an ocean-going hull. Alone of the Confederate ironclads, she had a modern power-plant in good operating condition. Captured after running aground, she was the only Confederate ironclad to be used against her former owners, joining the Federal squadron on the James River.*

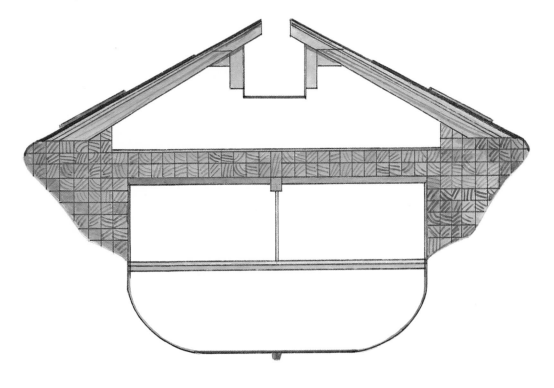

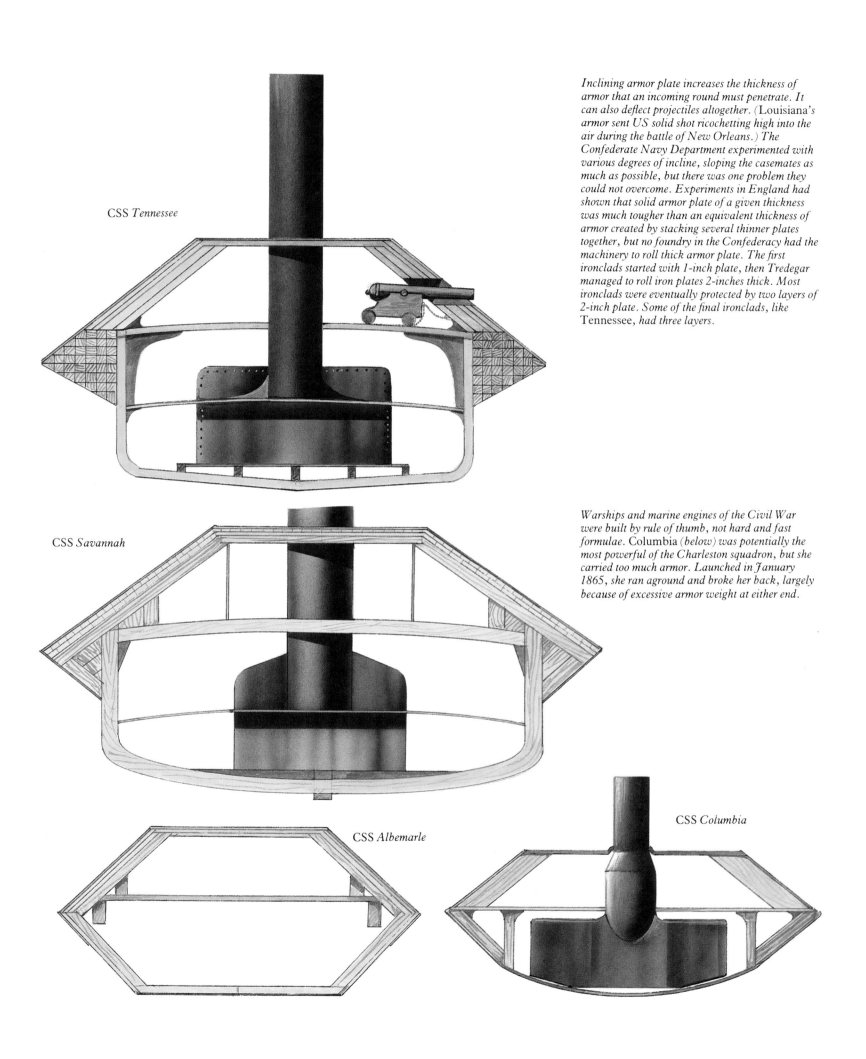

CSS *Tennessee*

Inclining armor plate increases the thickness of armor that an incoming round must penetrate. It can also deflect projectiles altogether. (Louisiana's armor sent US solid shot ricochetting high into the air during the battle of New Orleans.) The Confederate Navy Department experimented with various degrees of incline, sloping the casemates as much as possible, but there was one problem they could not overcome. Experiments in England had shown that solid armor plate of a given thickness was much tougher than an equivalent thickness of armor created by stacking several thinner plates together, but no foundry in the Confederacy had the machinery to roll thick armor plate. The first ironclads started with 1-inch plate, then Tredegar managed to roll iron plates 2-inches thick. Most ironclads were eventually protected by two layers of 2-inch plate. Some of the final ironclads, like Tennessee, had three layers.

CSS *Savannah*

Warships and marine engines of the Civil War were built by rule of thumb, not hard and fast formulae. Columbia (below) was potentially the most powerful of the Charleston squadron, but she carried too much armor. Launched in January 1865, she ran aground and broke her back, largely because of excessive armor weight at either end.

CSS *Albemarle*

CSS *Columbia*

Warships of the US and Confederate Navies

Of these warships, only the *Albemarle* was to be destroyed by a US weapon – the spar torpedo fitted to Cushing's steam launch. The *Tennessee*, pride of the Mobile squadron, was forced to strike her colors after her last stand against Farragut's fleet, and the rest of the Confederate warships there could offer little resistance. The other squadrons were blown up by their own crews as the Union armies overran their bases.

BELOW: Fredericksburg *was a 188-foot long ironclad built in Richmond to the shallow-draft* Albemarle*-type design. Fitted out in March 1864, she joined* Virginia II *and* Richmond *on the* James River, *forming a trio of powerful ironclads hemmed in by the line of obstructions laid by Union forces near City Point. She was armed with one 8-inch Brooke rifle in the bow, one 11-inch smoothbore in the stern, and a 6.4-inch rifle on either beam. During 1864* Fredericksburg *had several engagements with Union troops ashore and took part in the sortie of January 1865 when all three ironclads attempted to break through the obstructions after heavy rains increased the depth of the river.* Fredericksburg *was the only one not to go aground.*

Overseas shipbuilding

The Confederacy was unable to build ocean-going warships capable of defeating the blockading squadrons. Consequently, the very able Lieutenant North was dispatched to Europe to place contracts with private shipbuilding yards in England and France. His efforts were frustrated by heavy US pressure on the British and French governments. The most powerful warship ordered by the Confederacy was a 4700-ton broadside ironclad obviously designed to rival *New Ironsides*. Protected by 4½ inches of armor, she carried 12 8-inch muzzleloading rifles and 12 6-inch muzzle-loading rifles. Capable of 8½ knots, she was fully rigged and required over 500 crew, itself a serious problem for the Confederate Navy. However, the *Glasgow*, or *Santa Maria* as she was variously named, was eventually sold to Denmark after it was clear that Britain would never countenance her sale to the Confederacy.

This powerful ironclad was preceded in the Confederate European building program by two masted turret ships, the *North Carolina* and the *Mississippi*. Built by Lairds at Birkenhead, England, they were shallow-drafted to enable them to get up the Mississippi but had the

range to operate across the Atlantic. Displacing 2750 tons, they had two turrets – one between the mizzen and the main mast, the other between the main and fore mast; each carried two 9-inch rifles. Capable of 10½ knots, these eventually proved to be good sea boats but their low freeboard made it impossible to fight their guns in a seaway. Lairds and the Confederates went to great lengths to disguise the real identity of the purchaser after the British Government announced it would not permit shipyards to build warships for the Confederacy. The scheme eventually tried was to "sell" the ships to Egypt but have the Confederates take them over once at sea. Unfortunately, the British Government tumbled the plan, seized the ships, and in 1864 bought them for the Royal Navy. Completed in the fall of 1865, they served as HMS *Scorpion* and HMS *Wyvern*.

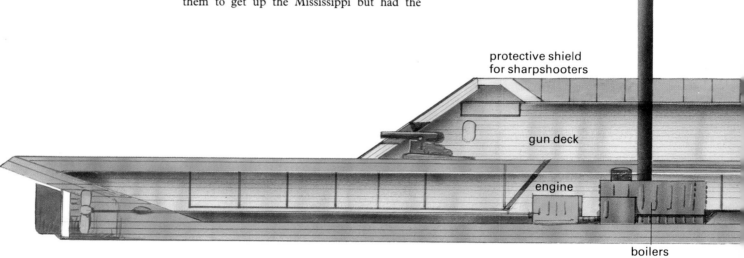

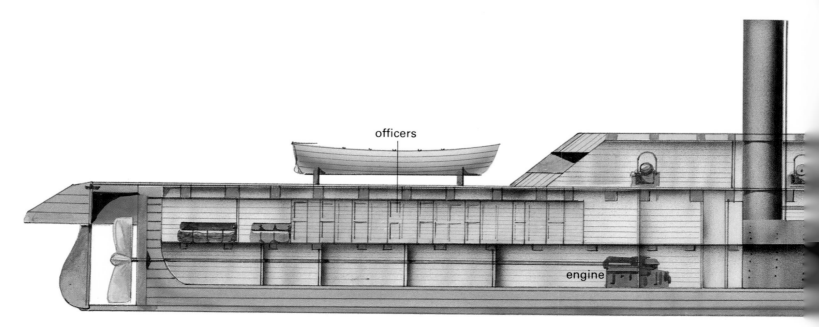

180

The only Confederate European-built ironclad to make it across the Atlantic was the much smaller 1500-ton armored ram *Stonewall*. Built in Bordeaux as part of a grandiose plan for four sloops and two rams, *Stonewall* had 4½–5½ inches of armor over 24 inches of wood backing. An armored housing at the bow pierced by three gun ports held an Armstrong 10-inch muzzleloading rifle that fired 300-pound shells. Abaft the main mast was a fixed turret with two 6.4-inch 70-pounder rifles. Both could fire astern, one to either broadside. The French Government stopped the shipyard from selling warships to the Confederacy, so the builders sold one ram to Denmark and the other to Prussia while these countries were at war. But the sale to Denmark fell through as the war ended. Sold back to her builders, *Stonewall* was secretly acquired again by the

Confederacy and slipped away from Copenhagen in January 1865.

Stonewall made for Spain and offered battle to the screw frigate *Niagara* and 2000-ton sloop *Sacramento* off Ferrol in March. The US warships declined to engage and the Confederate ram steamed west, reaching Havana in May. Learning that the war was lost, her captain sold her to the Spanish authorities to pay her crew.

Within two months of the US Navy establishing its blockade of the Confederacy, the Navy Department began to order additional wooden screw sloops. Twenty-three were ordered and the speed with which they were constructed led them to be known as the "90-day" gun boats. Schooner rigged and displacing just under 700 tons, the first four of the *Unadilla* class were commissioned by October 1861. Armament varied with up to four

heavy guns (100-pounder Parrotts or 9 11-inch Dahlgrens). *Sciota* had one 11-inch Dahlgren, one 20-pounder Parrott, two 24-pounder howitzers, and one 12-pounder smoothbore in 1863. This ship was mined off the coast of Texas in April 1865.

Larger warships were also under construction in 1861. Four 1500-ton screw sloops were launched during the fall and completed in early 1862. *Kearsage*, *Oneida*, *Tuscarora*, and *Wachusett* were to lead the hunt for Confederate commerce raiders. *Kearsage* destroyed *Alabama* in June 1864, while *Wachusett* captured the raider *Florida* in Bahia harbor, Brazil, four months later. *Oneida* fought at Mobile Bay. Armament varied: *Kearsage* had one 30-pounder Parrott, two 11-inch Dahlgrens, and four 32-pounder smoothbores at the time of her celebrated action off Cherbourg.

Four larger 1900-ton steam sloops were laid down at the same time. Launched between December 1861 and March 1862, the *Ossipee* class included *Housatonic*, *Juniata*, and *Adirondack*. As usual, their armament varied: *Housatonic* carried one 6.4-inch 100-pounder Parrott, three 4.2-inch 30-pounder Parrotts, one 11-inch Dahlgren smoothbore, and two 32-pounder smoothbores. Capable of 9–10

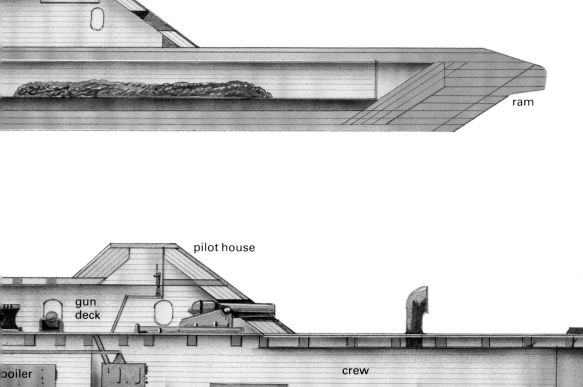

BELOW: Tennessee *is the best documented of Confederate ironclads. She put up one of the stoutest fights during the battle of Mobile Bay, taking on Farragut's whole fleet after the US warships had run past the forts. The heaviest guns in the US Navy hammered into the ironclad at point blank range but her armor withstood all but one of them.* Tennessee *had an Achilles' heel: her steering was unprotected and the stern chains were shot away, leaving the ironclad out of control. With the smokestack perforated, boiler pressure sank and* Tennessee *was a helpless target. Like many of the Confederate ironclads,* Tennessee *was too slow to use her ram against a moving ship.*

Warships of the US and Confederate Navies

knots, they were commissioned between June and November 1862. *Ossipee* fought at Mobile Bay, but the most memorable ship of the class was the *Housatonic*. On February 17, 1864 she became the first warship to be sunk by a submarine when the CSS *Hunley* made its suicidal attack with a spar torpedo.

BELOW: *Keokuk was an unsuccessful experiment – a 677-ton warship with sharply sloping sides and two non-revolving gun towers. These both contained a single 11-inch Dahlgren smoothbore able to be trained on either beam or fore and aft respectively. The gun ports were protected by 4½-inch iron shutters and the 4-inch iron plate protecting the towers was partly extended down the hull sides. Keokuk participated in the attack on Charleston and suffered some 90 hits, of which 19 penetrated her armor near the waterline. The Confederates were able to "skip" large-caliber solid shot across the smooth surface of the water to strike the ironclad's hull. She foundered the next day in a rising sea.*

Six further bark-rigged sloops were laid down in 1861. The four *Sacramento* class were enlarged *Ossipees*, displacing just over 2000 tons. Armed with one 8-inch 175-pounder Parrott, three 20-pounder Parrotts, two 11-inch Dahlgrens, and up to six lighter guns or howitzers, they were commissioned between August 1862 and July 1863. Two further sloops, the *Ticonderoga* and *Lackawanna*, were lengthened versions of the *Sacramentos*.

The above classes of wooden sloops commissioned between 1862 and 1863 were capable of a steady 9–10 knots at best. In 1863 a new class of very large screw frigate was laid down, designed for the unheard of speed of 17 knots.

The stated purpose of the *Wampanoag* class was the high speed pursuit of Confederate commerce raiders like the elusive *Alabama*. However, it was immediately obvious that these big Federal sloops would make good commerce raiders themselves. An Anglo-American war seemed more likely then that at any time since 1815. For their size, these ships were lightly armed, carrying 10 9-inch Dahlgrens and three 5.3-inch 60-pounder Parrott rifles, plus two 24-pounder howitzers. *Wampanoag* and *Ammonoosuc* were launched in 1864, *Madawaska* and *Neshaminy* in 1865. By this time there was no

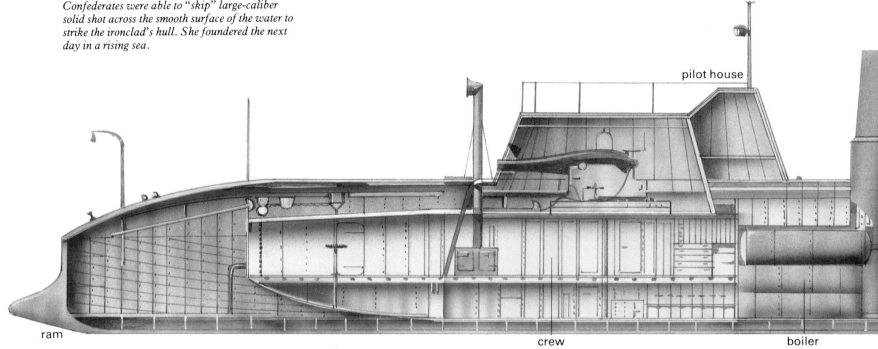

RIGHT: *Missouri was one of the few Confederate casemate ironclads to employ a sternwheel. At 183 feet long, she had a proportionally longer casemate than the other ironclads, and the 22-foot sternwheel was only partially protected; 8 feet of it projected above the armor. She had two engines and four boilers connected to one funnel, and was steered by three rudders under the fantail. The wheel was forward under the pilot house. Built of green timber caulked with cotton, with railroad T-rails for armor, and incapable of over 6 knots, Missouri was perhaps fortunate that the fall of the Red River stranded her at Shreveport.*

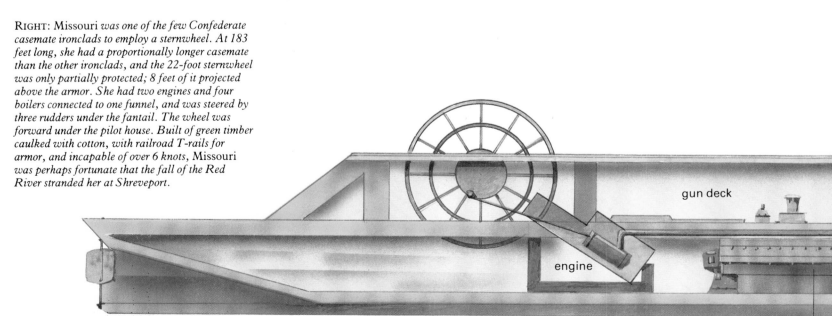

rush to commission them and *Wampanoag* did not begin her trials until 1868. She proved herself to be the fastest steamship in the world, but since this was achieved by devoting 30 percent of her displacement to machinery, it did not make her a successful warship. The British were sufficiently suspicious to retaliate with a three-ship class of larger, better armed, iron-hulled cruisers capable of 16 knots.

With this ever-expanding US fleet blockading its coastline, the Confederacy soon accepted that its ironclads could not drive the Federal squadrons away. No European-built

Confederate warships were due to be completed until 1863, so in the meantime, the only alternative was to run the blockade. Charles K. Prioleau, the Confederate fiscal agent in Liverpool, sent a steamer to Charleston as early as August 1861 and a flourishing industry grew steadily until late 1864. After the fall of New Orleans there were only three major ports left in the South: Wilmington, Charleston, and Mobile. Bristling with shore batteries and, in the case of the first two, offering more than one channel to the sea, they were difficult for the Federal warships to seal.

Purpose-built blockade runners were constructed as soon as it was realized just how monstrous the profits could be for a successful

voyage. Cargoes of brandy, silk, and luxury goods were unloaded from Europe at Nassau or Bermuda and transferred to shallow-draft vessels that could slip the sand bars in the harbor entrances. Painted low-visibility gray, like modern US Navy aircraft, they shipped only the lowest of masts and burned Northern or Welsh anthracite, fine coal that provided maximum thermal value but produced little smoke.

The early blockaders found a speed of 10 knots sufficient to outpace pursuers, but as the US Navy pressed captured blockade runners into service, speeds increased to 12, 14, and even 16 knots. Reaching port, the blockade runner auctioned its cargo, then stuffed its holds with cotton, buying at 6–8 cents a pound and selling in Bermuda for up to a dollar. Most granted part of their cargo space to the Confederate Government, while some government agencies like the Ordnance Department organized their own blockade-running ships.

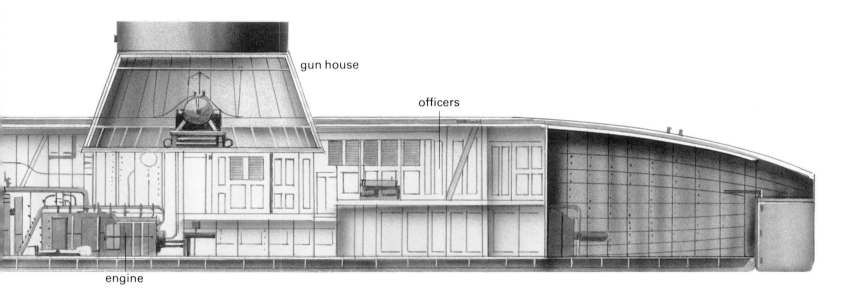

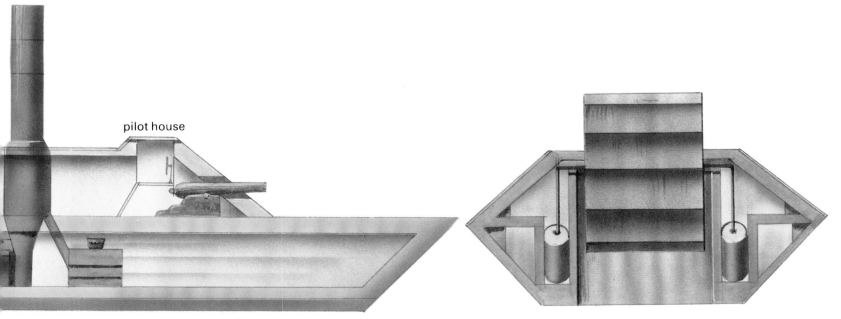

Warships of the US and Confederate Navies

Blockade runners were unarmed and while Federal warships might fire on them to enforce the blockade, these were non-belligerent merchant ships with their own legal rights, provided they did not carry weapons. Many were British-built, owned, and crewed. Royal Navy officers took leave to take part in blockade-running missions. For them it was often highly profitable and exhilarating, but the whole business was fraught with political problems.

The Confederacy began to strike back at Union merchant shipping from the earliest days of the war. The 450-ton bark-rigged steamer *Halbana* of the McConnell line was bought in New Orleans in April 1861 for conversion to a commerce raider. Renamed *Sumter*, she took 18 prizes in a career that began with a narrow escape from two much more powerful adversaries, USS *Brooklyn* and USS *Powhattan*. She eventually put into Cadiz, Spain, and was sold to become a blockade runner in Gibraltar.

Four 1500-ton fast corvettes being built in Bordeaux for the Confederacy were blocked by Union pressure on the French Government and the builder had to sell them to other clients. But several smaller, lightly armed raiders were finished in Britain and spirited to sea by the Confederates before the British Government or Federal officials could stop them. *Florida*, *Alabama*, *Georgia*, and *Shenandoah* inflicted very serious damage on the Union merchant marine and caused a protracted legal dispute between Washington and London after the

war. It was not the 69 prizes she took that made a raider like the famous *Alabama* so dangerous: the longer she continued to ply the world's oceans snapping up American merchant shipping, the fewer cargoes were entrusted to US shipping companies. Merchant ships were sold to foreign companies, so although the volume of trans-Atlantic trade increased steadily throughout the war, the size of the US merchant fleet declined drastically. It never recovered for the rest of the nineteenth century.

The warships of the Civil War spanned an incredible variety, from the graceful lines of the steam frigates to the unlikeliest-looking ironclad warships plying the great rivers of the western theater. The Union and Confederate navies were the first to fight a succession of battles with armored warships. Their use of the ram was observed with particular interest in Europe and helped spur a generation of naval officers down a tactical blind alley. Civil War ships were at the cutting edge of contemporary technology. Many were innovative, not to say experimental, but the sailors themselves seem to have taken it in their stride. Franklin Buchanan's idea of a trial cruise was to steam *Virginia* straight at the blockading squadron. When conventional tactics failed to defeat the *Albemarle*, Lieutenant Cushing lashed a bomb to a steam launch and blew up the Confederate ironclad in one of the most daring attacks of the war. This extraordinary era in naval operations certainly produced some extraordinary men.

BELOW: *The* David *was a semi-submersible torpedo launch that attacked the USS* New Ironsides *in October 1863, causing serious damage to the hull. The Confederates eventually built about 20 of these craft. Measuring 54 feet long and 5½ feet wide, they offered a very low profile to the target vessel. By taking water into their ballast tanks, the* Davids *submerged all but the 10-foot structure around the funnel. The explosive charge held 134 lb of black powder in a copper case, and were aimed to strike the target below the waterline.*

The Union responded to the threat of Southern submarine craft by experimenting with their own, which resembled the small submarines of today. Named Pioneer, *she was designed by Merriam & Halstead. This craft was 30 feet long, carried a crew of 6–13, and could travel at 4 knots under water. In 1872 she was put on display at the Washington Navy Yard.*

BOTTOM: Hunley *was the first submarine to attack a warship. Privately built, she was as lethal to her operators as to the enemy; the inventor himself and several nine-man crews perished during tests. Water ballast tanks at bow and stern were filled by valves and emptied by hand pumps. A candle provided light and warning as the oxygen ran out. On the night of February 17, 1864* Hunley *attacked USS* Housatonic *off Charleston. The spar torpedo exploded, sinking the warship in shallow water, but taking the submarine with it.*

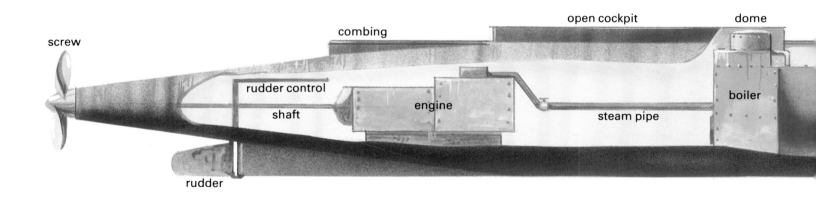

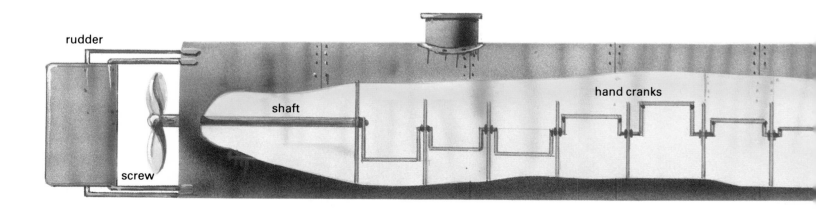

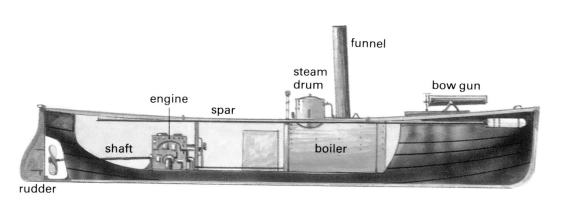

funnel

steam
drum

bow gun

engine

spar

shaft

boiler

rudder

ABOVE: Albemarle *was the only Confederate ironclad to be sunk by the US Navy during the Civil War, the victim of a 45-foot steam launch fitted with a spar torpedo. Lieutenant W. B. Cushing, a US Navy officer already renowned for daring boat raids, commanded a selected crew for an almost suicidal night attack. Spotted as it approached, the boat was received by a heavy fire of grapeshot and musketry but the shell struck* Albemarle *below the waterline and sank her. Cushing's crew were either killed or captured; he alone escaped.*

Lieutenant Cushing later went on to command the cruiser Wyoming *when, in 1873, he saved the lives of several Americans condemned to death after their capture by Spanish forces while trying to join Cuban rebels then fighting the Spaniards. Unfortunately, Cushing arrived too late to save 53 of the passengers and crew of the ill-fated* Virginius *already executed, but he threatened to fire on Spanish forces if more people from the* Virginius *were executed. This prompt action forced Spain to climb down and war was narrowly averted. Cushing lived for only one more year. He died at Washington in December 1874.*

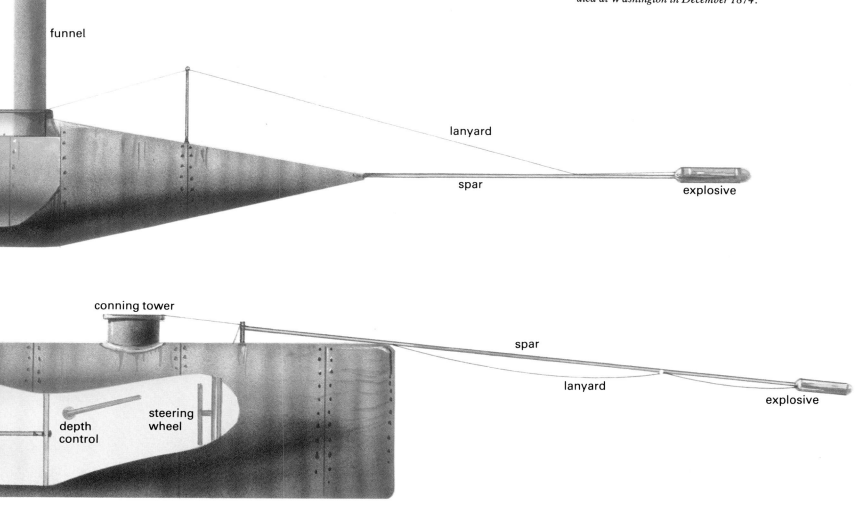

funnel

lanyard

spar

explosive

conning tower

spar

lanyard

explosive

depth
control

steering
wheel

Mine Warfare

Admiral Farragut's often quoted exhortation, "Damn the torpedoes, full speed ahead," was not actually credited to him until many years after his celebrated attack on Mobile Bay. But whatever his actual words, it was a courageous decision to brave the Confederate minefield that had just swallowed the monitor USS *Tecumseh*, Farragut was lucky. Officers aboard both *Hartford* and *Richmond* heard the pop of primers detonating as the ships' hulls struck further Confederate mines. Fortunately for them, the mines had been immersed so long that water had gotten to the powder charges.

Underwater mines were called torpedoes during the Civil War. Torpedoes in the modern sense were not in service until the 1870s. The Confederate "torpedo service," as it was termed, was ably led by Lieutenant Hunter Davidson and it was responsible for sinking some of the most powerful warships in the US Navy. Some Union officers, notably Admiral Farragut, condemned the use of mines as unworthy of a "chivalrous nation." But he did use them around *Hartford* when she lay off Mobile Bay just prior to the Union attack. There was a rumour that the ram *Tennessee* would sortie against the US fleet before it was concentrated and Farragut needed the protection conferred by a minefield.

Four monitors were sunk by mines. *Tecumseh* sank like a stone after running into the minefield at Mobile Bay. In January 1865 *Patapsco* was mined off Charleston. The Mobile area was choked with minefields and claimed two more victims on March 28, 1865. *Milwaukee* was sunk in the Blakely River and the

RIGHT: *Some of the various "torpedoes" employed during the war. The* drifting torpedoes *relied on a buoyant barrel or log to keep them ready to explode below an enemy's waterline. Set adrift in the path of oncoming shipping, the tarred barrel contained a time fuse that led to the explosive charge. When it burned down, the charge detonated.*

The keg torpedo *was covered with pitch inside and out. Containing up to 100 lb of powder, it was detonated by percussion or chemical fuses in the top and sides. The conical ends were made from pine and kept the torpedo streamlined to reduce the disturbance from the tide. The* copper torpedo *followed the same system.*

The clockwork torpedo *was another drifting mine. When swept against the target, the current began to turn the tin propeller. This released a spring-loaded plunger to detonate a percussion primer and fire the main charge.*

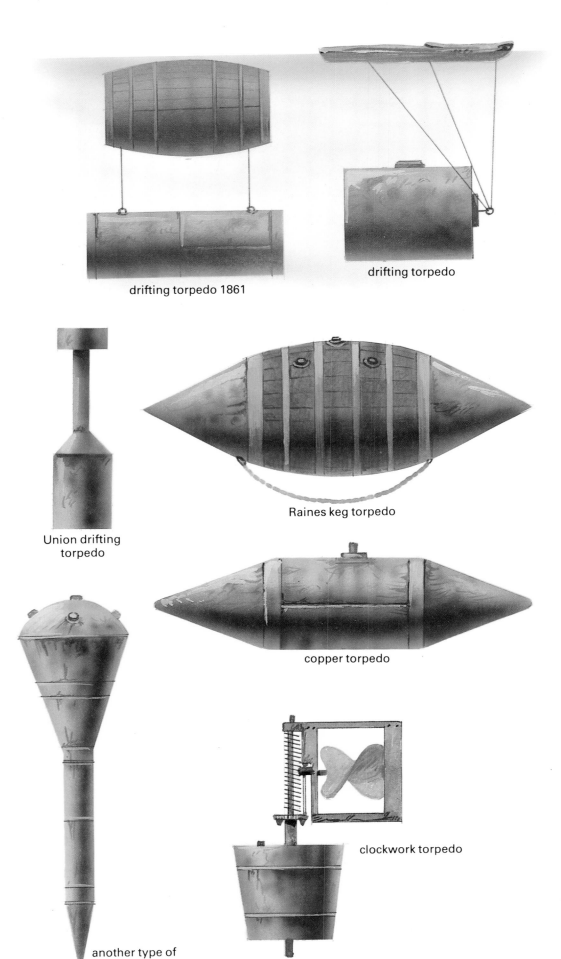

drifting torpedo 1861

drifting torpedo

Union drifting torpedo

Raines keg torpedo

copper torpedo

another type of copper torpedo

clockwork torpedo

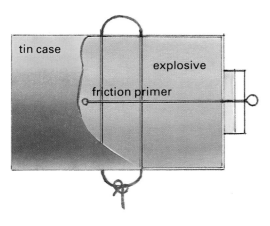

tin case

explosive

friction primer

explosive

coal torpedo

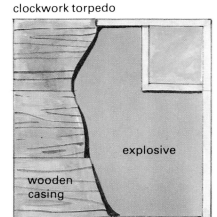

explosive

wooden casing

ABOVE: *A tin cylinder filled with gunpowder and containing a buoyancy chamber. Such "torpedoes" were anchored to the river bottom with percussion triggers, or triggers operated from ashore.*

The coal torpedo *was a Confederate sabotage weapon: an iron lump containing a powder charge, it was coated in tar and rolled in coal dust. Saboteurs infiltrated these into coal depots and they exploded in furnaces, blowing up ships' boilers.*

The Fretwell Singer torpedo *had a heavy iron cap on top. If displaced by a vessel striking it, it pulled out the pin projecting from the column below the mine. Pulling the pin released a spring-loaded firing pin against a detonator.*

The electric torpedo *was fixed to an anchor and had a (theoretically) watertight plug for its electrical wire detonator. These were fired from ashore.*

BELOW: *The* spar torpedo *was to have been fitted as standard to Confederate ironclads. Instead, their ironclad Albemarle was sunk by a spar torpedo mounted on a steam launch commanded by the intrepid Cushing. The torpedo was designed by engineer Lay and was fitted to the spar by an iron slide that could be detached from the launch. The torpedo was thus released and floated up against the target's hull. It was then fired by tugging a separate lanyard – all while under heavy fire at point-blank range!*

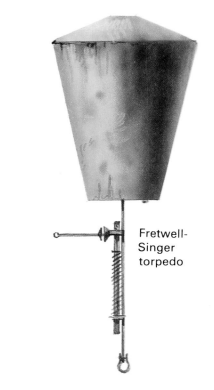

Fretwell-Singer torpedo

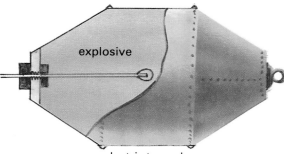

explosive

electric torpedo

Eads river monitor *Osage* was destroyed by a mine off Spanish Fort.

Confederate mines were improvised from all manner of containers. Many of those at Mobile were simply beer kegs filled with powder, detonated by a ships' hull striking small horns of fulminate that projected from the keg.

The first major loss to these new Southern weapons was the river ironclad *Cairo*. Captain Issac N. Brown, former commander of the ram *Arkansas*, was left to guard the Yazoo River after the loss of his vessel. Under his direction a 5-gallon glass demijohn was filled with gunpowder and fitted with a friction primer supplied by an artillery battery. The bomb was suspended on a wire secured to both banks and hung below the surface of the water. On December 12, 1862 the *Cairo* steamed up the Yazoo, keeping to midstream where she brushed against the wire, yanking the friction primer and detonating the mine. Although the ironclad settled rapidly, the crew abandoned ship in good order and no lives were lost. *Cairo* sank in 30 feet of water and in little over 10 minutes nothing remained but her smokestacks projecting folornly from the water.

Captain Brown's Yazoo minefield claimed its next victim in July as the advance of Union ground troops compelled the Confederate batteries covering the river to withdraw. Emboldened by the retreat of the cannon she had regularly duelled with, the ironclad *De Kalb* pressed forward only to run into a mine and sink within 15 minutes. Again no lives were lost. The crews of the river gunboats were more fortunate than those of the monitors whose lack of reserve buoyancy sent them plunging to the bottom if their hulls were pierced. *Tecumseh*

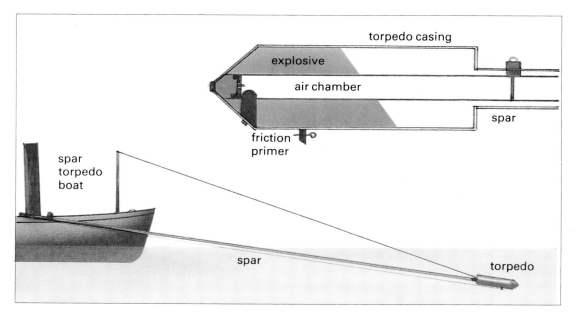

torpedo casing

explosive

air chamber

spar

friction primer

spar torpedo boat

spar

torpedo

Mine Warfare

sank in less than 30 seconds, taking 93 of her 114 crew to their deaths.

The Confederate torpedo service also employed command-detonated mines, fired by electric current. A thin wire placed inside a mine could provide sufficient heat to ignite fine-grade powder if an electric current was run through it. In August 1863 a Union flotilla made a reconnaissance of the James River, the monitor *Sangamon* leading the sidewheel ferry boat *Commodore Barney* and the small steamer *Cohasset*. The monitor anchored at Dutch Gap, unable to proceed further due to the low water, but the others pressed on to where Lieutenant Hunter Davidson and his men were waiting in ambush. The Confederates had placed several mines containing 500 pounds of gunpowder, connected by wire to the shore. When *Commodore Barney* was close enough, they detonated one. The wash from the explosion hurled 20 sailors overboard and the *Commodore Barney* was towed away by her consort.

The James River was even better provided with underwater defenses by May 5, 1864, when the army landed at City Point. The fleet was led by seven gunboats, dragging the river for torpedoes ahead of the troop transports and monitors. They found them the following day. *Commodore Jones*, a 542-ton sidewheel steamer, was blown up by a torpedo fired electrically from ashore and half the 88 men on board were killed. Sailors landed from the *Mackinaw* and managed to capture one of the Confederate torpedo operators, who promptly found himself in the bows of the leading vessel. He was unsurprisingly cooperative in locating further torpedoes in the path of the squadron.

No torpedoes used during the Civil War were self-propelled, although there were experiments with such weapons. One test on the Potomac resulted in the first sinking of a ship by a true torpedo, although it was not the target but a civilian-owned vessel that happened to be in the area. However, the Civil War did see the more extensive use of a short-lived class of weapon: the spar torpedo. This was an explosive charge on the end of a wooden spar projecting from a ship. Brought into contact with an enemy vessel, it could be detonated against the hull below the waterline either by percussion or by pulling a lanyard to fire a friction primer.

Spar torpedoes could be rigged from the hull sides or on the bow for a ramming attack. They were popular with the Confederate Navy and it was planned to equip all casemate ironclad rams with spar torpedoes as standard, although this was not achieved in practice. Spar torpedoes could be fitted to smaller, faster vessels, converting otherwise puny opponents into warships capable of destroying a major unit. The semi-submersible *David* class vessels were armed with spar torpedoes containing 100-pound warheads. The ill-fated submarine *Hunley* sank the *Housatonic* with a spar torpedo, but was consumed herself in the same explosion.

Although the Confederates made greater use of them, the most effective spar torpedo attack of the war was the Union attack on the ironclad *Albemarle*. This powerful ram had already

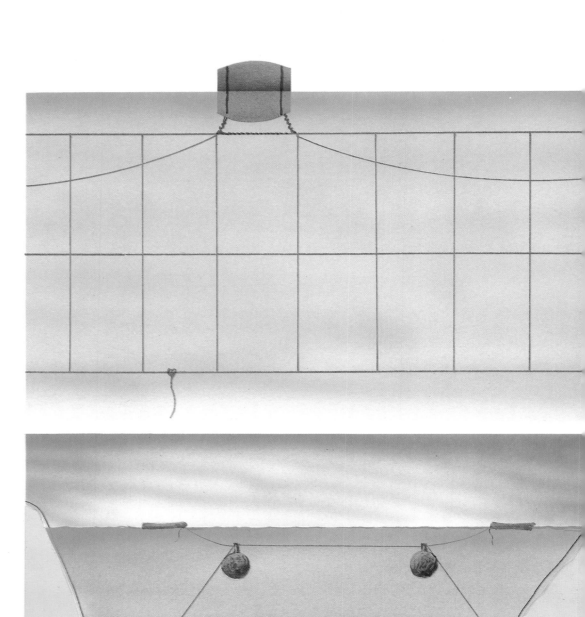

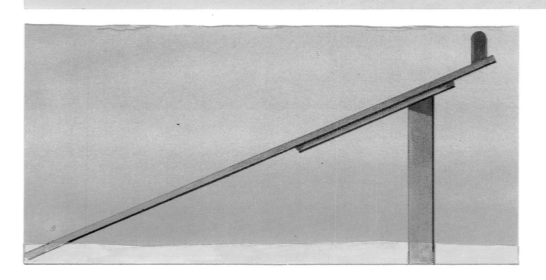

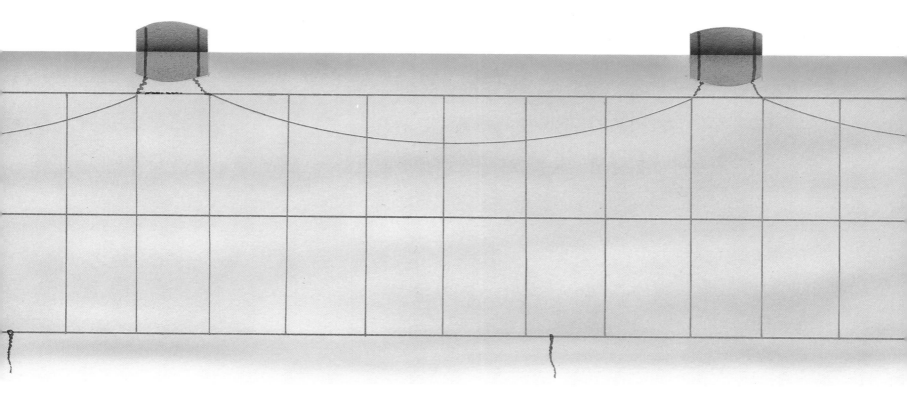

LEFT: *Demijohns filled with powder and exploded from the shore destroyed several US warships. One victim was the USS* Cairo *which sank in 30 feet of water in December 1862.*

BELOW LEFT: *Frame torpedoes were used in narrow waterways. Cast-iron shells with percussion detonators were fitted to heavy timbers and anchored to the bottom.*

ABOVE AND BELOW: *A typical Civil War minefield with the ropes holding the powder charges together, ready to drag them against the hulls of ships passing through. Used in combination with sunken blockships and other obstructions, these defenses were often the Confederacy's only hope of keeping out US warships. Only at Charleston and in the James River did the Confederates manage to assemble a squadron of ironclad warships.*

proved a tough opponent, sinking the *Southfield* and helping the Confederate Army recapture Plymouth, North Carolina. Lurking out of reach of the Union ironclads that could not cross the Hatteras bar, the *Albemarle* seemed secure, but Lieutenant William B. Cushing proposed to destroy her with a spar torpedo fired from a steam launch. The warhead, designed by a navy engineer, was mounted on the end of a pivoting spar. Under intense fire from the ironclad, Cushing succeeded in the delicate task of maneuvering the explosive charge against the *Albemarle*'s hull below the knuckle of her armor. The much-feared ram was holed and settled in shallow water so that her casemate was still visible above the surface.

Like most obstacles used in warfare, Civil War torpedoes could only form an effective barrier to enemy movement if they were covered by fire. Even the most mine-infested river could be cleared in time if the ships dragging the water for torpedoes were left unmolested. Passing through a mined area under fire prevented more leisurely methods of dealing with the torpedoes and special devices were produced for the US attack on Charleston harbor. The US monitors employed wooden rafts 50 feet long fitted over their bows with chains hanging down into the water. These were supposed to strike and detonate any mines that the monitor steamed into, but they seriously hampered the monitors' steering, not to mention speed. Later in the war, simple frameworks with cables attached were fitted in the bows of sidewheel steamers. Able to be raised when not in use, they could sweep the water directly in front of the warship without impeding progress.

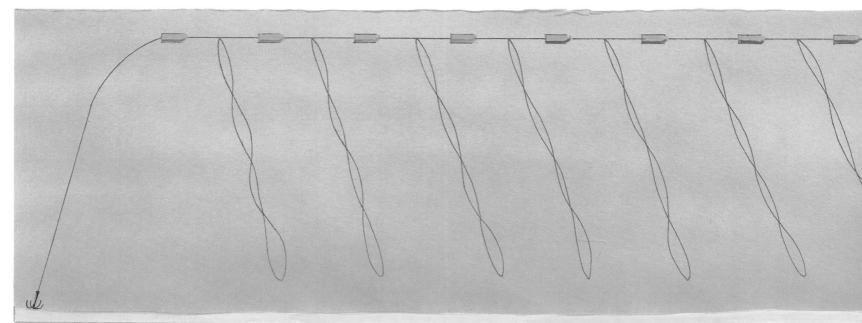

Index